Adapting the Canon
Mediation, Visualization, Interpretation

LEGENDA

LEGENDA is the Modern Humanities Research Association's book imprint for new research in the Humanities. Founded in 1995 by Malcolm Bowie and others within the University of Oxford, Legenda has always been a collaborative publishing enterprise, directly governed by scholars. The Modern Humanities Research Association (MHRA) joined this collaboration in 1998, became half-owner in 2004, in partnership with Maney Publishing and then Routledge, and has since 2016 been sole owner. Titles range from medieval texts to contemporary cinema and form a widely comparative view of the modern humanities, including works on Arabic, Catalan, English, French, German, Greek, Italian, Portuguese, Russian, Spanish, and Yiddish literature. Editorial boards and committees of more than 60 leading academic specialists work in collaboration with bodies such as the Society for French Studies, the British Comparative Literature Association and the Association of Hispanists of Great Britain & Ireland.

The MHRA encourages and promotes advanced study and research in the field of the modern humanities, especially modern European languages and literature, including English, and also cinema. It aims to break down the barriers between scholars working in different disciplines and to maintain the unity of humanistic scholarship. The Association fulfils this purpose through the publication of journals, bibliographies, monographs, critical editions, and the MHRA Style Guide, and by making grants in support of research. Membership is open to all who work in the Humanities, whether independent or in a University post, and the participation of younger colleagues entering the field is especially welcomed.

TRANSCRIPT

Transcript publishes books about all kinds of imagining across languages, media and cultures: translations and versions, inter-cultural and multi-lingual writing, illustrations and musical settings, adaptation for theatre, film, TV and new media, creative and critical responses. We are open to studies of any combination of languages and media, in any historical moments, and are keen to reach beyond Legenda's traditional focus on modern European languages to embrace anglophone and world cultures and the classics. We are interested in innovative critical approaches: we welcome not only the most rigorous scholarship and sharpest theory, but also modes of writing that stretch or cross the boundaries of those discourses.

www.legendabooks.com/series/transcript

TRANSCRIPT

1. *Adapting the Canon: Mediation, Visualization, Interpretation*, edited by Ann Lewis and Silke Arnold-de Simine
2. *Adapted Voices: Transpositions of Céline's Voyage au bout de la nuit and Queneau's Zazie dans le métro*, by Armelle Blin-Rolland
3. *Zola and the Art of Television: Adaptation, Recreation, Translation*, by Kate Griffiths
4. *Comparative Encounters between Artaud, Michaux and the Zhuangzi: Rationality, Cosmology and Ethics*, by Xiaofan Amy Li
5. *Minding Borders: Resilient Divisions in Literature, the Body and the Academy*, edited by Nicola Gardini, Adriana Jacobs, Ben Morgan, Mohamed-Salah Omri and Matthew Reynolds
6. *Memory Across Borders: Nabokov, Perec, Chamoiseau*, by Sara-Louise Cooper
7. *Erotic Literature in Adaptation and Translation*, edited by Johannes D. Kaminski
8. *Translating Petrarch's Poetry: L'Aura del Petrarca from the Quattrocento to the 21st Century*, edited by Carole Birkan-Berz, Guillaume Coatalen and Thomas Vuong
9. *Making Masud Khan: Psychoanalysis, Empire and Modernist Culture*, by Benjamin Poore
10. *Prismatic Translation*, edited by Matthew Reynolds
11. *The Patient, the Impostor and the Seducer: Medieval European Literature in Hebrew*, by Tovi Bibring
12. *Reading Dante and Proust by Analogy*, by Julia Caterina Hartley
13. *The First English Translations of Molière: Drama in Flux 1663-1732*, by Suzanne Jones
14. *After Clarice: Reading Lispector's Legacy in the Twenty-First Century*, edited by Adriana X. Jacobs and Claire Williams
15. *Uruguayan Theatre in Translation: Theory and Practice*, by Sophie Stevens
16. *Hamlet Translations: Prisms of Cultural Encounters across the Globe*, edited by Márta Minier and Lily Kahn
17. *The Foreign Connection: Writings on Poetry, Art and Translation*, by Jamie McKendrick
18. *Poetics, Performance and Politics in French and Italian Renaissance Comedy*, by Lucy Rayfield

Adapting the Canon

Mediation, Visualization, Interpretation

❖

Edited by
Ann Lewis and Silke Arnold-de Simine

LEGENDA
Transcript 1
Modern Humanities Research Association
2020

Published by Legenda
an imprint of the Modern Humanities Research Association
Salisbury House, Station Road, Cambridge CB1 2LA

ISBN 978-1-78188-708-0 (HB)
ISBN 978-1-78188-396-9 (PB)

First published 2020

Copy-Editor: Charlotte Brown

CONTENTS

ACKNOWLEDGEMENTS

❖

In the co-editing and writing of this project, we have incurred many debts. First and foremost, we would like to thank the contributors to the collection for their enormous patience, hard work, and good-natured collaboration over a number of years. Kate Griffiths, Bradley Stephens, Andrew Watts, and Bill Marshall provided incisive and invaluable advice in the formative stages of the project, when the volume was no more than a call for papers for the 2014 Legenda conference 'Adapting the Canon', from which it emerges. The executive committee of the MHRA have provided thoughtful and apposite guidance at every stage, and thanks are especially due to Malcolm Cook, Barbara Burns, and Alison Finch for their support over the years. Graham Nelson at Legenda has been generous and exceptionally kind in his steering of the project towards completion in what is a frantically busy period. We would like to thank our copy-editor Charlotte Wathey for her meticulous and careful work on the volume, her contribution to it is very much appreciated. Many thanks also go to Amanda Wrigley for her expert help in the compiling of the index.

Birkbeck has provided a collegial and friendly environment for our collaboration as co-editors, and allowed for many productive and thought-provoking dialogues. We are grateful for the institutional support which allowed us the scope to work on the volume (without a period of research leave, it simply would not have been possible to complete the project). Last but not least, we are very grateful for the patience, good cheer, and unfailing support of colleagues, friends, and family: and especially Toni, Andrew, Leo, and Rafi (who arrived mid-project, and in typically mischievous style, created havoc with our schedule).

March 2020

ABOUT THE CONTRIBUTORS

❖

Silke Arnold-de Simine is Reader in the Department of Film, Media and Cultural Studies at Birkbeck, University of London. Her research is concerned with (trans-) media aesthetics and ethics, tracing the pathways and following the transnational flow of practices of remembrance across different media outlets and art forms, such as photography, film/television, (digital) archives and museums. She is the author of *Mediating Memory in the Museum: Trauma, Empathy, Nostalgia* (Palgrave Macmillan, 2013, paperback 2016) and co-editor (with Joanne Leal) of *Picturing the Family. Media, Narrative, Memory* (Bloomsbury, 2018).

Juliane Blank is a teaching assistant at the Universität des Saarlandes (Saarbrücken, Germany), in the Department of German Literature. Her PhD thesis 'Literaturadaptionen im Comic: Ein modulares Analysemodell' (2015) provides a basic model for analysing graphic adaptations, but also examines recurring techniques and strategies of adaptation in comic books and graphic novels. In 2019 she finished her *Habilitation* thesis 'Katastrophe und Kontingenz: der Zufall in faktualen und fiktionalen Diskursen über Jahrhundertkatastrophen (Lissabon-Shoah-9/11)', which deals with coincidence and making sense in literary discourses on disasters.

Armelle Blin-Rolland is Lecturer in French and Francophone Studies at Bangor University. Her research interests include adaptation from and into literature, film and comic art; audiovisuality; intermediality; theories of voice across media; ecocriticism; and Breton comic art. She has published on these topics in *European Comic Art, Studies in Comics, Studies in French Cinema, Modern Languages Open* and *Modern and Contemporary France*. She has co-edited a special issue of *European Comic Art* on 'Comics and Adaptation', and, for *Studies in Comics*, on 'Comics and Nation'. Her monograph *Adapted Voices: Transpositions of Céline's 'Voyage au bout de la nuit' and Queneau's 'Zazie dans le métro'* was published by Legenda in 2015. She is review co-editor for *European Comic Art*.

Kamilla Elliott is Professor of Literature and Media in the Department of English and Creative Writing at Lancaster University. Her principal teaching and research interests lie in relations between British literature of the long nineteenth century and other media (painting, illustration, theatre, film, and new media). She is co-chair of the Association of Adaptation Studies, and author of *Rethinking the Novel/Film Debate* (Cambridge University Press, 2003), *Portraiture and British Gothic Fiction: The Rise of Picture Identification, 1764–1835* (Johns Hopkins University Press, 2012), and *Theorizing Adaptation* (Oxford University Press, 2020).

Christine Geraghty is Honorary Professorial Fellow at the University of Glasgow. She has published extensively on film and television with a particular interest in fiction and form. Her work on adaptation includes *Now a Major Motion Picture: Film Adaptations of Literature and Drama* (Rowman & Littlefield, 2008) and *Bleak House* (Palgrave/BFI, 2012) as well as essays on *Atonement* (2007), *The Knack ...* (1965) and *Tender is the Night* (1985). She is on the editorial board of the *Journal of British Cinema and Television* and on the advisory boards of a number of journals, including *Adaptation* and *Screen*.

Kate Griffiths is Professor of French and Translation at Cardiff University. She is author of *Émile Zola and the Artistry of Adaptation* (Legenda, 2009), *Émile Zola and the Art of Television: Adaptation, Recreation, Translation* (Legenda, forthcoming) and, with Andrew Watts, of *Adapting Nineteenth-century France: Literature in Film, Theatre, Television, Radio and Print* (University of Wales Press, 2013), and *The History of French Literature on Film* (Bloomsbury, forthcoming). Her work on adaptation has been supported by AHRC Research Leave, an AHRC Fellowship and she is currently leading an AHRC Collaborative Doctoral Award on BBC Radio Adaptation. She was academic consultant to BBC Radio 4's year-long adaptation of the works of Émile Zola.

Christina Ionescu is Director of the Visual and Material Cultures Programme at Mount Allison University in Canada. She is a *dix-huitiémiste* with an interest in book illustration, visual and material cultures, as well as word and image theory. She is the editor of *Book Illustration in the Long Eighteenth Century: Reconfiguring the Visual Periphery of the Text* (2011), co-editor of *Eighteenth-century Thing Theory in a Global Context: From Consumerism to Celebrity Culture* (2013), and co-editor of *Visualizing the Text from Manuscript Culture to the Age of Caricature* (2017). With Ann Lewis, she co-edited a special issue of the *Journal for Eighteenth-Century Studies* (*Picturing the Eighteenth-century Novel Through Time: Illustration, Intermediality and Adaptation*, December 2016). Her recent journal articles have appeared in *Cahiers du GADGES*, *Image & Narrative*, *Le Livre et l'estampe*, and *Journal for Eighteenth-Century Studies*. Her current research project focuses on the first publication of Random House, an edition of Voltaire's *Candide* designed and illustrated by Rockwell Kent, which was produced at the prestigious Pynson Printers under the direction of Elmer Adler. It is a collector's item that was subsequently declared a masterpiece of American book design and illustration.

Ann Lewis is Senior Lecturer in French Studies at Birkbeck, University of London. Her research focuses on eighteenth-century literature and culture, and text/image relations, especially illustration. She is author of *Sensibility, Reading and Illustration: Spectacles and Signs in Graffigny, Marivaux and Rousseau* (Legenda, 2009) and a number of articles relating to eighteenth-century fiction. She has co-edited several collections, including: *Picturing the Eighteenth-century Novel Through Time: Illustration, Adaptation and Intermediality*, with Christina Ionescu (special issue of *Journal for Eighteenth-Century Studies*, December 2016) and *Prostitution and Eighteenth-century Culture: Sex, Commerce and Morality*, with Markman Ellis (Pickering & Chatto,

2012). She is currently working on a monograph focusing on the figure of the prostitute in eighteenth-century France.

Jozefina Komporaly lectures in performance at the University of the Arts, London, and translates drama, fiction, and academic texts from Hungarian and Romanian into English. Her publications include the monographs *Staging Motherhood: British Women Playwrights, 1956 to the Present* (Palgrave, 2006) and *Radical Revival as Adaptation: Theatre, Politics, Society* (Palgrave, 2017), and numerous articles in edited collections and journals. Jozefina is editor and co-translator of the first English-language anthology of Matéi Visniec's plays, *How to Explain the History of Communism to Mental Patients and Other Plays* (Seagull Books, 2015) and of the critical anthology *András Visky's Barrack Dramaturgy: Memories of the Body* (Intellect, 2017). With Nicoleta Cinpoeş, she co-translated *'The Golden Round': Essays on the Politics of Power in Shakespeare* by Mihai Măniuţiu (Casa Cărţii de Ştiinţă, 2018).

Claire Pascolini-Campbell holds degrees in English and Comparative Literature from University College London and the University of St Andrews. Her research focuses on translation, influence, and medievalism, and the legacy of François Villon in particular. Her first book, *François Villon in English Poetry: Translation and Influence*, was published by Boydell & Brewer in 2018. Claire is Research Manager at the National Trust, where she oversees the organization's research department and leads on the delivery of the research strategy. Her next research project will look at how heritage organizations engage visitors in their medieval places.

Clive Scott is Professor Emeritus of European Literature at the University of East Anglia and a Fellow of the British Academy. His principal research interests lie in French and comparative poetics (*The Poetics of French Verse: Studies in Reading*, Oxford University Press, 1998; *Channel Crossings: French and English Poetry in Dialogue 1550–2000*, Legenda, 2002); in literary translation, and in particular the experimental translation of poetry (*Translating Baudelaire*, University of Exeter Press, 2000; *Translating Rimbaud's 'Illuminations'*, University of Exeter Press, 2006; *Literary Translation and the Rediscovery of Reading*, Cambridge University Press, 2012; *Translating the Perception of Text: Literary Translation and Phenomenology*, Legenda, 2012); and in photography's relationship with writing (*The Spoken Image: Photography and Language*, Reaktion Books, 1999; *Street Photography: From Atget to Cartier-Bresson*, I. B. Tauris, 2007). Translation and photography combine in his *Translating Apollinaire* (University of Exeter Press, 2014). In 2018, his *The Work of Literary Translation* was published by Cambridge University Press. He was President of the MHRA in 2014.

Bradley Stephens is Associate Professor (Reader) in French Literature at the University of Bristol. His research examines the history and reception of literature written in French from the nineteenth century onwards, with particular interests in Romanticism (especially the life and works of Victor Hugo), phenomenology, adaptation studies, and gender. He has published widely in these fields, including the co-edited volumes *'Les Misérables' and its Afterlives: Between Page, Stage, and Screen* with Kathryn M. Grossman (Routledge, 2015) and *Approaches to Teaching Hugo's 'Les Misérables'* with Michal P. Ginsburg (MLA, 2018). He is also the author of

Victor Hugo, Jean-Paul Sartre and the Liability of Liberty (Legenda, 2011) and a critical biography of Hugo (Reaktion Books, 2019).

Jeremy Strong is Professor of Literature and Film at the University of West London. Chair and co-chair of the Association of Adaptation Studies from 2010 to 2016, he serves on the editorial board of its journal *Adaptation* and other peer-reviewed journals. He is widely published in the field of literature-on-film, with a particular interest in questions of genre and narrative. He has edited several books, including *Educated Tastes: Food, Drink and Connoisseur Culture* (University of Nebraska Press, 2011); and is the author of *James Bond Uncovered* (Palgrave Macmillan, 2018), as well as his first novel *Mean Business* (Kindle, 2013, e-book).

LIST OF ILLUSTRATIONS

Every effort has been made to contact copyright holders; however should any errors or omissions inadvertently have been made, we would be pleased to correct this in future editions.

INTRODUCTION

❖

Adapting the Canon: Mediation, Visualization, Interpretation

Silke Arnold-de Simine and Ann Lewis

The emergence of 'adaptation' as a highly dynamic and growing field of research is amply evidenced by a rapidly expanding critical and theoretical literature. Since 2010, there have been at least seven substantial 'handbooks' and 'companions' surveying the field of adaptation studies, setting out some of its parameters as a distinct area of study and scholarship, and/or serving as an introduction to this area.[1] Since 2015 alone, a significant number of monographs and collections of essays focusing on adaptation in relation to less studied genres and media (such as television, comics, and illustration) have appeared,[2] while a number of important monographs and collections are just published or forthcoming in 2019–2020.[3] Two learned associations, three dedicated journals, and several book series focusing on adaptation have established a clearer identity for this body of critical writing, especially since 2008, and at any time one can find a number of international conferences and/or calls for papers focusing on this subject.[4]

At the interface between a range of disciplines (film and screen studies, media and cultural studies, digital humanities, modern languages and comparative literature, English studies, performance and reception history, history of the book and visual culture, and others), the study of adaptation foregrounds a range of key methodological questions, regarding the status of the 'text', the 'author' (or *auteur*), and the 'consumer' of literary and cultural artefacts. Interdisciplinary and comparative by its very nature, the study of adaptation encourages the bringing together of perspectives and approaches such as narratology, (visual) semiotics, and reception studies, and promotes the questioning of assumed 'norms' within each discipline. But this 'in between' status (rarely if ever is adaptation studies granted institutional recognition as a separate department or offered as a programme in its own right) can also provoke unease, and even hostility from other disciplines. Often relating to the perceived value or quality of 'adaptations', this is as much a feature of reactions from film or media studies as from literary scholarship, as well as resulting from the 'dysfunctional relationship between adaptation and theorization' evoked by Kamilla Elliott.[5] Much of this is bound up in problematic questions of definition — both how to define an adaptation, and adaptation studies as a field —

and its relationship to the (literary) canon with all that that notion implies about aesthetic values and hierarchies. Questions around focus and methodology have been at the centre of debates within adaptation studies since its early phase, and the move away from 'fidelity studies', broadly conceived, to approaches centred on adaptation's creative and subversive potential, have been usefully charted in several recent surveys of the different generations of 'adaptation studies'.[6] Although such debates suggest some ongoing unease and scepticism at the heart of the adaptation studies project, the richness and rigour of the voluminous output outlined at the start of this introduction, suggests that such sceptical self-awareness creates a productive dynamic. Or, as Thomas Leitch puts it, 'it is healthier for the field to be riven by debates than to produce methodological consensus'.[7] Indeed, his outline of a series of 'foundational questions' or unresolved tensions, may, as he suggests, be seen as the basis of a canon of thinking and writing which has been core to the establishment of adaptation studies, in their structuring of debates at different moments. These critical fault lines are summarized by Leitch roughly as follows: 1) what counts as an adaptation? should adaptation be defined as a particular group of texts? 2) is there any validity to approaches which assess the 'fidelity' between a 'source' and its 'adaptation'? 3) should adaptation studies be primarily analytical or evaluative (and given that no-one would seriously propose that we stop evaluating adaptations altogether, what place ought evaluation to play in the field)? 4) what is the value of the case study as a methodological tool? Especially where this can result in a simple 'compare and contrast' exercise, and 5) is adaptation scholarship better served by close readings or by more general synthetic, holistic approaches, and how can such approaches be integrated? (pp. 7–9).

The adaptation scholars who, at different stages, have engaged with these questions, producing very different responses, may be seen as the canonical authors of this discipline: Deborah Cartmell, Dennis Cutchins, Lars Elleström, Kamilla Elliott, Christine Geraghty, Kate Griffiths, Linda Hutcheon, Thomas Leitch, Julie Sanders, Robert Stam, Bradley Stephens, Imelda Whelehan, amongst many others. We understand this canon of critical and theoretical frameworks (like any form of canon) as a dynamic and fluid dialogue, constantly shifting in relation to new debates and new considerations; in short, an adaptive canon.

Canonization and Adaptation

The relationship between adaptation studies and notions of canonicity has, nonetheless, been fraught at the best of times. Julie Sanders brings out some of the double-edged nature of this relationship, in her discussion of adaptation and appropriation, simultaneously suggesting the ways in which adaptations rely on the authoritative status of an existing canon, and equally, their potential to reshape it, and to 'write back':

> The debate that has raged around canon formation in literary studies in recent decades is inescapable [...]. Adaptation both appears to require and to perpetuate the existence of a canon, although it may in turn contribute to its ongoing reformulation and expansion. [...] Adaptation becomes a veritable marker of canonical status; citation infers authority. To this end, adaptation could be

> defined as an inherently conservative genre [...]. Yet as the notion of hostile takeover present in a term such as 'appropriation' implies, adaptation can also be oppositional, even subversive.[8]

Despite its persistence in academic scholarship, the notion of the canon as a sanctioned corpus of established classics which excludes large segments of cultural production, has oft been considered ideologically suspect.[9] When considered in the context of adaptation studies, a key problematic is the way in which the notion of 'canonicity' (and adapting the canon) seems to privilege the literary text over its adaptations especially in visual media such as film, comics, or video games. Here, 'literature', especially the novel, often appears (or is constructed) as a prior, primary, and more culturally validated artistic form within a ranking of aesthetic value, promoting an hierarchical imbalance that the pursuit of studies focused on the question of fidelity in the early development of adaptation studies only exacerbated. Deborah Cartmell talks of 'the dominance of classic adaptations to adaptation studies and the elitism and sense of inferiority that this has perpetuated (good book = bad film, bad book = good film)', also noting that a focus on the adaptation of canonical literature has excluded a wealth of material still ripe for exploration, 'video games, advertising adaptations, [...] and film to theater'.[10]

From the perspective of cultural studies, moreover, questions of aesthetic value are broadly irrelevant, and the idea of bestowing a timeless or transcendent quality on texts/artefacts elevated to the canon risks disregarding their socio-cultural, economic, and industrial context and ignoring the wider networks within which they are located. In this light, both adaptation and canonization could be framed differently, as vital parts of the workings of cultural memory. Following this line of thinking, adaptation serves to keep narratives, characters, and themes alive through ongoing (re-)interpretations, transferring them from the potentiality of the archive into active memory through public circulation.[11] As Astrid Erll states, 'remediation tends to solidify cultural memory, creating and stabilizing certain narratives and icons of the past'.[12] These processes are involved in a form of modern mythmaking in which stories are told and retold, reconfigured in different media environments and across media platforms, enabling audiences to engage in creative activities such as gaming, reading, watching, listening, and indeed in rewriting and developing the narrative (in the case of fanfiction or creative reversionings via YouTube clips, for example).

The different chapters within the present volume interrogate these various premisses and problematics, exploring the multiple ways in which the relationship between adaptation and canonicity can be played out and complexified. Armelle Blin-Rolland provides a number of very suggestive remarks in her chapter (drawing on the work of E. Dean Kolbas, Brian Rose, and others), bringing out the ways in which the process of adaptation renews the canon within culture as an ongoing and unfixed 'constellation', continuing rather than preserving it:

> 'Serial adaptation' is involved in canon formation, in the sense that it contributes to the canonical text becoming culturally familiar. As a result, the palimpsestuous reading of adaptations of canonical texts, as Linda Hutcheon points out, may not rely on a 'direct experience' of the text, but rather on a

> memory partly shaped by its serial adaptation, and resulting ongoing presence of the story in culture. [...] Through the lens of adaptation, the canon appears as a constellation of texts that are repeatedly returned to and rearticulated in new historically-situated contexts, shifting meaning and shape, repeated with a difference. While adaptation perpetuates the canon, it 'continues' rather than preserves it, in the sense that it turns it into a hybrid and dynamic, un-final construction inscribed in broader intertextual and intermedial networks.

Adaptation, Mediation, and Intermediality

In our title, we have suggested that the adaptive encounter is one of 'mediation'. Mediation suggests not only a connecting link, an interface between two or more terms, but also potentially an abrasive or disruptive quality (one of the *OED*'s definitions is 'intervening between people in a dispute to bring about agreement or reconciliation'). The act of adapting is frequently one of 'writing back', subversion and revision — self-consciously and perceptibly bridging or building relationships between cultures, genres, languages, and media. Put another way, 'adaptation studies ought to focus on the space of disjunction between texts and media to ask what that space, that necessary difference enables'.[13] The essays collected within the present volume stage a number of encounters between texts, artworks, films, and other artefacts, all of which cross time and place. While transnational dynamics are one of the most fascinating aspects of the adaptive process, the dominance of Anglo-American corpora within studies on adaptation (whether collections or monographs) has often been noted by scholars.[14] In contrast, almost every chapter within this collection involves some kind of intercultural exchange (many centred on cross-Channel dialogues between France, Germany, Italy, and England, but also interactions between France and the US, Japan and the wider world). Correspondingly, one of the aspects of adaptation that comes to the fore in several chapters (such as Komporaly's discussion of Thomas Ostermeier's *Hamlet* in Chapter 9, or Pascolini-Campbell's analysis of Ezra Pound's radio play of François Villon's *Le Testament* in Chapter 10), is transformation through linguistic translation and invention. The bringing together of case studies which foreground the transnational dynamic is a central aspect of what this volume seeks to achieve, in the juxtaposition of a wider range of national perspectives than is often found in collections of this kind.

Likewise, our volume is also a reaction to the novel-to-film paradigm that, as oft noted, continues to dominate the field. Despite the increasing visibility of work focusing on other medial forms and a more varied range of transpositions (see n. 2 above), a quick examination of the works included in our bibliography immediately shows the preponderance of critical writing focusing on the text/screen interface. The contributions to our volume have generally moved away from this paradigm, to explore the adaptive process in connection with (relatively) less discussed media, such as apps, the radio, and comic books — indeed, a major focus is on visualization, especially within various forms of graphic adaptation. The chapters also bring together a much wider range of literary forms and genres than the novel:

the medieval *ballade*, the short story, the theatre, the mash-up. Furthermore, many of the chapters juxtapose several different media rather than focusing on a single transposition: in Chapter 4 Blin-Rolland looks at film together with comic-book versions of *Jekyll and Hyde*, in Chapter 5 Stephens traces *Les Misérables* in manga and anime, and in Chapter 11 Griffiths considers film, television, and radio reworkings of *Thérèse Raquin*.

The majority of chapters within this collection explore adaptation across media, which brings us to our last point: the relation between adaptation studies and 'intermediality'. As we have seen, defining adaptation and situating adaptation studies is one of the core problems at the heart of the discipline.[15] Whilst Linda Hutcheon's definition of adaptation as 'an extended, deliberate, announced revisitation of a particular work of art'[16] remains influential, the specificity of 'adaptations' as a particular form of transtextuality, or intertextuality, can be difficult to pin down.[17] If the model of intertextuality threatens to dissolve the specificity of adaptations as a recognizable form of cultural production, this porosity also applies to adaptation studies as a separate field of enquiry.[18] Given the central importance of different types of media interaction in processes of adaptation, several scholars (such as Lars Elleström) have, likewise, attempted to situate or subsume adaptation studies within the broader field of 'intermediality'.[19] There are, however, significant differences between these two concepts: not all forms of adaptation are intermedial — some adapt across genre rather than medium for example, as in the reworkings of *Pride and Prejudice* explored by Jeremy Strong in Chapter 8 of this collection; and not all types of intermediality correspond to forms of adaptation. Nonetheless, the connections and overlaps between adaptation and intermediality are suggestive and have given rise to some of the most exciting new work in the field.[20] Notwithstanding this, Leitch notes that the problem of getting adaptation scholars and intermedialists to engage with each other 'remains as urgent as ever' (p. 8), 'the search for a common language that would foster productive dialogue between the two approaches [...] continues to be maddeningly elusive' (p. 16). To see adaptation as an intermedial process allows us to think through the relationship between different 'media configurations' as 'relative, dynamic and interactive rather than unidirectional, fixed and hierarchical'.[21] Interpreting adaptations as hybrid intermedia and interart practices clearly signals a departure from traditional concerns such as the source text, its translation, and related questions of fidelity.

F. W. Murnau's film *Nosferatu — eine Symphonie des Grauens* (Germany 1922) provides us with an illustration of how adaptation and intermediality can function together as frameworks of analysis, whose combination produces multi-layered interpretations. This film not only references Bram Stoker's novel as source material in its credits but goes further by mimicking the medial qualities of the book or rather the way a reader 'performs' the book: *Nosferatu* starts with the turning pages of a chronicle. As we will suggest in the analysis to follow, the film demonstrates various different forms and aspects of intermedial relations, and their connection with adaptation. By applying Eckard Voigts-Virchow's analytical concepts of 'media combination, media transfer, and media contact'[22] (also termed 'media combination', 'medial transposition', and 'intermedial reference', and 'primary', 'secondary', and 'figurative intermediality' by Irina Rajewsky and Werner Wolf respectively),[23] we can see how these can potentially come together in one media product:

1. Media combination or what Wolf terms 'primary intermediality':[24] as a silent film *Nosferatu* combines different aesthetic practices in one media configuration: (moving) images, (written) text and (musical) score. The film itself draws attention to its intermedial nature through its subtitle 'a symphony' but also through the use of five acts, in their imitation of the structure of drama, a very common feature of films from that time.

2. Media transfer/transposition: as the first film adaptation of Bram Stoker's novel *Dracula, or the Undead* (1897), *Nosferatu* also fits Wolf's definition of 'secondary intermediality' which describes the subsequent transformation of a work into another medium (and is the closest equivalent to the 'adaptation').[25] Although Murnau had changed all the names of the places and characters from the novel, he mentioned his source in the credits: 'After the novel Dracula by Bram Stoker, freely composed by Henrik Galeen'. The legal issues that ensued prefigure what would become one of the central issues in the analysis of film adaptations: the question of whether it was only inspired by the original or whether it was indeed a direct media transfer. This lay at the heart of a law suit which Stoker's widow had instigated only two months after the film was released, not least because she had set her hopes on the traditional and respectable medium of the theatre and the Broadway adaptation of her husband's novel. In 1924 a German court decided that all negatives and prints of the film should be destroyed, but by then copies had been sold to different countries world-wide, the film had already spread and in a very similar vein to that of his protagonist it led a sort of illegitimate after-life as a revenant in damaged and varying versions and as a mere shadow of its former self, as befits the undead.

3. 'Media contact', 'intermedial references', or 'figurative intermediality' (to use the terms of Voigts-Virchow, Rajewsky, and Wolf respectively) describes the most specific and rarest of these intermedial relationships, when within the given parameters of a medium the structure is transformed so that it results in the simulacrum of another medium, e.g. freeze-frame in a film. A medium which is normally latent appears in another medium as form and thereby becomes visible. In this way the parameters of both medial frameworks are foregrounded. In *Nosferatu* the relationship between text and visuals seems to reverse the conventions of silent film in which the moving images are punctuated by intertitles which supply part of the narrative or the dialogue. Here, we would argue, the text is interspersed with images. *Nosferatu* suggests with its opening, that we are not watching a film but reading a chronicle. The film begins with the foxed title page of a handwritten diary which traces the events that lead to the outbreak of the plague *A Chronicle of the Great Death in Wisborg anno Domini 1838 by †††*, implying that the viewer is indeed a reader. Medial differences are made visible and are self-reflexively 're-inscribed'. In this sense, as Joachim Paech notes, intermediality can be seen as a self-reflexive commentary which, in highlighting medial capacities and restrictions, reflects on the general conditions of a medium.[26]

Many of the chapters of this volume specifically engage with questions of intermediality, providing examples of ways in which 'figurative intermediality' generates complex and highly self-referential meditations not only on media relations, but also more specifically on the adaptive process itself. By focusing on intermediality in this context, we hope to have shown how the synergies and convergences between analytical frameworks can produce new readings, and to have suggested how the openness of adaptation studies to other approaches — arising from its status 'in between' (disciplines, concepts, cultures, and media) — can be seen as a strength rather than a weakness.

Overview of the Chapters

The first chapters of this book present a series of opening lines and new perspectives, suggesting different ways in which the field of adaptation studies can be situated and can orient itself, looking to the future, as well as the past. Chapters 1 and 2 each foreground new epistemologies of consumption associated with the adaptive process, particularly its interactive dimension, and its capacity to dissolve the distinctions between reading and writing. The collection opens with Clive Scott's richly suggestive exploration of how we might approach an aesthetics of adaptation that could move beyond the drive towards presenting case studies or producing analytical methodologies (for example, by elaborating taxonomies), which has often characterized this field of study. In his teasing out of connections and differences between practises of translation and adaptation, he notes that both are capable of mitigating and even resisting the oppressive aspects of traditional notions of the canon, in their 'minoritarian' (as opposed to 'official' and 'major') status, and as arts of the dynamic and refractive. Key to his sketching out of an alternative model for approaching adaptation is the idea of the polyglot rather than the monoglot reader: the reader who is familiar with the source and does not need to look backwards to it, instead taking it 'into a world of new comparabilities, into new exercises in perception'. Seeing reading as aesthetic experience rather than comprehension, and the reader's activity as one of 'making sense' and engaging the senses rather than of retrieving meaning, allows for a more productive and dynamic encounter: translation and adaptation may be understood as 'adventures in perceptual consciousness which set the source in motion, projecting it into possible futures, understanding the source as as an unquiet field of forces and energies within ever changing contexts'. His chapter uses David Shenton's 1986 comic-book version of Wilde's *Salomé* (1891), and various re-versionings of Goethe's poem 'Über allen Gipfeln' (1780), as a way of exploring synaesthesia, metamorphosis, and montage as producers of a priasmatic aesthetics that embodies the posthistorical and digital mentality, and goes beyond the discussion of the limits and possibilities of medium specificity. Ultimately, Scott suggests that the relationship between source and adaptation may be conceptualized as one of reciprocation rather than derivation: 'works within the canon do not immobilize themselves in time-honoured aesthetic values, but are the initiators of self-proliferative creative partnerships and co-authorings which keep their values in constantly self-reconfiguring progress'.

Kamilla Elliott's argument, in Chapter 2, is similarly oriented towards future developments, and to the ways in which our engagements with the adaptive process are conditioned or even determined by new technologies and the digital mentalities which accompany them. She creates the portmanteau 'ad-app-tation' in her ground-breaking exploration of apps as a form of adaptation technology, focusing on the British literary canon. Considering the major significance of apps used on mobile devices within contemporary culture, she surveys a range of apps allowing readers to engage with literary texts — those allowing the purchase of and access to ebooks, those embodying virtual bookshelves, collections, and even libraries (such as *Free Books Ultimate Classics Library*); those delivering packages of 'snackable fiction' (such as *Dailylit*) and those providing an immersive experience (such as iClassics's *PoeYourself*). She contrasts the approaches of apps which present authors with different degrees of reverential awe, subversive playfulness, and/or haunting artistry (for example, *Eye Shakespeare* or *Dickens: Dark London*) with those focused on the critical presentation of their *œuvres* (*Explore Shakespeare, Shakespeare at Play, RE:Shakespeare*) or particular works such as Eliot's *The Waste Land* (Touch Press with Faber and Faber, 2011).

Elliott contrasts the conservative approach of many educational apps, which present the literary canon to an audience as a pedagogic and scholarly tool (often selecting texts from the traditional humanist canon rather than from the new canons which have emerged since the 1960s) with the more radical and creative apps designed for very young children, including 'augmented reality apps' such as *Alice in Wonderland AR Quest*. Even in those apps which aim for an unquestioned presentation of the canon, though, tensions emerge between authoritative and open interpretations, the latter a corollary of the interactive structures and media combinations which allow the reader a certain freedom to navigate their own path. Elliott explores the way in which ad-app-tation creates new epistemologies of consumption, charting the shift away from modalities of reading and vision arising from print culture and cinema (such as narrative) to haptic and interactive experiences (more characteristic of gamification). Ultimately, she argues, because they change the way in which the literary canon is produced and consumed, new technologies 'change not only the answers to prior questions' (as Siobhan O'Flynn does in her Epilogue to the second edition of Hutcheon's *A Theory of Adaptation*), 'they also require new questions'.

Chapter 3 moves away from the broader perspectives sketched out in the first two chapters, to provide a more archaeological account, excavating some of the historical critical positions that have been adopted in relation to adaptations. Here, Christine Geraghty considers the way in which a specific film, Vincente Minnelli's *Madame Bovary* (1949) produced for MGM and based on Gustave Flaubert's celebrated novel of 1857, can be used as a test case for contrasting the critical approach of writers from different disciplinary backgrounds, and uncovering some of the assumptions and preoccupations underlying their constructions of genre and canonicity. She focuses on five divergent interpretations of this popular Hollywood prestige picture and its fictional heroine — three by scholars in the field of adaptation studies at various moments of its development (Robert Bluestone in 1957, Robert Stam in 2005, and Mary Donaldson-Evans in 2009), and two from film studies as it emerged in the

1980s (Lesley Stern in 1981 and Robin Wood in 1986). Within these accounts, treated thematically rather than in date order, the status of the 'source' text shifts significantly, indeed Geraghty notes that 'film studies was itself predicated on a lack of interest in adaptations as adaptations'. This serves as an important reminder that the emergence of both adaptation studies and film studies as recent disciplines has determined tensions that underly some of the critical attitudes that are played out in the reception of particular works, and more generally. While Flaubert's novel has been the inspiration for many adaptations which have generated a significant body of critical writing, Geraghty's analysis in the present volume sheds particular light on the ways in which canonicity has been differently construed within the critical reception of a particular film: from Bluestone's traditional measuring of the (lack of) 'success' of the adaptation by reference to its relationship with the canonical source text, to Wood's attempt to establish the canonicity of *Madame Bovary* (1949) by elevating Minnelli to a pantheon of film directors (a status which has little or nothing to do with Flaubert or his novel).

As noted earlier, given the continuing dominance of the novel-to-film paradigm within studies of adaptation, the contributions to this volume have — with the exception of Geraghty's meta-critical analysis outlined above — tended to move away from this approach, deliberately foregrounding a broader range of relationships between texts and media, and combining discussion of film adaptation with other forms of visual interpretation. The following four chapters each focus, in different ways, on strategies of visualization in the adaptive process within the context of print culture, with a particular emphasis on comic books (manga, graphic novel, and comics) and — a different but related bimodal product combining text and image — the illustrated book.

In Chapter 4, Armelle Blin-Rolland provides an incisive analysis of Jean Renoir's 1959 film *Le Testament du Docteur Cordelier* (*Experiment in Evil*) and Lorenzo Mattotti and Jerry Kramsky's 2002 comic book *Docteur Jekyll et Mr Hyde*, inscribed within what she calls the 'ever-expanding polymedia network' created through the 'serial adaptation' (using Brian Rose's term) of Robert Louis Stevenson's popular tale *The Strange Case of Dr Jekyll and Mr Hyde* (1886).[27] Like many other encounters captured in the present collection, this chapter not only brings together adaptations in different media, closely analysing the creative possibilities opened up by the techniques and artistry of film and of comic books respectively, but it also bears witness to complex cross-cultural and linguistic dynamics: both film and comic book are non-Anglophone (indeed Mattotti and Kramsky's comic book was initially written in Italian, but first published in French), and both transpose the story through time and place — from Victorian England to 1950s France and Weimar Germany.

Through the close reading of particular scenes, which have become visually established as key points in the narration through the process of serial adaptation (despite being relatively short in the 'source' text), Blin-Rolland focuses her analysis on the ways in which the dual figure Jekyll/Hyde is used to re-articulate the notion of evil within very different contexts: through an explicit engagement with the historic moment in the case of Mattotti and Kramsky's comic art, and its occlusion in Renoir's 1959 film. Renoir's film makes no direct reference to recent French history, although this absence is itself read by Blin-Rolland, following Colin Davis, as a highly significant reflection on France still in denial about its war-time collaboration. In both the film and comic book, what has been termed 'figurative intermediality' or 'intermedial reference' (Wolf, Rajewsky) is an important dimension of the work and its capacity to generate multi-layered meanings. Renoir's film evokes theatricality and self-consciously dramatizes the audio-visual mechanisms of its own forms of representation to figure the duality of the character Cordelier/Opale; Kramsky and Mattotti's comic book references the visual arts, and Expressionism in particular, an association that both defamiliarizes the reader from their memories of the story and, through the recognizable artistic context, identifies the unleashing of evil that is depicted with the rise of Nazism. A key notion throughout this chapter is what Blin-Rolland calls 'adaptive reading': the reader's ability to perceive a complex play of 'repetition and difference' (Hutcheon) or 'interaction and transformation' (Miller) in relation to the genealogy of adaptations (and in the case of *Le Testament*, a performance tradition) within which each reworking of the tale is inscribed, and which, as we have seen, also connects outwards to the intertextual and intermedial weave more broadly.

The focus on visual culture, and the combined analysis of film animation with comic book adaptation continues in Chapter 5. Here, Bradley Stephens turns to a relatively unstudied facet of the vast array of adaptations provoked by Victor Hugo's *Les Misérables* (1862): those produced in Japan in the late twentieth century and early twenty-first century. His focus is on two specific adaptations: an animated television series of fifty-two half-hour episodes broadcast over the course of 2007 — *Les Misérables: Shōjo Cosette* [A Girl Named Cosette] — directed by Hiroaki Sakurai as part of Nippon Animation's World Masterpiece Theatre and within a recognizable *shōjo* genre destined for family viewing; and a 2009 graphic novel, *Re Mizeraburu*, by East Press within its *Manga de Dokuha* [Reading through with Manga] series of socially conscious titles, aimed at an adult audience (republished in French by Soleil Manga in 2011). Situating these works within the context of the reception of Hugo's novel in Japan more broadly, and within the culture of manga and anime, he shows how each version of the story is adapted to a different audience, and within a different production context (both producers examined here specialize in adapting classic literature for popular audiences of different kinds).

Stephens also provides a close comparative analysis of how visualization is used within the two media to produce powerfully emotive effects (for example, in the representation of Fantine's misfortunes). Throughout this chapter, he considers questions relating to the representation of cultural alterity in the adaptation process, especially pertinant in the case of a text whose Romantic vision of common humanity and of a unified human race is at stake. The complex negotiation of the relationship between cultures is an inherent aspect of manga and anime, which are directed at a transnational entertainment market and deliberately leave aspects of their representation culturally indeterminate while at the same time producing a unique aesthetic style in the context of a genre that is recognizably Japanese.

Chapter 6 further develops our collection's engagement with graphic adaptation and various forms of interplay between the verbal and the visual, with Juliane Blank's multifaceted survey of 'the Kafka image', as it has been explored within a new generation of comic books and graphic novels since the 1990s. She notes that Kafka, with Goethe, are the two most adapted German-speaking writers of all time. But rather than focusing on the adaptation of a single text, Blank brings together several of Kafka's most famous and popular works ('Das Urteil' ['The Judgement'], 1912, *Die Verwandlung* [*The Metamorphosis*], 1915, and *Der Process* [*The Trial*], 1914/15) and considers how, since the 1990s, comic books have engaged both with previous traditions of illustrating and adapting Kafka's works, and with the complex status of Kafka as an iconic figure (in respect of his personal appearance, as established by photographic portraits, and his reputation as a writer), within both academic and popular culture. Indeed, Blank notes that within popular culture, Kafka has achieved a kind of celebrity cult status, and has to some extent even come to embody the 'modern' or 'postmodern' condition.

The illustrated biography *Kafka for Beginners* (1993) by Robert Crumb and David Zane Mairowitz, which also includes short graphic adaptations of Kafka's most popular works, is seen as a cornerstone of the new approach, and as a canonical adaptation in its own right, which has strongly marked subsequent adaptations within the 1990s generation of graphic novels. Through a close analysis of the strategies of visualization adopted by this work, together with Peter Kuper's *The Metamorphosis* (2003) and Chantal Montellier and David Z. Mairowitz's *The Trial* (2008), Blank explores how they engage with the formal and aesthetic complexity of Kafka's texts, for example, by experimenting with the visual possibilities for conveying narrative perspective, rather than simply attempting to 'extract' the plot. She brings out their commitment to retaining some of the 'funny' dimension of comic strips, through visual humour and visual means of producing irony, and examines their interpellation of various frameworks of interpretation taken from popular and academic traditions, including the biographical approach, and the playfully post-modern attitude, for example. These self-conscious and experimental modes of visualization, she suggests, not only reflect on their own status as post-modern adaptations, but they also allow for a new understanding of graphic adaptation in its own right, whose rejuvenation in recent years owes much to the figure of Franz Kafka.

In Chapter 7, Christina Ionescu turns to the illustrated book as a relatively neglected example of the adaptative process. Despite the fact that illustrations of literary works are a very long-standing form of transposition from text to image, illustrations and the illustrated book as a whole have rarely been theorized from the perspective of adaptation studies, especially when compared to the burgeoning field of theoretical and critical work surrounding comics adaptations/the graphic novel. Ionescu notes that the illustrated book is of particular interest in that the visual adaptation is in this case 'source-bound', which is to say that the illustrations usually appear alongside the text which they adapt whereas most other forms of adaptation such as films, plays, and comic books, create a stand-alone product, which may incorporate text directly taken from the source, but do not do so in its integrality. Ionescu brings together the perspectives of book history, word-and-image, and adaptation studies, in order to explore illustrations and the illustrated book as a material object and consumer product that is adapted in multiple ways and arises out of a creative and collaborative process involving many different agents including artists, translators, editors, typographers, book designers, printers, binders, publishers, and booksellers, amongst others.

In this survey of the ways in which the visual presentation of the illustrated book is adapted for, marketed at, and sold to different audiences, Ionescu focuses on four illustrated editions of Voltaire's bestselling tale, *Candide* (1759), published in New York in the interwar period: the 1927 Bennett Libraries' *Candide*, illustrated by Clara Tice; the 1928 *Candide* by Random House, designed and illustrated by Rockwell Kent; Ives Washburn's 1929 *Candide*, illustrated by Howard Simon; and Williams, Belasco and Meyers's 1930 *Candide*, illustrated by Mahlon Blaine and Arthur Zaidenberg, which respectively adapt the text as a product for book collectors, for the art connoisseur, for more modest book lovers, and for the mass market. This fascinating corpus sheds light nor only on the complex ways in which illustrations function within different material supports (as well as in connection with their 'source text') and how different processes of adaptation are combined within each illustrated edition, but also on the way in which the adaptations of Voltaire's Enlightenment tale had a key role to play in the development of the arts of the American book and printing industry at an important moment of its history.

In Chapters 8 and 9 we move away from the model of adaptation across media, and specifically, from various forms of interplay between verbal and visual modes arising out of graphic adaptation, to forms of adaptation that remain broadly within the same medium (text, or theatre) but cross generic boundaries to produce striking effects, and create ideological ramifications that may change our understanding of both the source and its web of existing adaptations. Jeremy Strong brings together three recent textual re-versionings of Jane Austen's *Pride and Prejudice*, each of which occupies a different position within current literary hierarchies, and engages playfully with its status. For each of these re-versionings, a working knowledge of the original text is essential for the reader's construction of meaning in and enjoyment of the new work, while also knowingly referencing earlier adaptive trends. In Jo Baker's *Longbourn* (2013), this is achieved by creating a parallel narrative interwoven with the plot but focusing on characters who are marginal, and marginalized, in Austen's novel; in P. D. James's *Death Comes to Pemberley* (2011) a sequel is added which engages with Austen's plot, shifting to a 'murder mystery' genre and potentially unravelling the tidy resolution of *Pride and Prejudice*; lastly, Seth Grahame-Smith's *Pride and Prejudice and Zombies* (2009) is a comic mash-up which incorporates much of Austen's text but adds new material involving Britain's affliction by a plague of zombies, and generates comedy through a combination of gore and subtle social observation, while retaining central elements of Austen's plot. Through a comparative analysis of these works, Strong identifies major themes which are occluded — or only barely present — in Austen's novel such as 'domestic work', 'race', 'war', and 'the wider world', but are foregrounded in these adaptations, providing critical and at times subversive readings that, in Sanders's terms, 'write back' both to the source text and the interpretations offered by some of its screen versions.

In Chapter 9 we turn to the theatre. Jozefina Komporaly provides an overview and analysis of the adaptive strategies employed by Thomas Ostermeier, in his theatrical adaptation of Shakespeare's *Hamlet*, which combines an assertive linguistic translation with experimental forms of dramaturgy and *mise en scène*, and a self-conscious engagement with various forms of intermediality in performance. This production is characteristic of the German director's aim of shaking up theatrical conventions, approaching canonical theatre 'through the lens of Sarah Kane', and using it first and foremost as a vehicle to interpret contemporary society, with a strong political inflection and elements of ideological critique (he has also adapted a number of other European classics, by Ibsen and Büchner amongst others). His *Hamlet* was commissioned for the Avignon Festival, as a high-profile international production, and is a showpiece of the Schaubühne theatre company which he directs.

Komporaly examines the role of Marius von Mayenburg's translation for this production of Shakespeare's language into accessible down-to-earth contemporary German prose as a key aspect of the adaptive process, together with a *mise en scène* which updates the play's cultural contexts to the here and now, and a fragmented performance aesthetic which owes much to postdramatic theatre, and strongly emphasizes interaction with the audience and improvization. Concomitantly, the production as a whole privileges the avoidance of cliché and predictability. Ostermeier's refusal of traditional markers of genre, in his accentuation of comedy within the piece, is a significant aspect of how he disrupts hierarchies and expectations associated with canonical productions. Perhaps most interesting in the context of the present volume is the way in which this production stages other media, whether through the inclusion of television game shows, DJ performances, video recordings, or Hamlet's own filming via a hand-held camera, which allows for the juxtaposition of live action on stage and documented performance via recording (viewed alongside each other) — a self-reflexive dramatization of contemporary society's obsessive cult of the self and of celebrity and, more generally, a critique of consumer culture. Hamlet's descent into madness is shown to be intrinsically linked to all of this, and he is characterized as a spoilt brat (a 'tantrum-throwing talk-show host'). In terms of the cross-cultural dynamics that this adaptation embodies, as Komporaly notes, it is interesting that despite Ostermeier's international acclaim, he has been much criticized in Germany, where he is at odds with current institutional opinion regarding the theatre, and is considered 'an exiled artist of sorts' (George Banu), although he shares with a number of other directors an interest in experimenting with the boundaries of staging classical work.

Claire Pascolini-Campbell shifts our focus to radio adaptation, one of the least explored media within this field of study. She provides a detailed analysis of Ezra Pound's adaptation of the fifteenth-century French poet François Villon's *Le*

Testament as a radio melodrama for the BBC in 1931, noting that this was but one of a number of Pound's adaptive engagements with Villon through various genres and media including pastiche, translation, and opera amongst others (within a context of multiple adaptations of Villon's *œuvre* more generally, for example in sculpture, music, theatre). Pound's inclusion of Villon in his various critical works and anthologies similarly suggests both his fascination with this writer, and also a deliberate attempt to establish his position within a revised and re-evaluated literary canon. Pascolini-Campbell explores Pound's 1931 radio play as an adaptation of an adaptation (his 1924 opera of the same text, composed in collaboration with the avant-garde American composer George Antheil), at the centre of a complex weave of genres and media. At the same time it brings out different aspects of Pound's formal experimentation with the creative possibilities afforded by new technologies associated with radio, a relatively new medium at the time, and one with a potential to reach mass audiences (BBC radio broadcasting began in 1922).

The central status of language itself within this adaptation for the aural medium of radio is played out on many levels. Pound's interest in the musical qualities of poetry, his theory of 'melopeoia', which explores the capacity of its sounds to communicate meaning, is key to understanding his adaptive strategy. Pound's radio play combined the libretto of his opera (Villon's Old French *ballades* as sung poetry), based on the idea that the sound of the verse would convey its own emotion and beauty as well as meaning, with a new dialogue in English, in order to make the events of the story more accessible to an English-speaking public. Like Mayenburg's translation into German of Shakespeare's language, discussed in Chapter 9, Pound's additional dialogue navigates not only the shift between languages (French and English) but also the distance between medieval, early modern, and contemporary idioms. Pound opts for linguistic inventiveness, rather than straightforward modernization, attempting to create a simulacrum of 'Villonian' English which situates Villon and his companions 'as part of a timeless urban working class' through a medley of different influences (including modern slang, American, and cockney, archaic language redolent of medieval usage, amongst other registers). In conjunction with the Old French libretto and English script, Pound furnishes an aural 'landscape' for the audience through his experimental use of 'foley' and a range of other sound effects to communicate the aspects of time and place (assisted by his producer, Edward Archibald Harding, who was a pioneer in radio technologies). An examination of the possibilities allowed by radio also forms part of the next chapter, which is similarly centred on cross-channel dynamics, adapting from France to England.

In the final article of this collection, Kate Griffiths uses Harold Bloom's notion of 'the anxiety of influence' as a model for considering adaptive relations. Whereas Bloom's account is concerned with writers and their combative relationship with canonical forbears, here Griffiths explores how such dynamics are self-consciously played out in the adaptation's figuration of its own relationship with various sources, and as a theme within each work. Focusing her analysis on Émile Zola's novel *Thérèse Raquin* (1867), which has been a huge adapting phenomenon since its initial publication, she brings together a range of its afterlives in different media including films by Marcel Carné (1953) and Charlie Stratton (2013); television adaptations in 1980 and 2002, dramatized by Philip Mackie and by Caroline Huppert respectively; and a BBC radio adaptation in 1998, by Melissa Murray. She examines each in turn, starting with Zola's text, showing that in each case the self-reflexive celebration of intertextual and intermedial borrowings may suggest a creative rather than destructive vision of influence, despite the potential for anxiety — an anxiety which manifests itself more clearly within the critical reception of many of the adaptations. In its delineation of a dense and multilayered set of influences, in which celebrated adaptations themselves become canonical references to be reworked and reinvented in subsequent afterlives, this chapter provides a fascinating example of how influence cannot be understood as a simple linear movement from 'source' to 'adaptation', but rather as a more complex encounter between cultural products circulating within multiple intertextual and intermedial networks.

* * * * *

In a recent conference, on 'Illustration and Adaptation', Kamilla Elliott posed the question: 'is there — and can there be — a canon of adaptations'? Although many of the articles in this collection do take a (canonical) literary text as their starting point, the analysis of the intricate and interlocking networks of texts, images, and memories generated by the process of 'serial adaptation' in each case, has brought to the fore a number of adaptations that have themselves become canonical (and are themselves reworked, reconfigured, and remediated across a range of cultures and media): Carné's film adaptation of *Thérèse Raquin* is a good example of this, as is Crumb and Mairowitz's *Kafka for Beginners* (1993) discussed as a cornerstone of a new generation of graphic adaptation. The immense richness of the multiple cross-cultural adaptations brought together and viewed alongside each other in the context of a volume like this may go some way towards providing such a (provisional, and constantly expanding) corpus — allowing the reader to navigate between different generations of adaptation and to construct their own 'adaptation networks'.[28]

Notes to the Introduction

1. In reverse chronological order: *The Routledge Companion to Adaptation Studies*, ed. by Dennis Cutchins, Katja Krebs and Eckard Voigts (Abingdon & New York: Routledge, 2018); *The Oxford Handbook of Adaptation Studies*, ed. by Thomas Leitch (Oxford: Oxford University Press, 2017); *Adaptation Studies: New Challenges, New Directions*, ed. by Jørgen Bruhn, Anne Gjelsvic and Eirik Frisvold Hanssen (London & New York: Bloomsbury Academic, 2013); *A Companion to Literature, Film and Adaptation*, ed. by Deborah Cartmell, Blackwell Companions to Literature and Culture (Chichester, Oxford & Malden, MA: Blackwell Publishing, 2012); *Adaptation Studies: New Directions*, ed. by Christa Albrecht-Crane and Dennis Cutchins (Madison, NJ: Fairleigh Dickinson University Press, 2010); *Redefining Adaptation Studies*, ed. by Dennis Cutchins, Laurence Raw and James M. Welch (Lanham, MD: Scarecrow Press, 2010). We note the overlap in our title with that of Yvonne Griggs, *The Bloomsbury Introduction to Adaptation Studies: Adapting the Canon in Film, TV, Novels and Popular Culture* (London & New York:

Bloomsbury Academic, 2016); however, our subject was determined and follows from the 2014 Legenda conference in London on which the present volume is based: the two projects are in fact very distinct in their focus and approach.

2. For example, on television: Yvonne Griggs, *Adaptable TV: Rewiring the Text* (London: Palgrave Macmillan, 2018); Shannon Wells-Lassagne, *Television and Serial Adaptation* (New York & Abingdon: Routledge, 2017); on comics and comics books: *Transmédialité, bande dessinée & adaptation*, ed. by Evelyne Duprêtre and German A. Duarte (Clermont-Ferrand: Presses universitaires Blaise Pascal, 2019); *Comics and Adaptation*, ed. by Armelle Blin-Rolland, Guillaume Lecomte and Marc Ripley, special issue of *European Comic Art*, 10.1 (2017); *Bande dessinée et adaptation: littérature, cinéma, TV*, ed. by Benoît Mitaine, David Roche and Isabelle Schmitt-Pitiot (Clermont Ferrand: Presses universitaires Blaise Pascal, 2015) [*Comics and Adaptation*, ed. by Benoît Mitaine, David Roche and Isabelle Schmitt-Pitiot, trans. by Aarnoud Rommens and David Roche (Jackson: University Press of Mississippi, 2018)]; and on illustration or visual culture more generally: *Adaptation in Visual Culture: Texts, Images, and their Multiple Worlds*, ed. by Julie Grossman and R. Barton Palmer (London: Palgrave Macmillan, 2017); Kate Newell, *Expanding Adaptation Networks: From Illustration to Novelization* (London: Palgrave Macmillan, 2017); *Picturing the Eighteenth-century Novel Through Time: Illustration, Intermediality and Adaptation*, ed. by Christina Ionescu and Ann Lewis, special issue of *Journal for Eighteenth-Century Studies*, 39.4 (December 2016); *Dante on View: The Reception of Dante in the Visual and Performing Arts*, ed. by Luisa Calè and Antonella Braida (Aldershot & Burlington, VT: Ashgate, 2007). Following the *Illustration and Adaptation* conference held by Illustr4tio at the Université de Bourgogne, in Dijon, in October 2019, two volumes are projected for 2021.

3. See, amongst others, Kamilla Elliott, *Theorizing Adaptation* (New York & Oxford: Oxford University Press, 2020); Kate Griffiths, *Zola and the Art of Television: Adaptation, Recreation, Translation* (Oxford: Legenda, forthcoming); Laurence Raw, *Expanding Adaptation Studies* (Basingstoke: Palgrave Macmillan, forthcoming); *Adapting Endings from Book to Screen: Last Pages, Last Shots*, ed. by Armelle Parey and Shannon Wells-Lassagne (Abingdon: Routledge, 2019); Thomas Leitch, *The History of American Literature on Film* (New York: Bloomsbury Academic, 2019); *Intersemiotic Translation as Adaptation*, ed. by Vasso Giannakopoulou and Deborah Cartmell, special issue of *Adaptation*, 23.3 (December 2019).

4. Three journals focus exclusively on adaptation studies broadly conceived: *Adaptation* (originally, *Adaptation: The Journal of Literature on Screen Studies*) (first published 2008); *Journal of Adaptation in Film & Performance* (first published in 2008); *Literature/Film Quarterly* (first published 1973). (The two learned associations are: the Association of Adaptation Studies, founded in 2006, and the Literature/Film Association, founded in 1989.) Palgrave's series on Adaptation and Visual Culture is an important contributor to the field's visibility (its first volumes appeared in 2015); Bloomsbury Academic also includes a significant number of volumes focusing on adaptation of various kinds; Legenda's Transcript, within which the present volume appears, focuses on 'all kinds of imagining across languages, media and cultures: translations and versions, inter-cultural and multi-lingual writing, illustrations and musical settings, adaptation for theatre, film, television and new media, creative and critical responses' (and began publishing in 2015). Recent/forthcoming conferences include: *Illustration & Adaptation*, conference, October 2019, Université de Bourgogne, Dijon; *Borders in/of Adaptation*, conference, October 2020, Université de Bourgogne, Dijon; the IFTR Translation, Adaptation and Dramaturgy (TAD) Working Group meeting at the IFTR conference in Galway, Ireland, July 2020. Current calls for articles include: *Adaptation as Revision*, a special issue of *Adaptation* to be guest-edited by Wieland Schwanebeck (deadline April 2020) and *Essays on Adaptation Studies*, a special issue of *Literature/Film Quarterly* (deadline January 2020).

5. On 'adaptation as a poor relation of both literary and film studies', see Thomas Leitch, 'Is Adaptation Studies a Discipline?', *Germanistik in Ireland*, 7 (2002), 13–26. See also Deborah Cartmell '100+ Years of Adaptations, or, Adaptation as the Art Form of Democracy', in *A Companion to Literature, Film and Adaptation*, ed. by Cartmell, pp. 1–13. On the antagonistic relationship between 'adaptation' and 'theorization' and the inherent bias of the latter against the former, joined with the need for a more reciprocal discourse of 'adaptive theorization', see

Kamilla Elliott, 'The Theory of *Bad*adaptation', in *The Routledge Companion to Adaptation Studies*, ed. by Cutchins, Krebs and Voigts, pp. 18–27.

6. See Christa Albrecht-Crane and Dennis Cutchins, 'Introduction: New Beginnings for Adaptation Studies', in *Adaptation Studies: New Approaches*, ed. by Albrecht-Crane and Cutchins, pp. 11–22; Jørgen Bruhn, Anne Gjelsvik and Eirik Frisvold Hanssen, '"There and Back Again": New Challenges and New Directions in Adaptation Studies', in *Adaptation Studies: New Challenges, New Directions*, ed. by Bruhn, Gjelsvik and Hanssen, pp. 1–16; and especially Thomas Leitch's 'Introduction', in *The Oxford Handbook of Adaptation Studies*, ed. by Leitch, pp. 1–20, which identifies three specific waves or generations of 'Adaptation Studies' and their shifting preoccupations, since George Bluestone's foundational *Novels into Film* (1957).
7. Leitch, 'Introduction', in *The Oxford Handbook of Adaptation Studies*, ed. by Leitch, p. 17 (further references to this introduction are given after quotations in the text).
8. Julie Sanders, *Adaptation and Appropriation*, 2nd edn (London & New York: Routledge, 2006), pp. 8–9.
9. On debates around the canon within a literary context, see John Guillory, *Cultural Capital: The Problem of Literary Canon Formation* (Chicago: University of Chicago Press, 1993), Harold Bloom, *The Western Canon: The Books and School of the Ages* (New York: Papermac, 1995), Dean E. Kolbas, *Critical Theory and the Literary Canon* (Boulder, CO: Westview Press, 2001), and *Fame and Glory: The Classic, the Canon and the Literary Pantheon*, ed. by Elizabeth Benjamin and Jessica Goodman, special issue of *MHRA Working Papers in the Humanities*, 8 (2013) <http://www.mhra.org.uk/publications/Fame-Glory> [accessed 10 August 2019].
10. Cartmell, '100+ Years of Adaptations', p. 10.
11. Aleida Assman notes that: 'While emphatic appreciation, repeated performance, and continued individual and public attention are the hallmark of objects in the cultural working memory, professional preservation and withdrawal from general attention marks the contents of the reference memory. Emphatic reverence and specialised historical curiosity are the two poles between which the dynamics of cultural memory is played out', in 'Canon and Archive', in *Cultural Memory Studies: An International and Interdisciplinary Handbook*, ed. by Ansgar Nünning and Astrid Erll (Berlin: de Gruyter, 2008), pp. 97–107 (p. 101).
12. Astrid Erll, 'Literature, Film, and the Mediality of Cultural Memory', in *Cultural Memory Studies*, ed. by Nünning and Erll, pp. 389–98 (p. 393).
13. Albrecht-Crane and Cutchins, 'Introduction', p. 20.
14. See, for example, Leitch, 'Introduction', p. 6; Cartmell, '100+ Years of Adaptations', p. 7. A notable exception to this trend is the nineteenth-century French novel, which has recently generated a significant body of critical work in relation to adaptation. See, for example: Kate Griffiths and Andrew Watts, *Adapting Nineteenth-century France: Literature in Film, Theatre, Television, Radio and Print* (Cardiff: University of Wales Press, 2013); Kate Griffiths, Bradley Stephens and Andrew Watts, 'Introduction: Multimedia Adaptation and the Pull of Nineteenth-century France', in *Adaptation*, special issue of *Dix-Neuf*, 18.2 (2014), 126–33; Kate Griffiths, *Émile Zola and the Artistry of Adaptation* (Oxford: Legenda, 2009) and *Zola and the Art of Television* (Oxford: Legenda, forthcoming); *'Les Misérables' and its Afterlives: Between Page, Stage and Screen*, ed. by Kathryn M. Grossman and Bradley Stephens (Farnham: Ashgate, 2015); Mary Donaldson-Evans, *Madame Bovary at the Movies: Adaptation, Ideology, Context* (Amsterdam: Rodopi, 2009); and *L'Œuvre de Victor Hugo à l'écran: des rayons et des ombres*, ed. by Delphine Gleizes (Quebec: L'Harmattan/Presses de l'Université Laval, 2005). In the French context more generally, see also *Adaptation: Studies in French and Francophone Culture*, ed. by Neil Archer and Andreea Weisl-Shaw (Bern: Peter Lang, 2012), and *French Literature on Screen*, ed. by Homer B. Pettey and R. Barton Palmer (Manchester: Manchester University Press, 2019).
15. For a recent discussion of this, see amongst others, Timothy Corrigan, 'Defining Adaptation', in *The Oxford Handbook of Adaptation Studies*, ed. by Leitch, pp. 23–35.
16. Linda Hutcheon, with Siobhan O'Flynn, *A Theory of Adaptation*, 2nd edn (Abingdon & New York: Routledge, 2013) p. 170.
17. See Thomas Leitch, 'Adaptation and Intertextuality, or, What isn't an Adaptation, and What Does it Matter?', in *A Companion to Literature, Film and Adaptation*, ed. by Cartmell, pp. 87–104.

18. For an interesting discussion of this problem, see Sarah Cardwell, 'Pause, Rewind, Replay: Adaptation, Intertextuality and (Re)defining Adaptation Studies', in *The Routledge Companion to Adaptation*, ed. by Cutchins, Krebs and Voigts, pp. 7–17.
19. See, for example, Lars Elleström, 'Adaptation Within the Field of Media Transformations', in *Adaptation Studies*, ed. by Bruhn, Gjelsvik and Hanssen, pp. 113–32.
20. For influential accounts of 'intermediality', see Irina O. Rajewsky, 'Intermediality, Intertextuality, and Remediation: A Literary Perspective on Intermediality', *Intermédialités*, 6 (2005), 43–64, and 'Border Talks: The Problematic Status of Media Borders in the Current Debate about Intermediality', in *Media Borders, Multimodality and Intermediality*, ed. by Lars Elleström (Basingstoke: Palgrave Macmillan, 2010), pp. 51–68. See also Lars Elleström, 'The Modalities of Media: A Model for Understanding Intermedial Relations', in *Media Borders*, ed. by Elleström, pp. 11–48; *Handbook of Intermediality: Literature, Image, Sound, Music*, ed. by Gabriele Rippl (Berlin & Boston: de Gruyter, 2015); Werner Wolf, 'Intermedialität', in *Metzler Lexikon Literatur- und Kulturtheorie: Ansätze, Personen, Grundbegriff*, ed. by Ansgar Nünning (Stuttgart: Metzler Verlag, 1998), pp. 238–39, and the recently published collection of English translations of Wolf's essays: *Selected Essays on Intermediality by Werner Wolf (1992–2014): Theory and Typology, Literature-Music Relations, Transmedial Narratology, Miscellaneous Transmedial Phenomena*, ed. by Walter Bernhart (Leiden & Boston, MA: Brill Rodopi, 2018).
21. Regina Schober, 'Adaptation as Connection: Transmediality Reconsidered', in *Adaptation Studies*, ed. by Bruhn, Gjelsvik and Hanssen, pp. 89–112 (p. 95).
22. Eckard Voigts-Virchow, *Introduction to Media Studies* (Stuttgart: Klett, 2005), pp. 85–86.
23. See Rajewsky, 'Intermediality, Intertextuality, and Remediation', p. 50, and 'Border Talks', pp. 55–56.
24. Wolf, 'Intermedialität'.
25. Ibid., p. 238 ff.
26. Joachim Paech, 'Intermedialität: Mediales Differenzial und transformative Figurationen', in *Intermedialität: Theorie und Praxis eines interdisziplinären Forschungsgebiets*, ed. by Jörg Helbig (Berlin, Schmidt, 1998), p. 16.
27. Brian A. Rose, *'Jekyll and Hyde' Adapted: Dramatizations of Cultural Anxiety* (Westport, CT: Greenwood Press, 1996), pp. 15–16.
28. For an interesting discussion of the metaphor of 'networks' in adaptation studies, see Newell, *Expanding Adaptation Networks*, pp. 1–2, 8 & 20 (esp. n. 2).

CHAPTER 1

❖

Translation, Adaptation, and the Senses of Medium

Clive Scott

Initial Positions

Our suspicion of the canon relates directly to our suspicion of those presuppositions and consequences the canon seems to entail: the sense that history has, for one of its specific functions, a process of distillation; that the canon subjects art to ethnic atavisms; that it supports an oppressive ethic of touchstones and epitomes; that it serves state-administered institutional mindsets — the curriculum, the syllabus, the reading-list, authorization by academic ancestral rite, justification by expert interpretative criticism. But the canon has come to weigh less heavily thanks to the incursions of cultural studies, gender studies, postcolonial studies, the arts of the everyday, and more particularly thanks to the tutelary offices of translation and adaptation. While indicating some of the differences between these two latter activities, I want to treat them as a partnership, predominantly for two reasons. First, they share qualities which one might associate with what Deleuze and Guattari call the 'minor' or 'minoritarian', in that, as arts of the dynamic and the refractive, they resist 'official', 'major', aesthetic criteria, pursuing the variable and variational as against the constant; testing limits; favouring the experimental; 'deterritorializing' and disequilibriating codes and conventions. In this last respect, adaptation might be regarded as more interrogative and irreverent than translation: it sets the interests of the source work more competitively against its own self-interests as an adaptation. Second, both translation and adaptation seem to me to encourage, not to say institute, modes of knowing and perceiving inherently alien to canon-formation. This latter proposition grows from the observation that linear history is an inappropriate way of imaging our own personal relationships with the past. What happens when our own ways of wanting to know, that is, associatively, free-rangingly, do not coincide with those institutional ways of knowing which build up bodies of knowledge according to accredited methodologies? Translation and adaptation provide resources and behavioural modes for answering that question. Furthermore, adaptation in particular draws our attention to the fact that the relationship between disciplines and media-practice is not an ordered transaction with stable rules and procedures, but a free-for-all, a begetter of all kinds of hybrid, often collectively rather than individually created.

This article, then, proposes as a first move, that the act of translation/adaptation is the engineering of the shift from one kind of exercise of knowledge to another: from research knowledge to self-expressive knowledge, from public knowledge to private forms of knowing, from classificatory knowledge to self-constructive knowledge. The problem we are left with is how this new kind of knowledge might be seen to grow out of the old, and to complement it, and how the potentially anarchic forces released by new epistemological attitudes might be fruitfully and coherently harnessed.

Adaptation: Testing the Temperature

In first making the transition from translation to adaptation studies, one is confronted by some worrying lines of thought. The relevant critical literature suggests, either explicitly or implicitly, that adaptation is quite simply the modern mode of self-expression, that we live in an age in which hybridization, montage, bricolage, recycling, intermedial and intergeneric cross-over or convergence are standard creative mechanisms,[1] facilitated and accelerated by digital technology and by the hypermedial mentality.[2] Indeed, critics seem to be increasingly of the view that 'adaptation' is a misleading term, too single-minded in what it suggests of intention, too focused in what it presupposes of critical response, and that 'intertextuality' better captures the pluralistic, heterogeneous, and self-dispersive thing that adaptation really is.[3] All this immediately makes any stable evaluative criteria, and fidelity in particular, not worth pursuing, even though the very act of comparing source and adaptation unavoidably regenerates a discourse which sounds fidelity-orientated.[4] In fact, adaptation studies might here be reckoned to be the victim of its own regressive logic: if you insist that cinema, say, achieves effects equivalent to *or* divergent from those of the novel, either way and before you know it, you find yourself back with essentialist, medium-specific approaches. Furthermore the case for refusing to treat the source as a privileged origin has grown stronger,[5] largely because the source itself is seen as a welter of intertexts and adaptations,[6] quite without aesthetic 'purity', and this, in turn, has led to some inconsistencies of attitude: Linda Hutcheon, for example, wants to espouse poststructuralist responses to the notion of origin, to question the adapted text's inevitable priority, but declares shortly afterwards that adaptations will be examined in her book 'as deliberate, announced, and extended revisitations of prior works'.[7] Correspondingly, there is less and less the prospect of writing any meaningful teleological history of adaptation as a practice, and more and more the prospect of an adaptation studies which produces case studies, and analytical methodologies,[8] often based on structuralist accounts of the elements of narrative,[9] and which constructs taxonomies[10] and categories of different kinds and degrees of adaptation,[11] but which itself has no agenda, which aims at neither an aesthetics of adaptation, nor a consumer-response theory for adaptation.[12] Thus one is left with a sense of a promiscuity both of nature and purpose which it would be fruitless, and unjustified, to resist or undo. This is a very crude and perhaps faulty diagnosis, and merely echoes the charges already laid at adaptation's door by the likes of Robert Ray and Thomas Leitch.[13] Nonetheless, these fault lines in adaptation studies seem difficult to square with positive feelings about the new futures of its partner, translation, which might be envisaged.

Of course, various existing accounts of adaptation strongly suggest that adaptation and translation should be seen as rather different undertakings, on the following scores, among others:

1. Adaptation is an explicit response to the demands of its medium; it is the medium as much as the adapter that determines the transformative choices.

2. Adaptation is more acutely aware of its audience and is, therefore, more communication-orientated and more geared to its conditions of reception, including, especially, economic conditions.

3. Relatedly, adaptation has the task of telling us where we are, as a community, in relation to a work; in other words, adaptation is a form of cultural diagnosis and of cultural self-assertion, with active obligations to its context.

4. Adaptation is more driven towards its own autonomy and is, therefore, more goal-motivated and more self-serving.

There is some truth in these differentiations perhaps: adaptation has been seen as distinctively cross-medial, more justified by its reception than its exercise, more ambitious for itself in aims and objectives, and thus more appropriative. But such characteristics are, with translation's own development, becoming less defining. Some critics have indeed felt that there is a strong case for harnessing aspects of translation theory to the study of adaptation,[14] particularly where the two disciplines might share Lawrence Venuti's call to translators to develop 'innovative translation practices in which their work becomes visible to readers'.[15] These words are commendable, but such commendation puts me in a false position, since Venuti's translational persuasions are, in other respects, diametrically opposed to my own. Where he reckons that the business of translation is an interpretation of the source text, that it necessarily has something metatextual about it, that it is the source's signified, I favour a translation which translates the phenomenology of reading and produces not a signified for the source but a companion signifier, what a reader, armed with his/her own perceptual response, feels impelled to write. And the likelihood is that this new signifier will be counterfactual in relation to the source, will develop those virtual dimensions of the source, its what-ifs, or what its generic and medial choices had prevented it from seeing, or bringing to fruition. Translation and adaptation thus share the condition of being the source's blind field, its off-screen, part of its ever moving into its own possibility, precisely by moving out of itself.

Towards an Alternative Model

The underlying concern of this article is, then, to understand reading not as comprehension, but as experience, as the activity of the psychophysiological apparatus of the reader. But this activity, this set of responses, this exploration of proprioception and kinaesthetics, must itself be given body, be given objective substance, by its integration into the translation or adaptation. So when Venuti comes to suggest the ways in which translation theory can advance thinking about film adaptation, I find his hermeneutic model too mechanistic and immobilizing.[16] His 'interpretants', that is, the formal and thematic codes applied to the adaptation, imply the voluntary and intentional.[17] They can too neatly be isolated for scrutiny and presuppose the stability of productive and receptive frameworks.[18] None of these things square with my particular needs, namely, to treat translation and adaptation as adventures in perceptual consciousness which set the source in motion, in two senses: in projecting the source into its possible futures, and in understanding the source as an unquiet field of forces and energies within ever-changing contexts which constantly generate new refractive configurations.[19]

Leitch, it seems to me, sets us off on the right track: 'And the great thing about adaptations is that they're constantly rewriting [books]. You cannot read a book without rewriting it. And if you're not rewriting it, you're not really reading it'.[20] Every text desires to be inscribed with the writing of its readers; every text desires to be other than it is. The writerly text, as Barthes has taught us, is the resistant text, resistant to consumption and assimilation, mobile, plural and self-multiplying, a productivity rather than a representation. It may be that Barthes's redefinition of interpretation — 'Interpréter un texte, ce n'est pas lui donner un sens (plus ou moins fondé, plus ou moins libre), c'est au contraire apprécier de quel pluriel il est fait' ('To interpret a text is not to give it a (more or less justified, more or less free) meaning, but on the contrary to appreciate what *plural* constitutes it') — has affinities with my own rejection of interpretation: it is less the assignment of meaning and more the palpation of a protean field of *sense*, more the exploration of our own self-diversifying relationship with it.[21] As Barthes suggests, the writerly text spawns signifiers which do not resolve themselves into signifieds but, instead, summon up, interpellate, other signifiers, such that the reader can make no decisions about meaning, can only conjure up a performance of the text's very productivity.

To Leitch's injunction one should add that unless the reader of a translation or adaptation can read/has read the original (i.e. is a polyglot as opposed to a monoglot reader), then the translation or adaptation may technically be a translation or adaptation, but is not so experientially. Only the monoglot reader requires translation/adaptation to be a reliable copy of the source; only the monoglot reader, like the interpretative critic, looks backwards. For the reader familiar with the source, the polyglot reader, there is no point in its repeating itself; instead, the source must be taken into a world of new comparabilities, and into new exercises of perception. Translation and adaptation are about turning the retrospective into the prospective; they are prosthetic instruments which expand our capacities to see into sources and make possible new experiential and perceptual behaviours.

One might further add that translation and adaptation concern the conversion of the chronometric time of the source's physical existence into the Bergsonian duration of its reading. It is significant, therefore, that André Bazin chooses to subtitle his treatment of Henri-Georges Clouzot's *Le Mystère Picasso* (1956) 'un film bergsonien' [a Bergsonian film].[22] And just as Bergson's image of cumulative duration is the snowball, constantly gathering the past into itself, so that the past is always, and at all points of itself, simultaneous with the present, so, as Bazin points out, at any given moment of its making, the two-dimensional picture plane is a cross-section of three-dimensional time, of the temporal flow which is accumulating in it.[23] As Picasso himself puts it: 'Il faudrait pouvoir montrer les tableaux qui sont sous les tableaux' [One should be able to show the pictures which are beneath the pictures].[24]

The reading mind, operating in Bergsonian duration, is stimulated by the source to access many different materials from its internal repository, materials dislocated from history, from their place in a scheme of things, and available to be drawn on, compared, connected, navigated among, in any way that the reading consciousness desires or requires. In this way, the Bergsonian mind should be aligned with a post-historical line of analysis. This post-historical line can be traced from Valéry and Benjamin in the late 1920s and early 1930s, through Malraux in the late 1940s and early 1950s, to the digital age, after the anticipations of Vilém Flusser in the 1980s.[25] What Benjamin perceives in the early 1930s is a world in which the photograph has brought all art within reach of the masses and has destroyed ritual and the aura, to replace them with exhibition-value and proximity; the photograph and film not only promiscuously mix artworks and relocate them, but also confuse the senses of scale, age, and context, and act as a prosthetics which opens up the optical unconscious (enlargement, close-up, slow motion, zooming). This is not only to say that the original loses its authority by being photographed; it is also to say that the original is *already* multiform, or at least multiformable. Malraux, for his part, identifies the museum as that which dislocates the work from context and function, and thus delivers the originally incomparable to comparability; photography only intensifies that particular condition: 'En outre, la photographie en noir "rapproche" les objets qu'elle représente, pour peu qu'ils soient apparentés. Une tapisserie, une miniature, un tableau, une sculpture et un vitrail médiévaux, objets fort différents, reproduits sur la même page, deviennent parents' [Moreover, black-and-white photography relates objects more intimately however small their actual kinship. Medieval objects as different as a tapestry, a miniature, a painting, a sculpture and a stained-glass window, when reproduced on the same page, become members of the same family].[26] Furthermore, Malraux designates the distortions of scale to be found in photographs as a 'fictionalization' of art: 'La reproduction a créé des arts fictifs (ainsi le roman met-il la réalité au service de l'imagination), en faussant systématiquement l'échelle des objets, en présentant des empreintes de sceaux orientaux et de monnaies comme des estampages de colonnes, des amulettes comme des statues' ('Indeed reproduction (like the art of fiction, which subdues reality to the imagination) has created what might be called "fictitious" arts, by systematically falsifying the scale of objects; by presenting [impressions] of oriental seals [and coins] the same size as the decorative reliefs on pillars, and amulets like statues').[27] He also underlines photography's capacity to reshuffle our sense of periods and their styles, a capacity it shares with translation; indeed there are many senses in which the devices of translation have the same effects as photographic technology, that is, they can act as a prosthetics. Finally, Malraux's commentary on the contemporary art world is significant for three further observations: first, that we already base our artistic judgements on misconceptions, for example, we overlook the polychromatics of Greek sculpture or of Romanesque churches; second, that later artists necessitate a re-evaluation of earlier ones; and finally, that resuscitations of past artists or artworks occur piecemeal and depend on what backward glances new trends in the arts invite — history becomes a repository of opportunity, of opportunistic recovery, rather than a carefully sequenced progression; historical sequence becomes montage.[28]

All these comments invite us to anticipate, as a further contribution to the development, in translation and adaptation, of new modes of creative consciousness and experiential process, the arrival of the digital mentality, identifiable by, among others, the following characteristics:

1. Accelerated processes of retrieval based on universal informational accessibility and disposal, and predominance of the transitory.
2. Reality perceived as an assembly of discontinuous, isolatable fragments, as montage. Not the continuities of the long take, or of tradition, or of sequential narrative. The whole picture of temporal unfolding yields to a moment-by-moment read-off, the analogue clock-face to the digital screen.
3. The concomitant, increasing equalization of phenomena. To proceed not by concentration and penetration, but by distraction, dispersed and centrifugal attention — hypertext, hypermedia.
4. Everybody becomes an expert, nobody is a specialist. Nobody has to bear individual responsibility for knowledge. Everyone can become a writer.
5. Flusser says: 'inherited things no longer have any place in our milieu'. Correct this to: 'the inheritedness of things is no longer of constitutive significance'. Flusser says: 'the past no longer matters to us'.[29] Correct this to: 'the past no longer matters to us by virtue of its pastness'.
6. The replacement of the irreversible (linearity) by the reversible and the counterchronological.[30]

Rethinking the Medium

When, therefore, the title of this article refers to 'the senses of medium', I want to suggest that post-historical and digital attitudes encourage us to shift the emphasis from medium, from concern with medium-specific properties, from the wars between analogy and category traced by Kamilla Elliott, to sense and the senses.[31] What exactly does this shift entail? First, medium is condemned to retrospective modes of thinking precisely because of its preoccupation with the meanings of medium. Meaning is something which is seen to inhere in language and culture by virtue of historical embeddedness. It is something which, however ambiguous, however plural, must be respected and cannot be denied, something which has claims to make. But meaning is, by its nature, in a permanent state of obsolescence.

Sense, on the other hand, has constantly to be made. But it is elusive; it multiplies, diversifies, escapes, or holds itself just beyond our grasp. It is an integral part of the source's progress through time and space, a guarantee of that progress. Translation/adaptation, then, is not the extraction of meaning from a text, in order to perpetuate it, but, rather, an account of a sense-making, which has written into it the activity of the readerly consciousness and the play of the readerly senses. And if the source has to be made sense of, repeatedly, it is because sources cease to be comprehensible to themselves shortly after their production, and progressively lose their meaning. Sources are nomadic texts, in search of themselves, in search of a 'place' in the world, in search of an ever-renewed expressive energy. In a word, then, translation/adaptation does not recuperate meaning, but generates sense, as it generates the future of the source. In translation/adaptation of this kind, the medial ramifies into the multimedial, and beyond that, into the multidimensional, into the polymorphous, into the multi-sensory.

And this takes us to our second point. Arguments about medium are generally about the different ways in which they address the senses, the physical senses that is; the senses are differently triggered, their activity is differently summoned, by the particular 'technologies' and constraints that operate in the medium. If the hybridity and heterogeneity (cultural plurality) of the medium suggest that terms such as 'intertextuality' or 'intersystemicness' would be more accurate reflections of the processes involved than 'adaptation', then there may also be a sense in which 'synaesthesia' is a more helpful concept than 'intermedial transfer'.[32] Synaesthesia is the indispensable term, (a) because it is more about the different senses than it is about the different arts/media, and (b) because it relates the senses by metamorphosis, that is, by one sense morphing into another, rather than by jumping from one sense to the other. It is the image of the morph rather than the jump which governs my view of translation/adaptation: translation/adaptation is the discovery of variational continuities between languages and works and senses rather than any carrying across, or transfer.

In order to gather together some of these threads, I would briefly like to consider David Shenton's wonderfully resourceful 1986 comic-book account of Wilde's *Salomé* of 1891. The comic strip or *bande dessinée* is a mischievous cat to put among the canonical pigeons, precisely because it exploits this melting of intermedial boundaries, setting the 'reader' afloat on a polymorphous stream of both contending and centrifugal associative impulses. The different temporalities of painting, cinema, and literature, the different propulsive tempi of narrative, speech, and spectation, are not so much patiently orchestrated as released into each other in the constant variations of paginal design, in the different ways of distributing and framing (or unframing) images, and in the play of linguistic and paralinguistic effects made available by modulations in speech balloon and calligraphic style; our perceptual and psychophysiological and intertextual involvements in the 'text' are thus free to generate their own weave and meshwork.

Shenton's *Salomé*, in the tireless interactivity of text and image, plays with the central collision of speaking and looking that occurs in the play. Salomé's dance,

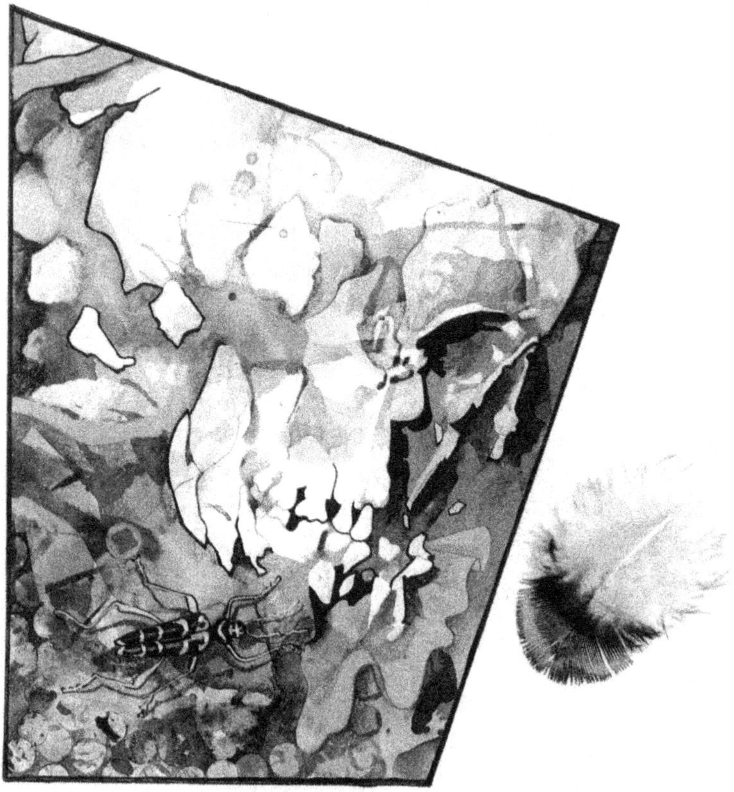

Fig. 1.1. Final page in David Shenton's comic-strip version (Quartet Books, 1986) of Oscar Wilde's *Salomé* (1891) © David Shenton.

the apotheosis of scopophilia, breaks the pact between Herod and John (Iokanaan), a pact based on the *word*, a pact already indicated in the biblical story; but that pact is restored when, in the final scene, Herod fulfils on Salomé the words Iokanaan has addressed to Herodias: 'Let them crush her beneath their shields'.[33] At the same time the visual, the sequence of vignettes, disintegrates and is erased (Figure 1.1). It is no surprise then that the image of Laocoön should figure in the text, not only because it recalls Lessing's 1766 essay 'Über die Grenzen der Malerei und Poesie' [On the Defining Limits of Painting and Poetry] also entitled 'Laokoon', but also because this depiction of Laocoön, devoured with his sons by serpents, refers back to an earlier image in which Iokanaan is enmeshed in the coils of Salomé's words. Has Salomé then, in her seduction of Iokanaan momentarily mastered the power of the word? Or is her language merely a language of the visual, of visual decoration, of simile, ultimately destroyed by Iokanaan's language of bare truth?

But these are the terms of the established debate between the visual and the verbal. Wilde, in Shenton's hands, has alerted us to another debate, another vocabulary, in which Salomé's dance acts as the point of departure. Salomé's dance is, ostensibly, a stripping down, a revelation of the objectives of voyeurism and scopophilia, a stark affirmation of a sexuality which is the unmanning and temporary unwording of Herod. But paradoxically the route to nudity is indeed the dance, a process of cinematic metamorphosis (Figures 1.2–3). As we look at these images we may be reminded of the drape dancing of Loie Fuller in the 1890s, dancing further animated by an underlighting of changing colours, helping to produce in the dance a sequence of unexpressed or virtual phenomena (butterfly, serpent, flame, waterfall, etc.), in a process of perpetual becoming. The very reading of the comic strip takes us through similar metamorphoses: the individual pages are governed by changing colour dominants and colour harmonies, each with their affective or spiritual connotations, just as changes in speech-balloon configuration capture variations of paralinguistic performance.

At the same time, we are encouraged to see the dance as a montage, or rather *démontage*, of materials (Figure 1.3). But the very act of looking/reading is also an act of montage (Figure 1.4). What I see on this page of heads of Salomé, in the smaller fourth image down on the left, is primarily Degas's *La Chanteuse au gant*, a pastel of 1878, remarkable for its depiction of the expressionist aggressions of underlighting: the foreshortening of the upturned face turns it to a skull, its song to a howl; and the densely black glove is suspended above the singer like an executioner's sword. But this is not all. Salomé's gloves will also remind us of the black gloves adopted by the cabaret *diseuse* Yvette Guilbert, black gloves lovingly depicted by Toulouse-Lautrec, which she wore because they were cheap, because they exaggerated the 'gracilité' [slenderness] of her arms, and because they introduced a note of elegance into the riff-raffish atmosphere of the café-concert.[34] But this is still not quite all. Salomé's second gloved hand, in the same image (Figure 1.4), laid across her forehead, begins to look like an 1890s bonnet, and that, with the upturned face and the decadent greenish tinge, takes us to Toulouse-Lautrec's oil, *Au Moulin Rouge*, of 1892–1893. In this painting, cut off by the frame in thoroughly photographic fashion, we see

FIG. 1.2. 'Cinematic' presentation of first moves in Salomé's dance © David Shenton.

Fig. 1.3. Continuation of previous image, across a two-page spread © David Shenton.

FIG. 1.4. The preliminaries of Salomé's dance: the mime of face and hands © David Shenton.

Fig. 1.5. Salomé's grand entrance: the 'unchaining' of her body © David Shenton.

the English dancer May Milton, in her strange, antenna-topped bonnet.[35] Milton is as if the clownlike doorwoman, or barker, for a gathering of the mute, inertial, joyless, moribund. Does Herod's banqueting hall indeed offer an equivalent of the funereal pleasure-seeking of the belle-époque Parisian café-concert?

But what makes the image on the facing page (Figure 1.5) equally familiar? Is this a slyly smiling allusion to Andromeda tied to her rock and awaiting the rescue of Perseus on Pegasus, the offspring of the blood from Medusa's decapitated head, an image endorsed, as it were, by Aubrey Beardsley's very Medusan depiction of the beheaded Iokanaan giving birth to a lily, in his own sequence of drawings for *Salomé*? Well, perhaps. But, more directly, it refers to the other Andromeda, the Angelica from Ariosto's *Orlando Furioso*, depicted in Ingres's painting of 1819, as Roger, mounted on a hippogriff, despatches the monster. But what does all this tell us? It tells two general truths: first, that these pictures, particularly where they postdate the action of Wilde's play, just as some of Beardsley's illustrations do, or as Shenton's attribution of a bubble-gum habit to Salomé and a chocolates habit to Herodias do, are not humorous anachronisms: rather, they generate corridors of time, of associative and transformational possibility through which we can view the source text and through which the source text can pass, in order to arrive at us; the source text is inevitably an uncontrollably expanding, increasingly inclusive work.[36] The work exists, we might say, expressly for its own proliferation. This is its *raison d'être*. This is what reading a text preparatory to translation, or to adaptation, brings about.

Secondly, as has been intimated in the earlier argument, adaptation perhaps finds new theoretical directions in the twinning of the principles of metamorphosis and montage, which together produce a prismatic aesthetics, indeed a cinematic aesthetics, that strange combination of juxtaposed images and uninterrupted sequence. Adaptation, like dance, is not a representation, but an agent of change. Metamorphosis is not concerned with categories and does not operate in the world of meaning; it is concerned with the production of sense, with the productivity of sense, which expands and permutates, in continuous variation, which rethinks language and expressive resource in heterogeneity, in conjunctive modulation. And the states or images through which the dance of metamorphosis passes occur in time, but a time that is cumulative, a Bergsonian time which paradoxically produces a simultaneity of available images.

Montage, for its part, pushes us out into n-dimensional or multi-dimensional space, a new unanchored and multiplied form of consciousness. Montage separates actions from their contexts, redesigns their equivalences, makes them agents in a complex and new rhythm of sense, dissociates them from a perceiving identity. But montage is an eraser of context only insofar as it makes available new contexts. Montage constructs new forms of perception, of life, out of an ease of accessibility to life, out of the incursions and interventions of life. Montage undoes the modernist principle of the work's autonomy. Dziga Vertov says of his new kino-eye, in 1929, that it 'uses every possible means in montage, comparing and linking all points of the universe in any temporal order, breaking, when necessary, all the laws and conventions of film construction'.[37] These remarks on metamorphosis and montage, together with the fact that cinema, as a multi-track medium, is naturally synaesthetic, begins to suggest that cinema is not just a partner in adaptation, but that it indeed enacts, in its own mechanisms, the very processes of, and the new directions for, adaptation.

An Aesthetics of the Signifier

I want with my final examples of adaptation to embrace the post-historical, or digital, condition even more fully, to plunge the source into the information stream, subjecting it to a variety of textual transformations and hypertextual insertions as explorations of its adaptability. When I set out to translate/adapt Goethe's 'Über allen Gipfeln' ('Wanderers Nachtlied II'),[38] a poem written in 1780 on the inside wall of a forester's hut on the Kickelhahn near Ilmenau, what intrigued me was the complexity of its music in relation to the simplicity of its syntax and lexis:

<table>
<tr><td>a</td><td>Über allen Gipfeln</td><td>(6)</td><td>/×/×/×</td></tr>
<tr><td>b</td><td>Ist Ruh,</td><td>(2)</td><td>×|/ – \(×)/(×) – /(×)/(×)</td></tr>
<tr><td>a</td><td>In allen Wipfeln</td><td>(5)</td><td>×|/×/× – \|/×/× – /××/×</td></tr>
<tr><td>b</td><td>Spürest du</td><td>(3)</td><td>/×× – /×/ – /×/(×) – /×\ (×)</td></tr>
<tr><td>c</td><td>Kaum einen Hauch;</td><td>(4)</td><td>/××/- /××/(×)</td></tr>
<tr><td>d</td><td>Die Vögelein schweigen im Walde.</td><td>(9)</td><td>×|/××/××/× – ×|/××/×<×/×</td></tr>
<tr><td>d</td><td>Warte nur, balde</td><td>(5)</td><td>/××</× – /×\</× – /××</×(\)</td></tr>
<tr><td>c</td><td>Ruhest du auch.</td><td>(4)</td><td>/××/ – /×/</ – /×/\</td></tr>
</table>

[Note on notation: lower-case letters to left = rhyme-scheme; bracketed numbers after lines = number of syllables; | = preceding upbeat (*Auftakt*); – = alternative reading; \ = secondary stress; (×) = silent off-beat; (/) = silent stressed syllable; < = pause]

<table>
<tr><td>Over the mountain peaks</td><td>/××/×× – /××/×\</td></tr>
<tr><td>Rest</td><td>/</td></tr>
<tr><td>   ful</td><td>× – \</td></tr>
<tr><td>   ness</td><td>× – \</td></tr>
<tr><td>In the tree-tops</td><td>××/× – ××/\</td></tr>
<tr><td>You feel</td><td>×/ – \/(××)</td></tr>
<tr><td>Hardly</td><td>/×</td></tr>
<tr><td>   a</td><td>×</td></tr>
<tr><td>   breath</td><td>/</td></tr>
<tr><td>The birds</td><td>×/(×) – (×)×/(×)</td></tr>
<tr><td>   are silent</td><td>×/× – (×)×/×</td></tr>
<tr><td>   in the woods</td><td>××/ – ××/(×)</td></tr>
<tr><td>But wait   a while</td><td>×/×/ – ×/×\</td></tr>
<tr><td>   soon</td><td>/</td></tr>
<tr><td>You too</td><td>/\ – /(×)\(×) – /(×)/(×)</td></tr>
<tr><td>   will find rest.</td><td>××/ – ×/(×)/</td></tr>
</table>

By 'complexity' I mean the change of rhyme-scheme from alternating to enclosed, the discrepancy between that scheme and the principal syntactic junctures, and, finally, the rhythmic uncertainty which roughly resolves itself into a pattern of dactyls, choriambs, and adonics as the poem proceeds. So I wanted to do a kind of textual musical setting. First I turned to Liszt's 1848 song-setting, which provided me with an expanded text, incorporating the repetitions of the score:

Over the mountain peaks
Rest
ful
ness
In the tree-tops
You feel
Hardly
a
breath
The birds
are silent
in the woods
But wait a while
wait soon
soon
soon
You too will find rest
soon
You too will find rest
you too
but wait
wait a while soon
You too will find rest
you too.

To this I added some of Liszt's markings for tempi and dynamics (in the musical sense), and also extracts from the slow third movement of Bruckner's Eighth Symphony, to get a different sense of scale and pace; but I also used handwriting, to capture a feeling of spontaneity, improvisation, an experimental and experiential here and now (Figure 1.6). Next, I converted the handwritten musical markings into an abstract graphics suggestive of pitch contours, suspensions, fades, and musical pointings of various kinds, loosely based on the notational practices to be found in the scores of avant-garde composers (Figure 1.7). These scores are themselves, to all intents and purposes, doodles, expressive of musical indeterminacy, or the translation of measurements of pitch-interval, note-value, tempo, into indications of the music's topography, or locomotive principles. Finally (Figure 1.8), I tried turning the music and the paralinguistic modulations into variations of typeface, whose names appear as if they were stage-directions, or a form of written musical markings. The accompanying series of handwritten words are the chromatic echoes (black, brown, green, blue) or shifting tonalities of the text, set to the choreography of a responsive body.

My next Goethe versions are to be found in Georges Perec's radio play *Die Maschine*,[39] written at the end of 1967 with Eugen Helmlé for Saarländischer Rundfunk and first broadcast on 13 November 1968.[40] It delivers Goethe's poem to a thoroughly deconstructive programming by a computer, among whose protocols

FIG. 1.6. Translation of Goethe's 'Über allen Gipfeln' on music paper, with handwriting and montaged fragments of score from Bruckner's Eighth Symphony, third movement.

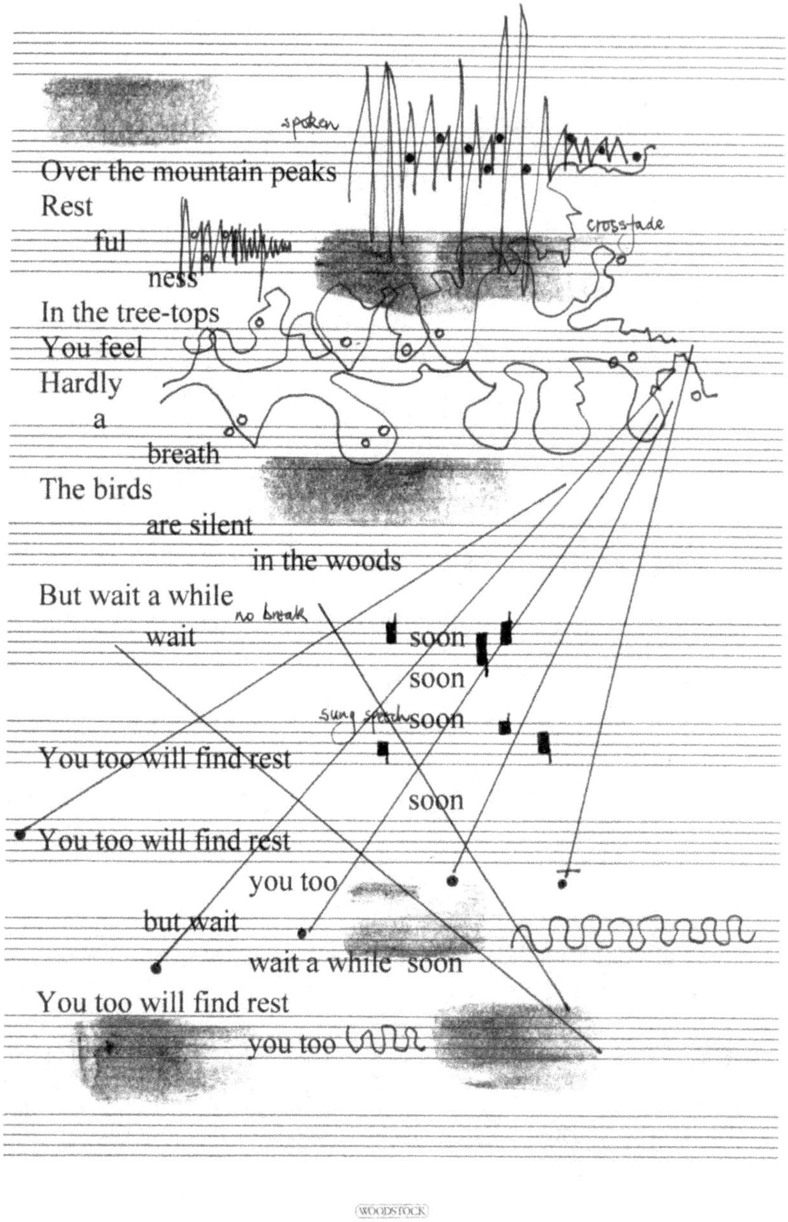

FIG. 1.7. Translation of Goethe's 'Über allen Gipfeln' on music paper, with graphite smudges and hand-drawn graphics loosely based on the notational practices of avant-garde composers.

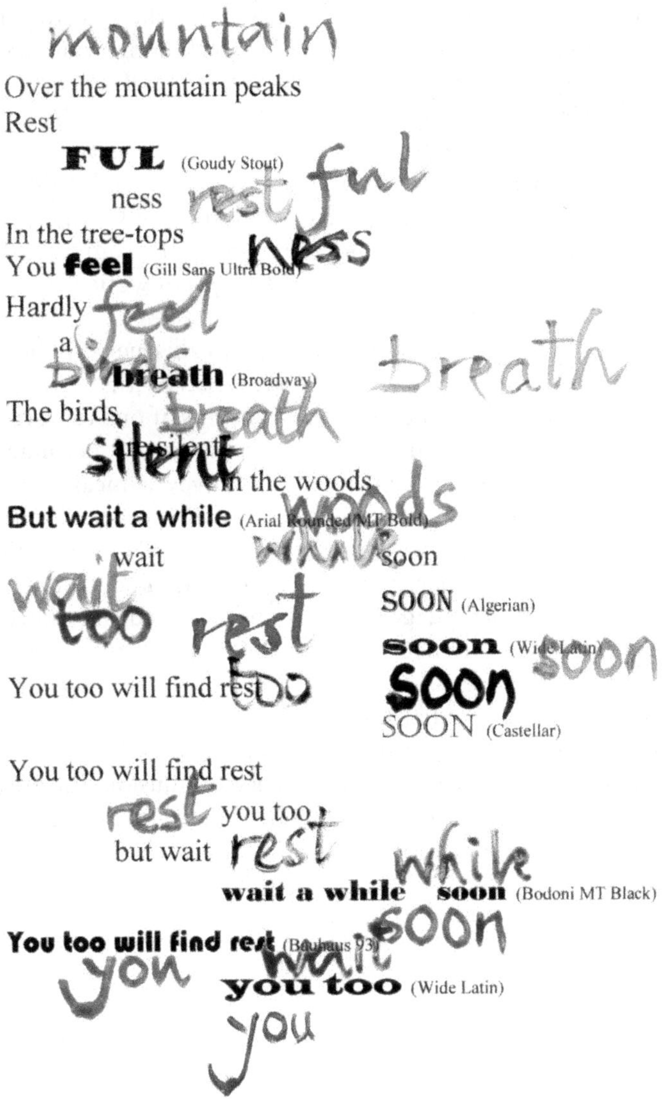
Over the mountain peaks
Rest
FUL (Goudy Stout)
ness
In the tree-tops
You feel (Gill Sans Ultra Bold)
Hardly
a
breath (Broadway)
The birds
silent
in the woods
But wait a while (Arial Rounded MT Bold)
wait
soon
SOON (Algerian)
soon (Wide Latin)
You too will find rest
SOON (Castellar)
You too will find rest
you too
but wait
wait a while soon (Bodoni MT Black)
You too will find rest (Bauhaus 93)
you too (Wide Latin)

FIG. 1.8. Translation of Goethe's 'Über allen Gipfeln', with watercolour handwriting and mixed typefaces.

are to be found one that analyses the poem quantitatively, one that produces text-internal permutations, one that explores permutation through imported materials, one that provides an alphabetic itemization of different aspects of Goethe's creative make-up (for example, 'goethe und aristoteles', 'goethe und die freiheit', 'goethe und der okkultismus'), and one that triggers an explosion of intertexts (for example, Baudelaire, Borges, Cummings, Dickinson, Neruda, Rimbaud, Izumi Shikibu (spelt 'Shibiku' in the text)). Perec's work contributes to the 'neue Hörspiel' [new radio play] because it promotes radiophonics, a technological or mathematical aesthetics, and new uses of stereophony (polyvocality), and it does so by adapting radio to the experimental, constructional techniques of Oulipo, into which Perec had been co-opted in 1966. Thus, Goethe's poem, the slightest of texts (in terms of verbal matter) begets linguistic and literary consequences of unimaginable proportions.[41]

What emerges from all this is what we might call a new aesthetics of the signifier, as opposed to an aesthetics of the whole sign. By that I mean: the choice of signifier is usually pre-constrained by what it means; if one removes that constraint then language's capacity to generate signifiers by purely permutational means is unbounded; language is not called upon to convey a meaning; it engenders or re-invents sense out of its own metamorphoses. Such a procedure puts us (alarmingly or exhilaratingly) in the hands of language; ironically, we devise methods for generating language which merely confirm our lack of control over language. But such a process also opens language up as an undiscovered and unoccupied territory, to renew perceptual experience, to embolden creativity, to activate projective possibility. And what we say here of language applies, of course, to all media: the signifier is a site of cross-medial multiplication, of the metamorphic ramification of sensory engagement. Within this world, intertexts and quotations are no longer motivated by referential function or specificity of allusion but are an area of free improvisation and association which gives the signifier greater temporal and spatial reach, and depth, and allows us to enter into relationships with periods and geographies outside our ken, to extend what reality is for us.[42]

Conclusion

So how, ultimately, are we to cure this critically embarrassing condition, this combination of, on the one hand, a loss of authoritative historical origins and, on the other, post-historical intertextual anarchy? For the loss of origins, the cure is easy. Any adaptation sets up a relationship with the source which is not one of derivation, but rather of reciprocation, a dialogue of equally contributory partners. If translation/adaptation is about the interaction of two 'texts', the source and the translation/adaptation, and not about the transfer of the one to the other, then the criterion of judgement, if one is deemed necessary, will not be whether the translation/adaptation is faithful (in whatever sense), but whether the interactivity between the two 'texts' is fruitful and to what degree.

And we also have ways of making sense of and giving purpose to the post-historical and the intertextual:

1. By developing a critical anthropology and a history of artworks as oceanic space rather than as land-masses, that is, as polymorphous and metamorphic relationships, as the free play of traversals, intersections, transactions, sedimentations, rather than as stable territories and mapped borders, settlement, and community.[43]

2. Relatedly, by understanding the relation between two works not as a comparison, but as a comparability, not as the careful measurement of similarities and differences, gains and losses, an application of double-entry accounting methods, but as the tracing of relationality, that is, of the dynamic of changing complementarities and synergies. Translation/adaptation is an intervention in the making, not of history, but of readerly relations to text and language, relations which are contingent, improvised, heuristic, piecemeal, of uncertain consequence.

3. By developing our understanding of the interval between source and translation/ adaptation in a more complex way. The phrase 'similarities and differences between' sets up juxtapositional relationships between the items compared, so that the interval is an interval of measurement. Such an interval sets apart, holds in tension. By contrast, the interval I have in mind is the interval of transition, in both directions; it is an inter-relational interval across which consciousness travels in a series of self-adaptations, finding connections, associations, trajectories, so that the function of the traversal becomes less and less about similarity and difference and more about variations, continuities, morphings. Part of the art, then, is filling out the interval, initiating the dialogue with the prospective audience, putting the audience at the heart of transition. By way of brief example, we might mention the publication in 2014 of Mike Poulton's adaptations for the stage of Hilary Mantel's *Wolf Hall* and *Bring Up the Bodies*, first performed in December 2013.[44] The play-script is accompanied not only by a short introduction in which Poulton explains aims, problems, solutions, the significance for the adaptation of the chosen theatrical space (the Swan, small with a deep thrust stage), but also by 'Notes on Characters' by Mantel herself, second-person addresses *to* the characters, rather as if she were a director drawing the actors into their roles, midwifing them into a new existence, handing them over to the stage, challenging them to substantiate their own particular dramas. It is in this animation of the genetics of an adaptation or translation, in making it an integral part of the 'work', that we make the processes of relocation and re-invention less arbitrary.

But underlying all this, of course, is our need to understand that we are engaged in a new epistemology; we need to know what the new nature of knowledge is, how it works, what its peculiar values are, and how it assigns value to the subjects it engages with. What *are* metamorphosis and montage as modes of knowledge? We also need to develop an adaptational aesthetics based not on stasis and achieved form, but on the dynamics of becoming. Thus the canon becomes significant not by any bequeathed authority but by what it can creatively put at stake, and translation/adaptation is our way of insisting that works within the canon do not immobilize themselves in time-honoured aesthetic values, but are the initiators of self-proliferative creative partnerships and co-authorings which keep their values in constantly self-reconfiguring progress.

Notes to Chapter 1

1. As Patrick Cattrysse reminds us: 'Even film adaptations of famous literary texts generally do not limit themselves to adapting the literary source alone. The story of such a book may have guided the film adaptation on the narratological level, but other aspects such as directing, staging, acting, setting, costume, lighting, photography, pictorial representation, music, etc. may well have been governed by other models and conventions which did not originate in the literary text and did not serve as a translation of any of its elements' ('Film (Adaptation) as Translation: Some Methodological Proposals', *Target*, 4.1 (1992), 53–70 (pp. 61–62)). For that reason, Cattrysse observes, adaptation studies gravitate naturally towards intertextual studies, or what, for him, might more appropriately be called 'intersystemic studies', since texts are not the only semiotic at stake.
2. See James Naremore, 'Introduction: Film and the Reign of Adaptation', in *Film Adaptation*, ed. by James Naremore (New Brunswick, NJ: Rutgers University Press, 2000), pp. 1–16 (p. 15); Robert B. Ray, 'The Field of "Literature and Film"', in *Film Adaptation*, ed. by Naremore, pp. 38–53 (p. 49); Robert Stam, 'Introduction: The Theory and Practice of Adaptation', in *Literature and Film: A Guide to the Theory and Practice of Film Adaptation*, ed. by Robert Stam and Alessandra Raengo (Malden, MA, & Oxford: Blackwell, 2005), pp. 1–52 (pp. 13–14).
3. Little is probably to be gained by preferring Gérard Genette's more non-committal terms 'hypertextuality' and the superordinate 'transtextuality' (*Palimpsestes: la littérature au second degré* (Paris: Seuil, 1982)), other than their more inclusive and non-prejudicial nature.
4. As David Kranz puts it: 'the heart of fidelity criticism is the *comparative textual method*, which allows critics to put a source and a film adapted from it side-by-side in order to see what the similarities and differences are' ('The Golden Continuum of Probability', in *In/Fidelity: Essays on Film Adaptation*, ed. by David L. Kranz and Nancy C. Mellerski (Newcastle upon Tyne: Cambridge Scholars Publishing, 2008), pp. 202–04 (p. 203)).
5. In *Émile Zola and the Artistry of Adaptation*, for example, Griffiths explores the ways in which the origin itself — in her case Zola — can undermine the sense of origins, whether origins of author, of text, of character, or of depicted reality.
6. See Griffiths and Watts, *Adapting Nineteenth-century France.*
7. Hutcheon, with O'Flynn, *A Theory of Adaptation*, pp. xv & xvi.
8. For example, Brian McFarlane, *Novel to Film: An Introduction to the Theory of Adaptation* (Oxford: Clarendon Press, 1996).
9. See, for example, Roland Barthes, *S/Z* (Paris: Seuil, 1970), and 'Introduction à l'analyse structurale des récits', in *L'Aventure sémiologique* (Paris: Seuil, 1985), pp. 167–206; Gérard Genette, 'Discours du récit', in *Figures III* (Paris: Seuil, 1972), pp. 65–273; Seymour Chatman, *Story and Discourse: Narrative Structure in Fiction and Film* (Ithaca, NY: Cornell University Press, 1978).
10. Deborah Cartmell and Imelda Whelehan are more 'understanding' of this habit: 'Yet the will to taxonomies is a distinctive feature of adaptation studies, which reflects more than anything its need to establish a critical perspective of its own' (*Screen Adaptation: Impure Cinema* (Basingstoke: Palgrave Macmillan, 2010), p. 6). Taxonomies are too convenient a short-cut to the establishment of a discipline.
11. For example, Geoffrey Wagner, *The Novel and the Cinema* (Rutherford, NJ: Fairleigh Dickinson University Press, 1975); Dudley Andrew, *Concepts in Film Theory* (New York: Oxford University Press, 1984); Hutcheon, *A Theory of Adaptation.*
12. Kamilla Elliott opens her fifth chapter with the blunt observation: 'Recent scholars conclude that adaptation studies lag deplorably behind the critical times' (*Rethinking the Novel/Film Debate* (New York: Cambridge University Press, 2003), p. 133), a view for which she goes on to give a variety of explanations.
13. Robert Ray, 'The Field of "Literature and Film"', and 'Film and Literature', in *How a Film Theory Got Lost and Other Mysteries in Cultural Studies* (Bloomington, IN: Indiana University Press, 2001), pp. 120–31; Thomas Leitch, 'Twelve Fallacies in Contemporary Adaptation Theory', *Criticism*, 45.2 (2003), 149–71.
14. Cattrysse, 'Film (Adaptation) as Translation'; Robert Stam, 'Beyond Fidelity: The Dialogics

of Adaptation', in *Film Adaptation*, ed. by Naremore, pp. 54–76 (p. 62); Kate Griffiths, '*Chez Maupassant*: The (In)Visible Space of Television Adaptation', in Griffiths and Watts, *Adapting Nineteenth-century France*, pp. 143–71 (p. 144).

15. Lawrence Venuti, *The Translator's Invisibility: A History of Translation* (London: Routledge, 1995), p. 311.
16. Lawrence Venuti, 'Adaptation, Translation, Critique', *Journal of Visual Culture*, 6.1 (2007), 25–43.
17. 'Locating a shift between an adaptation and its prior materials assumes some effort to fix the form and meaning of those materials in order to establish that a resemblance or divergence exists in the adaptation and reflects a specific interpretant applied by the filmmakers' (Ibid., p. 33). This also implies that interpretants are drawn from a fixed stock, a fixed critical taxonomy, that, therefore, can only confirm, if even by resistance, a certain Western taxonomy of critical attitudes.
18. 'The contexts in which the translation or adaptation was produced and received, the traditions and practices of translating and filmmaking as well as the social conditions of reading and viewing, must be taken into account to avoid rendering essentialist judgements that ignore historical contingencies [...]' (Ibid., p. 35). It is clear that Venuti's historical contingencies are not contingent enough, and that the contexts of reception are not sufficiently adjusted to the protean circumstances of individual performances.
19. As Stam puts it, in relation to adaptations: 'Yet if mutation is the means by which the evolutionary process advances, then we can also see filmic adaptations as "mutations" that help their source novel "survive"' ('Introduction', p. 3).
20. Thomas Leitch, 'Panel Presentations and Discussion: "The Persistence of Fidelity"', in *In/Fidelity*, ed. by Kranz and Mellerski, pp. 197–228 (p. 220).
21. Barthes, *S/Z*, p. 11; Barthes, *S/Z*, trans. by Richard Miller (New York: Hill & Wang, 1974), p. 5.
22. André Bazin, *Qu'est-ce que le cinéma?* (Paris: Éditions du Cerf, 2002), p. 193.
23. Henri Bergson, *Œuvres*, ed. by André Robinet and Henri Gouhier, 4th edn (Paris: PUF, 1984), pp. 495–500.
24. Cited in Bazin, *Qu'est-ce que le cinéma?*, p. 196.
25. I think here of Benjamin's reference in 'Das Kunstwerk im Zeitalter seiner technischen Reproduzierbarkeit', *Gesammelte Schriften* ed. by Rolf Tiedemann and Hermann Schweppenhäuser, 7 vols in 15 (Frankfurt a.M.: Suhrkamp, 1972–1989), I.2 (1974), 435–508 (p. 475), to Valéry's 'La Conquête de l'ubiquité': 'Comme l'eau, comme le gaz, comme le courant électrique viennent de loin dans nos demeures répondre à nos besoins moyennant un effort quasi nul, ainsi serons-nous alimentés d'images visuelles et auditives, naissant et s'évanouissant au moindre geste, presque à un signe' [Just as water, gas, and electricity are brought into our houses from far off to satisfy our needs with minimal effort, so we shall be supplied with visual or auditory images, which will appear and disappear at a simple movement of the hand, hardly more than a sign] (in *Œuvres II*, ed. by Jean Hytier (Paris: Gallimard, 1960), pp. 1284–87 (pp. 1284–85)). Valéry uses *ubiquité* in the following context: 'On saura transporter ou reconstituer en tout lieu le système de sensations, — ou plus exactement, le système d'excitations, — que dispense en un lieu quelconque un objet ou un événement quelconque. Les œuvres acquerront une sorte d'ubiquité' [One will be able to transport or reconstitute absolutely anywhere the system of sensations — or, more accurately, the system of excitations — which is generated somewhere by some object or event] (p. 1284).
26. André Malraux, *Les Voix du silence* (Paris: Galerie de la Pléiade/NRF, 1951), p. 19.
27. Ibid., p. 22; Malraux, *The Voices of Silence*, trans. by Stuart Gilbert (Princeton, NJ: Princeton University Press, 1978), p. 24.
28. Ibid., pp. 45–48, 66; pp. 47–50, 68.
29. Vilém Flusser, *Writings*, ed. by Andreas Ströhl, trans. by Erik Eisel (Minneapolis: University of Minnesota Press, 2002), p. 139.
30. Flusser gives, as an example, a reader of the history of science who summons up Aristotle and Newton: 'To the future reader, "Aristotle" and "Newton" are simultaneously accessible, both coded digitally. So he can access both systems at the same time, and in such a way that they

overlap and disturb one another. [...] The reader will be able to manipulate the two overlapping systems so that an intermediate stage emerges in which Aristotle's system could arise from Newton's as well as Newton's from Aristotle's. From the available data, the reader will find out that the Newtonian system is, in fact, more recent than the Aristotelian, but he can just as easily reverse the history' (*Does Writing have a Future?*, trans. by Nancy Ann Roth (Minneapolis: University of Minnesota Press, 2011), pp. 153–54).

31. Elliott, *Rethinking the Novel/Film Debate.*
32. See, for example, Cattrysse, 'Film (Adaptation) as Translation'.
33. 'For Herod feared John, knowing that he was a just man and an holy, and observed him; and when he heard him, he did many things, and heard him gladly' (Mark 6: 20).
34. See *Toulouse-Lautrec*, ed. by Caroline Larroche, exhibition catalogue (London: South Bank Centre; Paris: Réunion des Musées Nationaux, 1992), p. 318.
35. See Reinhold Heller, 'Rediscovering Henri de Toulouse-Lautrec's *At the Moulin Rouge*', *Art Institute of Chicago Museum Studies*, 12.2 (1986), 114–35 (p. 118).
36. *Pace* Eric T. Haskell, 'Fusing Word and Image: The Case of the Cartoon Book, Wilde and Shenton', in *The Pictured Word: Word and Image Interactions 2*, ed. by Martin Heusser and others (Amsterdam & Atlanta, GA: Rodopi, 1998), pp. 245–54 (p. 246).
37. Dziga Vertov, *Kino-eye: The Writings of Dziga Vertov*, ed. by Annette Michelson, trans. by Kevin O'Brien (London: Pluto Press, 1984), p. 88.
38. Johann Wolfgang von Goethe, *Gedichte*, ed. by Erich Trunz, 2 vols (Frankfurt a.M.: Fischer Bücherei, 1964), I, 142.
39. Georges Perec, *Die Maschine: Hörspiel*, trans. and ed. by Eugen Helmlé, afterword by Werner Klippert (Stuttgart: Philipp Reclam jun., 1972).
40. For circumstantial information, see David Bellos, *Georges Perec: A Life in Words* (London: Harvill/Harper Collins, 1993), pp. 378–86.
41. We might add, as a final example, John Ottman's incorporation of 'Über allen Gipfeln' into the music which runs over the final credits of Bryan Springer's 2008 film *Valkyrie*, an account of the assassination attempt on Hitler of 20 July 1944. The track is entitled 'They'll Remember You' and has been described as 'a stunningly beautiful modern choir piece with references to both Mozart and Monteverdi'. Ottman had already written the theme but felt that it might acquire a different filmic status if it were choral, the status of tragedy rather than suspense movie. But if it were choral, what lyrics were to be used? Ottman takes up the story: 'The person I was doing this piece with thought of Goethe and then we found this poem. The poem was a loose allegory for the movie and talks about little birds falling silent in the woods and the last sentence is "soon you too will be at rest". It just gave me chills. It was not "on the nose" but it was at least reflective of having a sacrifice and being at peace with what you just tried to do. The problem was that the melody had already been written, so we had to fit the lyrics into the melody, which was like trying to fit a square peg into a round hole' <www.tracksounds.com/specialfeatures/interviews/interview_john_ottman_2008.htm> [accessed 20 February 2020].
42. See Hans Hartje, 'Georges Perec et le "neues Hörspiel" allemand', in *Écritures radiophoniques,* ed. by Isabelle Chol and Christian Moncelet (Clermont-Ferrand: Cahiers de recherches du CRLMC/Université Blaise Pascal, 1997), pp. 73–86.
43. To gain a fuller idea of what might be involved in an oceanic anthropology, see Françoise Vergès, 'Writing on Water: Peripheries, Flows, Capital, and Struggles in the Indian Ocean', *positions*, 11.1 (2003), 241–57.
44. Hilary Mantel, *Wolf Hall and Bring Up the Bodies*, adapted for the stage by Mike Poulton (London: Nick Hern Books/Fourth Estate, 2014).

CHAPTER 2

❖

Ad-app-ting the Canon

Kamilla Elliott

All the world's a platform, and all its multimedia merely apps...

When I began researching adaptation in the early 1990s, the field was focused primarily on adaptations of the Anglo-American literary canon to film, with a growing interest in television adaptations of that literature and a modest interest in the literary sources of auteur films. In a series of edited collections from 1996, Deborah Cartmell, Imelda Whelehan, and associates extended adaptation studies to pulp fiction, popular film, cult television, and novelizations;[1] in 2006, Linda Hutcheon expanded the field to include: 'Musical arrangements and song covers, visual art revisitations of prior works [...] poems put to music and remakes of films, and video games and interactive art [...] theme park rides, Web sites, graphic novels [...] operas, musicals, ballets, and radio [...] plays'.[2] Six years later, Hutcheon's preface to the second edition of *A Theory of Adaptation* and its epilogue by Siobhan O'Flynn refer to:

> Seismic shifts with the emergence of new platforms, technologies, and industries that have widened adaptation studies still further. Among these are participatory media, blogs, and wikis, the increase in smart mobile devices [...] the viral dissemination of DIY content online through platforms such as YouTube, Facebook and Twitter, and the revolution of touch-screen interfaces.[3]

Hutcheon saw no need to update her theory of adaptation, devised prior to these technologies, in light of them; today even newer technologies render the bookended updates of her 2012 second edition outdated. This chapter argues that new technologies do require new theories, as they change the ways in which the literary canon is produced and consumed, reconfiguring its global dissemination, remediation, criticism, pedagogy, and epistemologies of consumption, and changing the answers to the questions that structure Hutcheon's book. Attending to only one relatively new technology, the 'app', my chapter argues further that new technologies change not only the answers to prior questions, but that they also raise new questions. For example, haptic technologies require going beyond adaptation theories based in phenomenologies of hearing and seeing; virtual and augmented reality technologies require us to go beyond epistemologies based in realism, cognition, and imagination; and, when technologies allow consumers to become producers (the two together construct them as prosumers), theories of production and consumption based in older technologies such as print culture and cinema are insufficient to explicate these processes.

Apps are no minor adaptation technology; more people globally use mobile devices today than any other form of technology. In 2014, for the first time, there were more mobile devices and mobile subscriptions than people on the planet, and they were multiplying five times as fast as the human population.[4] By 2016, 63 per cent of the world population owned a mobile phone; by 2019, that number increased to 67 per cent,[5] with more than half of these devices being smartphones.[6] To put these statistics into perspective, only one in three people had access to a toilet in 2018.[7] The number of apps downloaded annually is predicted to rise from 178.1 billion in 2017 to 258.2 in 2022. As of September 2018, 2.1 million Android apps and 2 million Apple apps were available for download. While in that month, games accounted for 24.86 per cent of Apple app sales, books and education combined were second, at 11.42 per cent. Moreover, a study of the most popular Android apps in June 2018 indicated that book and reference apps reached 70.68 per cent of users. Therefore, those who would understand literary adaptation generally, and how the British literary canon (this chapter's focus) is being adapted specifically, cannot afford to ignore 'ad-app-tations'.

By increasing access to literacy and the literary canon, apps can be educationally and economically democratizing forces. Their interactive technologies furthermore challenge hierarchical relations among authors, readers, critics, and texts constructed in older media, as readers, auditors, spectators, and consumers created by older media technologies become interactive users, writers, prosumers, reviewers, and marketers of books via apps. The regularity and ease with which apps are updated in response to user feedback further increase user agency in the production of apps.

Yet app technologies are often engaged to oppose and leapfrog over theories such as poststructuralism, postmodernism, and radical politics to reinstate traditional formalist, modernist, and humanist approaches to the canon. Apps not only adapt the literary canon, they also adapt its criticism and prior adaptations by older media. Literary ad-app-tations often present canonical manuscripts reverently under a high-art humanist lens; their editors confidently digitize 'definitive' editions accompanied by 'authoritative' scholarly commentaries. Yet at the same time, they revive the illustrations and multimedial adaptations eschewed by modernist and formalist critics during the twentieth century, and their networked technologies seem to confirm once controversial claims by adaptation scholars that criticism and adaptation undertake similar functions.[8] Conversely, Daniel Fischlin and Mark Fortier contend that 'any modern or historical production of Shakespeare, whether theatrical, critical, or editorial, is an adaptation'.[9] Apps literalize and conflate these claims. Even apps offering ultra-conservative scholarly commentaries rampantly engage in poststructuralist intertextuality and postmodern pastiche and/or palimpsest when they set traditional textual studies in networked digital relations with illustrations, audio, video, music, games, and interfaces that allow users to choose, combine, and ignore elements, destabilizing top-down scholarly and pedagogical traditions. Similarly, some apps maintain tensions between hagiographical and parodic approaches to authors and their works, both of which, scholars argue, construct and maintain literary canons.

One of the most surprising findings of this research is that the most radical canonical apps are often those designed for very young children, offering new ways of reading and engaging with canonical literature. Some apps require users to game rather than read, watch, listen to, or study the canon. GPS and augmented reality allow literary tourists to travel in time and space to engage in mutual hauntings of dead literary authors and their works, interweaving authors, characters, and locations in new ways. The chapter concludes with a consideration of the new literacies involved in the study of ad-app-tations. But before I pursue these arguments, some definitions of key terms are required.

Definitions, Debates, Contexts

Since definitions of the canon are inextricable from debates regarding it, I begin with the *OED*'s baseline definition. The *OED* offers the additional benefit of highlighting historical changes in definitions, as well as debates over terminology, in its illustrative examples.

Canon

Most definitions of 'canon' in the *OED* are religious; these definitions infuse and shape the literary canon. In 2002, the *OED* added a specific literary definition:

> *Literary Criticism.* A body of literary works traditionally regarded as the most important, significant, and worthy of study; those works of esp. Western literature considered to be established as being of the highest quality and most enduring value; the classics (now freq. in the canon). Also (usu. with qualifying word): such a body of literature in a particular language, or from a particular culture, period, genre, etc.

Yet even as this definition and its illustrative examples articulate the pseudo-religious thrust of the literary canon, they acknowledge challenges to it. Against claims to universality, they highlight the canon's historical, geographical, and formal localism and diversity. The *OED*'s final illustrative example ('The canon was under attack from feminists and social historians who saw it as the preserve of male and bourgeois dominance') figures canonical debates as militant political affairs. E. Dean Kolbas expands:

> By some accounts, the Western canon — the corpus of works comprising the 'classics' of art and literature, the very summit of cultural achievement in the West — once thought of as timeless and universal, is now being undermined by the combined forces of feminism, multi-culturalism, popular culture, and relativistic literary theories that have occupied schools and universities since the 1960s. By other accounts, the canon has been dominated by 'dead, white European males', excluding authors and artists from social groups that have historically been marginalized or that do not conform to the interest of the dominant culture. It is therefore condemned as an elitist, patriarchical [*sic*], racist, or ethnocentric construction.[10]

Although the cultural functions of the canon remain hotly contested, Kolbas assesses that 'both liberal pluralists and conservative humanists [...] seem to share a surprisingly uniform conception of the canon itself' (p. 3). Most of the authors and works treated in this chapter could feature on either side of the canon debate.

Adaptation

As with 'canon', the *OED* also offers a definition of 'adaptation' specific to arts and media: 'An altered or amended version of a text, musical composition, etc., (now *esp.*) one adapted for filming, broadcasting, or production on the stage from a novel or similar literary source'. This definition from the 1989 edition warrants updating to acknowledge Hutcheon's expansion of the field to a wider range of both older and newer media forms.

Adaptations have been integral to canon formation, dissemination, and perpetuation. Michael Dobson documents their centrality in establishing Shakespeare as 'national poet';[11] theatre historians, illustration, and film scholars alike attest to the role of adaptations in widening the reach of literary canons.[12] Julie Sanders reflects on how adaptation has functioned both to affirm and subvert the canon: 'Adaptation both appears to require and to perpetuate the existence of a canon [...]. To this end, adaptation could be defined as an inherently conservative genre [...]. Yet [...] adaptation can also be oppositional, even subversive'.[13] Conversely, the literary canon has been central to the development of both the practice and study of adaptation, serving to valorize and validate not only new media forms, but also adaptations themselves and adaptation studies as a field.[14] This chapter examines some ways in which apps have determined canon (de)formation and, concomitantly, some ways in which the canon has determined app formation. As the first work addressing these issues, it introduces a wide range of examples, all of which warrant further examination not within the scope of a single book chapter.

App

The word 'app' is relatively new, used from 1985 to refer to computer applications (*OED*), but from 2008 the term has referred almost exclusively to mobile device software. Although the thirteenth edition of the *BCS Glossary of Computing and ICT* (2013) offers a more up-to-date definition ('App is a computer program run on a smartphone or hand-held computer. App is an abbreviation of application used in the context of mobile computing'), even here, the definition does not encompass new mobile technologies such as iWatches and other wearable devices.[15]

As 'canon' and 'adaptation' mutually define each other, so too, 'adaptation' and 'app' interconnect. My title, 'Ad-app-ting the Canon,' makes a portmanteau (defined by Lewis Carroll as 'two meanings packed into one word') of 'adaptation' and 'application'.[16] The *OED* offers a general definition of 'adaptation' as 'making something suitable for a new use or purpose' and of 'application' as 'the action of putting something into operation or use'; the two words are remarkably similar, yet they diverge. 'Adaptation' foregrounds *making* a product for a new use; 'application' foregrounds *putting* the product into use; 'adaptation' emphasizes production; 'application' stresses consumption. In computing rhetoric, 'adaptation' refers to redesigning software so that it can operate on a new hardware platform, as in adaptations of videogames made for one type of gaming console so that they can work with another. An app or application allows a consumer to *use* that adaptation (as in apps that allow videogames designed for consoles to be played on a smartphone or tablet).

Beyond their technological uses, apps must have a practical *use* perceived and valued as such by consumers. Such use value simultaneously draws on and departs from Karl Marx's definition of 'use-value' in *Das Kapital*:

> The utility of a thing makes it a use-value. But this utility is not a thing of air. Being limited by the physical properties of the commodity, it has no existence apart from that commodity. A commodity, such as iron, corn, or a diamond, is therefore, so far as it is a material thing, a use-value, something useful. [...] Use-values become a reality only by use or consumption.[17]

However, software applications are neither material things nor things of the air (even air is a material entity, a combination of chemicals); they are material objects, but their uses are largely virtual; they are things of the digital airwaves, simulating and often displacing material things by fulfilling their uses virtually. Conversely, the practical, real-world uses of apps link them to, but also carry them beyond, Jean Baudrillard's theories of simulacra.[18] Apps have enabled mobile devices to simulate *and replace* telephones, typewriters, scanners, calendars, address books, documents, file cabinets, and meeting rooms; to become virtual pens, paper, envelopes, stamps, post offices, and mail boxes displacing the actualities; they have become our memos, notes, and diaries; our clocks and alarm clocks. They can monitor our health, vital signs, medication schedules, and fertility; they have become our barometers, pedometers, calorie counters, fitness coaches, dog whistles, restaurant and travel guides, traffic reports, train, flight and bus schedules, flashlights, maps, and GPS systems. Apps go beyond the hard objects they displace: there are apps that wake users at an appropriate point in their sleep cycles; they can turn on their lights and raise their thermostats as they travel home; they can find them a parking spot before they can see it.

Apps are also simulating and displacing professional tools. Carpenters use apps as spirit levels; coaches use them to analyse athletic performance; there are design apps for architects, and stock market apps for investors. Academics can use apps to access archives remotely, scan documents, format references, attend virtual meetings, edit, review, conference, and self-publish (*iAuthor* offers self-publication with a global advertising platform). Apps will translate both written and spoken languages instantly, if not perfectly.

Beyond their professional functions, they link users to social, ideological, economic, and recreational networks where they can engage in virtual encounters, debates, economic exchanges, and simulated activities. In addition to well-known apps connecting users to Facebook and Twitter, newer apps allow users to interact in virtual reality and to run into each other in the actual world, as with, for example, the *Pokemon Go* app, in a gaming context.

More specific to the concerns of this volume, apps are simulating and displacing the media through which we consume literature and its adaptations, becoming our books, newspapers, magazines, photo frames and albums, sound systems and music libraries, film and video players and archives, and game consoles; they are also enabling consumers to become producers of adaptations as they provide affordable desktop publishers, sound recorders and mixers, cameras, video cameras, and editors. There are apps to develop and design apps (for example, *AppMakr*, *TheAppBuilder*, and *Appy Pie*). Apps also provide access to platforms on which to disseminate one's adaptations globally. Windows has created an app called *Adaptations*, which instructs users how to make an adaptation.[19]

Jon Agar has written, 'You can tell what a culture values by what it has in its bags and pockets. Keys, combs, and money tell us that property, personal appearance, or trade matter'. In the eighteenth century, he notes, the pocket watch was a symbol of entrepreneurship and industry, a marker of independence from the town clock and church bell that symbolized land-based and religious authority.[20] Today, what we can carry in our pockets has multiplied exponentially. Mobile devices have miniaturized the world, allowing us to carry an immense array of useful commodities and technologies in our pockets; they place access to spaces that hitherto contained us — banks, shops, travel agencies, libraries, museums, archives, cities, nations, and even other planets — in our clothing and bags, reversing relations between persons and spaces, outside and inside, texts and contexts.

Beyond such historical and sociological functions, mobile devices are changing the epistemologies through which we engage with the world generally and with literary adaptation specifically. Virtual reality approximates actual sensory experiences of taste, sight, smell, sound, and touch. (There are limits, however, to the virtual's displacement of the physical: *iBeer*, an app that simulates drinking a pint of beer, however realistically visually and aurally, is unlikely to replace the actual activity.)[21]

The most prominent way in which apps are changing epistemologies of consumption is through haptic technologies. According to Gerard Goggin,

> The mobile phone very much emerged as a haptic technology, rather than primarily an aural, listening or speaking technology [...] underscored by the emphasis on the mobile as a 'hand' (or 'handy') technology, and especially through the text messaging 'thumb' culture.[22]

When the iPad was unveiled on 30 December 2009, the *Wall Street Journal* quipped, 'Last time there was this much excitement about a tablet, it had some commandments written on it'. The following month, when Steve Jobs presented the tablet to an expectant audience, he stood before a giant screen bearing the Wall Street quotation and Gustav Doré's engraving of Moses destroying the Ten Commandments.[23] In terms of the present volume, what is more canonical than the Ten Commandments? Mobile devices and their apps situate users as commanders at the centre of a virtual, custom-made world; hand-held, they bring everything, including canonical literature, to hand. Like God writing on the tablets, users issue commands and order virtual worlds with fingers rather than oral pronouncements, chisels, or pens.

Ad-app-ting the British Literary Canon

Ad-app-tations, while they participate in and simulate prior adaptations of the canon, by definition must do more than carry a work from one medium to another, or from one historical or cultural context to another, or from one demographic to another; they must do more than convey aesthetics, mythologies, narratives, or political ideologies: they must fulfil some practical, useful function for their users, whether a teaching tool to assist students in gaining academic credentials, a means of consuming multimedial adaptations on a single device, or a more convenient, accessible, and economic way to read, hear, view, touch, or even game the literary canon.

The discourse of ad-app-tations turns readers, viewers, audiences, and consumers into users. While consumers and users are often conflated in marketing rhetoric, especially when the focus is on exchange-value rather than use-value, the words connote different concepts. To consume is 'to use up'; to use is 'to make use of, employ, esp. habitually' (*OED*). Traditional marketing rhetoric speaks of 'end users'; most apps construct *ongoing* users, who purchase app updates and new app content. Apps themselves are constantly adapting and being adapted in order to remain useful and used. Returning several years on to revise this chapter, I did not find a single app that had not been updated in the interim period.

Literati have historically worried that new technologies and transmedial adaptations of literature will bring about the death of authors, literature, and readers.[24] Against the mainstream, Thomas Leitch argues that adaptation of literature to other media facilitates a shift from passive media consumption to an active literacy 'whose goal is engagement, analysis, and reasoned debate'.[25] Apps go further than these scholarly functions. Self-proclaimed as 'the world's most-loved storytelling platform', the *Wattpad* app claims to connect 'a global community of 65 million readers and writers through the power of story'. *Wattpad* users network over reading and writing, reviewing what they read and compiling recommended reading lists for fellow users. *Wattpad* offers not only free access to canonical literature in the public domain, but also hosts new writing by amateurs, promising to 'discover [...] untapped, unsigned, and talent writers and connect [...] them to global multi-media entertainment companies'. *Wattpad* also offers the promise of adaptation to new writers: 'See your story get published, get produced to movie or film, get adapted to a TV series'; below this are logos of Simon & Schuster, HarperCollins, Macmillan, NBC, Paramount, Entertainment One, and Turner.[26] *Wattpad* joins similar social networking reading apps such as *Litsy* and *GoodReads*, as well as fan fiction and YouTube apps, to reconstruct readers as writers, critics, and adapters.[27]

I have elsewhere discussed the theoretical and practical challenges that the layers of reading and writing in adaptation, as well as representations of authors in film adaptations of their work, present to Roland Barthes's death of the author and birth of the reader; since that time, apps and other digital technologies are bringing about the death of the reader and heralding the birth of the reader as user. What, then, are some uses of canonical ad-app-tations?[28]

Ad-app-ting Canon Reading

Jobs's selection of Doré's illustration featuring Moses on the verge of destroying the tablets rather than his engraving of Moses presenting them taps into widely expressed fears that mobile devices and their apps will be used to destroy the canon and reading. Similar fears that book illustration and film would render prose fiction obsolete were voiced in the early years of the twentieth century.[29] But the printed paperback and hardcover books that mobile book apps are replacing are not synonymous with either 'the canon' or reading. The canon is not a material object, but a hotly debated and constantly shifting concept, forged and flowing through many media. Nor are mobile devices and apps doing away with reading: they are offering new ways of reading.

Apps customize reading: as Jobs put it, they can do 'whatever you want'.[30] Readers can select fonts, line spacing and margins, screen themes and screen brightness, or to have books read aloud to them; they can annotate, highlight, search, and bookmark virtual books; apps also help users to manage and organize their virtual library, offering reading recommendations and in-app purchases.[31] One recent trend has been to bring canonical literature to users in smaller portions. The app *Dailylit* asks:

> Don't want to carry *Anna Karenina* on the train? *DailyLit* sends you just enough for your morning commute or coffee break. Find yourself with some extra time? Can't wait a whole day for the next chapter of *Moby Dick*? Just tap 'Next *installment*' and it'll be on its way. ... Before you know it, you'll be knee-deep in *Ulysses* and actually looking forward to your morning bus ride.[32]

Dailylit joins *Wattpad*, *Serial Box*, *Tapas*, *Radish*, and other apps in delivering what J. D. Biersdorfer has called 'snackable' fiction for the digital age.[33] Although this recalls older practices of serial publication, the portion sizes are much smaller. Ross Williams, creator of the *Sonnet Project* app, recounts: 'I started thinking about how I could deliver Shakespeare to people in small chunks, things that would be manageable and get people to experience Shakespeare in their day-to-day lives without having to make the commitment to go see a full show'.[34] Gina Bloom's study of Shakespeare videogame adaptations finds that games not only 'trade on the bard's cultural iconicity, using theatre to sell games', but also that 'increasingly theatre proponents have reversed this strategy, using games to sell theatre' — to encourage gamers to commit to seeing a 'full show'.[35]

Apps furthermore introduce new phenomenologies of reading. Presenting *iBooks* for the iPad in 2010, Jobs revealed a virtual bookshelf displaying books and containing a button which, when pressed, opens 'a secret passageway' to the virtual *iBooks* store, where users can browse and purchase ebooks by tapping and swiping their screens. Tapping also buys books, downloads them onto the virtual bookshelf, and navigates their pages. Joining new modes of consumption, apps have introduced new ways of reading: their technologies carry us from theories of Enlightenment vision and the psychoanalytic gaze to a haptic visuality (more literally haptic than the modes theorized by Laura U. Marks and others), in which reading unfolds through intersections of seeing and touching.[36] The union disrupts neoclassical hierarchies and segregations of the senses, which placed vision at the top and touch at the bottom. Building on somatic-cognitive processes of hand-eye coordination, the haptic visuality of reading virtual literature on apps is not so much a biological affair as it is an adaptation of how we consume other media forms, combining movements that used to read print books with techniques and conventions from cinematography, which in turn simulate visual practices associated with these media. Finger pincer movements zoom in and out on objects and texts like the lens of a camera or eye; dragging, swiping finger-movements scroll up and down pages like pan, tilt, and track shots in film; tapping the edge of a virtual page turns it — sometimes visually simulating an actual page turn, sometimes cutting to the next page like a new shot in film. Finger-movements make objects grow and shrink, appear and disappear, not only in imitation of film techniques, but also in imitation of supernatural and magical gestures that enchant reading. Reading via apps, then, forges not only hybrid phenomenologies of media consumption in which reading engages film techniques, but also hybrids of bodily movements and sheer magic.

iClassics claims that its series of *Tactile Tales* 'represents a new way of reading' enabled by its 'immersive' reading apps:[37]

> iClassics Productions has become famous for its artistic and technological enhancements of great literature, and our collection of Immersive Entertainment apps would be woefully incomplete if it did not include the works of Charles Dickens. While not quite as terrifying as the iPoe Collection ... the iDickens Collection is a family-friendly app, bursting with great horror moments that hook young readers to great Dickensian literature.[38]

iClassics's *Poe Yourself* app encourages immersion by role-playing Poe's characters.

Tactile Tales and other similarly immersive ebooks exceed print books in their capacity to contain embedded videos, music, sound effects, animations, and other media. A review of Push Pop Press's app, *Our Choice*, claims that 'this app really shows what the future of books could look like'. The app's 'first title is a revised version of Al Gore's 2009 book about the environment and it has been augmented with video, interactive charts and fun touches such as blowing into the iPad's microphone to trigger a demo of wind power'.[39] Augmented reality apps such as winner of the App Store Best of 2017 award, *Alice in Wonderland AR Quest*, superimpose digital images, texts, sounds, and animations on a camera recording of users' actual space, including a looking glass that not only shows them a view of Wonderland but also offers them entry into it if they step into the space it occupies in their real-world location.[40] As Gabriella Giannachi has written:

> The hypersurface is where the real and the virtual meet each other. It is materiality and textuality, real and representation ... Through the hypersurface the viewer can enter the work of art, be part of it, as well as interact with it ... while maintaining a direct rapport with [her] own environment.[41]

Once in that space, users can manipulate virtual objects and make narratives by doing so.

Ad-app-tations not only revolutionize the bodily movements and phenomenologies by which users engage with literature, they further revolutionize the movement of literature across societies and the globe. Their virtual nature allows users to carry the entire canons of many nations. Both the Amazon Kindle Paperwhite and the Kobo Aura H2O can hold up to six thousand ebooks, saving space at home, lightening luggage when travelling, rendering large libraries portable property.[42] A review of the *Play Shakespeare* app remarks: 'Sure, you could lug around several heavy books in your bag and read all of Shakespeare's extensive plays, sonnets, and poems. Or, you could save yourself the broken back and download this app instead'.[43] As Jobs demonstrates, apps allow users to purchase books anywhere on the planet with Internet access.

Sales figures show that ebooks are eating into print book sales almost everywhere: university libraries are increasingly opting to purchase electronic over print copies. Yet while in 2014 ebook sales were predicted to outnumber print book sales by 2017 in the US and 2018 in the UK, in 2017 the Association of American Publishers reported that 43.2 per cent of its sales were print and 27 per cent were ebooks, while the Publishers Association of the UK reported a 3 per cent rise in ebook sales compared to a 5 per cent increase in print book sales.[44] However, Piet van Niekerk advises that the figures do not indicate a loss of interest in e-reading, as the publishing industry has been substantially increasing ebook prices (possibly to drive up print sales) and has not tracked millions of its ebook sales. Major companies such as Amazon do not report their ebook sales at all.[45] Moreover, global sales of ebooks as a percentage of print books are increasing: in 2013, ebook sales constituted 12.3% of total book sales worldwide; by 2018, they had risen to 25.8%. The number of digital publishing product users worldwide rose from 479,700,000 in 2016 to 540,600,000 in 2018 and is projected to rise to 621,800,000 by 2022. Clearly, the figures do not indicate a decline in reading; rather, they document an increase. As theatrical, film, and television adaptations have all been shown to increase the sales of the books they adapt rather than threaten them with obsolescence, so too ad-app-tation has increased overall book sales and readership.[46]

Nigel Newton, chief executive of Bloomsbury Publishing, says: 'We live in a golden age of reading, where more recent works are consumed than at any time in history through digital delivery'.[47] While Newton emphasizes the increase in sales of *new* works; what of older, canonical works? Apps have increased their circulation by making access to the literary canons of many nations and periods easier than ever before. Most reading apps are free (for example, *Kobo Reading App*); as of 26 November 2018, *Free Books Ultimate Classics Library* by Digital Press Publishing hosted 51,305 free 'classic' ebooks; even on sites that charge for books, older canonical works are almost always in the public domain and can usually be downloaded at no cost. Therefore, apps make the literary canon more affordable as well as more accessible. Thanks to virtual storage, downloaded apps and books, whether purchased or free, resist theft, fire, floods, and war; even when the mobile device containing them is lost, stolen, or destroyed, virtual literature survives the death of the bodies containing it, persisting not only on millions of other devices, but also on thousands of systems that generate and support canonical literary apps. It would require a global apocalypse to destroy the canon in these forms.

Along with condensing, localizing, personalizing, customizing, and reducing the costs of vast quantities of literature for first-world users, apps make literature and literacy more accessible in developing nations. A study published in August 2017 found that 98.7 per cent of people in developing nations had a mobile phone subscription,[48] a staggering statistic when set beside the 83.8 per cent who owned one in the US in that year.[49] A UNESCO report, 'Reading in the Mobile Era', found that hundreds of thousands of people in developing countries are using mobile devices to learn to read and that mobile apps such as *iBooks*, *Google Play Books*, *Amazon Kindle*, *Nook*, and *Universal Book Reader* have substantially increased access to reading material. Sixty-two per cent of respondents in Ethiopia, Ghana, India, Kenya, Nigeria, Pakistan, and Zimbabwe said they are reading more as a result of mobile reading devices. Although the most common reason given was convenience (67 per cent), 13 per cent of respondents said that their primary reason for reading on their phone was because it was more affordable than reading in print, and another 9 per cent said it was because they do not otherwise have access to books:

> Digital networks, computer processors and liquid crystal display (LCD) screens remove production constraints that have kept reading material prohibitively expensive for centuries. Increasingly, paper and ink are being replaced by bits and bytes, and physical distribution channels are being streamlined by cables that can carry electronic information to the farthest corners of the planet almost instantaneously. At the same time ever-improving search tools are making the vast repositories of online text easy to use and navigate. Today a robust internet connection gives a person access to more text than in all of the physical libraries ever built.[50]

Users in developing countries often share mobile devices, increasing the reach of reading on a single device beyond single individuals.[51] Ad-app-tation, then, is providing access to literacy and books to those for whom print literature is out of reach, as well as offering new ways of reading.

Ad-app-ting Scholarship and Pedagogy of the Canon

In addition to democratizing access to literacy and books, digital technologies generally and apps specifically are democratizing literary scholarship, canonical and otherwise. Unfunded scholars can now use material from archives hitherto unavailable to them. It would have taken many years and copious funds to conduct the research for my 2012 monograph using conventional print libraries and archives; not only did Google Books, ECCO, NCCO, the Internet Archive, Project Gutenberg, and other electronic databases grant me access to works from collections all over the world, digital search technologies also saved me time.[52] While some sources were transcribed using html and similar technologies, most allowed me to view scanned pages of books as they would appear were I holding print versions. Although I used a laptop rather than a mobile device for my research, some of these companies, including Project Gutenberg and the Internet Archive, have produced apps, and more are likely to do so in future. Students who might not be able to afford a laptop or phone line broadband can use their phones to access these resources.

In contrast to the democratizing effects of digitization and apps on access to scholarly archives, pedagogical apps to date tend to fall on the conservative side of canon debates, treating canonical authors and texts reverentially and using traditional methods of textual scholarship inherited from studies of the religious canon. Most are reinstating the traditional canon at the expense of rival canons championed by progressive and radical scholars since the 1960s. About 78 per cent of silent era films were lost, destroyed, or discarded in the twentieth century; as silent fiction films were often selected on the basis of the canonicity of the literary works they adapted, so too in the early years of the twenty-first century, government bodies, universities, and commercial investors have opted to fund apps featuring works from the traditional canon rather than the new canons challenging it.[53] Thus while works by Petrarch, Shakespeare, Jonson, Austen, Scott, Dickens, Melville, Twain, and Jefferson have received ample financing, the Brown Women Writers' Project, founded in 1988 to recover forgotten women writers, for years languished unfunded and un-updated.[54] Today, scholars who resist the late twentieth-century poststructuralist, postmodern, and radical left-wing political theoretical turn in the humanities are flocking to the digital humanities in the same way that they flocked to adaptation studies in the 1970s, pursuing narratological, structural, and quantitative analyses of texts in an effort to understand style, influence, and greatness.[55] For example, at a symposium I attended in 2014, a leading digital humanities scholar (who will remain unnamed) argued that Jane Austen was probably not a great writer after all because she did not use that many different words. Here digital humanities methodologies were being used to discredit the only woman writer who has occupied an undisputed place in the British literary canon.

The conservative, high art, humanist canonical content of apps is often strikingly at odds with their innovative, populist technological forms. If canonical apps are ideologically conservative in their selection of texts and their commentaries upon those texts, they are technologically innovative in their media combinations: *The Waste Land*, released by Touch Press in partnership with Faber & Faber publishers in 2011, is one of the most elegant, sophisticated, and expensive British canonical apps on the market. Designed for scholars and advanced students, it treats the poem conservatively, as a sacred text, linking a navigable, searchable contemporary print version with embedded explanatory notes to the original handwritten manuscript and its earliest typescript, bearing annotations by Ezra Pound and Vivian Eliot. It also contains biographical information and images, hagiographically presented. In so doing, it functions as both virtual museum and archive. It goes beyond these functions to conjoin literary criticism and multimedial adaptation, supplementing its textual glosses and notes with adaptations of the poem to other media, including audio readings by T. S. Eliot, Ted Hughes, Alec Guinness, and Viggo Mortensen, and a filmed performance by Fiona Shaw. The app hosts a virtual community of poets, scholars, and actors, some long dead, some recently deceased, some living, maintaining a virtual scholarly afterlife for the poem.

Yet the app also creates interconnections between textual criticism and multimedial adaptation excoriated for violating medium specificity (and resented as rivals to their work) by high art modernists. Filmed commentaries by Seamus Heaney, Paul Keegan, Jim McCue, Craig Raine, Frank Turner, Jeanette Winterson, and Fiona Shaw engage the same media used for Shaw's dramatic performance. The poem's texts, textual criticism, performance, and performed criticism interpenetrate through networked technologies. In spite of the app's top-down pedagogical elements, its interactive structures allow users to choose how the poem is presented and to change that mode of presentation at any time. With traditional technologies, different devices would be needed to alternate between modes of representation; readers would have to put down the print poem and turn on an audio recording or audiovisual adaptation of it or go to a library or online to look up criticism on it. The app integrates these modes almost seamlessly, allowing the user to change the format in which she engages the poem at any line and to change it midline. Explanatory written notes and filmed commentaries on specific passages can be accessed simply by tapping or can equally easily be ignored.[56] While a user may choose to progress respectfully and sequentially, there is nothing to prevent her from engaging in any number of unconventional leaps across lines of poetry and media and the app's hyperlinked structure actively encourages digressions and shifts in focus.

Apps aimed at secondary school students too evince tensions between authoritative and open interpretation, between humanist critical methodologies and adaptation technologies, and convergences and divergences between scholarly criticism and aesthetic adaptation. Three pedagogical apps ad-app-ting that most canonical of authors, William Shakespeare, illustrate these tensions. Cambridge University Press's app, *Explore Shakespeare* (2012), targets general readers, actors, and secondary school students. Its promotional video simultaneously claims both interpretive innovation ('Explore Shakespeare as never before') and traditional top-down academic authority ('Discover the definitive Cambridge editions'). It combines aesthetic technologies and film celebrities ('Each play is beautifully presented with a full audio performance from stars like Michael Sheen and Kate Beckinsale') with traditional pedagogical tools ('Understand the stories with glossaries, activities, and summaries'). It conjoins verbal illustrations (scholarly commentaries) with pictorial illustrations of performed Shakespeare ('Visualise the action with hundreds of professional [production] photos').[57] In so doing, the app forges partnerships between traditional textual scholarship and multimedia adaptation that have elsewhere and in the past engaged in fierce rivalries.[58]

These tensions and alliances, however they may be resolved or persist in the apps, are palpable in marketing discourses. Henry Volans, head of Faber Digital, expresses concern about collaborating with a press deemed 'to have a scientific bias' in creating *The Waste Land* app (referring here to the quantitative 'science' of digital technology), but reassures himself that 'their interests are wide and the idea that people who are good with technology can't understand literature is thankfully beginning to melt away'.[59] Rivalries between quantitative digital and qualitative humanities methodologies are more pronounced in *Explore Shakespeare*'s marketing. The promotional video produced by the technological team asserts that the *quantitative* aspects of the app allow for 'deeper' analysis than the app's textual criticism ('Want to delve deeper? Use the theme line to trace the ebb and flow of the play's themes. Discover character relationships. Explore the language of each scene with interactive word clouds'). By contrast, the written promotion published by Cambridge University Press on its website excludes the app's quantitative technologies from its 'delve deeper' section, reserving that for traditional verbal criticism alone ('accessible articles by authoritative Cambridge sources', 'detailed notes', and text searching).[60]

Ideological tensions over interpretation and adaptation also emerge across different apps treating the same canonical materials. *Shakespeare at Play*, a Canadian app released in fifty countries one year later, targets 'students learning Shakespeare for the first time', using many of the same technologies deployed by the Cambridge app: audio description, verbal commentaries, in-line annotations, and performance by actors. Yet its marketing rhetoric clearly contests its competitor's pedagogical strategies. It prioritizes performed adaptation over textual criticism as the best means to understand Shakespeare's words:

> Shakespeare wasn't meant to be read, which is why his work can be so difficult and intimidating. His words were meant to be brought to life in performance. That's why our app provides a video of every scene, with simple staging to help keep the focus on the words.

It further protests against Cambridge University claims to 'definitive' readings, and in so doing challenges high art, humanist criticism via reader-response theory:

> Our app empowers students to tackle Shakespeare on their own terms. [...] Rather than attempting to offer a definitive reading, [Professor Noam] Lior [...] the dramaturge on all of our productions as well as the academic voice of *Shakespeare at Play* [...] challenges viewers and readers to make interpretational [*sic*] choices when a play demands it.[61]

The app further rejects the top down, language focused aspects of celebrity audio performances; in place of low-budget audio recordings of well-known actors, it offers low-budget video performances by unknown, but 'classically trained' actors.

For all the Canadian app's commitment to less hierarchical modes of representation and interpretation, it appears stuffily traditional by comparison to *RE:Shakespeare*, released on 30 June 2015. Co-produced by Samsung Electronics and the Royal Shakespeare Company and hosted by David Tennant, this free app targets 'young people between the ages of 11 and 18', foregrounding 'modern and entertaining elements' rather than traditional scholarly methods supplemented by low-budget audio and video performance.[62] Its promotional video announces the app as a meeting point for 'the world's favourite playwright' and 'some of the biggest names in popular culture'. Rather than adapt prior modes of textual criticism and audiovisual adaptation to app technologies, this app adapts Shakespeare to popular app technologies:

> Users can lip sync lines with street poet Indigo in a video mash-up, mix Shlomo's breakbeats with Shakespeare's verse to create their own unique track and see if they can tell rap from Shakespeare, with Akala's Hip-hop or

> Shakespeare quiz. [...] Drawing on the RSC's proven 'ensemble' technique, users meet and work together with [... a]ctor Tamsin Greig, RSC voice coach Nia Lynn, and top director Iqbal Khan.[63]

Following rehearsals, users can perform a scene opposite a virtual RSC actor. Finally, 'RE:Shakespeare users have a chance to explore the Royal Shakespeare Theatre and watch scenes from the 2015 RSC production of *Much Ado About Nothing* in amazing 360° action — a world first'. The app takes interactivity to a new level and radically modernizes the modes of adaptation through which users engage with Shakespeare, while maintaining a strong RSC theatrical tradition.

Study guides for A-levels and GCSEs have also been ad-app-ted. These apps are not designed solely to educate or to inculcate cultural ideologies, but also have pragmatic and economic uses: they help students pass exams and gain academic credentials. The apps in turn tout the value and pedagogical authority of those academics who have produced the app content and have passed exams and gained credentials themselves, creating a closed circle of cultural and economic value, in which those with academic credentials guide those aspiring to them and to the cultural and economic value that academic credentials are seen to provide.

Some pedagogical apps entice users with a rhetoric of professionalization and competition. The App Store preview for Foothills Education's *Fact Mountain* nineteenth-century British literature app calls the user to 'Become a true literature expert with Fact Mountain', 'Become deeply informed through hundreds of hyperlinks', and 'Challenge your knowledge with two games'.[64] Whilst Play Shakespeare's *Shakespeare* app is free, its *Shakespeare Pro* app offers users the chance to 'become a Shakespeare pro' for only $9.99.[65] These apps put themselves in competition with older pedagogical technologies: both previews tout the apps' superior technologies and new media techniques in the creation of expertise; both offer less expensive pathways to virtual expertise.

Intriguingly, canonical apps for young children are often more innovative and technologically sophisticated than apps for older students, possibly because they are less constrained by exams and gaining credentials. Apps based on Lewis Carroll's *Alice in Wonderland* illustrate this tendency. Some ad-app-tations engage traditional literacy pedagogies: for example, the *Kids Book Club Alice* app offers children a choice of 'autoplay', 'read it myself', and 'read to me'. The app supplements these traditional techniques of teaching print reading with audio, music, illustrations, and audiovisual adaptations of the text that go beyond the capacities of printed books.

Other children's canonical apps go further than simulating traditional media to engage young readers with new media. The *AvatarBook Alice in Wonderland* app allows children to photograph their own faces and superimpose them on Alice's head and body: 'Make your children the fairy tale star'.[66] The interpenetration of selfie face with character body changes the ways in which children identify with fictional characters, going beyond empirical identification of and projective identification with characters offered by traditional media to a multimedia pastiche of imaged, interactive, performing self and/as other.

When Atomic Antelope released *Alice for the iPad* in April 2010,[67] the *Huffington*

Post declared, 'It reinvents reading' and the BBC nominated it 'the future'.[68] Sections of John Tenniel's illustrations to Carroll's book are animated; users' haptic movements enhance and produce elements of those animations. Yet by January 2014, even that app appeared dated. The YouTube adverts for both apps make clear that the A1000Castles app is technologically light years ahead of its 2010 predecessor in the interactivity of its animations; it also carries the avatar technology of the *Alice AvatarBook* app further.[69] (That the only way to demonstrate this clearly is to direct my readers to audiovisual representations of them on YouTube in the footnotes suggests the limits of verbal criticism to explicate apps.)

Some apps use canonical literature to teach other subjects besides reading: the *Alice App* designed by Emmanuel Paletz combines Carroll's story with art history;[70] Miniville's *Sounds of Alice in Wonderland* teaches musical scales;[71] ITbooks' *Alice* app teaches English to Spanish children.[72] *Alice's Tea Cup Madness* gives users a joint lesson in capitalist economics and female servitude through gaming. Casting the user as Alice and locating her as a waitress where she must rush to meet the demands of impatient, mostly male, clients (March Hares, Mad Hatters, and more), her tasks are:

> Keep customers happy by serving them as fast as you can.
>
> The happier they are the more money you will earn.
>
> Purchase upgrades to improve the look of your tea house and get better equipment to meet increasing customer demand.

Like the pass-your-exams apps addressed above, this app creates a closed circle of educational and economic investment: the user needs to upgrade her skills and the app to upgrade her virtual profits; to do so she must *purchase* the upgrades. Implicitly, she must also be able to persuade adults to purchase them for her.

While the child user must know how to read to use the app, the skills it teaches are not primarily those of reading or textual analysis, but those of gaming. To date, adaptation studies has been principally concerned with the study of narrative, whether its formal and aesthetic aspects, or its ideological and political connotations. New media are shifting critical focus from a discourse of narrativization to a discourse of gamification in many disciplines; in education studies, game-based learning is being opposed to the story-based learning that dominated the eighteenth and nineteenth centuries.[73] In *The Gamification of Learning and Instruction*, Karl M. Kapp defines gamification as 'a system in which learners, players, consumers, and employees engage in an abstract challenge, defined by rules, interactivity, and feedback that results in a quantifiable outcome ideally eliciting an emotional reaction'.[74] Eric Zimmerman describes:

> An emerging set of skills and competencies, a set of new ideas and practices that are going to be increasingly a part of what it means to be literate in the coming century [...]. Literacy and media literacy are [...] not sufficient for one to be fully literate in our world today.[75]

These skills include competition, point-scoring and other rewards for acquiring gaming skills and achieving gaming goals, following rules, collaborating with others, role-playing, and problem-solving. The statistics with which this chapter opens attest that sales of gaming apps outstrip education and book apps combined. Sometimes the two overlap: the *Kids Book Club Alice* app not only teaches literacy, it also teaches gaming. At any point in the story, children can pause the reading to solve puzzles and jigsaws, play match games, count items, search images for hidden items, or make a painting. During gaming activities, the reading ceases, replaced by vocal praise when the child succeeds: 'Good job! Great! Great job!'. While gamification has not yet displaced narrativization, or gaming reading, and are unlikely to do so, they have a formidable presence in the canonical literary apps for the youngest readers and suggest that the future forms of pedagogical apps for older children will be vastly different from what they are today.

Ad-app-ting Authors: Parody, Hagiography, Haunting

Canonical literary games targeting older users are often parodic: *Angry Bards*, a parody of the popular game *Angry Birds*, calls bards into battle to 'defend the integrity of the fine arts' from regal censorship of their satire. Players are instructed to 'tap the battlefield to send musical notes to that location' and 'attack enemies with musical notes to defeat them'.[76] Such militant uses of the arts forge a double parody of battle games and political uses of the arts. *Flapping Bard* requires users to keep the long-dead William Shakespeare from plunging to a virtual bloody death. Even if he dies, he returns to live and die again in the endless afterlife afforded by gaming.[77] Parodic apps also parody the relationship between literature and gaming: there is a parodic video game of *Waiting for Godot*, in which nothing happens and no action on the part of gamers has any effect.[78] Parody not only undermines the seriousness of the literary canon and canonical authors: by critiquing cultural appropriations of canonical authors and works, it equally constructs the canon 'as a cultural force'.[79] The question of parody merits further consideration and extension from traditional media to gaming, work that is beyond the scope of this chapter.

Hagiography forges the reverential side of a canonical coin whose obverse is parody. The *Eye Shakespeare* app engages both sides of that coin. Developed by the Shakespeare Birthplace Trust, using GPS, the app acts as virtual tour guide in actual Stratford-upon-Avon, providing reverent commentaries and guides to tourist attractions as the user progresses on her literary pilgrimage. But when it goes further than the real-world tours it displaces, using augmented reality and QR scanning technologies to superimpose Shakespeare's last home (long destroyed) and Shakespeare (played by an actor) upon the actual landscape, it borders on parody. The actor playing Shakespeare is an everyman buffoon — a far cry from Shakespeare's grave and graven cultural images. Users can have their photographs taken with this buffoonish 'Shakespeare', but in order to have a material rather than a virtual photograph, it must be purchased from the birthplace gift shop. Its developers are transparent about their aims: 'We hope the app will prove a hit with visitors to Stratford and will also play its part in boosting tourism in the region'.[80]

Dickens: Dark London, an app published by the Museum of London in collaboration with Creative Brothers and Sisters, also uses GPS technology to take users around former authorial haunts. However, it is a far more serious and aestheticized affair than *Eye Shakespeare*. The app adapts *Sketches by Boz* (1836), ruminations on Dickens's night walks around London. Superimposing a contemporary satellite map of London on an 1862 map of the city, the app creates a palimpsest of historical and contemporary London, guiding the user to the locations written about by Dickens. The app allows users to do more than trace the past steps of a dead author on a tourist pilgrimage; it allows them simultaneously to inhabit a virtual authorial body and to be possessed by the words of the author. The app's selection of a first-person, quasi-autobiographical text foregrounds a Romantic expressivist view of authorship. The author's words haunt the user, entering her ears through actor Mark Strong's voiceover, while images by illustrator David Foldvari invade her eyes, including illustrations of Dickens, who appears with his characters within some scenes. Alexis Easley views illustrations 'as a device for collapsing fictional and extrafictional worlds'; imaging Dickens beside his characters collapses divides between author and character.[81] However, that he is the iconic Dickens of the 1860s rather than the Dickens of 1836 creates a sense of atemporal haunting in which a subsequent Dickens revisits scenes narrated by his younger self. A multimedial, intertextual pastiche and hagiographic palimpsest, the app combines fictional and artifactual locations and overlays authorial and character locations, past and present maps and authors, as well as print, spoken words, illustrations, and music. The multisensory, transtemporal media create a tug of war between nostalgia and futurity — between the literary and historical past and artistic and technological progressivism, constructing a reciprocal haunting, in which the past and old media haunt the present and new media, and vice versa, while 'Dickens' (the author and his writings) haunts the user even as the user haunts the locales visited and written about by Dickens. This is not spectral, abstract one-way haunting; this is mutual, interactive possession and multifaceted haunting. Yet it is by no means seamless or synchronized. Unlike the attempts of mainstream cinema and television adaptations to make their modes of representation (acting, costumes, production design, props, camera techniques, editing, music, and so forth) appear as a seamless, unmediated whole, the app's representations are fragmented, disjointed, and self-conscious. The verbal descriptions are often at odds with the drawn illustrations; 2012 real-world London bore very little resemblance to either. This is a palimpsest with all the seams showing; interactive as it may be, it precludes immersion when all of its modes of representation are engaged simultaneously.

Conclusion

If ad-app-tations render relations between authors, writings, and users simultaneously tangible and spectral, interactive and distancing, they equally raise the spectre of new and distancing literacies in which literary scholars may flounder. The *Shakespeare SwipeSpeare* app 'puts the words of the Bard into plain and simple English with a Swipe of a finger!'[82] Others remediate canonical literature through the language of new media. David Gaddy's *Poe Moji* app calls users to 'Enjoy your literary discussions with friends and Edgar Allen Poe! This pack of thirty-five emoticon stickers is great for expressing your meloncholy [*sic*] ... and your general love for all things gothic!'[83] The typo in the promo demonstrates a slipshod attitude to canonical language, counterpoised to a new hybrid literary language comprised of the author's face, his literary quotations, and new media emoticons.

Yet more fundamentally, the language of apps situates most literary scholars as illiterates. In *Dickens: Dark London*, not only are Dickens's writings palimpsestically overlaid by other words and other media created by other authors and artists, his writings are themselves laid over software coding, which is the ur-text, the origin, the deep structure, the universal language of this and all apps. Apps and other digital technologies challenge the transtheoretical position based on discourses of older media that form is inseparable from content maintained by formalist, structuralist, and poststructuralist theories (under poststructuralism there is no content).[84] Part of Henry Jenkins's definition of new media convergence culture includes 'the flow of content across multiple media platforms', independent of any specific delivery mechanism.[85] This is in part because underlying all new media is a universal language (in contrast to longstanding claims that the languages of different media are irreducible) — that of software coding.[86]

Apps thus require new theories of language, of authorship, and of media consumption. Computer programmers are the underlying authors of ad-app-tations. As with the scenarists and title-card writers in the early days of cinema and many screenwriters thereafter, their names lie buried beneath the names of the canonical authors they ad-app-t and the names of the production companies that employ them. More significantly, their software codes remain invisible and illegible to most literary critics. Ad-app-tations render scholars like myself illiterates in our own fields. For the first time in the history of our subject, a majority of academics cannot read the deep structures underlying the ad-app-tations of canonical texts. We have become users rather than readers. Even as they promote global literacy, apps create an illiteracy extending to academics — the illiteracy of 'iteracy' (the term used to describe knowledge of computer coding). If Marshall McLuhan is right and the medium is the message, it is a message we can no longer read.[87] If computer coding is the universal language, it is one in which we are not conversant. Almost all of us read digital literature in translation; almost all of us have become comparative scholars. Whether or not we learn to read computer coding, even at the level of its surface structures, this chapter has, I hope, shown that ad-app-tations require new modes of reading, analysis, and study, and new theories of adaptation.

Notes to Chapter 2

1. *Literature/Film Quarterly*, established in 1973, was the only dedicated field journal; Robert Giddings, Keith Selby, and Chris Wensley's *Screening the Novel: The Theory and Practice of Literary Dramatization* (London: Macmillan, 1990) addresses television adaptation; Neil Sinyard's *Filming Literature: The Art of Screen Adaptation* (New York: St. Martin's Press, 1986) treats auteur films; the first book-length study to focus on pulp fiction and popular film adaptation was *Pulping Fictions: Consuming Culture Across the Literature/Media Divide*, ed. by Deborah Cartmell and others (London: Pluto Press, 1996).
2. Linda Hutcheon, *A Theory of Adaptation* (New York: Routledge, 2006), pp. 9 & xiv.

3. Siobhan O'Flynn, 'Epilogue', in Hutcheon, with O'Flynn, *A Theory of Adaptation*, pp. 179–206 (p. 179).
4. Zachary Davies Boren, 'There are Officially More Mobile Devices Than People in the World', *Independent*, 7 October 2014 <http://www.independent.co.uk/life-style/gadgets-and-tech/news/there-are-officially-more-mobile-devices-than-people-in-the-world-9780518.html> [accessed 10 August 2015].
5. Unless otherwise referenced, all statistics are from *Statista* <www.statista.com> [accessed 2 November 2018].
6. Simon Kemp, 'Digital in 2018: World's Internet Users Pass the 4 Billion Mark', *We Are Social*, 30 January 2018, <https://wearesocial.com/blog/2018/01/global-digital-report-2018> [accessed 2 November 2018].
7. 'Figures Show More People in the World Have Access to a Mobile Phone Than a Toilet', Mead Johnson and RB, October 2018 <https://www.rb.com/media/news/2018/october/figures-show-more-people-in-the-world-have-access-to-a-mobile-phone-than-a-toilet/> [accessed 3 November 2018].
8. See, for example, Sinyard, *Filming Literature*; Wagner, *The Novel and the Cinema*, pp. 219–31.
9. Daniel Fischlin and Mark Fortier, 'General Introduction', in *Adaptations of Shakespeare: A Critical Anthology of Plays from the Seventeenth Century to the Present*, ed. by Daniel Fischlin and Mark Fortier (Abingdon & New York: Routledge, 2000), p. 17.
10. Kolbas, *Critical Theory and the Literary Canon*, p. 1.
11. Michael Dobson, *The Making of the National Poet: Shakespeare, Adaptation and Authorship, 1660–1769* (Oxford: Clarendon Press, 1992).
12. Elliott, *Rethinking the Novel/Film Debate*, p. 55; Greg M. Colón Semenza and Bob Hasenfratz, *The History of British Literature on Film, 1895–2015* (London: Bloomsbury, 2015).
13. Julie Sanders, *Adaptation and Appropriation* (Abingdon & New York: Routledge, 2006), pp. 8–9.
14. Richard Abel, *The Ciné Goes to Town: French Cinema 1896–1914* (Berkeley: University of California Press, 1998), p. 246; Sarah Cardwell, *Adaptation Revisited: Television and the Classic Novel* (Manchester: Manchester University Press, 2002), pp. 33–34.
15. Arnold Burdett and Dan Brown, *BCS Glossary of Computing and ICT*, 13th edn (London: British Computer Society Learning and Development Ltd., 2013), [n.p.]
16. Lewis Carroll, *Alice's Adventures in Wonderland* and *Through the Looking Glass* (London: Penguin 1998), p. 180.
17. Karl Marx, *Das Kapital* (Washington, DC: Regnery, 2009), pp. 1–2.
18. Jean Baudrillard, *Simulacra and Simulation*, trans. by Sheila Faria Glaser (Ann Arbor: University of Michigan Press, 1994).
19. Microsoft Corporation, *Adaptations, Microsoft Store*, [n.d.] <https://www.microsoft.com/en-us/store/apps/adaptations/9wzdncrddwg7> [accessed 16 July 2014].
20. Jon Agar, *Constant Touch: A Global History of the Mobile Phone* (Cambridge: Icon Books, 2003), p. 3.
21. hottrix, *iBeer 2.0. The REAL iBeer for iPod touch and iPhone*, YouTube, 10 July 2008 <https://www.youtube.com/watch?v=8b9PH55EtJI> [accessed 6 September 2014].
22. Gerard Goggin, 'Adapting the Mobile Phone: The iPhone and its Consumption', *Continuum: Journal of Media & Cultural Studies*, 23.2 (2009), 231–44 (p. 233).
23. EverySteveJobsVideo, 'Steve Jobs Introduces Original iPad: Apple Special Event (2010)', YouTube, 30 December 2013 <https://www.youtube.com/watch?v=_KN-5zmvjAo> [accessed 9 August 2014].
24. Elliott, *Rethinking the Novel/Film Debate*, p. 47, 51–52.
25. Thomas Leitch, *Film Adaptation and Its Discontents: From 'Gone with the Wind' to 'The Passion of the Christ'* (Baltimore, MD: Johns Hopkins University Press, 2007), p. 12.
26. *Wattpad* <https://www.wattpad.com> [accessed 2 November 2018].
27. Simone Murray, *The Adaptation Industry: The Cultural Economy of Contemporary Literary Adaptation* (New York & Abingdon: Routledge, 2012), pp. 188–91.
28. Kamilla Elliott, 'Screened Writers', in *The Blackwell Companion to Literature, Film, and Adaptation*, ed. by Deborah Cartmell (London: Blackwell, 2012), pp. 179–97; Roland Barthes, 'The Death

of the Author', in *Image, Music, Text*, trans. by Stephen Heath (New York: Hill & Wang, 1977), pp. 142–48.

29. Elliott, *Rethinking the Novel/Film Debate*, pp. 51–52.
30. Eric Stewart, 'Steve Jobs Introduces iBooks for the iPad', YouTube, 29 January 2010 <https://www.youtube.com/watch?v=3G31PSNhVUM> [accessed 6 September 2014].
31. John Corpuz, '15 Best E-book Reader Apps', *Tom's Guide*, 18 September 2018 <https://www.tomsguide.com/us/pictures-story/583-best-ereader-apps.html> [accessed 27 November 2018].
32. *Dailylit* <https://www.dailylit.com> [accessed 3 November 2018].
33. See also J. D. Biersdorfer, 'New Apps Provide a World of Literature, One Chapter at a Time', *The New York Times*, 12 May 2017 <https://www.nytimes.com/2017/05/12/books/review/new-apps-provide-a-world-of-literature-one-chapter-at-a-time.html> [accessed 2 November 2018].
34. Ashley Milne-Tyte, 'Shakespeare? There's an App for That', *VOA News*, 28 August 2013 <https://www.voanews.com/a/shakespeare-theres-an-app-for-that/1738809.html> [accessed 2 November 2018].
35. Gina Bloom, 'Videogame Shakespeare: Enskilling Audiences through Theatre-making Games', *Shakespeare Studies*, 43 (2015), 114–27 (p. 114).
36. Laura U. Marks, *Touch: Sensuous Theory and Multisensory Media* (Minneapolis: University of Minnesota Press, 2002).
37. iClassics, *Tactile Tales* <http://iclassicscollection.com/en/tactiletales/> [accessed 2 November 2018].
38. iClassics, *Charles Dickens* <http://iclassicscollection.com/en/project/charles-dickens/> [accessed 2 November 2018].
39. '250 Best iPad Apps: Books', *Daily Telegraph*, 3 June 2011 <http://www.telegraph.co.uk/technology/mobile-app-reviews/8552749/250-best-iPad-apps-books.html> [accessed 6 September 2014].
40. See, for example, Grn Pod, 'iOS 11 AR Game Play', YouTube, 17 October 2017 <https://www.youtube.com/watch?v=lXY4pBxYcXY> [accessed 25 November 2018].
41. Gabriella Giannachi, *Virtual Theatres: An Introduction* (London & New York: Routledge, 2004), p. 95.
42. *Wired*, 'The Best e-Readers and Kindles', 9 July 2018 <https://www.wired.co.uk/article/best-e-readers-kindles> [accessed 27 November 2018].
43. *Open Education Database*, 'The Very Best Book, Comics, and Manga Apps: Our Top 23 Choices', 18 December 2012 <http://oedb.org/ilibrarian/the-very-best-book-apps-our-top-15-picks/> [accessed 6 September 2014].
44. Mark Swaney, 'Ebooks on Course to Outsell Printed Editions in the UK by 2018', *Guardian*, 4 June 2014 <http://www.theguardian.com/books/2014/jun/04/ebooks-outsell-printed-editions-books-2018> [accessed 6 September 2014].
45. Piet van Niekerk, 'Is "Screen Fatigue" Really a Turn-up for the Books?', *Fipp: The Network for Global Media*, 13 November 2018 <https://www.fipp.com/news/features/screen-fatigue-books> [accessed 27 November 2018].
46. Elliott, *Rethinking the Novel/Film Debate*, pp.141–43.
47. Swaney, 'Ebooks on Course to Outsell Printed Editions in the UK by 2018'.
48. Simon Sharwood, 'Developing World Hits 98.7 per cent Mobile Phone Adoption', *The Register*, 3 August 2017 <https://www.theregister.co.uk/2017/08/03/itu_facts_and_figures_2017/> [accessed 27 November 2018].
49. *Statista*.
50. Mark West and Han Ei Chew, *Reading in the Mobile Era: A Study of Mobile Reading in Developing Countries* (Paris: UNESCO, 2014), pp. 15–16.
51. Jeffrey James, 'Sharing Phones in Developing Countries: Implications for the Digital Divide', *Technological Forecasting and Social Change*, 78.4 (May 2011), 729–35.
52. Kamilla Elliott, *Portraiture and British Gothic Fiction: The Rise of Picture Identification, 1764–1835* (Baltimore, MD: Johns Hopkins University Press, 2012).
53. Caroline Frick, *Saving Cinema: The Politics of Preservation* (Oxford: Oxford University Press, 2011), p. 65.

54. Amy E. Earhart, 'Can Information Be Unfettered? Race and the Digital Humanities Canon', in *Debates in the Digital Humanities*, ed. by Matthew K. Gold (Minneapolis: University of Minnesota Press, 2012). Recently, the abandoned Brown Women Writers Project was adopted by Northeastern University.
55. Thomas Leitch, 'Where Are We Going, Where Have We Been?', in *The Literature/ Film Reader: Issues of Adaptation*, ed. by James M. Welsh and Peter Lev (Lanham, MD: Scarecrow Press, 2007), pp. 327–33.
56. Touch Press, 'A Walk through *The Waste Land*', YouTube, 7 June 2011 <https://www.youtube.com/watch?v=rlhosnfP-Jw> [accessed 9 July 2014].
57. Cambridge University Press, 'Explore Shakespeare iPad Apps from Cambridge', YouTube, 28 November 2012 <https://www.youtube.com/watch?v=Uq9-OPDKtac> [accessed 6 September 2014].
58. See, for example, Elliott, *Rethinking the Novel/Film Debate*, Chapters 2–4.
59. Henry Volans, 'Building the Wasteland', *The Thought Fox*, Faber & Faber, 2011 <http://thethoughtfox.co.uk/building-the-waste-land/> [accessed 3 August 2015].
60. Citations from web page and video promos cited above.
61. *Shakespeare at Play*, 8 October 2013 <http://www.shakespeareatplay.ca/> [accessed 6 September 2014].
62. SamsungTomorrow, 'Samsung Reveals RE:Shakespeare App: An Encounter of Digital and Literature', 20 June 2015 <http://global.samsungtomorrow.com/samsung-unveils-reshakespeare-app-an-encounter-of-digital-and-literature/> [accessed 5 August 2015].
63. 'Bringing Shakespeare to Life Through Technology', 30 June 2015 <http://www.samsung.com/uk/discover/news/bringing-shakespeare-to-life-through-technology/> [accessed 5 August 2015].
64. iTunes Preview, *Fact Mountain: 19th Cent. British Literature* <https://itunes.apple.com/is/app/19th-cent-british-literature/id1422926555?mt=8> [accessed 2 November 2018].
65. iTunes Preview, *Shakespeare Pro* <https://itunes.apple.com/gb/app/shakespeare-pro/id341392367?mt=8 > [accessed 27 November 2018].
66. theavatarbook, 'Avatarbook *Alice in Wonderland* — iPad App', YouTube, 13 September 2011 <https://www.youtube.com/watch?v=FN67aEUb02M> [accessed 1 August 2015].
67. Atomic Antelope, '*Alice for the iPad*', YouTube, 12 April 2010 <https://www.youtube.com/watch?v=gew68Qj5kxw> [accessed 4 July 2014].
68. Reviews posted under '*Alice for the iPad*', *iTunes Preview*, 26 March 2015 <https://itunes.apple.com/gb/app/alice-for-the-ipad/id354537426?mt=8> [accessed 6 August 2015].
69. A1000Castles, '*Alice in Wonderland*, Arthur Rackham', YouTube, 24 January 2014 <https://www.youtube.com/watch?v=0vFweU5EA4M> [accessed 12 August 2015].
70. Emmanuel Palentz, '*The Alice App*: Renaissance Art Meets the Alice World', *The Alice App*, 4 April 2014 <http://thealiceapp.com/the-alice-app/> [accessed 14 July 2015].
71. iOS App Stats, 'Miniville's *Sounds of Alice in Wonderland*', 12 August 2015 <http://www.iosmobileapp.com/john_jumper/minivilles_sounds_of_alice_in_wonderland/appId422778394> [accessed 12 August 2015].
72. Itbooks, 'Once Upon a Time' [n.d.] <http://eraseunavez.itbook.es/> [accessed 12 August 2015].
73. Patrick Jagoda, 'Gaming the Humanities', *differences: A Journal of Feminist Cultural Studies*, 25.1 (2014), 189–215.
74. Karl M. Kapp, *The Gamification of Learning and Instruction: Game-based Methods and Strategies for Training and Education* (San Francisco: Pfeiffer, 2012), pp. 10–11.
75. Eric Zimmerman, 'Gaming Literacy: Game Design as a Model for Literacy in the Twenty-first Century', in *The Video Game Theory Reader,* ed. by Bernard Perron and Mark J. P. Wolf (New York: Routledge, 2009), pp. 23–31 (p. 23).
76. Sean Capelle, 'Party Like It's 1599 in *Angry Bards*', *AppAdvice*, 26 March 2013 <http://appadvice.com/review/quickadvice-angrybards> [accessed 12 August 2015].
77. Asinine Games, 'Flapping Bard', YouTube, 23 March 2015 <https://www.youtube.com/watch?v=REbHoa_yM3Y> [accessed 12 August 2015].
78. Funnel27, '*Waiting for Godot*: The Video Game', YouTube, 16 June 2010 <https://www.youtube.com/watch?v=5N1kqtum5rI> [accessed 14 July 2014].

79. Elin Diamond, 'Stoppard's *Dogg's Hamlet, Cahoot's Macbeth*: The Uses of Shakespeare', *Modern Drama*, 29 (1986), 593–600 (p. 594).
80. Shakespeare Birthplace Trust, 'Eye Shakespeare App', *Shakespeare Birthplace Trust*, [n.d.] <http://shakespeare.org.uk/visit-the-houses/eye-shakespeare-app.html> [accessed 14 July 2014].
81. Alexis Easley, *First Person Anonymous: Women Writers and the Victorian Print Media, 1830–70* (Aldershot: Ashgate, 2004), p. 31.
82. Google Play preview, *Shakespeare SwipeSpeare* <https://play.google.com/store/apps/details?id=com.swipespeare&hl=en > [accessed 27 November 2018].
83. David Gaddy, *Poe Mojis* <https://appadvice.com/app/poe-mojis/1182601024> [accessed 27 November 2018].
84. See Elliott, *Rethinking the Novel/Film Debate*, Chapter 5.
85. Henry Jenkins, *Convergence Culture: Where Old and New Media Collide*, rev. edn (New York: New York University Press, 2008), p. 243.
86. Elliott, *Rethinking the Novel/Film Debate*, p. 64.
87. Marshall McLuhan, *Understanding Media: The Extensions of Man* (London: Routledge & Keegan Paul, 1964), pp. 1–18.

CHAPTER 3

❖

Minnelli's *Madame Bovary* (1949): A Test Case for New Disciplines

Christine Geraghty

The many adaptations of Flaubert's *Madame Bovary* (1857) have provided fertile ground for teaching and analysis. The model for analysing an adaptation through a comparison of different versions is well established in adaptation studies and an exemplary approach to adaptations of *Madame Bovary* is provided by Mary Donaldson-Evans. Such analysis usually involves a discussion of the movement from novel to film in formal terms with an emphasis on key plot elements, narrative voice, and characterization. This kind of scrutiny can lead into debates about faithfulness but more fruitfully into discussions of medium specificity and the formal differences between the novel and the feature film. A comparison of adaptations of *Madame Bovary* also leads into other important areas. Questions about authorship come to the fore when analysing different film versions, placing Gustave Flaubert, as the author of the novel, in a relationship with key French film auteurs, Jean Renoir and Claude Chabrol, who adapted the book for cinema in 1934 and 1991 respectively. The range of adaptations of *Madame Bovary*, including television versions and a feature film from India (*Maya Memsaab*, 1993), also means that the act of comparison may highlight different aspects of the novel when studying adaptations from different historical periods and national contexts, making this approach useful for discussing the impact of particular production situations at different moments in time.[1]

In addition, a study of the adaptions of a classic novel such as *Madame Bovary* opens up particular issues about the relationship between literature and film in terms of artistic possibilities and canonical recognition. Flaubert's *Madame Bovary* undoubtedly belongs within the canons of world literature but the status of the many and various film and television versions is much more open to question. For adaptation scholars, the reputation of the novel makes it almost impossible to avoid debates about how far an adaptation of a classic novel can or should be mindful of its source and in particular how far Flaubert's ironic and ambiguous account of his heroine can or should be adopted in the adaptation. Film studies scholars though, as we shall see, are likely to be working with a different set of canonical repertoires in which the director, rather than the writer, is the key figure. Genre is also a factor, and an adaptation which takes on generic features of the romance or melodrama may be differently assessed from an art film. The study of different versions of this world classic thus opens up tensions about how canonical status is bestowed and the different disciplinary assumptions which underpin this process.

This article describes some of the early academic work on the Hollywood adaptation of *Madame Bovary* to open up questions about disciplinarity and the methods of analysis deployed in discussions of an adaptation in the context of a film made in the heyday of the studio system. My emphasis is not so much on the film itself but on the critical work it has generated.[2] I want to explore how Vincente Minnelli's 1949 adaptation for MGM has provided a test case for critics from different disciplinary backgrounds and to illustrate how these different traditions, even in their early manifestations, demonstrate different approaches to questions of production and audience. This case study is offered as one small but significant indication of how the relatively new disciplines of adaptation studies and film studies, often developing out of English or Modern Languages Departments, operated in parallel with each other and demonstrated very different attitudes to some key concepts. This may help to explain not only why adaptations studies found it difficult to draw on the insights of film studies but also suggests that that film studies was itself predicated on a lack of interest in adaptations as adaptations.

In terms of the critical commentary that surrounds Minnelli's *Madame Bovary*, adaptation studies is represented by three scholars: Mary Donaldson-Evans, as a scholar who has paid particular attention to adaptations of *Madame Bovary*, and two seminal critics, Robert Stam and George Bluestone, who used the film to express views on Hollywood adaptations more generally. Against this, I set the work of two film studies pioneers, Lesley Stern and Robin Wood, who represent two very different approaches in film studies which were being developed in the 1970/80s. Most academic work is modelled on a sense of development, of insights being built on the work that has gone before. Here though I am looking at work which did not follow this approach but refuted, ignored, or did not know what had gone before. Because of this, this article does not offer a chronological line starting with the first account, that of Bluestone in 1957, and showing how each critical account builds on its predecessor. Instead the task is more archaeological. It involves digging back in time and working retrospectively (though not in strictly chronological order) to find early readings made when film studies and adaption studies were first developing. It means unearthing accounts that have been buried or ignored, and using them to examine the issues that arise when critics assess the adaptation of an established classic in the context of popular cinema.

Madame Bovary (1949) is a late example of the MGM prestige pictures adapted from respected classics or from the middle-brow fiction promoted through the US Book of the Month Club. These prestige productions had worked, since the early silent days, to make cinema more respectable, but the 1930s saw a resurgence of this approach, as Guerric deBona notes: producers such as Irving Thalberg and David O. Selznik 'managed to combine MGM star glamour with literary property to secure prestige productions'.[3] Examples include *David Copperfield* (1935), *The Good Earth* (1937), and *Pride and Prejudice* (1940).[4] Such films were sold through their stars, their lavish costuming, and detailed, rich art design. In the case of *Madame Bovary*, MGM also used controversies over censorship and scandal to suggest that the film had the same kind of artistic prestige as its French source. Film studies scholars, as we shall see, are also likely to situate this *Madame Bovary* by paying attention to Vincente Minnelli as an admired director of musicals and melodrama. His films are firmly positioned within the Hollywood studio system at its most flamboyant when the wide screen and sophisticated sound systems were weapons in fighting off the challenge of television.

Two Critiques from an Adaptation Studies Perspective: Stam and Donaldson-Evans

The first critical account I refer to comes from the work of Robert Stam. Stam is an adaptations scholar whose work on intertextuality and the dialogic possibilities of adaptations has been very influential and helped to break up some log-jams in adaptation studies in the 2000s. In *Literature through Film*, his chapter on adaptations of *Madame Bovary* begins with a discussion of the source, pointing to its importance in literary history and commenting on Flaubert's development of a free, indirect style which moves in and out of its heroine's consciousness. Stam also discusses *Madame Bovary* as a 'proto-cinematic' novel, written with 'a film-script-like precision'; it is, he says, 'relentlessly visual' and, in a discussion of a passage from the novel telling of Emma's response to Rodolphe's rejection letter, he comments that Flaubert's verbal depiction 'has the remarkably prescient quality of being more "cinematic" than anything managed by the filmmakers' whose adaptations Stam is about to discuss.[5] Stam is not arguing that Flaubert's *Madame Bovary* should be kept inviolate; he emphasizes the inevitability of Flaubert's novel entering into 'the continuing processes of artistic dialogism and intertextuality, leaving new texts in its wake' (p. 161). But the very metaphor of the novel as a ship sailing ahead emphazises the status of the original source and the difficulty of keeping pace with it.

Stam finds some virtues in Minnelli's 1949 adaptation. He credits the film for having retained, and even foregrounded, the theme of the influence of literature on the heroine and notes how this has been visually rendered through the 'panoply of visual images' (p. 169) — book covers, magazines, portraits — which fascinate Emma. He notes also that 'like the novel, the film makes us feel Emma's corporeal sensations' (p. 171). But Stam's account is dominated by his general view that 'Hollywood adaptations perform what might be called an aesthetic mainstreaming' so that 'in the name of mass-audience legibility, the novel is "cleansed" of moral ambiguity, narrative interruption, and reflexive meditation'; this practice of 'mainstreaming' has ideological and aesthetic consequences but it also 'dovetails with economic censorship, since the changes demanded [...] are made in the name of monies spent and box-office profits required' (p. 43).

So far as Minnelli's *Madame Bovary* is concerned this means that 'the stylistic experimentalism of the novel [...] largely disappears' (p. 175). The film makes use of a framing device showing Flaubert, played by James Mason, defending his own book in court against charges of offence to public and religious morality; Flaubert's voice is then heard at various points in the film, commenting on his heroine's behaviour. Stam argues that, in the trial scene, Minnelli makes 'Flaubert, the consummate artist, express philistine positions about art' and, more generally, that Flaubert's irony is replaced by a simplifying 'clarity of judgement and motivation so that the spectator will not be confused by complexity' (pp. 168, 174). The film 'shies away from social critique' (p. 175), passing over questions of class and corruption. The voiceover problematically conflates author and narrator and 'the tone and content of the voice-over goes [*sic*] against the grain of Flaubert's own aesthetic' (p. 167). In respect of the heroine, Stam argues that Minnelli 'reproduces the mingled distance and sympathy' towards Emma which the novel elicits but concludes that this is overridden by the promotion of Emma (played by Jennifer Jones) as a star; thus, far from being a minor character at the Vaubyessard ball, as she is in the novel, 'the film's *mise-en-scene* [...] has all eyes converge on her, thus constructing her as a "star"' (p. 171). The filming of the ball is, in this account, an example of how Minnelli cultivates 'an aesthetic of crescendo and excess' which is 'in contradiction' to the novel but 'effective in terms of mainstream entertainment norms' (p. 173). As so often for adaptation scholars, the culprit here is Hollywood's dependence on melodrama. Stam argues that Minnelli 'mines' the novel 'not only for possible production numbers [like the ball], but also for potential melodramatic and spectacular scenes'; 'Music, dialogue, performance [...] all reinforce the same melodramatic effect' (pp. 173, 174). In this analysis, the economic base overdetermines the adaptation, forcing it to adopt the lineaments of melodrama to detrimental effect.

The later reading, offered by Donaldson-Evans, does not necessarily disagree with Stam's account of its Hollywood determinants, but she is more sympathetic to its production context. In particular, she reads the film as a challenge to the censorship codes in force in Hollywood in the 1940s. She takes the 'most important influence' on this adaptation to be Hollywood's adherence to the Motion Picture Production Code and argues that the use of the trial to show the unsuccessful prosecution of the book was a means of challenging the MPCC and aligning the prestige of MGM with claims for artistic freedom.[6] For Donaldson-Evans, 'Minnelli's genius — to have secured the spectator's esteem for the author [...] was a powerful weapon against the Code' (pp. 83–84), and he worked effectively to undermine the influence of censorship. She considers the film a remarkable achievement for the time and suggests that Minnelli as a director was working against the mores of the Hollywood which Stam describes.

Donaldson-Evans argues that although the challenge was successful, in that the film got made and screened, 'the deepest imprint' (p. 100) on it was made by censorship since Minnelli and the producers were aware that its sexual content and social commentary were under extreme scrutiny. This success came at a cost to his heroine who, she argues, is positioned as manipulative and conniving; as the film progresses, Emma emerges 'not as victim, but as victimizer' of the men she seduces so that 'the conduct of the character on screen leaves the spectator increasingly cold' (p. 96). The audience is invited not to identify or sympathize with her but to observe her descent into narcissism and self-destruction; Donaldson-Evans compares Emma to the femmes fatales of 1940s films noirs and argues that for her, like them, death can be considered a just punishment. She concludes that the film is 'black and white in more ways than one' and that 'it provides an unmistakably moral viewpoint, clearly reflecting the ideology of its era' (p. 100). Like Stam, Donaldson-Evans does more than offer a rigid comparison between novel and film. She offers an analysis which indicates that the film has a status in its own right and, in a sensitive account of its production situation, comes close to analysing the film on its own terms. But her reading of the film, as offering a negative and punishing characterization of its heroine, indicates that for Donaldson-Evans, as for Stam, the status of the novel, both as a great book and the primary source, has had a strong impact on her judgements.

Two Film Studies Interpretations: Stern and Wood

The interpretations offered by the two film studies scholars offer accounts based on different theoretical models. These essays did not enter the mainstream of adaptations work on *Madame Bovary*. Stam does not refer to either essay in his chapter, while Donaldson-Evans footnotes one, the 1981 work by Lesley Stern, but does not cite Robin Wood's 1986 essay. These articles are tucked away in obscure film journals but it may also be that the names of the authors, who were well known in early film studies, are less significant to adaptation studies scholars. Both articles are, however, revealing as examples of how film studies was developing in different ways in the 1980s and it is notable that, unlike the approaches adopted by Stam and Donaldson-Evans, there is little here to indicate that the film might be noteworthy because of its source in a canonical novel.

Stern's account of Minnelli's *Madame Bovary* is an example of the radical direction some scholars in early film studies, working outside traditional academic departments, were taking in the 1970s and early 1980s. The essay, in two parts, is an exploratory one, arising out of discussions in an informal group and work on a university course.[7] The analysis uses intellectual frameworks which are also typical of its time: semiotics and psychoanalysis. Writing in the early 1980s, Stern and her co-authors use semiotics to emphasize the instability of the text and the difficulty of establishing Emma's significance. The article starts from the premise that with 'Madame Bovary' we have 'a sign with at least three possible signifieds': Madame Bovary the character who dies at the end of the story, but is perhaps immortalized by *Madame Bovary*, the novel, which, itself, is declared immortal at the end of the film, *Madame Bovary*. No one signified takes precedence here since 'as soon as the possibility of more than one signified is suggested, the stability and unity of the signifier is called into question'.[8] Stern draws attention to this kind of slippage throughout her discussion of the film, examining the framework of Flaubert's trial, for instance, in terms of the interplay of fact and fiction. She suggests that the framing of the film through the trial and the use of Flaubert's voice-over are attempts to root the film in an historical event. But she argues, 'the trial itself is fictionalized and portrays a fictional Flaubert' who presents the story of Emma as if she were real with his words '"Let me take you back to the time when Emma was twenty"'. His version is presented as 'more true than the official [prosecutor's] version, as though the film will give us the "true story"' (p. 53). 'What is on trial?' the article asks:

> Hollywood, the novel *Madame Bovary* by Gustave Flaubert, Gustave Flaubert himself (either historical or fictional), the author of the film (either the historical or fictional Minnelli), a character designated Madame Bovary, a category which we will call femininity which is not reducible to the nomination Emma Bovary, or finally, fiction itself? (p. 54)

Unlike Donaldson-Evans, Stern does not see Minnelli's Emma as a 'victimizer' but argues that she is a heroine who creates and is destroyed by fiction. The paper draws on the work of Freud to provide a psychoanalytic framework centring on the concept of hysteria. The aim is not to define Emma as an hysteric but to show how hysteria emerges as a consequence for the character, and the film, of the attempt to tell a story of female sexual desire through a woman who is trapped by femininity: 'Emma is disposed to hysteria which is linked to feminine desire. She lives in a fiction, but her death is written in her desire, it is already inscribed as her destiny' (p. 68). Unlike Donaldson-Evans's emphasis on punishment, Stern suggests that Emma is 'indicted for sins of the senses' in the trial but is 'forgiven for those same sins in her death scene' (p. 68). On her deathbed, Madame Bovary achieves some kind of apotheosis; the ineffability of her death is expressed through the excesses of melodrama: music soars as the dying Emma kisses the cross presented by the priest and the camera moves up and out of the open window, leaving the house and showing the sky above the small town. This final shot expresses feeling rather than thought; 'her desire is not tied to the body — in fact it is a pursuit for something beyond'. For Stern, this scene, in which the persistence of Emma's desire cannot be denied, is 'one of the most erotic moments of the film' (p. 68).

'Fiction/Film/Femininity — Paper Two' is characteristic of how work in film studies was developing, at this point, in relation to adaptations. The article expresses little interest in the practice of adaptation; it does not offer explanations for the adaptation based on the production set-up or on censorship as Stam and Donaldson-Evans will do. But neither is it concerned to claim a canonical status for the film or its director. Instead, it seeks an understanding of the film, based on analysis of its handling of representation and narrative, within a framework which is being applied to but did not develop out of cinema. In terms of methods, it is an early example of the use of psychoanalysis and critical theory so important to the development of film studies as a discipline in the 1980s; puzzles and wordplay feature as well as shot analysis and syntagmatic narrative analysis. Typically, it ends with a question: 'One further speculation — does Emma Bovary die *because* of fiction or *in the cause* of fiction?' (p. 68). Given the complexity of the analysis and the impenetrability of some of the language, it is perhaps not surprising that the article did not later speak to adaptation scholars.

Robin Wood's article was published after Stern's but it arises out of an earlier wave of activity in the development of film studies. Wood was closely associated with the journal *Movie*, launched in June 1962 with a challenge to what the young editors saw as the complacency of British film culture. With the new journal, they sought to change the criteria for the evaluation of films and to challenge the established canon of directors. Following the emphasis on auteurism promoted by *Cahiers du Cinéma* and influentially taken up by the US critic Andrew Sarris, *Movie*'s first issue featured a pantheon of directors which depressed the status of British directors and gave a high evaluation to the directors of Hollywood's studio system.[9] *Movie*'s methods of analysis involved close attention to the visual organization of the film and a commitment to looking for the meaning of a film through its style. Controversially, *Movie*'s writers devoted serious analysis to popular cinema and particularly valued genre films made by directors whom they respected. And they challenged the prevailing negative view of Hollywood that only by accident could 'anything good escape from this industrial complex'.[10]

The importance of Minnelli as an example of the kind of director who could be recognized through this approach can be seen in the first issue of *Movie*. Minnelli was placed in the histogram as 'Brilliant', the second category in the list and behind only Howard Hawks and Alfred Hitchcock who were in the first category of 'Great'.[11] A (much-ridiculed) interview with Minnelli was also published in this first issue in which he answered questions while watching an extract from one of his films.[12] Although Wood wrote about *Madame Bovary* (1949) over twenty years later, he could still begin the article by taking up again the argument that 'Minnelli was among the most neglected and misrecognized of the major Hollywood directors and *Madame Bovary* is perhaps the most neglected and misrecognized of his major works'.[13] Wood makes a shift from the book to the film early on in the article and his commitment to the director is at the heart of his argument that, as the director of the film, Minnelli is not attempting to re-present the original author's intentions by other (filmic) means. He has to make the source material his own even if he does so in a way that is quite different to, and even at odds with, that of the writer:

> By far the most important difference between novel and film lies in the author's (and reader's) relationship to the central figure: Flaubert's celebrated detachment [...] is replaced by Minnelli's passionate commitment to and identification with his (and Jennifer Jones') Emma Bovary; the Flaubertian assumption of clinical objectivity [...] gives way to an all-pervasive, precariously controlled hysteria. (p. 76)

Wood, like Stern, takes hysteria as the organizing principle of the film, seeing it as 'a major component of both Minnelli's directorial personality and Jones's screen persona' (p. 76). He celebrates the film as a melodrama with Jones as an identification figure and argues that, like other great female stars, she embodies and is punished for her transgressiveness. That transgressiveness is not so much based on the repression of sexual desire but on the thwarting of her 'essentially creative aspirations [which] can find no form worthy of them within her social environment'. Hysteria is therefore a legitimate response, 'the instinctive response to powerlessness and the stifling of creativity' (p. 78).

Wood is thus at odds with the later accounts by Stam and Donaldson-Evans in terms of his appreciation of Minnelli's full-blown use of Hollywood's spectacle. Unlike Stam, Wood embraces the concept of stardom and sees the identification of the audience with Jones as integral to the film rather than an unfortunate consequence of its production context. And unlike Donaldson-Evans, Wood argues that the film's female audience will feel Emma's punishment to be unjust and unfair: 'We cannot even begin to appreciate *Madame Bovary* unless we accept and share Minnelli's identification with Jennifer Jones. [...] Emma cannot be blamed for breaking the rules of patriarchal capitalist society; she had no say in the making of them' (p. 78). Like Stern, Wood draws attention to the final shot of the death scene with its camera movement out of the window 'towards freedom, the final celebration of her spirit at the moment of her final defeat' (p. 80). The audience is invited to identify not with the punishment but the escape.

Having established his overall argument, Wood goes on to demonstrate the film's 'richness of connotation' (p. 79) by isolating a series of motifs which allows him to discuss Minnelli's *mise en scène*. Unlike that of Stern, this account is keen to evaluate Minnelli's directorial gifts and to praise the film as one of his key works. The ball scene is for Wood 'at once one of Minnelli's finest musical "numbers" and a supreme enactment of the "hysterical text"'. The smashing of the windows is diegetically motivated but more importantly, in terms of the film's guiding principle of hysteria, it is 'cogently *demanded*' and 'brilliantly orchestrated' (p. 80). The film is a success because the director has been able to work with, rather than in opposition to, the conventions of genre, spectacle, and stardom and at the same time offer its audience an account of *Madame Bovary* which invites passionate identification with the heroine's frustration and transgressions rather than masochistic alignment with her punishment.

George Bluestone and the 'Dreams of Hollywood'

It was long a practice in adaptation studies to refer back to the work of George Bluestone whose book, *Novels into Films*, originally published in 1957, became a foundation stone of adaptation studies. The republication of the book in 2003, over forty years after its first appearance, indicates its significance as a continually referenced point of origin in adaptation studies. Bluestone offers an example of the kind of adaptation analysis which was heavily premised on the adaptor being true to the spirit of the original source and finding visual expression for the novel's themes. Stam does comment briefly on Bluestone's account of the film while Donaldson-Evens does not; both are in some ways moving away from his approach though both retain an element of his moralism about Hollywood. For me, however, what is most interesting about Bluestone's analysis is that his attempt to impose his version of the process of adaptation on Minnelli's film almost unwittingly exposes the film's most interesting ambiguities in a way that provides a surprising link with accounts by Stern and Wood.

Bluestone used *Madame Bovary* (1949) to develop further his account of the medium specificities of the novel and the film, pursuing the argument that 'interior-subjective novels', such as those by Flaubert, refuse the transition to cinema and, even more broadly, that given cinema's facility for rendering physical reality 'the attributes of language [the narrator's voice, in particular] must be suppressed in favor of plastic images'.[14] For Bluestone, *Madame Bovary* is a great work of art and the film can only achieve greatness if it finds a way of matching its achievements. He criticizes Minnelli's film for 'a marked failure of the pictorial imagination' (p. 198) and ascribes this to the failure of Robert Ardrey's script and Minnelli's direction. He believes that the adaptation should pursue the 'difficult task' of 'finding visual equivalents for Flaubert's language' so that, as with the novel, 'it is not Emma's *story* we would primarily remember, but the lovely *rendition* of it' (p. 205). He finds no attempt to achieve this end in Minnelli's film.

Bluestone particularly objects to the film giving Flaubert a star appearance in the trial and his function as a voice-over. He goes so far as to speak for the author when he comments that 'for Flaubert [...] this retailing of Emma's story would seem appalling' (p. 198). He objects to the film's melodramatic excesses, particularly in the sound; the film covers up the inability of 'of the images [...] to convey the inner content of the narrative [...] by supplying a *noise*, and usually a loud one' (p. 205). In seeking to show how the director should 'strive to refine himself out of his film as Flaubert strove to refine himself out of his book', he seems to feel quite at liberty to tell Minnelli how he should have created the camera shots and done the editing: '[The director] will recreate [...]. He will alternate [...]. He will mount his images'. To criticize this film as an adaptation is, for Bluestone, 'to write a new scenario' (p. 212). In this account, the status of Flaubert as the author of a recognized classic novel overrides any acknowledgement of Minnelli's status as a director and his right to make his own aesthetic decisions.

Wood calls Bluestone's account 'one of the most misguided and misconceived pieces of writing perpetrated by an evidently serious and intelligent critic' and challenges the assertion that 'one of the American cinema's most fully formed and masterly stylists [...] "must" find visual equivalents for Flaubert's language' as 'a singular piece of effrontery' (p. 75). Bluestone's patronizing rhetoric about how different the film should have been finds its roots in the hierarchical assumptions that place words above images and are so difficult to overturn when assessing the adaptation of a canonical text. Nevertheless, as Bluestone pushes on to his final comments, something interesting happens. Having demonstrated to his satisfaction that the film was a failure, he tries to diagnose why the film went wrong. 'Something must have troubled the film-makers,' he ponders, 'to move them to alter so seriously the historical facts' of the court case. The answer he suggests lies in the kinship between Emma and 'prototype of the perennial movie-goer' (p. 213). He has argued that Minnelli ignored Flaubert's analysis of nineteenth-century French society but now he asks whether the figure of Flaubert's Emma Bovary comes too close to the romantic visions and mundane lifestyles of the film audiences of the mid-twentieth century, in particular the female audience at which the film was aimed. Did the film-makers, he asks, see 'and therefore refuse Flaubert's surgical portrait of their own patrons?' (pp. 213–14) He concludes his analysis by suggesting that the novel cannot or perhaps should not be filmed in Hollywood because of this:

> Perhaps [...] Flaubert's Emma cannot be rendered cinematically [...]. For to do so would be to expose the face of the industry itself. Emma's dreams would become the dreams of Hollywood; her demise would correspond to our perpetual disappointment. [...] Perhaps the film-makers failed so utterly because they realized, in some profound way, that Madame Bovary, to paraphrase her creator, was ourselves. (p. 214)

Bluestone thus ends his account of a film he suggests cannot be made by identifying himself with the female film audience, 'the perennial movie-goer' (p. 213). There is something troubling about the film that *was* made which leads him to these reflections. And this sense of trouble is a pre-cursor of themes that are then scattered across the later analyses offered by the other critics I have discussed here. It centres on the anomalies and contradictions which attach themselves to its heroine and it is explained in various ways: by her transformation into a film star (Stam); by her solipsism and self-destruction (Donaldson-Evans); by her living in a life of fantasy (Stern); and by the hysteria which expresses her frustration (Wood). The trouble is created by the pulling-together of themes of femininity, transcendence, and identification, and filming them with all the spectacle and emotion that Minnelli and MGM could offer.

Bluestone presents his insight as a block, this is the end of the analysis and the film fails. Stam suggests that Bluestone is right in remarking on the 'strangeness' of some of Minnelli's decisions and himself comments on the 'tensions and contradictions' he finds in the melodramatic film (pp. 167 & 170). But neither critic can get past its failure to present the social critique and stylistic experiments of the novel. Stern and Wood represent the different stirrings of early film studies; Stern seeks an explanation in the unconscious of the film while Wood demonstrates how much the film owes to Minnelli's conscious handling of the material. But in conclusion I would argue that another strand of the early film studies tradition allows us to move on further and to focus more particularly on the troubling nature of the film.

Conclusion

Stam and Bluestone both emphasize the commercial considerations which, they argue, shape Hollywood's products. For me, the most useful theoretical framework for looking at this film which, Bluestone suggested, 'expose[s] the face of the industry itself' (p. 214) can be found in the 1969 categorization of Hollywood cinema developed by the *Cahiers du Cinéma* editorial group. The Marxist commitment of the editorial group led its members to an analysis of Hollywood films which sought to demonstrate that the economic determinants of the base could only produce films which took on the ideological values relating to that base. But the *Cahiers* editors found that there were some Hollywood films which did not fit this base-superstructure model. These were films which 'seemed at first sight to belong firmly within the ideology and to be completely under its sway, but which turn out to be so only in an ambiguous manner'.[15] In such films, the internal contradictions turn the apparent ideological function of the film against itself and potentially expose the workings of ideology:

> One can see two moments in it: one holding it back within certain limits, one transgressing them. An internal criticism is taking place which cracks the film apart at the seams. If one reads the film obliquely, [...] one can see that it is riddled with cracks: it is splitting under an internal tension [...]. The ideology thus become[s] subordinate to the text. It no longer has an independent existence: it is *presented* by the film. (p. 33)

The importance of this for film studies was its argument for the practice of reading against, rather than with, the text; such reading put an emphasis on contradiction, a lack of unity, on the gaps and fissures in the narrative, on structured absences, excessive reaching for effect and disconnections between the story and the form. While Bluestone clearly had not done this, what he had stumbled over and been so disconcerted by was something of that order: a reaching for effect which seemed to indicate a contradiction at the heart of Hollywood's promise to its female audience. Minnelli's *Madame Bovary* takes a story of a woman to whom nothing happens and who dreams of other lives. It makes her a film star who wears wonderful dresses, seduces men, and triumphs at the ball. Through camera work and *mise en scène*, the audience of film goers is asked to identify with her desires and her triumphs since that is what Hollywood cinema consistently offers us; at the ball, we share Emma's vision in the mirror of herself transformed. But the intensity of that experience reveals its inadequacy; we actually cannot be film stars and Emma's romantic and maternal failures run the risk of rupturing the identification mechanisms that underpin the Hollywood machine which relies on an ideology of fiction and femininity, as Stern had indicated. The hysterical quality of the film indicates how the ideological repression is being tested; there is a risk that our desires will be exposed as unfulfillable, that the ideological project will be presented by the film, made visible and knowable. The film's hysterical qualities are a mark of how hard it needs to work to avoid this.

Bluestone gestures towards this but in his determination to describe the film as a failure he misses the point that it so nearly succeeded in exposing how Hollywood's star system could not ultimately fulfil the desires of its audience. By encouraging identification with the heroine's romantic fantasies, the film potentially turns the audience's need for escapism against itself and runs the risk of subverting the pleasures offered by the films of the Hollywood studio system. It is interesting that Stam, Bluestone, and Donaldson-Evans emphasize not just the translation of book into film but also the monolithic nature of the Hollywood studio system and the conscious decisions it makes in pursuit of profits. Wood, Stern, and the *Cahiers* editorial group offer, by contrast, accounts in which Hollywood's efforts at controlling popular identification and pleasure are put at risk by the film's demonstration of the impossibility of its heroine achieving fulfilment through the femininity embodied in the Hollywood star system. Such an approach emphasizes what film studies analysed as the unconscious mechanisms associated with Hollywood's dependence on genres and stars and offers an understanding of how melodramatic spectacle often indicates points of ideological crisis.

This brief account of the critical commentary on Minnelli's adaptation of *Madame Bovary* demonstrates the different routes taken by early film studies and adaptation studies. While both disciplines struggled for academic status, adaptation studies seemed to accept the canonical status of key texts and classic authors while film studies made a break by either establishing a new canon via the auteur theory (Wood) or by refusing questions of aesthetic evaluation altogether (Stern). For adaptation studies, the price for this accommodation was the long-running dominance of questions of evaluation and fidelity to the primary source. As late as 2007, adaptations scholar Thomas Leitch both expressed his 'skepticism' about using 'fidelity to a given precursor text as an unquestioned criterion of value' and a more general ambition to 'dethrone evaluation as the unmarked or central activity of adaptation study'.[16] But perhaps film studies also missed out by eschewing evaluation and by insisting on the stand-alone status of the adaptation, treating many films, from films noirs to westerns, musicals to science fiction, as if any relationship to the other works which preceded them was only cursory.

The development of adaptation studies means that now the adaptation of a classic novel, such as *Madame Bovary*, no longer dominates the field and there may be a deliberate attempt 'to avoid even the appearance of a tendency to reinscribe the superiority of the literary source'.[17] The emphasis is on what an adaptation adds to the hypotext rather than what is lost or left out, and the established conventions of popular cinema — the interplay of genres, the editing and camerawork, the presentation of performers as stars — are analysed rather than wheeled out as explanations for failure. Film studies has also changed, placing more emphasis on context in terms of production processes and audience expectations as well as on broader historical and social contexts. With maturity, both disciplines can now offer fuller explanations of a more diverse range of material. Nevertheless, my archaeological digging into the passionate responses provoked by the melodrama of Minnelli's *Madame Bovary* is a reminder that while popular films can be read with the grain of their context, we need also to read their incoherences and excesses against the grain in order to explore the contradictions which they are often seeking to reconcile.

My thanks to the editors and readers for their help with this article.

Notes to Chapter 3

1. For discussion of *Maya Memsaab* see Mary Donaldson-Evans, 'The Colonization of Madame Bovary: Hindi Cinema's *Maya Memsaab*', *Adaptation*, 3.1 (2010), 21–35.
2. There is not space in this short article to deal with the full complexity of the arguments of my chosen critics. I am drawing out particular aspects of their work for analysis here.
3. Guerric deBona, *Film Adaptation in the Hollywood Era* (Urbana, Chicago & Springfield: University of Illinois Press, 2010), p. 27.
4. These and other prestige adaptations are discussed in Christine Geraghty, *Now a Major Motion Picture: Film Adaptations from Literature and Drama* (Lanham, MD: Rowman & Littlefield, 2008).
5. Robert Stam, *Literature through Film: Realism, Magic and the Art of Adaptation* (Malden, MA, & Oxford: Blackwell, 2005), pp. 148, 159. Further references to this book are given after quotations in the text.

6. Donaldson-Evans, *Madame Bovary at the Movies*, p. 71. Further references to this book are given after quotations in the text.
7. Lesley Stern, 'Fiction/Film/Femininity: Paper One', *Australian Journal of Screen Theory*, 8 (1981), 37–48 (p. 47). For an account of similar groups in a British context in the 1970s, see Terry Bolas, *Screen Education from Film Appreciation to Media Studies* (Bristol: Intellect Books, 2009).
8. Lesley Stern, 'Fiction/Film/Femininity: Paper Two', *Australian Journal of Screen Theory*, 9–10 (1981), 51–68 (p. 52). Further references to this article are given after quotations in the text.
9. [Anon.], 'The Talent Histogram', *Movie*, 1 (1962), 10–11.
10. Ian Cameron, 'Films, Directors and Critics', *Movie*, 2 (1962), 4–7 (p. 5).
11. [Anon.], 'The Talent Histogram', p. 10.
12. Mark Shivas, 'Method: Vincente Minnelli', *Movie*, 1 (1962), 20–24 (p. 20). For a defence of the interview and *Movie*'s position see Cameron, 'Films, Directors and Critics', pp. 4–7.
13. Robin Wood, 'Minnelli's *Madame Bovary*', *CineAction!*, (December 1986), 75–80 (p. 75). Further references to this article are given after quotations in the text.
14. George Bluestone, *Novels into Films* [1957] (Baltimore, MD: Johns Hopkins University Press, 2003), pp. 211, 203. Further references to this book are given after quotations in the text.
15. Jean-Luc Comolli and Paul Narboni, 'Cinema/Ideology/Criticism', trans. by Susan Bennett, *Screen*, 12.1 (1971), 27–36 (p. 32). Further references to this article are given after quotations in the text.
16. Leitch, *Film Adaptation and Its Discontents*, p. 21.
17. Mireia Aragay, 'Reflection to Refraction: Adaptation Studies Then and Now', in *Books in Motion: Adaptation, Intertextuality, Authorship*, ed. by Mireia Aragay (Amsterdam: Rodopi, 2005), pp. 11–34 (p. 26).

CHAPTER 4

❖

Polymedia Jekyll & Hyde: The Dual Character in Renoir's Film and Mattotti and Kramsky's Comic Book

Armelle Blin-Rolland

Robert Louis Stevenson's *The Strange Case of Dr Jekyll and Mr Hyde*, a 'crawler' published in 1886 and an instant popular success, stands as a canonical text of Victorian fiction. The figure of Jekyll and Hyde, a reputable, yet morbidly ashamed of his 'pleasures', doctor who turns into a man with 'Satan's signature upon [his] face' has become a modern cultural myth, a standard bearer for the duality of man.[1] This chapter will approach dynamics of rewriting and rereading the canon through a focus on two versions of the tale, Jean Renoir's 1959 film *Le Testament du Docteur Cordelier* (*Experiment in Evil*) and Lorenzo Mattotti and Jerry Kramsky's 2002 comic book *Docteur Jekyll et Mr Hyde*,[2] that are inscribed in an ever-expanding polymedia network of Jekyll/Hydes, created through a process of 'serial adaptation' that has been examined by Brian A. Rose.[3]

As a classic with a mythical or archetypal dimension that has been repeatedly transposed across time, nations, and media, *Jekyll and Hyde* provides a richly suggestive case study to reflect on the relationship between canonicity and adaptation. As Julie Sanders argues, adaptation 'both appears to require and to perpetuate the existence of a canon', while having the capacity to reformulate and expand on it, and, in the case of appropriations in particular, to subvert, challenge, and write back to it.[4] Moreover, serial adaptation is involved in canon formation, in the sense that it contributes to the canonical text becoming culturally familiar. As a result, the palimpsestuous reading of adaptations of canonical texts, as Linda Hutcheon points out, may not rely on a 'direct experience' of the text, but rather on a memory partly shaped by its serial adaptation, and the resulting ongoing presence of the story in culture.[5] Understanding the canon through adaptation therefore enables us to examine canonical texts as un-final, being (like all other texts, but explicitly) 'eternally written *here and now*'.[6] Through the lens of adaptation, the canon appears as a constellation of texts that are repeatedly returned to and rearticulated in new historically-situated contexts, shifting meaning and shape, repeated with a difference.[7] While adaptation perpetuates the canon, it 'continues' rather than preserves it, in the sense that it turns it into a hybrid and dynamic, un-final construction inscribed in broader intertextual and intermedial networks.[8]

Iterations of Stevenson's tale, which is 'periodically "injected"' into culture, reflect various facets of the complex relationship between canonicity and adaptation as outlined above.[9] The 1943 *Classics Illustrated* comic book version, for example, is part of a collection with the aim of enticing the young reader to turn to the source text and therefore 'real' literature, in this way reinforcing the cultural capital of the literary canon (and of literature over comics). More broadly, that the last few years have seen new versions notably on radio, television, and in film shows that the process of serial adaptation is still ongoing, 'activating and reactivating' the text's canonical status.[10] Jekyll/Hyde is present in series that draw on and reinvent characters from fairy tale, folklore, and/or the literary canon, such as on television ABC's *Once Upon a Time* (2011–18) and Showtime's *Penny Dreadful* (2014–2016), and in comics Alan Moore and Kevin O'Neill's *The League of Extraordinary Gentlemen* (since 1999). These highly intertextual series weave a web of adaptations of earlier characters, positing and contributing to Jekyll/Hyde's place as part of a constellation of figures that are both citable and malleable, recognized and transformed. Jonathan Holloway's 2013 stage adaptation, which turns Jekyll into a female scientist transforming into a male-female Hyde to escape the gender boundaries of Victorian society, can be seen as subverting the source text by articulating its rewriting around issues of gender that were seemingly absent from it. Film adaptations such as John S. Robertson's 1920 and Rouben Mamoulian's 1931 versions have contributed to making the scene of Jekyll's first transformation into Hyde, which is rather short in the source text, into a key passage of the story — especially if it is told visually — that is arguably anticipated by the viewer or reader of iterations of the tale, and of which, as we will see, Mattotti offers a strikingly creative interpretation.

The present chapter will explore how Renoir's film and Mattotti and Kramsky's comic book adaptations, which are part of this polymedia network of Jekyll/Hydes, reread and rewrite Stevenson's tale in terms of meaning and shape. While Brian Rose's analysis of the geneaology of adaptations of the novella focuses exclusively on US works, this chapter will explore how two non-Anglophone versions of the tale re-articulate its key motifs of the duality, and even plurality, of man and the nature of evil, through the new geographical, cultural, and historical settings in which they place the story, and through the creative uses of the specificities of the media of film and comic art (which I will examine via close readings of several key scenes). Following Colin Davis's analysis, I will consider how Renoir's film can be read as reflecting its contemporary context of a late 1950s France still in denial over the extent of its World War II collaboration, while making no direct references to recent French history.[11] I also explore the construction of an asymmetrical, disjunctive Jekyll/Hyde through the combination of cinematic voices and bodies, in the scene of the doctor's confession. In contrast to Renoir's film, Mattotti and Kramky's comic engages explicitly and aesthetically with the historical and national context in which it sets the story, namely Germany at the end of the Weimar Republic and during the rise of Nazism, in the sense that it offers a re-vision of history through art, the text becoming a 'voyage into Expressionist culture'.[12] Through the analysis of the key scene of Jekyll's first transformation into Hyde, I will argue that this version exploits the medium's potentialities for adaptation, as an 'art of both iteration and transformation', in the words of Ann Miller, encouraging the reader to perform what I term an 'adaptive reading'.[13] By focusing on the rearticulation of the notion of evil in these transpositions of the tale, and the aesthetically innovative translations of this culturally familiar story of a dual figure, this chapter will suggest that Renoir's film and Mattotti and Kramsky's comic are productive case studies to examine the canon, through adaptation, as a polymedia and dynamic construction.

Renoir's Cordelier/Opale

Le Testament du Docteur Cordelier is part of Renoir's late career, after his return to France in the early 1950s, following his American period in the 1940s. *Le Testament*, like Renoir's subsequent film *Le Déjeuner sur l'herbe* (*Picnic on the Grass*) (shot and released in 1959), was made using television multi-camera techniques, with longer rehearsal times and a short shooting period.[14] My reading of Renoir's film will centre on the transposition of the complexities of the dual figure. Jekyll and Hyde, renamed 'Cordelier' and 'Opale', are played by Jean-Louis Barrault, a major stage actor whose extremely physical acting is strongly influenced by mime. Roxane Hamery, who identifies a 'rhétorique du double' [rhetoric of the double] in Barrault's career in film, points out that Barrault's acting is based on 'l'expressivité gestuelle' [gestural expressiveness].[15] This is seen in *Le Testament*, where Barrault renders the duality of Jekyll/Hyde through the use of his body and voice in performance. The characters of Doctor Cordelier and Mr Opale are differentiated by obvious uses of make-up and costume, Mr Opale being dark- and curly-haired, extremely hairy, and wearing a suit that is too big for him. This stark physical difference is emphasized by Barrault's gestural repertoire. He plays Cordelier, an upper-class psychiatrist, in an extremely stiff, austere manner (Figure 4.1). On the other hand, his Opale is hunched and characterized by disarticulated and sudden movements, a vocal style with a lower tessitura than Cordelier's, and frequent grunts that contrast with Cordelier's verbal confidence and eloquence. Mr Opale is also announced and accompanied by a theme tune on the soundtrack, a kind of jaunty and slightly dissonant tune that fits with his gestures and way of moving, music here being used to accompany and supplement the actor's performance in the construction of the audio-visual character.

The centrality of Barrault's performance as Cordelier/Opale in the film is of course inscribed in the genealogy of Jekyll and Hyde adaptations, which, as Leitch states, often served as 'star vehicles for actors eager to show their range by playing both Jekyll and Hyde'.[16] This can be traced back to the primacy of dual performances by Richard Mansfield in Thomas Russell Sullivan's 1887 stage adaptation, or John Barrymore in John S. Robertson's 1920 film.[17] While Barrault's performance therefore echoes a performance tradition of Jekyll/Hydes, a crucial difference between this and previous versions of the character is that while

FIG. 4.1. Jean-Louis Barrault as Doctor Cordelier. Jean Renoir, *Le Testament du Docteur Cordelier* (1959). Dir. Jean Renoir: RTF, Sofirad, Compagnie Jean Renoir.

Opale appears as the embodiment of pure evil, Cordelier, who anaesthetized and raped his female patients before he even started creating the potion, is far from representing pure goodness. The representation of Jekyll as 'monodimensionally positive', with which *Le Testament* contrasts, is in fact, as Rose notes, 'entirely the invention of adaptation', starting with Barrymore's 1920 version. It has since been repeated in a large proportion of subsequent versions, the process of serial adaptation transforming the story into an 'illustration of the diametricality of good and evil'.[18] Renoir's Cordelier, on the other hand, echoes Stevenson's Jekyll, who is 'committed to a profound duplicity of life'.[19] The complexity of the Cordelier/Opale duality in contrast with other filmic Jekyll/Hydes is, I argue, key to reading *Le Testament* in relation to its transposition of the story in a new contemporary context, and the use of the specificities of the medium.

Despite the fact that Renoir transposes Stevenson's story across time and nations by setting it in post-war, late 1950s Paris, one aspect that is striking in *Le Testament* is its complete lack of any explicit references or allusions to recent history or contemporary events, neither to World War II nor the Algerian War of Independence (1954–1962). This would seem to be at odds with Rose's characterization of Stevenson's story as a 'tracer-text' whose adaptations are dramatizations of contemporary cultural anxieties.[20] That *Jekyll and Hyde* is continuously being reread and rewritten through adaptation can in fact be related to the ambiguities of the novella, which enables multiple interpretations in the sense that the nature of Jekyll's pleasures, and therefore what Hyde indulges in, is never specified. It has however been widely read as pertaining to Victorian sexual repression, and the resulting illicit homosexual and/or heterosexual activities.[21]

Le Testament's lack of references to the complexities of its historical context, and, through the characters of the devoted servants, its presentation of a rigid class society with no sense of revolt or contestation from the lower classes, may be seen to confirm Renoir's supposed 'depoliticization' in the later stage of his career. However this analysis has been challenged by Martin O'Shaughnessy, who argues that one should look beyond the 'escapist surface' of Renoir's late films.[22] This is echoed by Colin Davis who, in his examination of postwar Renoir through trauma theory, provides an insightful analysis of the ways in which *Le Testament* can be seen to engage with post-World War II France while not making any explicit references to it. Davis argues that Opale's violence may be understood to allude to recent history, as his victims are primarily 'the young, the old, the disabled, the sick and the defenceless', groups that 'were picked out for quick elimination in the German death camps'.[23] Reflecting on the complete absence of overt criticism of the rigid class society the film depicts, Davis suggests that *Le Testament* presents what he calls a 'post-fascist society', arguing that 'it is *post*-fascist because fascism has done its work, and can now afford to make itself invisible'. In this context, Opale's evil has in fact been 'preempted by a society whose hidden violence he reenacts'. According to Davis, Renoir reinvents *Jekyll and Hyde* for a 'post-Holocaust audience', and Opale functions as the trace of the violence that made possible this society with clean, empty streets, and compliant citizens. This reading resonates further with the context in which the film was made, as old divisions regarding the Occupation era resurfaced in France during the Algerian War, which was perceived as another civil war.[24]

In order to further understand how the film may be seen to speak of its contemporary context while purporting to be a 'flight into fantasy' in O'Shaughnessy's words,[25] it is perhaps productive to read it in relation to not only the resurfacing of the Occupation past in the decolonization era, but also its repression, as part of the second phase of the 'Vichy syndrome' as theorized by Henry Rousso.[26] During the phase of 'repression' (1954–1971), memories of the 1940–1944 civil war were repressed in French cultural and political life with the aid of the resistencialist myth, which identified the Resistance with the nation as a whole and minimized the importance of the Vichy regime. De Gaulle returned to this vision of the Occupation era in the 1950s, having already articulated it in his speech at the Liberation of Paris on 25 August 1944. It was in the 1960s, after the end of the Algerian War of Independence, that the Gaullist resistancialist myth would be crystallized.[27] *Le Testament* was made in 1959, towards the beginning of this period of repression but as 'old Occupation wounds' were reopened, so it is arguably productive to read the Cordelier/Opale duality through a dynamic of conflict and tension between the repression and resurfacing of the memory of violence and Fascist collaboration.[28]

The theme of repression is key to the film, and of course more broadly to the story of Jekyll and Hyde. Cordelier creates the potion in order to cure himself of his sexual urges, and as O'Shaughnessy points out, Opale is therefore a 'product of repression and hypocrisy'.[29] This resonates not only in relation to Renoir's critique of bourgeois 'morality' (a theme present throughout his *œuvre*, such as in his 1939 *La Règle du Jeu* (*The Rules of the Game*)), but also in the historical context outlined above.[30] Indeed, what the potion unleashes is, more than a surrender to sensual pleasures, a need for violence that, as we have seen, may be linked to the memory of the atrocities committed during World War II. The Cordelier/Opale duality, as it is constructed by Barrault in performance, and the way in which both characters are treated by others within the film, resonates further within this context of tension between the past being repressed, and resurfacing. Due to Barrault's exaggerated physical acting, it can be argued that his Opale is *posited* as performance, in line with what Hamery sees in Barrault's acting in film as 'l'idée d'un personnage qui se constitue en dehors de toute tentation illusioniste' [the idea of a character that is constituted outside any illusionistic temptation].[31] Hamery's argument relates to the way that the viewers may perceive Barrault's acting as theatrical and therefore at odds in a filmic context, but the idea of Opale as an exaggerated character is also interesting within the diegetic world of the film. Characters who come across Opale easily recognize diabolical evil in his strange, almost cartoonish figure — though he is, as Hyde in Stevenson's novella, difficult to describe.[32] However, there is a general failure, and refusal, to explore and confront the connections between the exteriorized evil of Opale, and Cordelier, an illustrious psychiatrist who is described by his friend Joly as a 'bienfaiteur de l'humanité' [benefactor of humanity] and who hosts parties attended by the elite and ambassadors. Only one person, Cordelier's rival fellow doctor Dr Séverin (who functions as a Dr Lanyon figure from Stevenson's novella), challenges Cordelier and his medical experiment, calling him a 'danger pour l'humanité tout entière' [danger for mankind as a whole] and his theories 'monstrueuses' [monstrous]. By contrast, the police officers in charge of the case are keen not to involve Cordelier in a scandal, even though they have been made aware by Joly that he is connected to, and, as far as they know, might be sheltering a criminal. When Joly learns of Cordelier's experiment during the confession scene to which I will turn in detail shortly, he first cries out that 'le complice et le receleur de l'immonde, ce n'est pas Cordelier!' [Cordelier cannot be the accomplice and the receiver of evil!]. After initially rejecting Cordelier's confession, Joly must however confront the truth as it can no longer be denied.

We may therefore argue that while the film portrays a post-Fascist society, through the ways in which it reacts to the Cordelier/Opale duality, it is also a society that attempts to repress its resurfacing Fascist past. It projects diabolical evil onto an exaggerated character, but fails to see where it originates from. Denying what powerful and highly integrated members of their own society could and can do, French people in *Le Testament* project their fear onto an obvious incarnation of, and even a performance of, evil, which prevents them from looking inwards. If Opale functions as a disturbing reminder of a past whose memory is resurfacing,

FIG. 4.2. Mr Opale takes the audio-recording of Dr Cordelier's confession back from Mr Joly before playing it. Jean Renoir, *Le Testament du Docteur Cordelier.* RTF, Sofirad, Compagnie Jean Renoir. 1959.

Cordelier may be understood as a symbol of duality and internal divisions, showing how evil is part of the fabric of man and nation and how this can be repressed and hidden. In this regard, *Le Testament*, in spite of its complete lack of references to historical context, can be situated in relation to later cinematic portraits of evil in French cinema that openly engage with Vichy France, and, as analysed by Esther Rowlands, 'challenge and interrogate the location of horror and the nature of monstrosity' through philosophical interrogations of evil.[33] *Le Testament* offers a version of the canonical story that arguably resonates in the historical context on which it is apparently silent, and the film goes beyond the simplistic, Manichean version of a clear distinction between good (Cordelier/Jekyll) and evil (Opale/Hyde).

The complexities of the Cordelier/Opale duality are articulated in a striking way in the relation between cinematic voice and body during the very long confession scene, which takes up the last third of the film (Figure 4.2). Joly (who functions as an Utterson figure in the film) is called by Cordelier's butler, who is alarmed by the screams coming from the laboratory in which the doctor has locked himself. When Joly enters the room, he finds only Opale and no Cordelier. Convinced that the monster has attacked his friend, Joly confronts him. Opale explains that he intends to tell him the truth about his relationship with Cordelier and, after the servants have left the room, produces an audio recording, and starts playing Cordelier's confession.

It is significant that the doctor's letter in Stevenson's novella has become an audio recording in the film, and that Cordelier therefore only appears as a prerecorded (and, in Michel Chion's terms, 'acousmatic') voice. Cordelier's voice is not only disembodied as a recording, but is also, in a sense, bodiless, as he can at this stage no longer retain his shape without morphing into Opale, unless he drinks a lethal amount of potion. Yet the relationship between voice and body is more complex here due to the duality of the character. As Chion argues, 'the effects of acousmatic perception vary widely depending on whether or not we have previously seen the source of the sound'.[34] Indeed, while the *acousmêtre* is a 'kind of voice-character [...] [which] derives mysterious powers from being heard and not seen',[35] if the viewer has seen the source of the acousmatic voice, it then 'carries along with it a mental visual representation'.[36] In the case of this audio confession, not only does the viewer have a mental visual representation of Cordelier's body (which can now only reappear in death), but via the palimpsestuous viewing, they know that Opale, who is inscribed in the scene's visual field, is Cordelier's other body.

In order to analyse this scene further, it is fruitful to refer to the complexity of the relationship between voices and bodies in film, which is partly due to the heterogeneity of the channels of sound and image. In modern cinema the sound image and the visual image become autonomous elements, as analysed by Deleuze, and it is the heautonomous and asymmetrical relationship stemming from this disjunction that constitutes the audio-visual image.[37] Britta H. Sjogren stresses the 'parallel' status of sound in film, rather than its unity with the image.[38] This implies a division between the voices (as elements of the sound track) and the bodies (as elements of the image), between which, as Chion points out, there is a necessary 'incision or cut' due to the 'physical nature of film', which is then restitched together at the seam.[39]

In this confession scene, Renoir's film self-reflexively exploits the heterogeneous relationship between image track and sound track to adapt the duality of the character. As the recording is being played, the acousmatic voice of Cordelier and the transformed, monstrous body of Opale coincide in the same space, and Barrault's Cordelier voice and his Opale body are restitched into an impossible, disjunctive being. In this sense, Cordelier/Opale is constructed as an audio-visual dual character, as the doctor's voice and the 'monster's' body (his 'autre corps' [other body]) are combined by the viewer in an irrational and asymmetrical relationship. The Opale/Cordelier audio-visual duality is further complexified as Opale starts to react to Cordelier's pre-recorded voice (and therefore his other voice). Opale adds his own voice to the recording, his primal cries of pain contrasting with Cordelier's poised, very articulate confession. Opale is then as if directed by the acousmatic voice: when Cordelier talks of perversity and evil, Opale steals Joly's wallet from his pocket; and when Cordelier talks of a battle, Opale lies down and cries in pain.

After the recording ends with Cordelier saying 'je décidai de nommer cette nouvelle partie née de moi Opale' [I decided to name this new part born out of me

Opale], Opale does indeed seem to exist independently from Cordelier, outside of him. He tells the visibly shocked Joly, who first refuses to believe the story, that he indeed is not Cordelier, stating that any trace of the doctor is gone from within him. However, as Joly declares that he needs to understand, Opale starts speaking as Cordelier ('quand je suis devenu Opale pour la première fois' [when I became Opale for the first time]) in voice-over. Now that the acousmatic voice has gone quiet, it is as if it had been absorbed by Opale, who starts telling the rest of their story.

First forming a disjunctive duality, Opale and Cordelier then merge into what Joly perceives as an aberrant unity, the merging of two voices and two bodies into one. While throughout his voice-over narration Opale switches between pronouns (echoing the same process in the novella, through here it is Opale/Hyde who switches between 'he' and 'I' rather than Cordelier/Jekyll) but retains his distinctive vocal style, at the very end of the film, as he prepares to mix and drink the lethal amount of potion that will enable him to recover Cordelier's body in death, Opale's movement and vocal style gradually become closer to Cordelier's, and he is addressed as Cordelier by Joly. It is as if the two had imperfectly merged, or rather as if the dual character were in constant oscillation between Cordelier and Opale. This can be seen as continuing the shifting between pronouns in Stevenson's novella, as Opale also oscillates between voice(s) and movement(s). Hyde is a part of Jekyll; here, Cordelier and Opale are both parts of each other, and together form a disjunctive, heautonomous whole.

As Reader points out, this confession scene does more than 'bring the novella "up to date" somewhat fatuously', in the sense that through the relationship between voice and body it 'calls the very antithesis of presence and absence into question'.[40] It plays with the fact of Jekyll and Hyde's co-existence, but the impossibility of their simultaneous embodiment, by disjunctively combining Cordelier's audio presence with Opale's visual presence, and later, through performance, rendering Cordelier's voice and movement through Opale's voice and body. Renoir's adaptation, therefore, rearticulates the complexities of the duality of Jekyll/Hyde, through a dramatization of cultural anxiety regarding the (unsuccessful) repression of memories of Fascist collaboration and colonial violence in 1950s French society, and through the slippage between Jekyll's and Hyde's cinematic voice/s and body/ bodies, as violence can no longer be contained in another voice and another body.

Mattotti and Kramsky's *Jekyll & Hyde*

In the same way that Renoir's film is inscribed in a genealogy of filmic versions of Stevenson's story, Mattotti and Kramsky's *Docteur Jekyll et Mr. Hyde* is part of a network of comic adaptations of Stevenson's story. In order to understand Mattotti and Kramsky's approach to adaptation into comics, it is useful to contrast it with the use of the medium in the *Classics Illustrated* series. As explained in the introduction to this chapter, the aim of *Classics Illustrated*, a series of comic book adaptations of works from the literary canon, is to entice the readers to eventually turn to the source text; a note at the end of all issues published between 1941 and 1971 exhorted the young reader to borrow the literary source from their school or public library.

The series is, then, as Rocco Versaci argues, characterized by a 'paradoxical attitude — to simultaneously use and efface the comic book medium'.[41] By contrast, Mattotti and Kramsky's version, rather than being positioned as a consciously inferior and simplified introduction to a canonical text, is a revisualization of a cultural reference and memory that openly exploits the potential of comics as an art form and as an adaptive medium.

In this regard, it is interesting to situate Mattotti and Kramsky's version in relation to graphic adaptations by Alberto Breccia, to whom their *Jekyll and Hyde* is dedicated. Breccia, a prolific adapter of literary classics (including Stevenson's novella, short stories by H. P. Lovecraft and Bram Stoker's *Dracula*), is described by Mattotti as a reference with regard to graphic experimentation.[42] In Breccia's as in Mattotti's work, adaptation into comics is used, not to borrow from, and reinforce, the cultural capital and legitimacy of literature and the literary canon, but as a means of experimenting with the medium and exploring its potentialities, retelling oft-adapted stories and cultural references in renewed ways.[43] Mattotti, who cites as major influences movements such as Expressionism, Futurism, and metaphysical art,[44] has developed his striking graphic style (or 'Mattoptics', to use Barbara Uhlig's translation of art critic's Enrico Ghezzi's term) across comics, illustration, and painting.[45] His work in comics is characterized by the fact that he uses the medium very consciously, and creatively, as a language. He summarizes his conception of comics as follows in an interview with Paul Gravett:

> It's important to think of comics not like a genre but as text, images, writing, melody, colour, form. If you take it in a pure way, you can make so many things. Little by little, young authors are thinking about it and it is very interesting when artists are able to really use the language of the sign, the form. Texts are important and can be great but comics is also the language of images, of styles, of forms. We must use everything to communicate the depth of the subjects and the emotions.[46]

Mattotti describes a medium with artistic and emotional possibilities that need to be explored in depth, including through intermediality, in relation not only to literature, but also the visual arts and music. This attention to image, style, and form, is evident in his work on *Docteur Jekyll & Mr. Hyde*, which offers a striking visual reformulation of the story.

By contrast with *Le Testament*'s post-World War II setting, Mattotti and Kramsky's version is set in Germany towards the end of the Weimar Republic and the rise of Nazism, rather than in the authors' contemporary and national context of twenty-first-century Italy. This transposition of *Jekyll and Hyde* can therefore be read as a retrospective look at a period during which Nazism would become part of the fabric of the nation. This sets the release of evil in the individual (Hyde) prior to the institutionalization and systematization of evil (Nazism). Here, Hyde arguably functions as a sign of what is to come, rather than as a reminder of the past as in *Le Testament*. While Renoir's, and Barrault's, Opale/Hyde can be seen as a *performance* of evil, instantly identifiable and recognizable, Mattotti's Hyde is a shifting, permanently morphing, and unstable form. Aesthetically, this Hyde is not an aberration in his historical context as was Opale (a reminder of what has been repressed), but is visually coherent with it, part of a world of distortion and 'wild, unusual' colours.[47]

What is perhaps most striking in Mattotti and Kramsky's re-contextualization of the story is the way in which it engages with the historical context through art, in the construction of an Expressionist visual text. Mattotti explains that the book became a 'voyage into Expressionist culture', and mentions in particular the influence of Otto Dix, Max Beckmann, and George Grosz on the artwork, notably with regard to colour and form, to give a 'hysterical idea of reality'.[48] Uhlig has analysed the references to Expressionism in Mattotti's work on *Jekyll and Hyde* in the 'flattened pictorial space, organic brushwork, and the vivid, unconventional colors that appear independent of their real-world objects'.[49] In Mattotti's Expressionist-inspired graphics, Uhlig differentiates between 'filtered memories' that simulate aesthetic aspects of Expressionism and do not refer to a specific artwork, and 'direct references'. Filtered memories include the use of a colour palette similar to that chosen by the art group 'Der blaue Reiter' [The Blue Rider] (1911–1914) at the beginning of the comic, or of tilted angles reminiscent of German Expressionist cinema such as in Robert Wiene's 1920 *Das Cabinet des Dr. Caligari*. Mattotti also includes direct references, such as to George Grosz's 1917/18 *Widmung an Oskar Panizza*, or Otto Dix's 1927/28 *Grande Ville* and 1933 *The Seven Deadly Sins*. This shows Mattotti's exploration of comics through intermediality, in this way inscribing comics in a dialogue between art forms. The comic book combines the three subcategories of intermediality in the 'narrow sense' as theorized by Irina O. Rajewsky. Indeed, there is firstly a process of medial transposition, from a literary source text to a comic book (that is of course inscribed in the polymedia network of versions of the tale). Secondly, comic art is itself shaped by media combination, in the medial constellation of text and image that constitutes it. Finally, through intermedial references to individual paintings and more broadly to Expressionism, the comic 'thematizes, evokes, or imitates elements or structures' of other media, transposed into the specificities of comic art.[50] In this regard, the panel, which is one of the formal specificities of comic art, may also echo the shape of a screen or a frame if the reader perceives the 'filtered memories' of, and 'direct references' to, Expressionist cinema and art. As cinema and art are referenced as medial systems, the comic in a sense both displays and figuratively bridges the 'intermedial gap' between comic art and other media.[51]

The intermedial references to German Expressionism are to be understood as, following Rajewsky, 'meaning-constitutional strategies', in the creation of a visual text that explores comic art's relation to other media, and graphically echoes key motifs in *Jekyll and Hyde* and the new setting of the story.[52] Indeed, as Anton Kaes explains, the Expressionists 'explored that part of existence that lies behind the conventional masks of observable reality', their preoccupation with 'inner states of mind, with dreams, delusions, and madness [conveying] a disorienting sense of impending crisis'.[53] The artwork participates in the re-telling of a story of a literal exteriorization of inner evil, through the embodiment of Jekyll's 'hidden nature'.[54]

Uhlig points out that Mattotti includes an unfiltered reference to Otto Dix's *The Seven Deadly Sins*, a painting that contains 'thinly veiled allusions to the rising Nazi regime', such as in the skeleton holding a scythe to form a shape reminiscent of a swastika.[55] In the comic, this is graphically referenced and juxtaposed with *récitatifs* in which Jekyll talks of his crimes as Hyde.[56] Hyde stands as a mythological, archetypal force of evil that also takes on historical resonance in the era in which the comic is set. This is perceived by the twenty-first-century reader of the comic, who retrospectively sees Expressionism in the context of the impending collapse of the Weimar Republic and the rise of Nazism, echoing the ways in which the canon adapts and is adapted across time to take on renewed meanings and resonances.

Kaes argues that in its violation of realist conventions 'Expressionist art wanted to shock the viewer into experiencing the world in a new defamiliarizing light'.[57] Mattotti and Kramsky's *Docteur Jekyll & Mr. Hyde* similarly confronts the reader with a graphic text that defamiliarizes them with their memory of *Jekyll and Hyde*, and, at the same time, with what might be their habitual reading practise in relation to comics, in the sense that the text invites them to perform a reading that goes beyond narrative construction. In her analysis of Mattotti and Kramsky's comic, Caraballo examines how it, in places, 'breaks' with figuration by tending towards abstraction, resulting in a partly non-narrative comic that turns the reading process into a realization of possible significations and sensations.[58] My discussion of this process will be articulated in relation to understanding comic art as a language and an adaptive medium, engaging the reader in what I term an 'adaptive reading'.

In order to explore how Mattotti and Kramsky use the possibilities offered by the medium in their re-utterance of the oft-adapted story of Jekyll and Hyde, and how the adaptation of a canonical text is used to experiment with the medium, I shall focus on the scene of Jekyll's first transformation into Hyde (Figure 4.3).[59] As explained at the beginning of this chapter, this has become a key scene through serial adaptation, and the reader is therefore likely to have already a visual mental representation of it. Comics are defined by Ann Miller as 'an art of both iteration and transformation',[60] which echoes Hutcheon's characterization of adaptation's formal structure as a mixture of repetition and difference.[61] The process of adaptation into comics as iteration/repetition and transformation/difference is used productively in this scene to engage the reader in an adaptive reading, in the reconstruction of the steps of the metamorphosis of Jekyll into Hyde, and the renewed vision of this episode in cultural memory.

The fact that the transformation is presented on a double page is highly significant. It suggests the duality of the character through a diagonal reading from the top of the left-hand page at the start of the process, to the end result on the bottom of the right-hand page. At the same time, it isolates in panels various stages of the transformation, hinting at Jekyll's potential plurality. In Stevenson's novella, Jekyll, after stating that 'man is not truly one, but truly two', '[hazards] the guess that man will be ultimately known for a mere polity of multifarious, incongruous and independent denizens'.[62] In the graphic transformation, the 'non-fugitiveness' of the comic images (to use Thierry Groensteen's term) arguably renders this

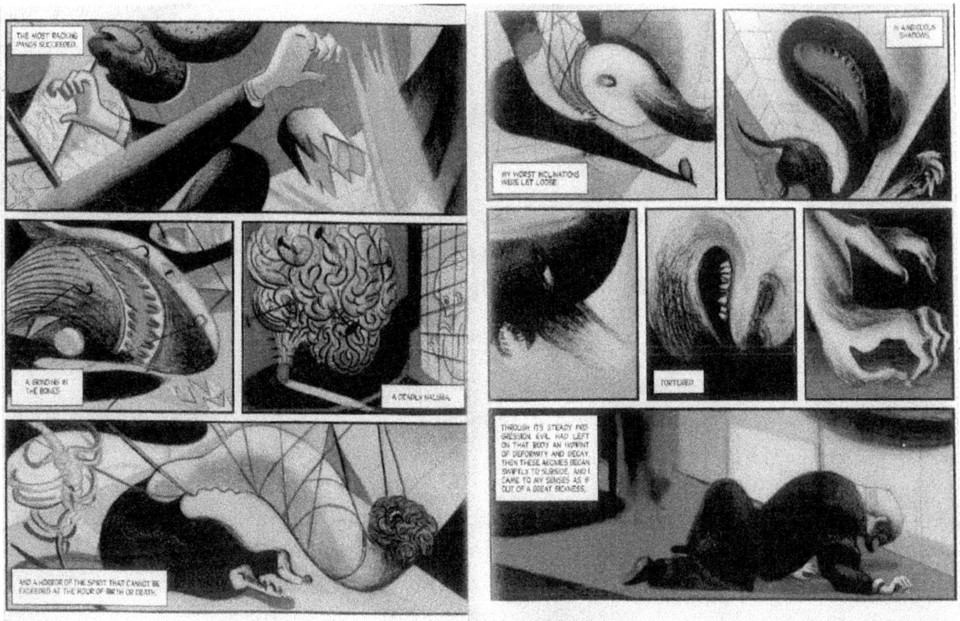

FIG. 4.3. 'Jekyll's first transformation into Hyde'. Extract from Mattotti and Kramsky, *Dr. Jekyll & Mr. Hyde* © Casterman. With the kind permission of the authors and Editions Casterman / Avec l'aimable autorisation des auteurs et des Editions Casterman.

plurality, by confronting the reader with the co-presence of all that is inside Jekyll, broken up into panels and juxtaposed on the double page.[63] These are shown as all potential forms of Jekyll, rather than simply as glimpsed stages of the transformation process, as fugitive filmic images would be perceived. Moreover, the double page of open mouths of varying shapes, all seemingly screaming, can be seen to echo Jekyll's later shocking realization that within him, 'the slime of the pit seemed to utter cries and voices'.[64] When this line is voiced by Jekyll in a *récitatif* at the end of the comic, it may remind the reader of the visually striking transformation scene, which can be retroactively understood in the comic as a network (as theorized by Groensteen) as showing this pit within Jekyll, and his potential multifariousness, including the in/un-human within him.[65]

The presentation of the transformation scene on the double page also actively encourages the reader to adapt their reading of the scene as a block, by exploring the possibilities offered by comic art as a medium whose reading process allows for not only linear but also translinear and plurivectoral reading.[66] The first panel on the left-hand page, in which Jekyll is seized with 'the most racking pangs' after drinking the potion, and the last four panels on the right-hand page, which show the final stage of the transformation into Hyde, with the 'monstrous' but recognizable shaping of his face and hands, are easily interpretable, in particular in a palimpsestuous reading. However, the five panels in between move away from figuration to represent Jekyll/Hyde's subjective experience of the transformation process. Jekyll/Hyde's hands and mouth become graphic motifs across the double page, but in these five panels they morph into shapes evoking rather than representing hands and a mouth, the former have become distorted claws, and the latter, a gaping hole in what barely resembles a body anymore.

This encourages the reader to relate parts of panels to parts of other panels in order to decipher and reconstruct the transformation process. The process of sequential reading is supplemented by an active and conscious plurivectoral reading, across the page, or back to previous panels, in order to identify the iterated elements and understand their transformation, thereby relating the non-fugitive comic images to their 'perifield' (in Benoît Peeters's terms).[67] Here, the reader actively engages both with comics as an art of iteration and transformation and with the mixture of repetition and difference that is inherent to adaptation, as this strikingly different metamorphosis scene nonetheless repeats motifs recurrent in other versions, for instance through the close-up on Jekyll/Hyde's hands, which is a feature of Mamoulian's 1931 version.

The relationship between text and image also encourages the reader to adapt the pace of their reading to the graphic text. Indeed, the reader is encouraged to eschew a purely narrative, linear reading to reflect on text-image relations, in the sense that the image seems to suggest visual metaphors rather than direct illustrations of the text visible alongside it. This invites the reader to contemplate the panels further in an attempt to decipher the relationship between the two. A reading of the text as text-image poetry becomes more fruitful than focusing solely on narrative progression. For instance, the *récitatif* containing the words 'a grinding in the bones' is juxtaposed with the image of a shark being caught; 'a deadly nausea' is juxtaposed with the image of the brain that was in the doctor's laboratory, and in this panel now seems to be growing, covered in nails, and turning into smoke. The breaking-down of Stevenson's source text into what resembles a prose poem, and its combination with Expressionist images highlights not only the multiplicity of possible visualizations of words (the visuality of the text), but also the evocative power of the drawing. The combination of text and image does not close off the reader's visual interpretation of the text, but foregrounds the multiple possibilities for the deciphering and interpretation of the text-image syntax.

Lastly, it is useful to reflect on the potentialities of the gutter on this double page in relation to this adaptive reading. Groensteen points out that 'the gutter, insignificant in itself, is invested with an arthrologic function that can only be deciphered in light of the singular images that it separates and unites', and he compares the progressive construction of meaning in comics to the similar process structuring the reading of a literary text.[68] I would like to suggest that the gutter functions not only as a blank space for the construction of narrative meaning, but also potentially as a space of openness for the reader to practice a palimpsestuous reading, inscribing this version in their own intertextual and intermedial network. Comic art can then be understood as an adaptive medium not only in terms of its hybridity and its potential for intermediality, but also as a participative art form, through which readers can realize multiple possible readings. The adaptation of a canonical text and a cultural reference here becomes a process through which to explore the graphic and emotional potential of comics, as a language, as an art form, and as an adaptive medium.

Conclusion

Renoir's and Mattotti/Kramsky's 'generations', in Leitch's terms, of *Jekyll and Hyde* adaptations, offer creative re-articulations of Stevenson's novella in terms of content and form.[69] Both versions can be read to engage in different ways with a context where notions of evil have been redefined, the comic through an Expressionist voyage into pre-World War II Germany, and the film by seemingly presenting a largely atemporal fantastic context that can however also be analysed in terms of the tension between the repression and resurfacing of France's Fascist past. Going beyond a clear division between good and evil and exploring the complexities of the dual figure, Renoir's film further constructs Cordelier/Opale as an audio-visual double, in the asymmetrical, heautonomous relationship between cinematic voice and body. Mattotti and Kramsky's adaptation exploits the potential of comics as an art form to render the plurality of the character, and to engage the reader in the re-vision of his transformation.

These two case studies serve to highlight the eternal, unfinal process of rereading and rewriting the canon through adaptation. *Jekyll and Hyde* appears as both malleable, in the sense that it is repeatedly transposed and its meaning and form shifted; and already partly shaped by the meanings and forms given to it by serial adaptation. The authorship of this canonical text seems both vacant in the Foucauldian sense, and always filled, decentred, and multiplied. It is shared with participative readers and viewers, who must restitch Cordelier/Jekyll's voice to Opale/Hyde's body in the filmic context, or retrace the steps of Jekyll's transformation in the comic, in each case, inscribing old and new versions in their own intertextual and intermedial networks. By retelling the story across time, media, and nations, Renoir's film and Mattotti/Kramsky's comic contribute to the unfinal becoming of the dual character Jekyll/Hyde into a polymedia myth, and of the canonical text into a shifting, dynamic construction.

Notes to Chapter 4

1. Robert Louis Stevenson, *The Strange Case of Dr Jekyll and Mr Hyde*, in *The Strange Case of Dr Jekyll and Mr Hyde and Other Tales of Terror*, ed. by Robert Mighall (London: Penguin, 2002), pp. 1–70 (pp. 55, 16).
2. *Le Testament du Docteur Cordelier*, dir. by Jean Renoir (Studio Canal, 2007), DVD (English titles for the film are *Experiment in Evil* and *The Doctor's Horrible Experiment*). Jerry Kramsky and Lorenzo Mattotti, *Docteur Jekyll & Mr. Hyde*, trans. by Marc Violine (Tournai: Casterman, 2002). While Mattotti and Kramsky wrote the comic in Italian, using Carlo Fruttero and Franco Lucentini's 1988 translation of Stevenson's novella, their comic book adaptation was first published in French. References in this chapter are to the English translation of the comic: Jerry Kramsky and Lorenzo Mattotti, *Dr. Jekyll & Mr. Hyde*, trans. by Adeline Darlington (Nantier: NBM, 2002). Other than this, and unless otherwise indicated, translations into English in the present article are my own.
3. Rose, *'Jekyll and Hyde' Adapted*, pp. 15–16.
4. Sanders, *Adaptation and Appropriation* (2006), pp. 8–9.

5. Hutcheon, with O'Flynn, *A Theory of Adaptation*, p. 122. John Ellis refers to this memory of the canonical text as a 'generally circulated cultural memory' (quoted by Hutcheon in her study), while Rose refers to the same notion in terms of 'popular-cultural memories and associations', reflecting his focus on popular culture. See John Ellis, 'The Literary Adaptation', *Screen*, 23 (1982), 3–5 (p. 3) and Rose, *'Jekyll and Hyde' Adapted*, p. 15.
6. Barthes, 'The Death of the Author', p. 145.
7. On the concept of an historical constellation of elements as a metaphor for canon formation, see Kolbas, *Critical Theory and the Literary Canon*.
8. As Thomas Leitch argues, 'the most exciting prospect offered by contemporary adaptation studies is [that they offer a new way of understanding] all texts as intertexts, all reading as rereading, all writing as rewriting, and so turn the classical canon [...] into a field of intertextual energy past, present, and future' ('Everything You Always Wanted to Know about Adaptation: Especially if You're Looking Forwards rather than Back', Literature/Film Quarterly, 33.3 (2005), 233–45 (p. 239)).
9. Rose, *'Jekyll and Hyde' Adapted*, p. 15.
10. I am borrowing the expression from Sanders, *Adaptation and Appropriation*, p. 22. For recent adaptations, we can note a 2015 ITV series, a 2016 BBC Radio 4 drama, and Serge Bozon's 2017 film *Madame Hyde*.
11. Colin Davis, *Postwar Renoir: Film and the Memory of Violence* (New York & Abingdon: Routledge, 2012).
12. Lorenzo Mattotti, in Paul Gravett, 'Lorenzo Mattotti: The Magic & Music of Comics' <http://www.paulgravett.com/articles/article/lorenzo_mattotti> [accessed 14 December 2014].
13. Ann Miller, *Reading Bande dessinée: Critical Approaches to French-language Comic Strip* (Bristol: Intellect, 2007), p. 88.
14. Davis, *Postwar Renoir*, p. 80. In his reading of the film, Keith A. Reader argues the film is an example of an agonistic text, in part through the relationship of competition and rivalry between four artistic media, namely cinema, literature, the theatre, and television ('Literature/Cinema/Television: Intertextuality in Jean Renoir's *Le Testament du Docteur Cordelier*', in *Intertextuality: Theories and Practices*, ed. by Michael Worton and Judith Still (Manchester: Manchester University Press, 1990), pp. 176–89).
15. Roxane Hamery points out that Barrault's characters are often seized with madness, and she links in particular his performances in *Le Testament* and in Jeff Musso's 1937 noir *Le Puritain*, in which he plays a fanatical journalist who murders a young woman ('Rhétorique du double: les figures inquiétantes de Jean-Louis Barrault', in *Les Cinéastes français à l'épreuve du genre fantastique: socioanalyse d'une production artistique*, ed. by Frédéric Gimello-Mesplomb (Paris: L'Harmattan, 2012), pp. 109–28 (pp. 109–10)).
16. Leitch, Thomas, 'Jekyll, Hyde, Jekyll, Hyde, Jekyll Hyde, Jekyll, Hyde: Four Models of Intertextuality', in *Victorian Literature and Film Adaptation*, ed. by Abigail Burnham Bloom and Mary Sanders Pollock (Amherst, NY: Cambria Press, 2011), pp. 27–49 (p. 31).
17. On Barrymore's performance, see Richard J. Hand, 'Paradigms of Metamorphosis and Transmutation: Thomas Edison's *Frankenstein* and John Barrymore's *Dr Jekyll and Mr Hyde*', in *Monstrous Adaptations: Generic and Thematic Mutations in Horror Film*, ed. by Richard J. Hand and Jay McRoy (Manchester: Manchester University Press, 2007), pp. 9–19 (p. 13).
18. Rose, *'Jekyll and Hyde' Adapted*, pp. 23–24.
19. Stevenson, *The Strange Case of Dr Jekyll and Mr Hyde*, p. 55.
20. Rose, *'Jekyll and Hyde' Adapted*, p. 7. Rose identifies a shift from an understanding of evil as violence against domestic foci in the early adaptations, to the consequences of personal degradation on society in adaptations released between 1932 and 1948, and finally, between 1955 and 1990, as potentially releasing chaotic violence and causing mass destruction.
21. See Katherine Linehan, '"Closer Than a Wife": The Strange Case of Dr Jekyll's Significant Other,' in *Robert Louis Stevenson Reconsidered: New Critical Perspectives*, ed. by William B. Jones, Jr. (London: McFarland & Company, 2003), pp. 85–100.
22. Martin O'Shaughnessy, *Jean Renoir* (Manchester: Manchester University Press, 2000), p. 193.
23. Davis, *Postwar Renoir*, pp. 89–90.

24. Ibid., pp. 90–92. Davis uses the term 'post-Holocaust audience' in his article 'From Psychopathology to Diabolical Evil: Dr Jekyll, Mr Hyde and Jean Renoir', *Journal of Romance Studies*, 12.1 (2012), 10–23 (p. 10).
25. O'Shaughnessy, *Jean Renoir*, p. 208.
26. Henry Rousso, *The Vichy Syndrome: History and Memory in France since 1944* (Cambridge, MA: Harvard University Press, 1991). The period of repression (1954–1971) followed that of 'unfinished mourning' (1944–1954), and was followed by 'contestation' (1971–1974) and 'obsession' (after 1974). Davis refers to the era of 'repressions' in his analysis of Renoir's 1960 play *Carola* and 1962 film *Le Caporal épinglé* [The Elusive Caporal] as postwar works that directly depict World War II (Davis, *Postwar Renoir*, pp. 117–36).
27. See Rousso, *The Vichy Syndrome*, pp. 82–97. Landmark films that challenged the resistancialist myth include Marcel Ophuls's 1969 *Le Chagrin et la pitié* [The Sorrow and the Pity], and Louis Malle's 1974 *Lacombe, Lucien*.
28. Rousso, *The Vichy Syndrome*, p. 82.
29. O'Shaughnessy, *Jean Renoir*, p. 208.
30. On the film's depiction of the 'untrustworthiness of the bourgeoisie' and how this relates to Renoir's *œuvre*, see Reader, 'Literature/Cinema/Television'.
31. Hamery, 'Rhétorique du double', p. 110.
32. A young woman, asked to describe Opale to the police, cannot give any defining features, apart from the fact that his clothes were too big for him, and says: 'tout ce que je sais, c'est qu'il faisait peur' [all I know is that he was frightening]. This recalls Mr Enfield's description of Hyde to Utterson: 'He's an extraordinary-looking man, and yet I really can name nothing out of the way. No sir; I can make no hand of it; I can't describe him' (Stevenson, *The Strange Case of Dr Jekyll and Mr Hyde*, p. 10).
33. Esther Rowlands, *Cinematic Portraits of Evil: Christian de Chalonge's 'Docteur Petiot' and Jean-Pierre Jeunet's 'Delicatessen'* (Amherst, NY: Cambria Press, 2009), p. 26. Rowlands is here referring specifically to the 1990 film *Docteur Petiot*.
34. Michel Chion, '100 concepts pour penser et décrire le cinéma sonore', trans. by Claudia Gorbman <http://michelchion.com/download/new> [accessed 1 October 2015].
35. Michel Chion, *Audio-Vision: Sound on Screen*, trans. by Claudia Gorbman (New York: Columbia University Press, 1994), p. 221.
36. Chion, '100 concepts pour penser et décrire le cinema sonore'.
37. Gilles Deleuze, *Cinema 2: The Time-Image*, trans. by H. Tomlinson and R. Galeta (London: Athlone Press, 1989), p. 256.
38. Britta H. Sjogren, *Into the Vortex: Female Voice and Paradox in Film* (Urbana: University of Illinois Press, 2006), pp. 5–6.
39. Michel Chion, *The Voice in Cinema*, trans. by Claudia Gorbman (New York: Columbia University Press, 1999), p. 125.
40. Reader, 'Literature/Cinema/Television', p. 185.
41. Rocco Versaci, *This Book Contains Graphic Language: Comics as Literature* (New York: Continuum, 2007), p. 187.
42. Lorenzo Mattotti, in Alberto Breccia, 'Alberto Breccia, 20 ans après: entretien avec Lorenzo Mattotti' <http://www.alberto-breccia.net/breccia-20-ans-apres-entretien-lorenzo-mattotti/> [accessed 3 October 2015].
43. The increasing number of innovative graphic adaptations of canonical texts can be linked to the changing status of comic art in terms of cultural legitimacy, and therefore the changing relation of the medium to the literary canon.
44. Lorenzo Mattotti, in Florian Rubis, 'Lorenzo Mattotti: "Je n'ai pas honte de le dire: le dessin est, quand même, une discipline spirituelle!"', *ActuaBD* <http://www.actuabd.com/Lorenzo-Mattotti-Je-n-ai-pas-honte> [accessed 10 August 2017].
45. Ghezzi's term is 'Mattottica pinottica' (Barbara Uhlig, 'Hidden Art: Artistic References in Mattotti's *Docteur Jekyll & Mr Hyde*', *Image [&] Narrative*, 17.4 (2016), 43–56 (p. 43)).
46. Gravett, 'Lorenzo Mattotti'.
47. Ibid.

48. Mattotti also mentions Francis Bacon as an influence, and Laura Cecilia Caraballo offers an analysis of the comic through Deleuzian concepts from his work on Bacon. See Laura Cecilia Caraballo, '*Docteur Jekyll & Mister Hyde* de Mattotti et Kramsky: briser la figuration', in *Bande dessinée et adaptation*, ed. by Mitaine, Roche and Schmitt-Pitiot, pp. 137–54.
49. Uhlig, 'Hidden Art', p. 45.
50. Rajewsky, 'Intermediality, Intertextuality, and Remediation', pp. 52–53.
51. On the 'intermedial gap', see Rajewsky, 'Intermediality, Intertextuality, and Remediation', p. 55. Rajewsky analyses the use of a picture-frame-like device to reference the medial system of painting in Sasha Waltz's 2000 dance theatre production *Körper* [Bodies] (ibid., p. 57).
52. Ibid., p. 52.
53. Anton Kaes, 'The Expressionist Vision in Theater and Cinema', in *Expressionism Reconsidered: Relationships and Affinities*, ed. by Gertrud Bauer Pickar and Karl Eugene Webb (Munich: Wilhelm Fink, 1979), pp. 89–98 (p. 89).
54. Frau Elda, who is pursuing Jekyll, tells him she wants to discover his 'hidden nature'. Jekyll first attempts to avoid temptation, but quickly tells Elda to meet him in Hyde's lodgings, therefore consciously planning to 'delve into the depths of our darkness together' in Hyde's form, and probably anticipating that he will brutally murder her as Hyde (Kramsky and Mattotti, *Docteur Jekyll & Mr. Hyde*, pp. 39–41). This shows that as in Renoir's *Le Testament du Docteur Cordelier*, there is no diametrical opposition between Jekyll and Hyde with the doctor standing as a symbol of 'good'.
55. Uhlig, 'Hidden Art', pp. 52–53.
56. Kramsky and Mattotti, *Docteur Jekyll & Mr. Hyde*, p. 56.
57. Kaes, 'The Expressionist Vision in Theater and Cinema', p. 89. Sanders identifies a 'mechanism of defamiliarization' in appropriations, in the sense that many of them '[invite] us as readers or spectators to look anew at a canonical text that we might otherwise have felt we had "understood" or interpreted to our own satisfaction' (*Adaptation and Appropriation*, p. 99).
58. Caraballo, '*Docteur Jekyll & Mister Hyde* de Mattotti et Kramsky'.
59. Kramsky and Mattotti, *Docteur Jekyll & Mr. Hyde*, pp. 16–17.
60. Miller, *Reading Bande dessinée*, p. 88.
61. Hutcheon, *A Theory of Adaptation*, p. 142.
62. Stevenson, *The Strange Case of Dr Jekyll and Mr Hyde*, pp. 55–56. These lines are retained in Kramsky and Mattotti, *Docteur Jekyll & Mr. Hyde*, p. 12.
63. Groensteen points out that, unlike filmic images, comic images are non-fugitive, and 'every panel exists, potentially if not actually, in relation with each of the others' (*The System of Comics*, trans. by Bart Beaty and Nick Nguyen (Jackson: University Press of Mississippi, 2007), p. 146).
64. Groensteen, *The System of Comics*, p. 69. Retained in Kramsky and Mattotti, *Docteur Jekyll & Mr. Hyde*, p. 63.
65. See Groensteen, *The System of Comics*. For an analysis of the potential of comics as an adaptive medium in relation to Régis Loisel's prequel to Peter Pan (another cultural myth constructed in a proliferating multimedia network of adaptations), drawing on Sanders's and Groensteen's uses of the concept of the network in adaptation studies and comics studies respectively, see Armelle Blin-Rolland, 'Re-inventing the Origins of the Boy Who Wouldn't Grow Up: Régis Loisel's *Peter Pan*', *Studies in Comics*, 5.2 (2014), 273–90.
66. Groensteen, *The System of Comics*, p. 155.
67. Benoît Peeters, *Case, planche, récit* (Tournai: Casterman, 1991), p. 15.
68. Groensteen, *The System of Comics*, p. 114.
69. Leitch, 'Jekyll, Hyde, Jekyll, Hyde, Jekyll Hyde, Jekyll, Hyde', p. 44.

CHAPTER 5

❖

Turning Japanese? *Les Misérables* from Meiji to Manga

Bradley Stephens

Victor Hugo's novel *Les Misérables* has consistently lent itself to adaptation across different generations, cultures, and media. The story of the convict Jean Valjean and his struggle for salvation amidst the social injustices of early nineteenth-century France has proven itself to be one of the country's most prosperous exports. Since its first appearance in 1862 and the global publishing sensation that followed, audiences worldwide have shown a lasting appetite for *Les Misérables*, from the theatrical play by the author's son Charles in 1863 to Alain Boublil and Claude-Michel Schönberg's immensely successful 1980s stage musical, which itself was adapted into a blockbuster film in 2012. Such demand suggests that the canonicity of *Les Misérables* is sanctioned as much by popular opinion as it is by critical orthodoxy. In live-action film and television series alone, *Les Misérables* has inspired well over sixty international adaptations, beginning at the dawn of motion pictures when the Lumière brothers presented their short film *Victor Hugo et les principaux personnages des 'Misérables'* in 1897, just two years after developing their cinematograph.[1] This select sample of the novel's prodigious legacy of adaptations reflects a capacity for crowd-pleasing that shows no signs of decline in the twenty-first century.

It is a legacy that promises to garner closer critical attention at a time when digital archives and resources are making material more widely available than ever before, and when the field of adaptation studies has become both more visible and more aware of its own multidisciplinarity. As I have argued elsewhere, the insights that the history of *Les Misérables* brings to adaptation studies can only be brought into focus through recent conceptual and methodological developments.[2] As a 'growth area in the Arts and Humanities [...] with a new theoretical richness and interdisciplinary confidence',[3] adaptation studies has stepped beyond its early origins in novel-to-film studies to think more about 'adaptation as process':[4] as a creative rather than simply imitative practice that takes into account a broad network of determining factors, including media specificity, economic circumstance, and cultural preference. In the case of a work as internationally recognizable as *Les Misérables*, perspectives that look across cultures are essential to exploring how and why that story becomes part of a global cultural memory. In so doing, those vantage points cannot become restricted to the single critical criterion of fidelity. The question of how faithful an adaptation is to its source is supplanted by a less hierarchical appraisal of their relationship that accepts an adaptation as an autonomous work in its own right. Furthermore, the range of media cannot remain limited to live-action film and theatre, no matter how plentiful that resource may be. Long-established forms such as radio, animation, and comics have sustained retellings of *Les Misérables* for over a century and a half, and while interactive media forms (such as video games) and audience-made content of digital platforms (such as fan fiction sites and YouTube) are now making their own contributions, these outlets can easily remain marginalized in discussion. To read adaptations solely in terms of their fidelity to a source and to concentrate exclusively on film and stage adaptations would be akin to skim-reading only one section of a larger narrative.

The present chapter seeks to address some of these gaps in scholarship by considering adaptations originating on the other side of the world from where Hugo originally wrote his novel. Japan presents a noticeably intriguing angle from which to grasp the global and diverse reach of *Les Misérables*, especially through its internationally renowned animated and graphic media. The historical relationship between *Les Misérables* and Japan has to date not been closely examined but this chapter will argue that, within such a context, the Japanese culture of anime and manga in particular help to outline the transnational dimensions of adaptation as an artistic and cultural process. In turn, this relationship obliges a nuanced appreciation of how well-known stories that find a global audience can travel across different media forms and cultural spaces.

Les Misérables in Japan

Hugo's story has been noticeably popular in Japan. Beyond mainland Europe, the United Kingdom, and North America, which between them have unsurprisingly produced around half of all cinematic adaptations of the novel, Japan has produced more than one in ten of the live-action screen adaptations of *Les Misérables*, reaching back to the silent period and featuring stars of early Japanese cinema such as Masao Inoue and Denjirō Ōkōchi.[5] More recently, the Boublil and Schönberg musical has been in demand since its initial three-month run sold out at Tokyo's Imperial Theatre in the summer of 1987. The origins of such popularity arguably lie in the 1860s, when *Les Misérables* first appeared and when Japan was on the verge of a major transformation into a modernized nation state, which in part helps to explain the novel's strong appeal in Japan at this time. Hugo's beliefs in equality of opportunity and human dignity proved as attractive in Asia as they did in Europe and the Americas. He was the best known of all the Western literary greats of the period, not least because he was one of the few to have condemned the sack of the Summer Palace in Beijing by the British and the French in 1860 as an act of barbarism during the Second Opium War (an intervention that continues to resonate in modern China).[6]

The restoration of imperial rule with Emperor Meiji in 1868 opened Japan up to the West after two centuries of isolationism under the Tokugawa shogunate, and France was considered to be a model of enlightened ideals with whom the empire could establish various cultural, political, and military ties. The famous Iwakura Mission to the West, which played a central role in this modernization programme, visited France as part of its itinerary in the winter of 1872, several years before the heralded reception of Japanese art at the 1878 Paris Exposition universelle.[7] Hugo's standing as France's most iconic living writer ensured that his work, by way of his reputation, did not go unnoticed in this intercultural dialogue. In addition to translations of other French luminaries like Alexandre Dumas and Jules Verne, Shiken Morita's accessible translations of Hugo's fiction, including *Claude Gueux* (1834) and *The Last Day of a Condemned Man* (1829) in 1890 and 1896 respectively,[8] influenced a generation of writers during the Meiji restoration, while Hugo's Romantic drama *Hernani* (1830) helped to invigorate *shinpa* (or 'new school') theatre at the turn of the century.[9] The first prominent translation of *Les Misérables* itself came in October 1902. Shūroku Kuroiwa (under the pseudonym Ruikō Kuroiwa) serialized his rendering of the novel over ten months in Tokyo's largest newspaper *Yorozu chōhō* [Morning Report for the Masses]. Kuroiwa favoured ease of reading over accuracy, reworking the prose from Isabel Hapgood's 1887 English translation to suit Japanese tastes while preserving the central plot. Kuroiwa believed that Hugo's novel was ideally suited to the tabloid's combination of popular entertainment with social commentary.[10] Counting the less privileged levels of Japanese society amongst its readership, including labourers and farmers, alongside the emerging urban middle class, he rightly predicted that Hugo's narrative of the dispossessed would find a wide and devoted audience. A two-volume edition of Kuroiwa's version followed in 1906, with novelist Shūsei Tokuda's abridged translation appearing eight years later.

Hugo's voice was therefore being echoed and heard at a formative period in the history of Franco-Japanese relations, and it has continued to resonate to the present day. By the start of the twentieth century, Western influence, an 'optimism for a new day of "civilization and enlightenment"', and an industrial revolution, had propelled Japan ahead of its Asian neighbours, but this prosperity did not come without a price: urban investment exacerbated rural poverty, and the gap between rich and poor widened.[11] 'In afflicted areas loss of land and employment, vagabondage, and a desperate search for sustenance at the lower levels of drudgery in mines and among the urban proletariat changed the face of rural life.'[12] The subsequent Taishō period oversaw the further development of democracy within the empire, introducing universal male suffrage in 1925, only to be followed by the rise of nationalist conservatism during Emperor Hirohito's reign from 1926 onwards. Throughout these shifts, *Les Misérables* often casts a pertinent spotlight onto the need for socially responsible government in a number of different ways. In April 1938, to take but one example, Mansaku Itami's film *Kyojin-den* [Life of a Giant] — the fourth screen adaptation of the novel to appear in interwar Japan — suggested how timely Hugo's story had become for Japanese culture by transposing the narrative to the Satsuma Rebellion of 1877 and giving the characters Japanese names, such as Sanpei Onuma for Jean Valjean.[13] At this time of social upheaval, Hugo's French novel contributed in potent ways to Japan's self-fashioning.

Such an extensive reception across the nineteenth and twentieth centuries prompted Tōru Tsuji and Naoki Inagaki to translate a broad selection of Hugo's poems into Japanese for the first time in 1984 in order to draw attention to the man behind *Les Misérables*. Twelve years later in 1996, a major exhibition on Hugo's colourful life and immense body of works was presented by four different museums in Tokyo, Osaka, Koriyama, and Hiroshima, with support from the Ministry of Foreign Affairs, the French Embassy, and Japan's best-selling daily newspaper *Yomiuri*. The exhibition, in which one of the eight display halls was dedicated solely to *Les Misérables* with photographs of the original manuscript, attracted some 53,000 visitors.[14] Japan's enduring interest in *Les Misérables* confirms how readily Hugo's work has travelled outside its native France into new environments and forms. The extent to which *Les Misérables* has 'turned Japanese' in these adaptations, to paraphrase the 1980 pop song by The Vapors, points to questions of reception and appropriation that are central not only to the novel's afterlife but also to the cultural process of adaptation itself.

Les Misérables in Anime and Manga

Notwithstanding the many examples that Japanese film and stage productions offer for analysis, this chapter looks beyond those versions to media that have become synonymous with Japanese popular culture both within the country and abroad, namely animated film and comic books. They are forms which embody the distinctive style of Japan's anime and manga traditions: a revered and lucrative part of the transnational entertainment economy since the 1990s that has contributed to the idea of *Kūru Japan* [Cool Japan] and to the ushering-in of what has been called a 'new Japanism' in the West.[15] From *Akira* (1982–1990) and *Princess Mononoke* (1997) to the *Pokémon* franchise, these cartoons on screen and in print use arresting visuals to create a world that resembles our own and yet alters its physicality and dimensions through the exaggeration of movement, gesture, and bodily appearance, for example through disproportionately large eyes and expressive hairstyles. Adapting the minimalism of traditional Japanese brush-painting and monochrome line drawing, and tapping into the rich lineage of *Toba-e* picture-books and *kibyōshi* [yellow-jacket books] of the eighteenth and early nineteenth centuries, each tends towards a different palette: anime (an abbreviation of *animēshon*) often displays colourful graphics, whereas manga favours black and white composition.[16] Together, they embody a visual culture that is dissimilar to the often more mimetic cartooning of Western producers such as Walt Disney Studios or Marvel Comics, and one that attracts audiences of all ages. Over half of all Japanese studio productions were anime by the new millennium, and Japanese adults of both genders regularly read pocket-sized manga.

Although they commonly manifest a playful temperament through their imagery, animated film and manga books in particular are widely acknowledged to represent more than facile distraction from their audience's daily routines.[17] Through imaginative character development and by running a gamut of genres from tragedy to science fiction, anime and manga serve the same multiple functions of self-reflection and commodification that other, more traditional genres and media (such as literature and painting) fulfil within Western high culture. Susan Napier makes a compelling case for the reasons behind this status: 'Japan is a country that is traditionally more pictocentric than the cultures of the West, as is exemplified in its use of characters or ideograms, and anime and manga fit easily into a contemporary culture of the visual'. The breadth of subjects across these media in turn becomes 'a useful mirror on contemporary Japanese society, offering an array of insights into the significant issues, dreams, and nightmares of the day'.[18] Mark MacWilliams stresses this line of thinking yet more emphatically: 'Rather than just serving up fantasy escapes from the real world, [anime and manga] are potentially a source for political, ethical, or existential critical reflection', in no small part thanks to post-war manga such as *Astro Boy* (1952–1968) from the pioneering cartoonist Osamu Tesuka.[19] Even the most fantastic of works touch upon questions of Japan's national identity: manga and anime have consistently probed the intense social and political uncertainty arising from such crises as the legacy of the Second World War to the prolonged economic collapse of the 1990s in what Dani Cavallaro describes as 'a fundamental human drama'.[20]

Within this culture, the attraction towards reworking a popular novel such as *Les Misérables*, with its powerful social criticism, should come as no surprise. Whereas to some Western critics, 'the combination of high literature — "the classic" — and the "cartoon" still seems an unholy alliance', Japanese culture is far less sceptical about graphic media.[21] Since the 1970s there have been at least six anime and manga versions of *Les Misérables* in Japan, accounting for over half the total number of the novel's cartoon adaptations worldwide. These late twentieth-century and early twenty-first-century Japanese versions of *Les Misérables* have yet to receive close critical attention. Two examples are especially relevant to the current discussion, since they come from producers who specialize in adapting classic literature: *Les Misérables: Shōjo Cosette* [A Girl Named Cosette], an animated television series of fifty-two half-hour episodes that was directed by Hiroaki Sakurai and broadcast as part of Nippon Animation's World Masterpiece Theatre throughout 2007; and East Press's *Re Mizeraburu*, a 2009 graphic novel in its Manga de Dokuha (or 'Reading Through with Manga') series that was republished in French by Soleil Manga in 2011.[22]

There have been over thirty adaptations in the World Masterpiece Theatre since it was founded in 1975: each series retold popular stories like Mark Twain's *The Adventures of Tom Sawyer* (1980) and Louisa May Alcott's *Little Women* (1987) and was screened weekly at 7.30 pm on Sundays on Fuji Television to allow for family viewing, akin to parents and their children reading stories together. In keeping with this family focus, *Shōjo Cosette* frames the story not around Jean Valjean but around the *shōjo* [girl] he adopts, the waif Cosette: a central character with whom the primary target audience of pre-teenage and teenage girls could identify, and whose trials through puberty dramatize Hugo's narrative interest in self-determination. The *shōjo* often personifies a transitional identity in anime and manga between childlike powerlessness and adult agency that is illustrated in how Cosette reckons with an upsetting past and an uncertain future. The entire novel is played out in full, making it one of the very longest adaptations of *Les Misérables*, but the plot is restructured and at times altered, notably regarding the fates of the street urchin Gavroche, whom Cosette saves from his wounds after the storming of the barricade, and the relentless police inspector Javert, who resists his suicidal thoughts thanks to a more positive epiphany after his final confrontation with Valjean. The result is a child's odyssey through Hugo's world that follows Cosette from the first episode, when her mother Fantine leaves her in the care of the Thénardiers, through to the last, when Valjean dies, and the now grown Cosette retraces that initial journey to Montreuil-sur-Mer from the opening scenes, but this time to visit her mother's grave together with her husband Marius and their own daughter. Each episode ends with a short preview of the next, narrated by two spirited young spectators who express their responses to the story, such as their fury with the Thénardiers' brutal treatment of Cosette. In addition, the sprightly opening theme song and the nostalgic end credits are both delivered by a female voice who sings of maternal love and the inevitability of growing up, which itself was in part reflected by the real-time viewing experience of watching the series (screened weekly over fifty-two weeks) across an entire year. The series as a whole risks affirming a normative femininity through Cosette, as might be expected from a character who has been accused of mere ornamentalism in Hugo's hands,[23] but it also relies on the ambiguous combination of strength and vulnerability that is emblematic of *shōjo* works and their 'consciousness-raising' of women's agency in post-war Japan.[24]

East Press's manga offers a quite different experience of *Les Misérables* in both its concerns and its structure. The Manga de Dokuha series adapts a more overtly adult selection of socially conscious titles, selling its books through convenience stores such as 7-Eleven. Series producer Kosuke Maruo and his collaborators 'thought that maybe we could get people to read well-known works perceived as tough reads by turning them into manga', preserving their subject matter but creating a fast-moving and easily accessible adaptation.[25] The first seventeen titles, from foreign novels such as Tolstoy's *War and Peace* (2007) to Japanese texts like Takiji Kobayashi's *Kanikōsen* [The Cannery Boat] (2007), sold over 900,000 copies, enabling this manga series to branch out and adapt non-literary titles such as Karl Marx's *Das Kapital* (2008) and John Stuart Mill's *On Liberty* (2011). Soleil's short preface introduces the series's goals, stating that this manga is not intended to replace Hugo's 'fabulous work' but to appeal to new and familiar readers alike with 'a new and yet valid take' on the novel.[26] If *Shōjo Cosette* mimics the scale of its source text but not strictly its focus, this 200-page manga rapidly contracts the dimensions of Hugo's 1500-page epic. Cutting out many characters like Éponine and narrative arcs such as her love triangle with Marius and Cosette, it shifts attention firmly onto Valjean to set the themes of individual accountability and social injustice more squarely within the context of adulthood. Beginning with Valjean's arrival at Bishop Myriel's and ending when he is finally set free by Javert, Valjean's ongoing redemption is central. Occasional reminders appear between the panels to note differences or omissions as regards Hugo's novel, such as when Javert commits suicide in front of Valjean (Figure

Fig. 5.1. 'Javert's suicide'. *Les Misérables*, by Victor Hugo © Variety Art works, East Press Co Ltd © Éditions Soleil for the French edition. Translation: Anne Mallevay

5.1), although such annotations are not comprehensive. In these closing pages, no explanation is given for the altered ending. Frames of a teary-eyed Valjean, staring smilingly into a new dawn now that he is free from his pursuer, unfold alongside images of Marius embracing Cosette as he recovers from his injuries, hinting at the marriage to come but giving no similar indication of the events it triggers and of Valjean's death. (Figures 5.2.i & 5.2.ii) In a clear instance of adaptations interacting with one another as much as with their primary source, the climax is strikingly similar to that of Bille August's 1998 Hollywood film adaptation and borrows the same uplifting denouement in order to reiterate the values of human compassion in a seemingly uncompassionate world.

These different narrative approaches to adapting the themes of *Les Misérables* are actualized through each version's use of different medial forms. *Shōjo Cosette* and *Re Mizeraburu* accentuate the aesthetic possibilities allowed by Japanese anime and manga in their retelling of Hugo's story, thereby revealing both continuity and originality in their relationships to that novel. As cartoons, both adaptations find inspiration in what Laurence Porter has called Hugo's 'extraordinary visual imagination', which is 'both impressionistic — sensitive to changes of light — and cinematic, aware of varying angles of vision'.[27] These attributes are often visible in tandem. After Fantine loses her job and is forced to sell her hair for Cosette's upkeep, contrast and viewpoint work together to evoke her ever-worsening degradation as she faces the harsh conditions of winter: 'The sky is a basement window. The whole day is a cellar'. Hugo's narrator temporarily pulls back his gaze from the destitution and positions the reader in the doorway to Fantine's room as Marguerite arrives so as to intensify the shock that both she and the reader feel upon realizing that Fantine has now sold her two front teeth: 'The candle lit her face. It was a bloody smile. Reddish saliva besmirched the corners of her mouth and inside her mouth was a black hole' (I.5.x: 155–56).[28] How each adaptation handles this notorious episode typifies their uses of the anime and manga style.

Although *Shōjo Cosette* is not averse to showing scenes of bloody suffering, such as the massacre at the barricade, the material violence of Fantine's descent is softened. Rather than sell her teeth and then her body, episodes 7 and 8 see her evicted from her room and forced to live in riverside shacks with the other *misérables*. Understandably for a family television series, Fantine's prostitution is avoided entirely. She only commits the public assault that will catch Javert's eye when two drunken men mistake her for a beggar and mockingly force snow down the back of her dress. The emotional power of her misfortune is, however, greatly emphasized by this adaptation's characteristic modes of representation. By using twelve drawings per second, as opposed to much Western animation which favours up to double that figure, anime treats time in a ponderous manner, whereby movement becomes more limited, and both gesture and facial expression are elementary rather than complex. Such 'animetism', as Thomas Lamarre categorizes it, favours design over movement and flattens the layers of the image, obliging the eye to slide across the whole frame rather than concentrate on one particular aspect.[29] Fantine's farewell to Marguerite feels agonizingly slow as she walks out onto the street. The camera alternates between interior and high-angle shots before

Fig. 5.2. (i) 'Marius and Cosette reunited'. *Les Misérables*, Victor Hugo © Variety Art works, East Press Co Ltd © Éditions Soleil for the French edition. Translation: Anne Mallevay

FIG. 5.2. (ii) 'Valjean's freedom'. *Les Misérables*, by Victor Hugo © Variety Art works, East Press Co Ltd © Éditions Soleil for the French edition. Translation: Anne Mallevay.

Fig. 5.3. 'Fantine loses her home'. *Les Misérables: Shōjo Cosette* (2007). Dir. Hiroaki Sakurai: Nippon Animation.

resting at street level, leaving the viewer free to consider both Fantine's fate and the town's apparent indifference towards her: nearly a dozen people are standing along the roadside, several with their backs turned, while tall townhouses loom above, their dull beige and grey hues sharply contrasting with the warm peach and violet tones of the early evening sky above (Figure 5.3). Later, as Fantine sells her hair, the frame slowly pans across an extreme close-up of her welling eyes, moving from the left, where her long golden locks can still be seen, to the right, where her hair has now been sheared. 'Cosette, now you won't be cold. My hair will clothe you,' she quietly declares, her voice giving way to the sound of the scissors' blades which continue to echo even as the image fades to black (Figures 5.4.i & 5.4.ii).

Where *Shōjo Cosette* utilizes colourful paintwork, a contemplative pace, and measured dialogue thanks to its animated and episodic form, *Re Mizeraburu* relies on a yet more heavily visualized mode to convey its meanings as simply and as instantaneously as possible.[30] Dialogue is kept to a minimum so that the panels do not become cluttered, and each image is made all the more striking thanks to its monochrome artwork. After her hair has been cut off, a stern-faced Fantine stares out from the page, her head slightly tilted downwards but her eyes looking directly ahead as open-mouthed onlookers behind her on each side look aghast (Figure 5.5). Her determination to provide for Cosette is further stressed by two thought bubbles on either side of her head, circled not in the usual crisp line seen with dialogue but with a coarse, almost throbbing border to suggest the pulsating nature of her mind: 'The hair only got me six francs! I must find the rest' (p. 39). She is

FIG. 5.4. (i) 'Fantine sells her hair'. *Les Misérables: Shōjo Cosette* (2007). Dir. Hiroaki Sakurai: Nippon Animation. (ii) 'Fantine sells her hair'. *Les Misérables: Shōjo Cosette* (2007). Dir. Hiroaki Sakurai: Nippon Animation.

Fig. 5.5. 'Fantine sells her hair'. *Les Misérables*, by Victor Hugo © Variety Art works, East Press Co Ltd © Éditions Soleil for the French edition. Translation: Anne Mallevay.

next seen with darkened lips and eyeliner, escorting a grotesque man off the street whose grinning mouth becomes his defining feature in a symbolic association of the sex trade with male consumerism. The subsequent revelation that she has sold her teeth entails fewer than one hundred words of dialogue, devoting more space to the visual portrayal of her misery (Figures 5.6.i & 5.6.ii). Fantine first appears in a near full-body image, her eyes closed in resignation and the strap of her nightdress slipping down her left shoulder after reading the latest letter from Thénardier demanding more money for Cosette's needs. In the page's largest panel, a close-up of her face then depicts her gaping and bloodied mouth, with her teeth missing and tears crowning her cheeks, alongside a final extreme close-up of that mouth and her tear-drenched nostrils (p. 51). In effect, little dialogue is required for these scenes to be swiftly understood, and the discomfort that Hugo intended his reader to feel when witnessing Fantine's troubles is made all the more forceful by the hauntingly frozen nature of each image.

Otherness and Alterity in the Adaptive Process

As seasoned adaptors, both World Masterpiece Theatre and the Manga de Dokuha series provide a revealing corpus for any discussion of how works like *Les Misérables* adapt to new aesthetic, cultural, and historical spaces. In the first instance, turning to these versions responds to the widely recognized need within adaptation studies for an intermedial and intercultural approach, itself directly relevant to a novel that has been adapted as prolifically as *Les Misérables.* At the same time, anime and manga engage with questions of otherness that are significant not only within *Les Misérables* and throughout its afterlives, but are also germane to their own status within the global market. In an account of the transnational practices of translation and adaptation that, like the present argument, cites The Vapors's 'Turning Japanese' song, Mark O'Thomas persuasively highlights the ethical importance of respecting alterity when importing source texts into new spaces, in this case through the media of film and theatre. Referencing Robert Lepage's concept of 'tradaptation', 'where the intentionality is not to censor or make palatable the original for the target culture but in a sense to force the target culture to confront itself through its exposure to the rewritten "original"', O'Thomas teases out the cultural power relations inherent in the tensions between strategies that either 'domesticate' or 'foreignize' a source, to recall Lawrence Venuti's influential formulation. Rather than colonize a source's cultural difference within a narrative of sameness, he advocates Venuti's use of translation as a means of preserving rather than eradicating that otherness: 'By foregrounding both its relation to its own culture as well as the culture and text of the original, the adaptation could provide a new, foreignized voice that speaks in a language other than, but paradoxically of, its own'.[31] The idea of paradox that O'Thomas raises in the name of complex relationships between cultures is particularly discernible where adaptations of *Les Misérables* are concerned, although in ways that further problematize the binary opposition of 'domestic' and 'foreign'.

Indeed, the anime and manga versions of *Les Misérables* at once reinforce the ethical imperative of acknowledging human difference and self-consciously complicate the

Fig. 5.6. (i) 'Fantine sells her body, including her teeth'. *Les Misérables*, by Victor Hugo © Variety Art works, East Press Co Ltd © Éditions Soleil for the French edition. Translation: Anne Mallevay.

FIG. 5.6. (ii) 'Fantine sells her body, including her teeth'. *Les Misérables*, by Victor Hugo © Variety Art works, East Press Co Ltd © Éditions Soleil for for the French edition. Translation: Anne Mallevay.

signalling of such difference. This paradox is a necessary consequence of both the source novel's narrative commitment to promoting social inclusion and the ability of anime and manga to dissolve rather than consolidate cultural specificity: Hugo's understanding that all peoples are not equal in the modern world is matched by his desire to overcome such differences and promote a human commonality. Such a desire finds a highly effective channel in anime and manga, since these are forms that Koichi Iwabuchi, amongst other critics, has defined by way of their *mukokuseki* [statelessness]: a 'culturally odourless' condition in which ethnicity and national identity are purposely effaced so as to broaden the appeal of anime and manga in a global market, but through a genre that is recognizably Japanese.[32] In these respects, if The Vapors' song title is understood literally (in the sense of actually becoming Japanese), its chorus is not as straightforward an articulation of what happens to *Les Misérables* in these adaptations as it first appears. But if it is read figuratively, as in the sensation of simply becoming different thanks to a transformative experience (like falling in love in the song's verses), then the notion of fully fixed categories of identity is productively challenged. This more metaphorical interpretation could be brought out more explicitly in O'Thomas's otherwise revealing argument concerning the function of alterity in the adaptive process.

As anime and manga adaptations, *Shōjo Cosette* and *Re Mizeraburu* might be said to 'turn' *Les Misérables* Japanese through a unique aesthetic style, but this style is not in itself 'oriental'. Anime and manga involve 'racial mixing and cultural blurring', as Amy Shirong Lu outlines: 'It is hard to detect any typical Japanese physiognomy from the characters — instead, a kind of hybrid global "look" hovers on their faces and bodies'.[33] In *Shōjo Cosette*, the blonde-haired and pale-skinned heroine is strikingly un-Japanese, but her large eyes, oval face, and sharp profile prevent her from being entirely Western either, as is true for all the characters (Figure 5.7). The

Fig. 5.7. 'Cosette as a waif'. *Les Misérables: Shōjo Cosette* (2007). Dir. Hiroaki Sakurai: Nippon Animation.

settings and costumes recall the tastes of nineteenth-century Europe, but greater attention is paid to creative colouring and emotional expression than to carefully researched historical or cultural distinction. Likewise, prolific anime composer Hayato Matsuo's romantic score draws on orchestral signatures that are conventional in Western adaptations of classic literature, but the theme tune, which sets the tone for each episode, mixes more contemporary percussion, wind-instruments like the recorder, and soft vocals, which are more reminiscent of Asian musical traditions. Similar traits are evident in *Re Mizeraburu*. Even though Valjean eventually ties his hair back into a neat ponytail that faintly recalls feudal nobility in Japan, for example, the Western style of his costume (his top hat and cravat) contrasts with other aspects of his appearance. The book's implied soundtrack is equally lacking in clear particularity. Manga's characteristic use of onomatopoeia, including the emboldened 'Waaaaahh!' that increasingly imprints itself across Fantine's later frames, distils human emotions to a basic, if not primal, form, and is enhanced by a corresponding use of commonly recognized symbols, such as when Marius first sees Cosette: an exclamation mark bursts forth next to his head and hearts appear in both his eyes (Figure 5.8). The simplicity of visuals, expressions, and gestures in each version ensures their openness to multiple cultures at once.

The appropriation of *Les Misérables* in these forms encourages a less anxious response to the 'cultural blurring' inherent in anime and manga than some commentators have put forward. Where Iwabuchi wonders whether these media have progressively erased Japan's specificity in order to succeed within a transnational entertainment culture, and others fret that 'the exportation of a frilly youth culture' trivializes the country's identity as 'infantile and superficial', Lu proposes models of cultural politics through which Japan positively creates 'everywhere-nowhere' narratives.[34] These are 'imaginary spaces of identification' that travel easily across international markets by softening national idiosyncrasies, precisely to intensify Japan's cultural influence and to allow it to be integral to, and individual within, East Asia as a central point between East and West.[35] When reviewed with an eye towards Japan's history with France, such narratives take on increased ideological power and point towards the persistent lure of the French Revolutionary dream for a universal republic. In her reflections on the ground-breaking success of Riyoko Ikeda's shōjo manga *The Rose of Versailles* (1972–1973), Anne McKnight discusses the series's historicist focus on 'the emergence of the "people"' before and during the Revolution through the experience of both noble and commoner girls. Rather than perpetuate the defeatism and disillusionment that many male activists explored on Japan's Left, Ikeda developed 'an appeal to "Frenchness" as a site of universal popular rights' in this manga, through which France is perceived as 'the historical origin of one discussion of rights that provides an alternative to, and supersedes, the version of "rights" at play in the American-imposed Constitution of post-war Japan'.[36] France, in turn, offers a rupture within the post-war geopolitical power axis through its historically idealized associations with popular sovereignty.

FIG. 5.8. 'Marius falls in love with Cosette'. *Les Misérables*, by Victor Hugo © Variety Art works, East Press Co Ltd © Éditions Soleil for the French edition. Translation: Anne Mallevay.

A Franco-Japanese Fraternity

The ways in which anime and manga resist particularism in favour of an imagined melting pot of identities resonate with the democratic ethos that pervades *Les Misérables*. To listen to Hugo's voice necessarily brings Japanese translators and adaptors into contact with this writer's notion of a unified human race. Unlike Balzac and Dickens, who used the phonetic potential of writing to let readers hear different accents in their novels, Hugo elided such possibilities so that all his characters sound the same. Their different registers are but linguistic counterparts to social strata, enabling the novel to stress an underlying shared quality in this fictional world.[37] The unity that the novel posits within France is one that reflects the wider connections between all countries, as symbolized by the hybrid nature of the French capital: 'Paris is Athens, Rome, Sybaris, Jerusalem, Pantin' (III.I.X.: 488). *Les Misérables* thus discloses a worldview that seeks to look both towards and, moreover, past the borders between cultural spaces and national identities. 'Through the transformational power of both empathy and metaphor, *this* can be *that*, the self can also be another', as Kathryn Grossman has demonstrated in what she defines as Hugo's 'system of continuous permutations' in the novel.[38] Hugo depicts not only a world divided by prejudice and self-interest, but also one in which disjunction generates harmony through 'the hidden connections beyond apparent gaps, differences, and antitheses' in order to allow for his Romantic vision.[39]

Looking deep into the past and gazing ahead beyond the present, the narrative confirms that 'the view from the top of the barricade', to recall one chapter title (V.I.V), is spatially and temporally panoramic. From this perspective, the divide between vice and virtue collapses. A criminal outcast like Valjean transforms into a heroic martyr as surely as Inspector Javert's law-abiding honour betrays 'all the bad of good' (I.8.iii: 243). The corresponding qualitative distinction between the worthless and the valuable is similarly complicated by the narrator's digressions on various topics that elaborate upon the transformative logic of his Romantic vision: the seemingly tangential becomes central when the French defeat at Waterloo heralds France's potential triumph in a new democratic age, or when the sewage of Paris converts into the nurturing manure of French agriculture in a powerful metaphor for the value of society's detritus and what Victor Brombert sees as the novel's ethos of 'salvation from below'.[40] The contexts of such a poetic vision were social and spiritual for Hugo, inherited from the inclusive mindset of the 1789 Declaration of the Rights of Man and of the Citizen, and also invoking the sensibility towards man's shared divine origins that touched so many members of his Romantic generation. For Hugo, no element of the world exists in isolation: all things are part of an endlessly creative cycle that is the work of an unknowable divine power, as intuited by the kindly Bishop Myriel in the edifying opening chapters. In *Les Misérables*, freedom, equality, and brotherhood stipulate both moral justice and cosmic truth.

Hugo's egalitarian stance against capital punishment, social poverty, slavery, imperialism, and military violence made him a champion for all peoples and especially for victims of discrimination. After his novel was published, he described himself as a 'patriot of humanity', observing the Revolution's 'principle of radiation' — the transmission of fundamental human rights outwards from revolutionary France to the modern world entire:

> Social problems transcend borders. The wounds of the human race cover the globe — they are not contained within the blue or red lines marked on the world map. Wherever men are in ignorance and in despair, wherever women sell themselves for bread, wherever children suffer for lack of an instructive book or a warming hearth, *Les Misérables* knocks at the door and says: 'Open me, I am here for you'.[41]

Not only did he craft archetypal characters for a breadth of reader identification; he also maximized his novel's capacity to incorporate different genres, from classical epic to romantic melodrama, blending numerous tastes at once. The goal, as stated in the preface, was to inform and to transform the future: 'as long as ignorance and misery exist in this world, books like the one you are about to read are, perhaps, not entirely useless' (xlv). By narrating a story in which all fates interconnect, Hugo uncovers a shared and changeable existence in which we are all implicated. This plea for a more humane world where human compassion would know no limits, and where misery would no longer blight society, is undeniably romanticized. As one of France's 'great men', Hugo's devotion to the values of 1789 to immunize the human race against the social and ideological diseases of the past has been criticized for its utopianism.[42] But in seeking to access an all-encompassing view of the world around him throughout his literary and political career, he made a firm impression upon different classes and cultures. The international outpouring of grief for his massive state funeral in 1885 accentuated Hugo's ability to strike a connection with readers everywhere.

Both *Shōjo Cosette* and *Re Mizeraburu*, as part of the latest chapter in Japan's appropriation of *Les Misérables*, demonstrate that artworks with universalizing aspirations like Hugo's novel galvanize the transcultural, multimedial, and transmedial process of adaptation. As examples of media with a characteristically indeterminate style, they do so with marked vigour. Hugo designed *Les Misérables* not simply to 'be' French or to 'turn' foreign in its travels, but to question such divisive lines so that a common humanity could be appreciated from different angles. In its very form, the novel contains practical encouragements of various sorts for its own adaptation: up to a third of the text is digression, so can quickly be cut for forms where such narrative discussion would be difficult to represent, such as the stage, while adaptors can dilate or contract their own visions of the narrative around the dramatic focal point of Valjean's plight just as the narrator himself does. But it is the novel's humanist dream that is the lifeblood of its afterlife. The famous preface is a stimulus for the novel's reception: it spurs audiences and adaptors alike into action by implying that any reading and retelling of the story is a humanitarian obligation. Anime and manga set a less aggrandized but equally universal agenda in which 'turning' source material Japanese through the act of adaptation ultimately problematizes the binary opposition of foreign/domestic. Works are 'othered' rather than simply foreignized in order to afford a glimpse of a different way of being along an undetermined horizon. In a twenty-first century that, paradoxically, is becoming ever more connected and yet remains ever divided, that horizon is as important now as it was in the nineteenth century.

Notes to Chapter 5

1. In comparison, there have been nearly eighty live-action film adaptations of the *Carmen* story since 1906, which is considered to be probably the most adapted story on screen after Bram Stoker's *Dracula* (1897) (Phil Powrie and others, *Carmen on Film: A Cultural History* (Bloomington: Indiana University Press, 2007), p. x). *Les Misérables* scores highly in such terms, especially as it is a more sprawling source text in comparison.
2. See Bradley Stephens, '*Les Misérables* and the Twenty-first Century', in *'Les Misérables' and its Afterlives*, ed. by Grossman and Stephens, pp. 191–204. In the introduction to this volume, Kathryn Grossman and I also note that, even though adaptations of Hugo's fiction and theatrical plays have been the subject of considerable discussion, *Les Misérables* had previously not been considered in isolation or beyond the media of stage and screen that have tended to dominate adaptation studies. Moreover, such discussion for the most part was open only to Francophone readers (p. 4). Due to constraints of coverage and expertise at the time of publication, Japanese culture was only touched upon in *'Les Misérables' and its Afterlives.*
3. Deborah Cartmell and Imelda Whelehan, 'A Short History of Adaptation Studies in the Classroom', in *Teaching Adaptations*, ed. by Deborah Cartmell and Imelda Whelehan (Basingstoke: Palgrave Macmillan, 2014), pp. 1–10 (p. 1).
4. Dennis Cutchins, Lawrence Raw and James M. Welsh, 'Introduction', in *The Pedagogy of Adaptation*, ed. by Dennis Cutchins, Lawrence Raw and James M. Welsh (Lanham, MD: Scarecrow Press, 2010), pp. xi–xix (p. xi).
5. The 1923 film *Ah! Ah! Mujō* ('Ah! Misery') is usually noted as the first Japanese screen adaptation, directed in two parts by Kiyochiko Ushihara and Yoshinobu Ikeda. When recalling her work as Akira Kurosawa's principal assistant, however, Teruyo Nogami claims that the first Japanese film of *Les Misérables* was produced in 1910 by the M. Pathe Company (*Waiting on the Weather: Making Movies with Akira Kurosawa*, trans. by Juliet Winters Carpenter (Berkeley, CA: Stone Bridge Press, 2006), p. 35). However, this film is not listed elsewhere, including in the comprehensive filmography that is available in *L'Œuvre de Victor Hugo à l'écran*, ed. by Gleizes, pp. 245–52. Nogami may have been referring to a Japanese release of a foreign version. In 1906, Shōkichi Umeya used profits from the exhibition of films from the Pathé Brothers' Singapore office to set up the M. Pathe studio, echoing the name in order to harness the French producers' reputation without their knowledge (Jasper Sharp, *Historical Dictionary of Japanese Cinema* (Lanham, MD: Scarecrow Press, 2011), p.153). That year, the Pathé Brothers's short *Le Chemineau* (directed by Albert Capellani) premiered in America, and there were also two multi-part American shorts released in 1909 which could equally have been redistributed by M. Pathe.
6. Hugo's outrage is noted in many Chinese history textbooks, and a bronze bust of the writer, with words taken from his attack on the British and French governments in a letter dated 25 November 1861, was unveiled in the old palace for the one hundred and fiftieth anniversary of the looting, as reported in 'On the 150th Anniversary of the Sacking of the Old Summer Palace, China Reflects', *China Daily*, 18 October 2010 <http://www.chinadaily.com.cn/china/2010-10/18/content_11425824.htm> [accessed 24 October 2019].
7. See Richard Sims, 'France', in *The Iwakura Mission in America and Europe: A New Assessment*, ed. by Ian Nish (Richmond: Curzon Press, 1998), pp. 45–55.
8. Akira Mizuno, 'Stylistic Norms in the Early Meiji Period: From Chinese Influences to European Influences', in *Translation and Translation Studies in the Japanese Context*, ed. by Nana Sato-Rossberg and Judy Wakabayahsi (London: Continuum, 2012), pp. 92–114 (p. 108).
9. See M. Cody Poulton, *Spirits of Another Sort: The Plays of Izumi Kyōka* (Ann Arbor: Michigan Centre for Japanese Studies, 2001), pp. 25–27; and Siyuan Liu, 'The Impact of *Shinpa* on Early Chinese *Huaju*', *Asian Theatre Journal*, 23.2 (2006), 342–55.

10. Mark Silver, *Purloined Letters: Cultural Borrowing and Japanese Crime Literature 1868–1937* (Honolulu: University of Hawaii Press, 2008), pp. 64–65. This version was the basis for Lu Xun's Chinese translation in 1903, although it was overshadowed by Su Manshu's very loose serialized translation of the French original that same year.
11. Marius B. Jansen, *The Making of Modern Japan* (Cambridge, MA: Harvard University Press, 2002), p. 484.
12. Ibid., p. 490.
13. Nogami, *Waiting on the Weather*, p. 38.
14. Naoki Inagaki, 'Victor Hugo aujourd'hui au Japon', *Revue des Deux Mondes*, (January 2002), 94–98 (p. 98).
15. Olivier Vanhée uses the term 'New Japanism' to convey Western excitement in his conference paper 'The Production of a "Manga Culture" in France', *Asia Culture Forum* (2006) <http://www.ceri-sciencespo.org/themes/manga/documents/texte_production_vanhee.pdf> [accessed 24 October 2019]. Frederik L. Schodt, in contrast, deploys it in a more uncertain context, asking if the slowdown of the manga market since its peak in the 1990s might constitute a late twentieth-century equivalent of how nineteenth-century Western art collectors pursued *ukiyo-e* or woodblock prints just as their popularity was dying out in their native country ('The View from North America: Manga as Late-Twentieth-century Japonisme?', in *Manga's Cultural Crossroads*, ed. by Jacqueline Berndt and Bettina Kümmerling-Meibauer (New York & Abingdon: Routledge, 2013), pp. 19–26.
16. See the art historian Brigitte Koyama-Richard's *Mille ans de manga* (Paris: Flammarion, 2007), which tracks the history of Japanese narrative art as the ancestor of manga.
17. The creative resources that animators and cartoonists foster, in addition to their status as 'artist-entrepreneurs', have also been essential to the emergence of Japan's video-game industry (Yuko Aoyama and Hiro Izushi, 'Hardware Gimmick or Cultural Innovation? Technological, Cultural, and Social Foundations of the Japanese Video Game Industry', *Research Policy* 32.3 (2003), 423–44 (p. 439)). *Les Misérables* was, in fact, adapted into a fan-made Japanese combat game by the developer Takase in 1998 entitled *ArmJoe* (a play on the novel's Japanese title of *Aa Mujō* [Ah! Misery]).
18. Susan J. Napier, *Anime: From Akira to Howl's Moving Castle*, 2nd edn (New York: Palgrave Macmillan, 2005), pp. 7–8.
19. Mark W. MacWilliams, 'Introduction', in *Japanese Visual Culture: Explorations in the World of Manga and Anime*, ed. by Mark W. MacWilliams (Armonk: M. E. Sharpe, 2008), pp. 3–25 (p. 10).
20. Dani Cavallaro, *Anime and the Art of Adaptation* (Jefferson, NC: McFarland, 2010), p. 14.
21. Paul Wells, 'Classic Literature and Animation: All Adaptations are Equal, but Some are More Equal than Others', in *The Cambridge Companion to Literature on Screen*, ed. by Deborah Cartmell and Imelda Whelehan (Cambridge University Press, 2007), pp. 199–211 (p. 199).
22. Victor Hugo, *Re Mizeraburu*, Manga de Dokuha (Tokyo: East Press Co. Ltd, 2009); *Les Misérables: manga de Dokuha*, trans. by Anne Mallevay (Paris: Éditions Soleil, 2011). The others I have identified are: two anime adaptations for the television programme *Manga Sekai Mukashi Banashi* entitled *Shōjo Cosette* (1977) and *Aa Mujō* (1978); another anime, *Jean Valjean Monogatari* (1979), from Toei Animation; and Takahiro Arai's serial manga version, which began appearing in September 2013 in *Monthly Shōnen Sunday* magazine.
23. See Nicole Savy, 'Cosette, un personnage qui n'existe pas', in *Lire 'Les Misérables'*, ed. by Guy Rosa and Anne Ubersfeld (Paris: Corti, 1985), pp. 173–90.
24. Fusami Ogi, 'Female Subjectivity and Shōjo Manga', *Journal of Popular Culture*, 36.4 (2003), 780–803 (p. 783).
25. 'Novels Under Manga Cover: Convenience Stores Go Literary', *Daily Yomiuri Online*, 25 July 2008 <http://web.archive.org/web/20080802010605/http://www.yomiuri.co.jp/dy/national/20080725TDY13001.htm> [accessed 24 October 2019].
26. Hugo, *Les Misérables*, trans. by Mallevay, p. 4. Future references will be given in parentheses. Translations, as for all this chapter's French citations, are my own unless otherwise stated.
27. Laurence M. Porter, *Victor Hugo* (New York: Twayne, 1999), p. 30.
28. Quotations from *Les Misérables* are taken from Julie Rose's English translation (London:

Vintage, 2008) and are referenced by part, book, and chapter number in alternating Roman and Arabic numerals in parentheses, followed by the page number.

29. Lamarre contrasts this state with 'cinematism' in his book *The Anime Machine: A Media Theory of Animation* (Minneapolis: University of Minnesota Press, 2009), pp. 9–10.
30. Schodt estimates that a 320-page manga may be read in around twenty minutes, enabling these books to be consumed with considerable stealth (*Dreamland Japan: Writings on Modern Manga* (Berkeley, CA: Stone Bridge, 1996), p. 26).
31. Mark O'Thomas, 'Turning Japanese: Translation, Adaptation, and the Ethics of Trans-National Exchange', in *Adaptation Studies*, ed. by Albrecht-Crane and Cutchins, pp. 46–60 (pp. 50–51).
32. Koichi Iwabuchi, '"Soft" Nationalism and Narcissism: Japanese Popular Culture Goes Global', *Asian Studies Review*, 26.4 (2002), 447–69 (p. 455).
33. Amy Shirong Lu, 'The Many Faces of Internationalization in Japanese Anime', *Animation*, 3.2 (2008), 169–87 (p. 172).
34. Lu, 'The Many Faces of Internationalization in Japanese Anime', pp. 176–83.
35. Christine R. Yano, 'Wink on Pink: Interpreting Japanese Cute as it Grabs the Global Headlines', *Journal of Asian Studies*, 68.3 (2009), 681–88 (p. 684).
36. Anne McKnight, 'Frenchness and Transformation in Japanese Subculture, 1972–2004', in *Mechademia 5: Fanthropologies*, ed. by Frenchy Lunning (Minneapolis: University of Minnesota Press, 2010), pp. 118–37 (pp. 122–29). This link may in part explain why France has the largest manga market outside Japan.
37. See David Bellos, 'Sounding Out *Les Misérables*', *Dix-Neuf*, 20.3–4 (2016), 241–51.
38. Kathryn M. Grossman, *Figuring Transcendence in 'Les Misérables': Hugo's Romantic Sublime* (Carbondale: Southern Illinois University Press, 1994), p. 118.
39. Ibid., p. 4.
40. Victor Brombert, *Victor Hugo and the Visionary Novel* (Cambridge, MA: Harvard University Press, 1984), pp. 86–139.
41. Victor Hugo, 'Lettre à M. Daelli', 18 October 1862, in *Œuvres complètes: Roman II*, ed. by Annette and Guy Rosa (Paris: Laffont, 1985), p. 1154.
42. One oft-cited blind-spot lies in the colonial consequences of nineteenth-century France's 'civilizing mission'. Hugo's opinions on European colonialism are far from unquestioning, however. Both his support of the need to disseminate the right to freedom to all regions (in socio-political, economic, and religious terms), and his outrage at the violence into which that 'mission' descended, need to be taken into account. See Franck Laurent, *Victor Hugo face à la conquête de l'Algérie* (Paris: Maisonnneuve & Larose, 2001).

CHAPTER 6

❖

The Kafka Image: Interpretations of a 'Classic' in the New Generation of Graphic Adaptation

Juliane Blank

As one of the most popular German-speaking authors of world literature, Franz Kafka has been the centre of a veritable celebrity cult in popular culture. Photographs of the author with the 'intense, creaturely gaze', especially his last portrait from 1924, have become icons of modern literature, and even, one might say, of modernity itself.[1] On the internet it is possible to buy an endless variety of t-shirts, mugs, tote bags, and other merchandise products with Kafka's face on them.[2] Images of the author play an important part in the Franz Kafka 'picture show' we see in present-day popular culture.[3]

One of the first writers to consider the relevance of Kafka's photographs to the interpretation of his works was Walter Benjamin who, in his 1934 essay on Kafka, set out to 'read' a childhood photograph as a key to his writing.[4] In her study on *Kafka and Photography*, Carolin Duttlinger also comments on the role of photographs of the author, both as an inspiration to those interpreting Kafka's texts and as objects of literary fandom:

> Kafka's photographs have always had a peculiarly iconic status in relation to his work. In themselves collectors' items, they are amongst the most recognizable of all authors' portraits, and continue to bear a persistent yet unfathomable significance for his writings in the minds of his readers.[5]

Under these circumstances it is not surprising that graphic adaptations of Kafka's works also rely on the power of photographic representations of the author, most notably the famous portrait taken only months before Kafka's death in 1924 (Figure 6.1).[6] In recent graphic adaptations, from the 1990s onwards, this canonical photographic image of Kafka is featured in more than one sense. It does not only provide a picture of the author, it also evokes Kafka's 'image' — in the sense of reputation — in popular discourse. It summons stereotypical popular notions of Kafka as a cryptic, even hermetic, writer whose works revolve around issues of psychological alienation, depression, loneliness, and the terrors of the modern world.

FIG. 6.1. Kafka in 1923/24, age forty © Archiv Klaus Wagenbach.

In this chapter, I will argue that popular notions of Kafka have had a substantial influence on recent adaptations of his works in comic books and graphic novels. While absorbing established approaches to adapting Kafka's works, however, these comic books and graphic novels also create new strategies of visualization.

This article will focus on three types of 'image': the image of Kafka's appearance and its use in visual adaptations; the 'image' in the sense of the notion of Kafka as a writer and as a person; and the 'iconography' of visual adaptations that forms new traditions incorporating the two former kinds of image. Comparing various adaptations of Kafka's works, primarily of 'Das Urteil' ['The Judgement'] (1912), *Die Verwandlung* [*The Metamorphosis*] (1915), and *Der Process* [*The Trial*] (1914/15), I will argue that since the 1990s we have witnessed a new generation of graphic adaptation and that this generation has formed distinctive strategies of adaptation. These strategies seem to be indicative of a new, distinctly postmodern approach to canonical literature that is particularly vivid in graphic adaptation.

Kafka, Adaptation, and Canonicity

How does graphic adaptation relate to the concept of a literary canon? Referring to adaptation in different media, Julie Sanders states that it 'both appears to require and to perpetuate the existence of a canon'.[7] Adaptation serves as a marker of canonicity, but it does not necessarily bestow canonical status on the adapted work of literature.[8] Adaptations into comics seem to require the concept of canon even more than, for example, adaptations into film: graphic adaptations primarily choose well-established, 'classic' literary texts. The titles of anthologies and adaptation series often reflect this fact — from the famous *Classics Illustrated* series (1941-1971) to the anthology *The Graphic Canon* (2012-2013).[9]

As a Jewish writer who lived in Prague and wrote in German, Kafka has been claimed as a 'classic' of German literature, of modern literature of the Western world, and of Jewish literature.[10] His relevance as an iconic figure for the twentieth century is practically a cliché and part of his 'image' in the Western world. As early as 1941, W. H. Auden referred to Kafka as 'the artist who comes nearest to bearing the same kind of relation to our age as Dante, Shakespeare, and Goethe bore to theirs'.[11] But unlike many other important modern authors, he is not only known to literary critics and scholars: Kafka has become a representative of the modern, or rather postmodern world itself, a part of the collective cultural memory and of popular culture. His works have been adapted into various media of popular culture, including film and comics. In fact, Kafka is one of the two most adapted German-speaking authors, the other being Johann Wolfgang von Goethe.[12] But even in an international context, the number of Kafka adaptations in different countries is remarkable: there are examples from the United States, Mexico, the United Kingdom, France, Italy, the Netherlands, the Czech Republic, and even Japan. The number of appropriations picking out selected aspects of Kafka's works (for example, characters, motifs, or recognizable plot elements) and developing them into their own stories is considerably higher.[13]

One might ask why, of all authors, has Kafka become such a celebrity in the realm of adaptation? Monika Schmitz-Emans argues that his novels and stories are predestined to be visualized because these texts have a visual dimension from the start: 'Kafka's texts are themselves composed of many imaginary pictures suggested by language'.[14] Kafka and his works have always had a special relationship with the visual arts.[15] Not only did the author himself leave numerous expressive drawings, he was also interested in visual media such as photography and film. But whereas his fascination with film only becomes apparent in his letters and diaries, photography is a recurring motif in his literary works.[16] Considering his fascination with visual media, it is not surprising that Kafka often uses techniques of 'detached visual descriptions' in his writings.[17] The beginning of *The Metamorphosis* presents a vivid example: although the scene is depicted from Gregor's point of view, the passage does not focus on his reactions to the surprising and possibly frightening experience of transformation. Instead, the narrative voice merely describes the unfamiliar body of the insect in great detail. Critics have suggested that this visual quality is at least partially responsible for Kafka's continuing popularity. Therefore it is to be expected that his works have triggered an enormous number of illustrations and visual adaptations — from comic books to the cinema, to short films available on YouTube.[18]

Comic books and graphic novels based on Kafka's works are a relatively new form of visual adaptation that has been thriving for years. Russ Kick, the editor of the anthology *The Graphic Canon* even claims that we live in a 'golden age' of graphic adaptation.[19] Since its beginnings in the 1940s, graphic adaptation has changed significantly. Rocco Versaci argues that 'literary adaptations have gone through a distinct evolution, ranging from paradoxical self-effacement of the comics medium, to embracing the unique formal and stylistic elements that comics have to offer'.[20] This 'evolution' took place in the wake of the so-called graphic novel boom that has brought about a new market for conceptually and aesthetically ambitious comic books and graphic novels in the United Kingdom and the United States, but also in Germany.[21]

The term 'graphic novel' was not coined by Will Eisner, as is still claimed by some scholars, although he was the first to use it on the cover of a published book, *A Contract with God and Other Tenement Stories: A Graphic Novel* (1978). The term 'graphic novel' rapidly caught on and is now used ubiquitously by publishers in English- and German-speaking countries (i.e. in languages that use a word still connected to the 'comical' roots of comics), although some artists have criticized publishers' use of the term 'graphic novel' to sell more comic books at higher prices.[22] Before the graphic novel boom, graphic adaptations could be roughly divided into two categories: they either identified themselves with an educational mission — as is the case, for example, with the *Classics Illustrated* series — or they tended to be singular examples of an idiosyncratic artistic approach based primarily on the personal interest of an adapting artist, such as Dino Battaglia's adaptations of nineteenth-century classics of world literature in Italian magazines during the 1970s. Looking back on the changes the graphic novel boom has brought about since the 1990s, there seems to have been a wave of new adaptations that bring together the educational commitment to 'classic' stories and the individual artistic approach. Throughout this period of rejuvenation in the field of graphic adaptation, Franz Kafka has been a hugely important inspiration and a challenge to this new generation of adaptations in comics.

One of the first examples of this new wave is Robert Crumb and David Zane Mairowitz's illustrated Kafka biography originally titled *Kafka for Beginners* (1993).[23] Combining short graphic adaptations of Kafka's most popular works with an illustrated biographical text, it is not an adaptation in the classical sense. Nevertheless, *Kafka for Beginners* is a cornerstone of the new generation of Kafka adaptations. The book still contains traces of the educational mission of introducing the readers to the author's life and works, yet it also presents visual interpretations of Kafka's texts by the underground comix artist Robert Crumb. Looking back on the history and development of Kafka adaptation in comics, Crumb and Mairowitz's book has gained 'canonical status' itself, and has become an influence that later adaptations could not ignore.[24]

The innovations that *Kafka for Beginners* contributed to the field of Kafka adaptation in comics quickly solidified into a range of strategies of adaptation that are representative of a new generation of graphic adaptation. I will focus on four characteristics of the new generation of Kafka adaptation in comics, as established by Crumb and Mairowitz and used in many subsequent adaptations: 1) a respectful attitude towards Kafka's writings as complex works of art, which I will designate as 'taking Kafka seriously'; 2) the complementary approach of not taking him too seriously, i.e. creating and maintaining an ironic distance from the author, his works, and the canonical status of each of these; 3) recognition of the significance of popular readings of Kafka, which can themselves be considered canonical, for graphic adaptation; and 4) the playful, eclectic, and self-consciously postmodern attitude towards academic 'schools' and their interpretations.

Taking Kafka Seriously: Visualizing Aesthetic and Narrative Complexity

What does it mean to take Kafka seriously? As a devoted Kafka reader, one might be tempted to ask how you could take him in any other way. In the field of adaptation, however, it has been an established practice to 'reduce' an adapted work to its plot while widely ignoring its aesthetic and narrative characteristics. In contrast to that practice, in *Kafka for Beginners* Crumb and Mairowitz show a heightened interest not only in Kafka's stories, but also in their specific form. Mairowitz was one of the first to try and stay as close to Kafka's 'sound' as possible, using his own translations of the texts and often emphasizing memorable quotations like the famous first sentence of *The Metamorphosis*: 'Als Gregor Samsa eines Morgens aus unruhigen Träumen erwachte, fand er sich in seinem Bett zu einem ungeheueren Ungeziefer verwandelt' ('As Gregor Samsa awoke one morning after disturbing dreams, he found himself transformed in his bed into an enormous bug').[25] While it may seem natural for a literary adaptation to work directly with textual material from Kafka's work, earlier adaptations in fact tended to paraphrase the source text in order to make the story more accessible to the reader. Newer adaptations created in the 1990s or later, however, tend to incorporate a substantial amount of direct material from the source text or its translation.

Furthermore, many of the newer graphic adaptations experiment with techniques that create a visual equivalent to Kafka's use of narrative perspective, or rather, its effects on the reader. To a certain extent, Kafka's modernity is constituted by his predominant use of internal focalization which has been called 'einsinniges Erzählen' [narration from a single fixed perspective].[26] In visual media, the effect of internal focalization can be achieved by creating what in film is called a 'point of view' (POV) shot, 'where the camera assumes the spatial position of a character in order to show us what the character sees; the camera lens, so to say, becomes the eye of the character'.[27] In comics, the effect of 'seeing through a character's eyes' is not created by a camera, but by the manipulation of perspective in the panel. More often than using a POV perspective, though, internal focalization is recreated by using a perspective of visual narration that Martin Schüwer — modifying observations of Jean Mitry and Gilles Deleuze — has called 'halb-subjektiv' [half-subjective].[28] Adapted from the 'shot reverse shot' technique used in film dialogues, the 'half-subjective' perspective is best described as the effect of looking over a character's shoulder at what is happening in a specific scene. We do not actually see through the character's eyes, but we are presented with his or her experience, we see *with him*, as Gérard Genette put it.[29] In Crumb and Mairowitz's short adaptation of Kafka's story 'The Judgement' included in *Kafka for Beginners*, the escalating conflict between Georg Bendemann and his father, which results in Georg being sentenced to death by his father and drowning himself, is presented primarily from Georg's subjective perspective, thus reflecting the dominant narrative perspective of Kafka's text.[30] We are presented with Georg's father as Georg sees him, as a surprisingly vital man of impressive physicality. His significance is not only accentuated by the room he takes up within the panel, but also by the aureole around his head (Figure 6.2).[31] This depiction of the father seems to be infected by Georg's subjective perspective in which the supposedly old and weak man changes into the 'Schreckbild' [horrible image] of his judge.[32]

The 'half-subjective' perspective employed in this and many other panels in the adaptation, provides an opportunity to present the events as the protagonist experiences them. Many graphic adaptations use such techniques of visual narration to create effects equivalent to those of internal focalization. Graphic adaptations of *The Metamorphosis* since 2000, for example, often experiment with presenting the confusing events in the Samsa family from the perspective of the son who has suddenly been transformed into an 'Ungeziefer' (*Die Verwandlung*, p. 115).[33] Experiments like these bear witness to a certain respect shown by these new adaptations in relation to a literary text which is seen not only as the source of a good story, but also as a work of art. They are expressions of a principle of adaptation which I have referred to as 'taking Kafka seriously'. One might even ask if this attitude reflects a new idea in graphic adaptation about what exactly can be considered canonical about a text.

Fig. 6.2. Crumb and Mairowitz, *Kafka* (Berlin: Reprodukt, 2017), p. 30
© Reprodukt. Printed with kind permission.

Not Taking Kafka Too Seriously: Visual Humour and Irony

Taking Kafka seriously can also mean not taking him too seriously. Adaptations of the new generation often have a keen eye for the humorous aspects of Kafka's works, and they sometimes create new comical effects by generating visual irony.[34] In *Kafka for Beginners*, Crumb and Mairowitz pay reverence to Kafka as a unique writer and person, but at the same time they take on a humorous and sometimes ironic attitude, especially when it comes to Kafka's notorious issues regarding his body and his identity as a Jewish man.[35] The ironic attitude apparent in Crumb and Mairowitz's approach to the famous author soon became one of the recurring features of new Kafka adaptations, for example, Peter Kuper's *The Metamorphosis* (2003) or Chantal Montellier and David Zane Mairowitz's *The Trial* (2008). Following *Kafka for Beginners*, they have often emphasized the absurd and grotesquely comical aspects of his works by making extensive use of the 'funny' vocabulary of comics.

It should be noted that traditionally comical elements, as frequently used in comic strips, are actually not as customary in graphic adaptations as one might think. In fact, graphic adaptations of canonical texts often refrain from stressing the 'comical' heritage of comics which is deeply rooted in popular culture, and instead seem to be trying to achieve a more distinguished style appropriate for the treatment of 'high literature'. This means that they often avoid using techniques such as caricature, sound words, speed lines, and visual metaphor that are primarily associated with funny comic strips. Under these conditions, the use of comical elements in adaptations of Kafka's works is worth looking into. Peter Kuper's adaptation of *The Metamorphosis* provides a striking example of how graphic adaptation can uphold the comical traditions of comics that are mainly associated with popular culture, thus presenting a contrast to the high-brow expectations regarding the literary canon. In Kuper's adaptation, Gregor Samsa is depicted as an anthropomorphic animal and thus evokes the tradition of humorous comic strips with their popular characters like Mickey Mouse or Donald Duck (Figure 6.3). In contrast to these popular characters, Gregor Samsa does not have an animal's head and a predominantly human body. Instead, Kuper illustrates Gregor Samsa's irritation with his transformed body by presenting him as an insect with a human face that often expresses confusion about his current state.

It has almost become a tradition in its own right to point out that Kafka himself firmly resisted the idea of showing the 'Ungeziefer' Gregor Samsa in illustrations to the first edition. In a letter to his editor's office he claims: 'Das Insekt selbst kann nicht gezeichnet werden' [The insect itself cannot be drawn], and suggests a different pictorial solution.[36] Gregor's transformation and the resulting confinement should only be hinted at by showing the door to his room from the outside. Adaptations in visual media are of course unable to adhere to Kafka's wishes since they automatically entail a change from the 'telling mode' to the 'showing mode'.[37] Kuper, however, uses a very specific kind of showing mode which is distinctly non-realistic. Instead of conforming stylistically to the cultural status of the adapted text, his adaptation of *The Metamorphosis* plays to the caricaturist strengths of comics in order to bring out the absurd qualities of the story (Figure 6.3).

In only three successive panels Kuper shows us the events rapidly unfolding after Gregor's attempted 'outbreak' at the end of the second chapter which will result in his ultimate imprisonment.[38] Trying to make room for the insect's crawling around, his sister has planned on taking out the furniture. Gregor, who usually hides under the sofa when someone enters the room, misunderstands this gesture and feels threatened. In order to protect his belongings, he 'breaks out' from his hiding place and shields some random item — ironically, a *picture* of a lady in fur — with his body. Having been spared the sight of her son in his transformed insect state up to this point, Gregor's mother appears to be fainting. His sister runs from the room to fetch some medicine, and Gregor follows her,

> Als könne er der Schwester irgendeinen Rat geben, wie in früherer Zeit; mußte dann aber untätig hinter ihr stehen, während sie in verschiedenen Fläschchen kramte; erschreckte sie noch, als sie sich umdrehte; eine Flasche fiel auf den Boden und zerbrach; ein Splitter verletzte Gregor im Gesicht, irgendeine ätzende Medizin umfloß ihn; Grete nahm nun, ohne sich länger aufzuhalten, soviel Fläschchen, als sie nur halten konnte, und rannte mit ihnen zur Mutter hinein; die Tür schlug sie mit dem Fuße zu. (*Die Verwandlung*, pp. 166–67)

> [Then he too ran into the next room, as if he could give his sister some kind of advice, as he used to do in the past; but he could only stand behind her, doing

FIG. 6.3. Kuper, *The Metamorphosis* (New York: Three Rivers Press, 2003), p. 46 © Peter Kuper. Used by kind permission of the author.

> nothing; while she was hunting among various little flasks, she was startled the moment she turned round; one bottle fell to the ground and broke in pieces; a splinter hurt Gregor in the face; some sort of medicine spilled around him, smarting; without waiting any longer, Grete took as many little flasks as she could hold, and ran with them to her mother; she slammed the door shut with her foot.][39]

While Kafka strings these elements together using semicolons, the cartoonist creates a rapid sequence by using the traditional visual language of comics, especially sound words and speed lines, to condense the dynamic action: Gregor's sister turning around, the bottle falling and breaking, the sister rushing back to Gregor's room and slamming the door. Gregor's reaction to the unpredictable behaviour of his sister is presented as a close-up; his emotions (shock, pain/disgust, confusion) can be deduced from his exaggerated facial expressions. Additionally, Kuper uses visual metaphors like Gregor's 'seeing stars' or the spiral line above his head to indicate dizziness in the third panel.

In their 2008 graphic novel *The Trial,* Chantal Montellier and David Zane Mairowitz create a different ironic effect by adding a visual level of reflection. On almost every page, the protagonist Josef K., who is trying to figure out the court system which is persecuting him, is accompanied by little skeletons (Figure 6.4). These skeletons directly quote the work of Mexican artist José Guadalupe Posada, who was specialized in *calaveras* — folkloristic depictions of skeletons originally

FIG. 6.4. Montellier and Mairowitz, *The Trial* (London: SelfMadeHero, 2008), p. 36 © 2008 SelfMadeHero, illustrated by Chantal Montellier and adapted by David Zane Mairowitz.

belonging to the context of the Mexican *día de los muertos* festivities. In Montellier and Mairowitz's *The Trial*, the skeletons are not part of the story and apparently cannot be seen by the characters, especially not by Josef K. Even though he cannot see them, all their actions (for example, laughing about K., mocking him, sometimes even addressing him), are reactions to his arrogant demeanour and his stubborn ignorance.

The skeletons can be interpreted as symbols of K.'s impending death; one might even say that they establish his fate as a visual fact. Ironically, he is unaware of this fact — unlike the readers who cannot ignore what is 'going on right under [their] nose'.[40] The addition of a meta-level of narration (the skeletons commenting on Josef K.'s actions), can be considered an equivalent to the complex narrative perspective of the adapted text. The narrative effect Kafka created in his first novel *The Trial*, left unfinished in 1915, is quite ambiguous. On the one hand, he uses the protagonist Josef K. as a focalizer, thus providing an opportunity for the reader to share K.'s experience of being arrested, persecuted, and finally executed by a legal system that he is unable to comprehend. On the other hand, it becomes clear that Josef K. is actually often quite wrong in his perceptions and resulting assumptions. On the one hand, the readers are invited to share Josef K.'s experience; on the other, they are encouraged to keep their critical distance.[41] In a very similar way, the adaptation aims at creating an ironic distance from its protagonist who is nonetheless present in almost every panel. Through this strategy, the skeletons have the function of ridiculing the protagonist and exposing him as a limited and self-righteous character.[42]

At the beginning of his first visit to the court offices, K. feels quite confident that his situation is not nearly as dismal as that of the other defendants whom he perceives as shabby individuals waiting submissively in the hallways. Both the reaction of K.'s 'colleague' and the laughing skeleton that he cannot see (Figure 6.4) expose his patronizing behaviour as utterly inappropriate and make it clear to the reader that K., who believes the courtroom visitors take him for a judge, is misjudging his own position. Later in the novel, Block reveals to K. that the defendant he was talking to was not confused because he was intimidated by K.'s superior status, but because he was convinced he could see the sign of K.'s and his own conviction on his lips.[43] The irony of K. *not* seeing and not realizing the severity of his situation becomes a visual leitmotif and a kind of inside joke between the adapting artist and the reader. The adaptation by Montellier and Mairowitz seizes on an ironic effect that is already implied by the ambiguous narrative perspective of the adapted text, but it creates irony in its very own way, using the full potential of surrealist representation that is available to the artists of comics.

Adopting and Adapting Canonical Readings of Kafka's Work: Popular and Academic Interpretations

Crumb and Mairowitz's groundbreaking *Kafka for Beginners* (1993) does not only present visual interpretations of Kafka's most popular works, it also deals with his life and his afterlife as a canonical writer and popular character. In terms of the ironic attitude discussed above, the passages about Kafka's popularity show the most pronounced tongue-in-cheek attitude. As Iris Bruce notes in her essay on *Kafka and Popular Culture*, Crumb and Mairowitz's book is basically 'a critique of modern consumer society, demythologizing Kafka by poking fun at the Kafka industry in academic circles and popular culture'.[44] As part of this 'demythologizing' project, the artist and the writer make fun of the academic approach to Kafka's works (ironically dubbed 'Kafkalogy'), and of the trivialized use of the adjective 'Kafkaesque' in popular discourse.[45] Two illustrations at the beginning and at the end of the book serve to illustrate this trivialization. They show a group of apparently educated people at a party. 'Yes, it's a very Kafkaesque situation over there right now,' claims a bearded man in the first illustration, presumably talking about one of the many crisis zones of the modern world (p. 5). At the end of the book, the same group of people reappears, this time discussing popular (half-) knowledge about Kafka: he was from 'Czechoslovakia', and he wrote 'weird stuff' (p. 156). Mairowitz's text ironically comments on Kafka's afterlife in academic and popular discourse:

> K himself was slowly becoming The ADJECTIVE, which would be known by many more people than would ever read his books. Of course — let's face it — this has not a little to do with the sound of his terrific name and its terrific GermaniK 'K's, Kutting their way like Kutlasses through our Kollective Konsciousness. (p. 156)

Apart from ironically reflecting on Kafka's role in academic and popular discourse, the book also takes on a critical attitude towards the more consumerist aspects of Kafka's fame in post-Cold War Prague. On one of the last pages of the book, we see Crumb and Mairowitz in the role of tourists wearing identical t-shirts adorned with

FIG. 6.5. Crumb and Mairowitz, *Kafka* (Berlin: Reprodukt, 2017), p. 165
© Reprodukt. Printed with kind permission.

the famous last photograph of Kafka (Figure 6.5). In the concluding sentence of the book, the growing 'Kafka industry' is presented as part of the Prague 'Kitsch': 'After years of ignoring him as a pariah, the new Czech Republic is finally discovering its strange Jewish son, no longer a threat and suddenly BANKABLE as a tourist attraction. The irony would not have been lost on him' (p. 175).

While Crumb and Mairowitz make fun of the cultural mechanisms and clichés that come with Kafka's popularity, they themselves draw on clichés of the popular discourse on Kafka, first and foremost the common notion that Kafka's works and his life are inextricably linked.[46] In order to grasp fully the significance of popular interpretations of Kafka's works for the new generation of graphic adaptation, it is necessary to discuss the most canonical readings of Kafka's works.

Kafka's works have often been described as notoriously hermetic and non-interpretable. In his *Notes to Kafka*, Theodor W. Adorno wrote: 'Every sentence says "interpret me", and none will permit it'.[47] Adorno's verdict, however, has not kept Kafka critics from interpreting — in fact, he has 'been subjected to a mass ravishment by [...] armies of interpreters', as Susan Sontag stated in 1966.[48] From the perspective of today's Kafka criticism, Manfred Engel distinguishes six basic approaches to the author's works that have shaped both critical and popular discourse: the 'biographical', the 'psychoanalytical', the 'socio-historical', the 'poststructuralist-deconstructivist', the 'religious-existentialist', and the 'Jewish interpretation'.[49] Judging from the lasting popularity of these approaches in literary criticism, they might be considered canonical in themselves. With the exception of the specifically academic poststructuralist-deconstructivist and the historical religious-existentialist approach, they have also found their way into popular discourse on Kafka and have shaped the popular notion of the author and his works. Adaptations of Kafka by the new generation, following Crumb and Mairowitz's example, often draw on well-established readings like these, most often the biographical and/or the socio-historical reading. In their indirect reception of literary criticism, Kafka adaptations seem to present a special case within the area of literary adaptations. The fact that Kafka adaptations often also draw on popular readings of the adapted novels and stories seems to confirm the canonical status of these established interpretations. In the analysis to follow I will focus on the biographical, and then Jewish interpretative frameworks.

Reading K. as Kafka: Visual References to the Author and his Hometown

The biographical approach has dominated the popular reception of Kafka from the start and is the most fashionable approach in graphic adaptation. Crumb and Mairowitz, again setting an example for later adaptations, create a link between Kafka's works and his life by embedding miniature adaptations within a biographical text. The seventeen-page adaptation of *The Metamorphosis*, for example, is included in a chapter on Kafka's difficult relationship with his physical appearance.[50] In the paragraph directly preceding and thus introducing the adaptation, Mairowitz reflects on Kafka's relationship with his body, using free indirect speech:

> What was there to do with his body which he saw as too thin, gangling, graceless, an offence to the eyes and, what's more, in everyone's way? It would have to be reduced, starve itself, go into hiding or simply transform itself into a beast, preferably one whose belly touched the ground and could scurry away without causing the world too much unpleasantness. (*Kafka for Beginners*, p. 38)

The image of a 'beast' whose belly touches the ground directly evokes the idea of the 'enormous bug' Gregor Samsa in *The Metamorphosis*. This passage is a perfect example of Crumb and Mairowitz's strategy of biographically embedding the adaptations, thus presenting Kafka's writing as an outlet for his issues with his father, his body, his Jewish heritage, women in general, and Felice Bauer in particular. But embedding is not the only way a graphic adaptation can establish a biographical interpretation of the adapted text.

Comicbook artists have developed certain techniques of visualization that serve the biographical interpretation. One of the basic techniques is to identify the author visually with his characters. Several Kafka adaptations in comics from around the world model their protagonists more or less closely on Kafka's personal appearance (as in, for example, Montellier and Mairowitz's *The Trial*, see Figure 6.6), or at least try to present him as a 'Kafka type' according to the popular iconography: slight of build and with full dark hair, dressed in dapper suits.[51] The implication is clear: the character's conflict is to be read as Kafka's own.

Another way to imply that the adapted text can and should be read biographically is to set the adaptation in Kafka's home town Prague, a strategy that is also deployed in film adaptations.[52] Although the author himself hardly ever describes specific locations in his works, adaptations in visual media generally have to provide more explicit information on where the story takes place. Graphic adaptations — again following the example of Crumb and Mairowitz — often use this technical requirement to create yet another connection between Kafka's life and times and his works, by quoting images of recognizable Prague landmarks and sights like the Charles Bridge, the Týn Church, or the Hradčany (the Prague castle).[53] Some adaptations take the task of recreating Kafka's Prague even more seriously. They do not only refer to recognizable tourist attractions, but also to biographically significant places, such as the building of the insurance company Kafka worked for (*Arbeiter-Unfall-Versicherungsanstalt für das Königreich Böhmen in Prag*).[54] In this way, the artists suggest that Kafka's description of his characters' working life — most prominent in *The Metamorphosis* and in *The Trial* — is really a reflection on the oppressive nature of his own position in the insurance agency.

Localizing a Kafka adaptation in Habsburg Prague creates a period setting that focuses on recreating the world in which Kafka would have lived and written. While the above-mentioned techniques of biographical interpretation, i.e. identifying characters with their author and quoting landmarks of his home town, are used in Kafka adaptations all over the world, the adaptations in which Mairowitz has been involved as a writer also engage with more specifically academic interpretations of Kafka's works, first and foremost canonical socio-historical and Jewish readings, while at the same time opening up new contexts in which Kafka and Kafka adaptation can, quite literally, be seen.

Fig. 6.6. Montellier and Mairowitz, *The Trial* (London: SelfMadeHero, 2008), cover illustration © 2008 SelfMadeHero, illustrated by Chantal Montellier and adapted by David Zane Mairowitz.

Playing with Contexts: Jewish Reference Points Within Different Frameworks for Interpretation

Kafka for Beginners paved the way for a differentiated perspective on the contexts in which Kafka was living and writing. A closer look at *Kafka for Beginners* as well as Mairowitz's next Kafka-related adaptation project *The Trial*, reveals that the setting they aim to create is not simply 'Habsburg Prague', but more specifically the milieu of assimilated Jewish life in which Kafka grew up and became a writer. By referencing historical photographs from the Jewish quarter Josefov, Crumb and Mairowitz suggest that Kafka's writing is inextricably linked to his life in early twentieth-century Jewish Prague. While in *Kafka for Beginners* the biographical passages are mainly linked to the Jewish context, *The Trial* takes this connection to the level of the narrative: Josef K.'s trial itself takes place in a distinctly Jewish Prague. Montellier and Mairowitz's use of historical photographs from Josefov repeats a strategy already used in *Kafka for Beginners*, and is thus to be considered a tip of the hat from Montellier to Crumb's visualization as an iconic contribution to Kafka adaptation.[55] The same can be said for the small detail of a kosher butcher that K. and his wardens pass on their way to the execution.[56] In *Kafka for Beginners* this image symbolizes Kafka's ambivalent relationship to family traditions: Kafka's grandfather on his father's side was a butcher ('Fleischhauer'), whereas he chose to become a vegetarian.[57]

The reference to the butcher in the background anticipates the imagery of Josef K.'s execution. In this scene, Montellier and Mairowitz choose to digress from the text of the novel in a highly meaningful way: instead of being stabbed in the heart, Josef K. has his throat cut like an animal.[58] Although the pointed knife depicted by Montellier would not be appropriate in this context, the image could be a reference to the ritual of *shechitah* according to Jewish dietary laws as it would have been practised by Kafka's grandfather in his *shtetl*. At the same time, the arrangement of the scene explicitly references Artemisia Gentileschi's painting *Judith and Holofernes* (1620/21), thus simultaneously evoking a range of different contexts. For example, Gentileschi's painting tells the myth of Judith who beheaded the general Holofernes to save her town and her people, and who was declared a heroine of ancient Judaism: 'Judith's success against all odds epitomizes the charter myth of Judaism itself — cultural survival through the commitment to the preservation of the Mosaic Law, with the help of God'.[59] Does the reference intend to establish a parallel between the Mosaic Law and the elusive 'Law' in *The Trial*? Does it try to point out the relativity and instability of death sentences legitimized by 'the Law'? The adaptation does not present an elaborate interpretation, but only hints at different possibilities for reading *The Trial* in a Jewish context. Given the fact that the adaptation itself as well as the preface and the afterword refer to a substantial number of different interpretations, the act of referencing contexts of interpretation seems to aim at opening up the range of possible readings instead of representing one specific interpretation.

So far, the references I have identified in *The Trial* seem to suggest that it is not only the context of Jewish life in Prague during Kafka's lifetime that is important

Fig. 6.7. Montellier and Mairowitz, *The Trial* (London: SelfMadeHero, 2008), p. 18
© 2008 SelfMadeHero, illustrated by Chantal Montellier and adapted by
David Zane Mairowitz.

for the adaptation, but also the context of Jewish history and the history of Judaism in general. Against this backdrop, it is not at all surprising that Montellier and Mairowitz also refer to the Shoah as the great Jewish catastrophe. Since many of the individual references are relatively subtle and often ambiguous in themselves, it is helpful to present them as a group in order to show the patterns that emerge. Many of these references occur in Chapter Two of Montellier and Mairowitz's *The Trial* which includes the first investigation of K.'s case, his return to the investigation room, and his first visit to the court offices.[60]

A close examination of Montellier's depiction of the investigation, suggests a certain resemblance between the examining magistrate and Adolf Hitler, at least concerning his moustache and haircut (pp. 24–27). At first, this resemblance may seem no more than a questionable joke. Later on, however, this moustache and haircut are applied to the vision of a menacing skeleton that haunts K.'s inner thoughts (p. 58). This suggests a pattern. Other references are hidden in the detail. Arriving at Juliusstrasse, where the investigation is to take place, K. seems to be irritated by the appearance of a passer-by — a strangely gaunt, bald creature which could recall the iconic images of concentration camp prisoners (Figure 6.7). Is this a coincidence? Taking a closer look at the details of this panel, we can discover three numbers on the wall behind K. If we recognize the references to Hitler and the concentration camps, these numbers are very likely to refer to a specific date: 14 March 1939, which was the day Nazi Germany began to establish the protectorate of Bohemia and Moravia, thus making the former Czech Republic a place in which Jews were officially repressed, persecuted, and ultimately deported and murdered.

Kafka died in 1924, but his sisters, as the biographical essay at the end of the adaptation points out, were deported and died in concentration camps (p. 119). It is possible that, had he survived the tuberculosis, Kafka would also have been murdered by the Nazis twenty years later. By means of subtle visual references, Montellier and Mairowitz present the world in which Josef K.'s trial takes place as a world heading towards the great catastrophe of the twentieth century. This impression is supported by the preface to the adaptation which quotes Jean-Paul Sartre's interpretation of *The Trial* as an 'allegory of Jewish identity in a world of latent anti-Semitism' (p. v). As one of several canonical approaches I have explored in the present chapter, it seems to provide one possible frame within which a range of scattered references can meaningfully be interpreted.

References to the Shoah are not completely new, when considering adaptations of Kafka's work in different media. They were also part of Orson Welles's canonical and iconic film *Le Procès* (1962) which is not set in Habsburg Prague, but in an unspecified present. Welles includes a scene in which Josef K., also on his way to the investigation, passes a square filled with very strange people, apparently waiting for something.[61] They are all half-naked, carrying their clothes under their arms and wearing a sign with a number around their necks. This scene has been read as an allusion to the visual representation of concentration camp victims.[62] Thus, the film by Welles, as well as the graphic novel by Montellier and Mairowitz more than forty years later, places Josef K.'s trial in a world of which the Shoah is an important part, whether in the future or in the past.

At the same time, this form of representation also establishes a very specific, political notion of the 'Kafkaesque'. From this perspective, the 'nightmarishly complex, bizarre, or illogical quality' associated with the term is applied to the mechanisms of the neatly organized machinery of death that enabled the Nazis to kill millions of people of Jewish heritage in only a few years.[63] Welles interprets Kafka as a 'prophet of fascism'.[64] As a document of Kafka reception, his vision of Josef K. as the object of and rebel against state terror is also representative of a historical shift from the metaphysical, existential readings of Kafka to socio-historical, political interpretations.[65]

Montellier and Mairowitz obviously draw on this interpretation, but they do not exclusively commit to it. Instead, they play with a number of possible contexts for reading Kafka. While the biographical reading is omnipresent through the ubiquitous use of Kafka's face, we also find traces of a socio-historical reading of the adapted novel as a portrait of Jewish life in a 'world of latent anti-Semitism' (p. v) which in fact overlaps with a political interpretation as a critical and prophetic depiction of the police state and bureaucratic terrors. It is equally possible to consider the depictions of K.'s inner world, such as his visions of being punished (pp. 57–61), as part of a psychological interpretation. In its eclectic attitude towards and playful rearrangement of canonical interpretations, the adaptation is truly a part of a postmodernist reception of Kafka.

Although this chapter has focused on adaptation strategies in their relation to concepts of canon, the strategy of placing Kafka in a certain interpretative context by means of visual reference is not limited to the context of canonical interpretations. In fact, it is not unusual for graphic adaptations of the new generation to quote an astonishing number of works from the visual arts, as well as a wide range of previous adaptations.[66] By quoting images from Crumb and Mairowitz's *Kafka for Beginners*, but also from Orson Welles's 1962 film, Montellier and Mairowitz pay homage to the impact these adaptations had on 'Kafka iconography'.[67] At the same time, they present their own work as part of a tradition of Kafka adaptation in various media of high and popular culture. As a representative of the new generation of Kafka adaptation, *The Trial* does not only reflect on its own status as an adaptation, but also on the way we see Kafka as a canonical author today — as an image in the mirrors of postmodern culture.

Conclusion

As I have argued in the present chapter, the 'Kafka image' has a special significance for academic and popular discourse, both in its literal and metaphorical sense. Photographs of the author continue to inspire interpretations of his works in an academic context, but also in the field of graphic adaptation. Kafka adaptation is connected to the concept of canon in more than one way. Not only is Kafka as an author considered a 'classic' of modern literature, his notoriously complex works have been subjected to several academic approaches which have formed interpretations that today can be considered canonical themselves. Last but not least, the field of Kafka adaptation seems to have formed its own canon. Like Orson Welles's film adaptation of *The Trial*, Crumb and Mairowitz's *Kafka for Beginners* has visibly influenced succeeding graphic adaptations in their general attitude towards the adapted texts.

The respectful and the ironic attitude, the adoption of the most popular interpretation of Kafka's works as biographical, and the playful attitude towards canonical academic approaches, have all formed distinctive strategies of visualization. As a product of popular culture in the wake of postmodernism, however, the new generation of graphic adaptation is not committed exclusively to a single approach or strategy, but instead experiments with a range of popular and canonical perspectives on the adapted text, while at the same time reflecting on its own status as an adaptation. In their eclectic attitude, the Kafka adaptations discussed in this chapter are prime examples not only of a new understanding of graphic adaptation, but also of a new approach to canonical literature. Merging elements from high and popular culture, they reflect today's perspective on canonical literature that cannot ignore the multitude and ubiquity of (cross-)media representation.

Notes to Chapter 6

1. Philip Roth, 'I Always Wanted You To Admire my Fasting, or, Looking at Kafka', in *The World of Franz Kafka*, ed. by J. P. Stern (London: Weidenfeld and Nicolson, 1980), pp. 202-17 (p. 202), quoted in Carolin Duttlinger, *Kafka and Photography* (Oxford: Oxford University Press, 2007), p. 2.
2. Study of the commercial use of images of Kafka, of quotations from his works and of references to him as a writer and as a character, has been shamefully neglected even in recent contributions to the field of Kafka's reception in new media and popular culture. As literary studies catch up with the digital world, it is possible that phenomena such as Kafka t-shirts, mugs, caps, badges, but also memes and posters will become the object of research. Hopefully, these studies will do more than simply judge such commercial items in terms of aesthetic value (see, for example, Idan Yaron and Omri Herzog, 'Kafka's Ruins in Popular Culture: A Story of Metamorphosis', *The Journal of Popular Culture*, 46.5 (2013), 1092-1105).
3. Monika Schmitz-Emans, 'Kafka in European and US Comics: Intermedial and Intercultural Transfer Processes', *Revue de littérature comparée*, 78.4 (2004), 485-505 (p. 485).

4. See Walter Benjamin, 'Franz Kafka: zur zehnten Wiederkehr seines Todestages', in *Gesammelte Schriften*, ed. by Rolf Tiedemann and Hermann Schweppenhäuser, 7 vols in 15 (Frankfurt a.M.: Suhrkamp, 1972–1989), II.2 (1977), 409-38 ('Ein Kinderbild', pp. 416-25).
5. Duttlinger, *Kafka and Photography*, p. 1.
6. The photograph is included in: Klaus Wagenbach, *Franz Kafka: Bilder aus seinem Leben* (Berlin: Verlag Klaus Wagenbach, 1983), p. 187. It is referenced in a range of different adaptations, examples of which can be seen in figures 6.5 and 6.6.
7. Sanders, *Adaptation and Appropriation* (2006), p. 8.
8. Ibid., p. 9.
9. *The Graphic Canon: The World's Great Literature as Comics and Visuals*, 3 vols, ed. by Russ Kick (New York: Seven Stories Press, 2012-13).
10. *'Der Kanon': die deutsche Literatur. Erzählungen*, ed. by Marcel Reich-Ranicki, 10 vols (Berlin: Insel Verlag, 2003). Among other stories by Kafka, this anthology also includes *The Judgement* and *The Metamorphosis*. Reich-Ranicki's collection of the twenty most important novels in German also features Kafka's *The Trial* (*'Der Kanon': die deutsche Literatur. Romane*, ed. by Marcel Reich-Ranicki, 20 vols (Berlin: Insel Verlag, 2002)). See also Harold Bloom, *The Western Canon: The Books and School of the Ages* (New York: Harcourt Brace & Co., 1994), pp. 447-62, and Ruth R. Wisse, *The Modern Jewish Canon: A Journey Through Language and Culture* (New York: Free Press, 2000), pp. 65-98.
11. W. H. Auden, *Prose and Travel Books in Prose and Verse*, in *The Complete Works*, ed. by Edward Mendelson, 6 vols (Princeton, NJ: Princeton University Press, 2002), II, 110. See also Lamping's remarks on Kafka as a 'modern classic' and as an example to modern writers like Auden (Dieter Lamping, 'Franz Kafka als Autor der Weltliteratur', in *Franz Kafka und die Weltliteratur*, ed. by Manfred Engel and Dieter Lamping (Göttingen: Vandenhoeck & Ruprecht, 2006), pp. 9-23 (pp. 16-17)). It should be noted that the English-speaking reception of Kafka's works preceded the reception in Germany by more than a decade. Kafka only rose to canonical status in (West) Germany after the Second World War.
12. In Goethe's case, adaptation concentrates on his drama *Faust: Der Tragödie erster Teil* (1808).
13. For an overview of graphic adaptations of Kafka's works in an international context, see: Monika Schmitz-Emans, *Literatur-Comics: Adaptationen und Transformationen der Weltliteratur* (Berlin: de Gruyter 2012), pp. 175-217; for an overview of adaptations of *The Metamorphosis*, see Christopher Hohlbaum, *Kafka im Comic* (Würzburg: Königshausen & Neumann, 2015), pp. 309-415. Appropriations are works that are based on literary texts and/or their authors, but take 'a more decisive journey away from the informing source into a wholly new cultural product and domain' (Sanders, *Adaptation and Appropriation*, p. 26).
14. See Schmitz-Emans, 'Kafka in European and US Comics', p. 485.
15. On this point, see: Heinz Ladendorf, 'Kafka und die Kunstgeschichte', *Wallraf-Richartz-Jahrbuch*, 23 (1961), 293-326, & 25 (1963), 227-62; Hartmut Binder, 'Anschauung ersehnten Lebens: Kafkas Verständnis bildender Künstler und ihrer Werke', in *Was bleibt von Franz Kafka? Positionsbestimmung. Kafka-Symposion, Vienna 1983*, ed. by Georg Kranner and Wendelin Schmidt-Dengler (Vienna: Braumüller, 1985), pp. 17-41.
16. On Kafka's drawings, see: *Einmal ein grosser Zeichner: Franz Kafka als beeldend kunstenaar*, ed. by Niels Bokhove and Marijke van Dorst (Utrecht: Salon Saffier Saffier, 2002), and Friederike Fellner, *Kafkas Zeichnungen* (Munich: Wilhelm Fink, 2014). On the question of photography, see Duttlinger, *Kafka and Photography*, and Gesa Schneider, *Das Andere schreiben: Kafkas fotografische Poetik* (Würzburg: Königshausen & Neumann, 2008). On Kafka's interest in film, see: Hanns Zischler, *Kafka geht ins Kino* (Reinbek: Rowohlt, 1996), and Peter-André Alt, *Kafka und der Film: Über kinematographisches Erzählen* (Munich: C.H. Beck, 2009). See also, Carolin Duttlinger, 'Film und Fotografie', in *Kafka Handbuch: Leben, Werk, Wirkung*, ed. by Manfred Engel and Bernd Auerochs (Stuttgart & Weimar: Metzler, 2010), pp. 72-79 (p. 75); and *Kafka and Photography*, p. 10.
17. Leena Eilittä, 'Kafka and Visuality', *KulturPoetik*, 6.2 (2006), 222-33 (p. 233).
18. See Schmitz-Emans, 'Kafka in European and US Comics', p. 485.
19. Russ Kick, 'Preface', in *The Graphic Canon*, ed. by Kick, I, 1.
20. Versaci, *This Book Contains Graphic Language*, p. 183.

21. See Schmitz-Emans, *Literatur-Comics*, p. 17.
22. See Juliane Blank, *Vom Sinn und Unsinn des Begriffs Graphic Novel* (Berlin: Ch. A. Bachmann, 2014).
23. Robert Crumb and David Zane Mairowitz, *Kafka for Beginners* (Cambridge: Icon Books, 1993). Newer editions of the book have been titled differently — the current title is simply *Kafka* (Berlin: Reprodukt, 2017).
24. See Torsten Hoffmann on the 'anxiety of influence' in Kafka adaptation: '"Das nicht, bitte das nicht!" Körperdarstellung in Comicversionen von Schnitzlers *Fräulein Else* und Kafkas *Verwandlung*', in *Graphisches Erzählen: neue Perspektiven auf Literaturcomics*, ed. by Florian Trabert, Mara Stuhlfauth-Trabert and Johannes Waßmer (Bielefeld: Transcript, 2015), pp. 42-63 (p. 59).
25. Franz Kafka, *Die Verwandlung*, in *Drucke zu Lebzeiten*, ed. by Wolf Kittler, Hans-Gerd Koch and Gerhard Neumann (Frankfurt a.M.: Fischer, 2002), pp. 115-200 (p. 115); English translation by David Zane Mairowitz in Crumb and Mairowitz, *Kafka for Beginners*, p. 39.
26. Friedrich Beißner, *Der Erzähler Franz Kafka* [1952] (Stuttgart: Kohlhammer, 1958), p. 42. Translation by Silke Horstkotte, 'Seeing or Speaking: Visual Narratology and Focalization, Literature to Film', in *Narratology in the Age of Cross-disciplinary Narrative Research*, ed. by Sandra Heinen and Roy Sommer (Berlin & New York: de Gruyter, 2009), pp. 170-91 (p. 173).
27. Edward Branigan, *Point of View in the Cinema: A Theory of Narration and Subjectivity in Classical Film* (Berlin, New York & Amsterdam: de Gruyter, 1984), p. 6.
28. Martin Schüwer, *Wie Comics erzählen: Grundriss einer intermedialen Erzähltheorie der grafischen Literatur* (Trier: Wissenschaftlicher Verlag Trier, 2008), p. 178.
29. See Gérard Genette, *Narrative Discourse: An Essay in Method*, trans. by Jane E. Lewin (Oxford: Blackwell, 1980), pp. 188-89. In this context, Genette quotes Jean Pouillon's term 'vision avec', which has been translated as 'vision with' the character.
30. See Richard T. Gray, 'Das Urteil: unheimliches Erzählen und die Unheimlichkeit des bürgerlichen Subjekts', in *Franz Kafka: Romane und Erzählungen*, ed. by Michael Müller (Stuttgart: Reclam, 2009), pp. 11-41 (p. 19). On *Kafka for Beginners* and visual focalization, see Juliane Blank, 'Erzählperspektive im Medienwechsel: visuelle Fokalisierung in Comic-Adaptionen von Texten Franz Kafkas', *kunsttexte.de*, 1 (2011) <https://edoc.hu-berlin.de/handle/18452/8106> [accessed 24 March 2020].
31. The thought bubble reads: 'My father is still a giant...'. Due to copyright issues, Figure 6.2 is taken from the latest edition of the German translation of the book: *Kafka* (Berlin: Reprodukt, 2017).
32. Franz Kafka, 'Das Urteil', in *Drucke zu Lebzeiten*, ed. by Kittler, Koch and Neumann, pp. 43-61 (p. 56).
33. Examples of internal focalization by means of 'half-subjective' perspective can be found in Crumb and Mairowitz, *Kafka for Beginners*, pp. 39-55; Peter Kuper, *The Metamorphosis* (New York: Three Rivers Press, 2003), for example, pp. 25, 41, 47, 57 & 59; Eric Corbeyran and Richard Horne, *La Métamorphose* (Paris: Guy Delcourt Productions, 2009), for example, p. [17] (my own pagination; no page numbers in the original).
34. The issue of humour is an aspect of Kafka criticism that has recently gained popularity. See for example: Astrid Dehe and Achim Engstler, *Kafkas komische Seiten: ein Lesebuch* (Göttingen: Steidl Verlag, 2011); Joseph Vogl, 'Kafkas Komik', in *Kontinent Kafka: Mosse-Lectures an der Humboldt-Universität zu Berlin*, ed. by Klaus R. Scherpe (Berlin: Vorwerk 8, 2006), pp. 72–87; Ute Friederich, *Komik — Comic: komische Elemente in den Texten Franz Kafkas und ihre bildliche Umsetzung in verschiedenen Comic-Adaptionen* (unpublished Masters thesis, Universität Bonn, 2009) <https://docplayer.org/43758272-Komik-comic-magisterarbeit-zur-erlangung-des-grades-einer-magistra-artium-m-a.html> [accessed 24 March 2020].
35. See Crumb and Mairowitz, *Kafka for Beginners*, pp. 60-63.
36. Franz Kafka, letter to G. H. Meyer (of Kurt Wolff Verlag), 25 October 1915, in *Briefe April 1914–17*, ed. by Hans-Gerd Koch (Frankfurt a.M.: Fischer, 2005), p. 145.
37. Hutcheon, *A Theory of Adaptation*, p. 23.
38. See Sandra Poppe, 'Die Verwandlung', in *Kafka Handbuch*, ed. by Engel and Auerochs, pp. 164-74 (pp. 166-67).

39. Franz Kafka, *The Metamorphosis and Other Stories*, trans. by Joyce Crick (Oxford: Oxford University Press, 2009), p. 56.
40. Chantal Montellier and David Zane Mairowitz, *The Trial: A Graphic Novel* (London: SelfMadeHero, 2008), p. 94.
41. See Manfred Engel, 'Der Process', in *Kafka Handbuch*, ed. by Engel and Auerochs, pp. 192-207 (p. 198).
42. See Friederich, *Komik — Comic*, pp. 58-60.
43. Kafka, *Der Proceß*, ed. by Malcolm Pasley (Frankfurt a.M.: S. Fischer Verlag, 2002), p. 237.
44. Iris Bruce, 'Kafka and Popular Culture', in *The Cambridge Companion to Kafka*, ed. by Julian Preece (Cambridge: Cambridge University Press, 2002), pp. 242-46 (p. 244).
45. Crumb and Mairowitz, *Kafka for Beginners*, p. 157. Further references to this book are given after quotations in the text.
46. See Bruce, 'Kafka and Popular Culture', p. 244.
47. Theodor W. Adorno, 'Notes to Kafka', in *Prisms*, trans. by Samuel and Shierry Weber (Cambridge, MA: MIT Press, 1967), p. 246.
48. Susan Sontag, 'Against Interpretation', in *Essays of the 1960s & 70s*, ed. by David Rieff (New York: Library of America, 2013), pp. 10-20 (p. 14). Sontag counts 'no less than three armies of interpreters' which have read Kafka's works as 'social allegory', 'psychological allegory', and 'religious allegory'.
49. See Manfred Engel, 'Kafka lesen: Verstehensprobleme und Forschungsparadigmen', in *Kafka Handbuch*, ed. by Engel and Auerochs, pp. 411-27 (esp. pp. 419-24).
50. See Hoffmann, '"Das nicht, bitte das nicht!"', p. 55.
51. See, for example: Guido Crepax, *Il processo* (Casale Monferrato: Piemme, 1999); Variety Art Works, *Henshin* [= *Metamorphosis*] (Tokyo: East Press, 2008); and Montellier and Mairowitz, *The Trial*. All three adaptations in which Mairowitz is involved as a writer — *Kafka for Beginners*, *The Trial* and a 2013 adaptation of *The Castle* with Czech artist Jaromir 99 — feature specific photographs of Kafka on their covers, but only *The Trial* uses the cover photograph for character design as well. Both of the film adaptations of *The Trial* star actors who are at least vaguely Kafkaesque in type. In Orson Welles's *Le Procès* (1962), Josef K. is portrayed by Anthony Perkins while Kyle MacLachlan took on the role in *The Trial*, dir. by David Jones (BBC, 1993).
52. Jones's *The Trial* also creates a period 'Bohemian' atmosphere and was shot in Prague.
53. For the Charles Bridge, see Kuper, *The Metamorphosis*, p. 77; Corbeyran and Horne, *La Métamorphose*, p. 35. The Týn Church can be seen in the background of the splash panel that opens the adaptation of *A Hunger Artist* in Crumb and Mairowitz, *Kafka for Beginners*, pp. 144-45. The Hradčany features in Corbeyran and Horne, *La Métamorphose*, p. 33. Corbeyran and Horne do not only rely on the images, but they insert a sign at the train station explicitly stating that Gregor Samsa has just arrived in his home town, Prague (p. 9); Montellier and Mairowitz refer to a part of the Prague castle ensemble when they depict the cathedral in which K.'s talk with the prison chaplain takes place as St. Vitus Cathedral (*The Trial*, pp. 91 & 102).
54. See Montellier and Mairowitz, *The Trial*, pp. 11 & 90; Variety Art Works, *Henshin*, p. 28.
55. In two scenes, Montellier draws back on images linked to the Jewish quarter, both times quoting *Kafka for Beginners*. For example, Montellier and Mairowitz, *The Trial*, p. 17: street scene from the part of town where the court offices are located, quoting Crumb and Mairowitz, *Kafka for Beginners*, p. 17, image of the fence around the Prague Ghetto; Montellier and Mairowitz, *The Trial*, p. 63: street scene from the part of town where Titorelli lives, quoting Crumb and Mairowitz, *Kafka for Beginners*, p. 16, street scene from the Ghetto quoting a historical photograph from Josefov, available at Prague Minos guide <http://www.digital-guide.cz/de/realie/die-stadtviertel-der-hauptstadt/die-judenstadt---josefov-1/> [accessed 24 March 2020].
56. See Montellier and Mairowitz, *The Trial*, p. 105.
57. Ibid., p. 61.
58. Ibid., p. 111.
59. Kevin R. Brine, 'The Judith Project', in *The Sword of Judith: Judith Across the Disciplines*, ed. by Kevin R. Brine, Elena Ciletti and Henrike Lähnemann (Cambridge: Open Book Publishers, 2010), pp. 3-21 (p. 3).

60. Montellier and Mairowitz, *The Trial*, pp. 17-37. Further references to this book are given after quotations in the text.
61. *Le Procès*, dir. by Welles, 33:14–33:53 (DVD).
62. See Anne-Marie Scholz, *From Fidelity to History: Film Adaptations as Cultural Events in the Twentieth Century* (New York: Berghahn, 2013), pp. 93-116 (p. 96).
63. *Merriam-Webster Dictionary*, 'Kafkaesque' <http://www.merriam-webster.com/dictionary/kafkaesque> [accessed 24 March 2020].
64. See Scholz, *From Fidelity to History*, p. 93.
65. On the impact of Welles's interpretation on German Kafka reception, see: Scholz, *From Fidelity to History*, p. 97. Engel also comments on the initial dominance of the existential interpretation and the rise of socio-historical approaches to Kafka's works (Engel, 'Kafka lesen', pp. 421–23).
66. For example, Crumb and Mairowitz, *Kafka for Beginners*, p. 134 (explicitly quoting George Grosz's satirical drawing *Friedrichstraße*, 1918); Montellier and Mairowitz, *The Trial*, p. 111 (quoting Artemisia Gentileschi's painting *Judith and Holofernes*, 1620–21).
67. Schmitz-Emans, *Literatur-Comics*, p. 182.

CHAPTER 7

The Illustrated Book as Source-Bound[1] Adaptation: A Case Study of New York Editions of *Candide* Published Around the Stock Market Crash[2]

Christina Ionescu

> 'Most studies of illustration are performed within the context of illustration only.'[3]
>
> 'The book is demonstrably *as much* the product of institutions, agents and material forces as is the Hollywood blockbuster.'[4]

In the second edition of her seminal study *A Theory of Adaptation* (2012), Linda Hutcheon refers to book illustration as a form of adaptation, but she does not elaborate on this form of transmedial crossover from text to image, which normally has the particularity of remaining materially bound to its literary source of inspiration in its disseminated form.[5] Recent scholarship in adaptation studies places the spotlight on theatre and film, while relying primarily on post-1800 source texts as examples, therefore setting aside a priori a large segment of cultural production that emerges from and is shaped by the processes of appropriation and remediation in the form of 'graphic afterlives', in particular illustrations designed for editions of eighteenth-century classics.[6] Interestingly, a similar resistance to considering book illustration from the theoretical perspective of adaptation studies is shown by researchers focusing on images that accompany the text in its material incarnation. In contrast, Lars Elleström passionately argues in favour of opening the theoretical framework of adaptation studies to 'the transfer and transformation of form and content between all kinds of art forms and media', and he concludes that the field itself should be relocated 'in the wider context of intermediality', a proposition that is not likely to gain favour with proponents on either side of the divide (adaptation studies on the one hand and intermediality on the other).[7] In an innovative monograph dealing with the still popular works of eighteenth-century author Laurence Sterne, which constitutes a notable exception to the prevailing exclusion of book illustration from adaptation studies, Mary-Céline Newbould implicitly places graphic responses under the umbrella of adaptation studies, but she chooses to engage critically with a wide range of visual Sterneana without deliberating at length on the theoretical ramifications of her choice.[8] Book illustration, one of the earliest forms of adaptation, consequently remains broadly untheorized from the perspective of adaptation studies despite important developments in recent years.[9] What further complicates this lacuna is that book illustration is only one of the components of the illustrated book, itself an adapted material object — created, published, marketed, sold, and consumed as a product.

The objectives of the present study are more modest than a theorization of the illustrated book from the perspective of adaptation studies. Inspired by Simone Murray's call for 'a long-overdue *materialising* of adaptation theory', this chapter positions the illustrated book as the result of a creative process of adaptation undertaken within a production context that is dynamic, collaborative, and transformative.[10] Text-to-illustrated-book adaptation is fashioned by a network of forces acting in specialized roles and with varying degrees of involvement — artists, translators, editors, agents, typographers, book designers, paper suppliers, printers, binders, publishers, booksellers, dealers, critics, readers, and so forth. This process operates on four interdependent and, in practice, partially overlapping levels: textual, artistic, material, and editorial. In the course of this adaptation process, a source text is visually interpreted by a principal artist, on his own or as part of a team, and typographically set and physically laid out on a page by a book designer and his associates, resulting in a consumer product that is materially packaged and strategically marketed by a publishing house that seeks to gain monetary profit and, occasionally, recognition or prestige. In some cases the original text (as opposed to the illustrated book artefact as a whole) is also the product of adaptation, which aims to render it accessible in a target language, to a specific segment of the reading public, or within different social, cultural, and political contexts through translation, abridgement (for example, chapbooks), or in extreme circumstances, censorship. From this perspective, four components forming the illustrated book-object are the direct result of adaptation: the text in its typographic presentation, material layout, and, in some cases, linguistic transfer or transformation; its illustration as transposition and interpretation of the source text; the book as physical support (produced in a specific combination of paper, ink, binding, dust wrapper, etc.); and the editorial add-ons that may introduce the text and its author, present the visual complement and comment on the artist's creative process, address the significance of the literary work for the intended readership, describe the material presentation of the edition, and generally enhance the appearance of the book to increase its value as a consumer product and draw attention to its unique qualities. The illustrated book, as a material object, is thus adapted for the benefit of a reader-viewer-consumer — this last qualifier being crucial in the process of adaptation.[11]

This case study will focus on a transitional period in the history of the interwar American book, the four years surrounding the Wall Street Crash of 29 October 1929 that marked the beginning of the Great Depression and left a permanent mark on the book arts and the printing industry. I will use examples of illustrated editions of a world classic that has emerged through time as particularly adaptive, Voltaire's *Candide*, and I will zoom in on a specific geographic location: New York City, the epicentre of the American printing industry at the time. In spite of its French author's proclaimed resistance to illustration, this staple of the Western literary canon was repeatedly illustrated in France and America as well as throughout the world in the more than 250 years following its publication.[12] Moreover, it is worth noting that *Candide* is but one text in an extensive corpus of canonical works belonging to cultural and historical contexts distant and different from the American one, which were textually, graphically, and materially adapted across the Atlantic as illustrated books for a large and diverse range of readers-viewers-consumers during the interwar period.

The Bennett Libraries' *Candide* (1927), Illustrated by Clara Tice: Adaptation as Typographical Replica and Iconographic Provocation

From a visual perspective, book illustration as source-bound adaptation operates somewhere between two extreme reference poles within the production field of the illustrated book: in complete fusion with the source text and in absolute disjunction with it. At one end of the spectrum are illustrators who seek to imitate or capture visually as closely as possible the leading textual features of the original, and at the other, artists who opt for severing all ties with the source text to rewrite it anew and assert their creative vision. The example of the edition of *Candide* illustrated by Clara Tice (1888–1973), an illustrator who indisputably belongs to the latter category, demonstrates that it would be a mistake to value fidelity or imitation over creativity and individuality, fusion over disjunction when considering the aesthetic qualities and interpretive acuity of such artefacts.

As expected by the connoisseur of the artist's books, Tice's aesthetic choices are deliberately unconventional and at times even provocative. When she received this commission, Tice was known as 'the uncrowned queen of Greenwich Village'.[13] A resident of the district that housed the artistic and intellectual bohemia of the Big Apple, the artist became an overnight sensation through a shocking affair: in 1915, her minuscule drawings of female nudes were judged immoral by New York City's Society for the Suppression of Vice led by Inspector Anthony Comstock, who ordered their immediate seizure at Polly's Restaurant, where they were hanging on the walls. During the 1920s, a prolific Tice exhibited her work in galleries, completed an array of commissions in art and design, and illustrated several literary works, including Giovanni Boccaccio's *The Decameron* for Boni & Liveright (1925) and Pierre Loüys's *The Adventures of King Pausole* (1926) for the society bearing the French author's name. The artist's notoriety and her irreverence for tradition were unquestionably the determining factors in Whitman Bennett's decision to choose her as the sole illustrator for his edition of the world classic. Her name is prominently displayed in the paratextual component: first, on the spine below the author's name ('Etchings by Clara Tice' in deluxe copies and 'Illustrated by Clara

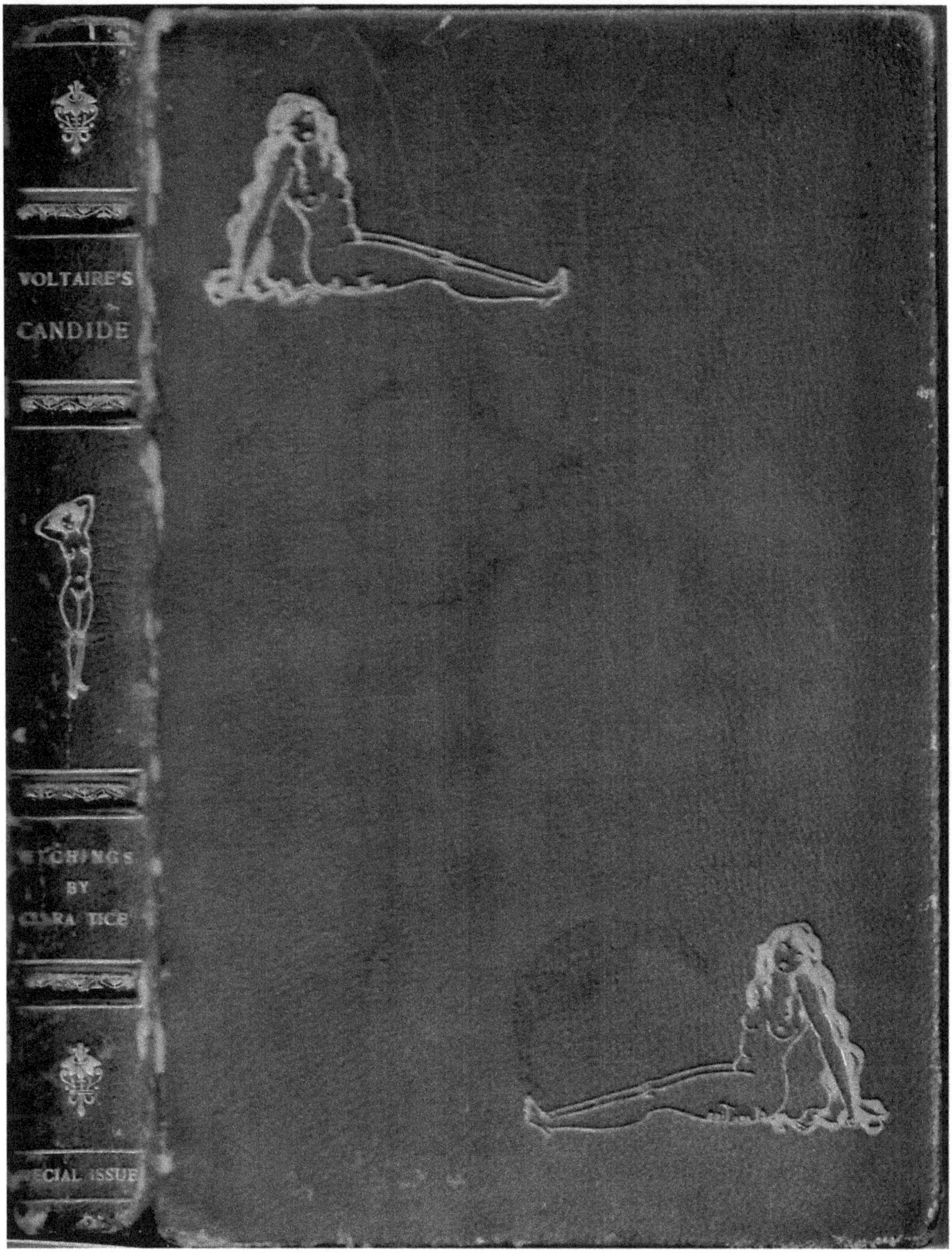

FIG. 7.1. Binding with Clara Tice's drawings of female nudes for Voltaire, *Candide* (Haarlem: Joh. Enschedé en Zonen, 1927), from the deluxe print run, unnumbered copy. Private collection.

Tice' in the ordinary print run), whereas the publisher's name is not inscribed under it, as was customary; second, on the title page, underneath Voltaire's name ('With 10 etchings by Clara Tice'). Reminiscent of the censored designs that had caused so much controversy, two gilt-stamped reclining female nude figures with long, wavy hair decorate the front cover of the binding executed for special copies in Bennett's bindery, and a standing unclothed female, similar in design and appearance, is imprinted in the middle section of their spine (Figure 7.1). The deluxe copies I have examined also contain Tice's signature on the verso of the half-title page. Just like a high-profile actor's popularity with the public today drives a Hollywood blockbuster from its development stage to its worldwide distribution, so must Clara Tice's star power have steered the production of and marketing campaign for this illustrated book, as evidenced by the visual-paratextual features that valorise her name, reputation, and art.

Aside from the unusual binding and visual complement, the edition of *Candide* published by the Bennett Libraries is inspired by eighteenth-century book design and even replicates some of its distinguishing features, including the conventional Dutch title page printed in black and red, with colour and font size used to add visual emphasis to key bibliographical details. Voltaire's literary masterpiece is presented to the American public in a limited octavo edition of '1000 copies, of which numbers 1 to 250 are on special deckle-edge Pannekoek paper; and numbers 251 to 1000 are on papier à la cuve'.[14] Moreover, there are eleven unique copies, unannounced on the ordinary colophon page, which are extra-illustrated and described as follows: 'These are the only copies containing the original etchings of which there are eleven; one especially made for this edition. Each copy contains one of the original drawings after which the etchings were made'.[15] The special copies, as well as the ones forming the deluxe print run, were intended for the book collector.

Published in a single octavo volume, this *Candide* is divided into two parts, but its pagination is continuous: announced as an 'exact reprint of the earliest English text' on the title page, the first part reproduces the first translation of Voltaire's tale into Shakespeare's language (with its original title, *Candide; or, All for the Best*, pp. 7–119; an anonymous translation publicized within the *Gentleman's Magazine* in May 1759); the other section features the *Second Part* (pp. 123–82; an apocryphal continuation initially published in 1760 and often appearing alongside the original).[16] This edition was printed abroad by the prestigious Dutch firm Joh. Enschedé en Zonen, founded in Voltaire's century as the title page informs the reader, a production detail that would have impressed the book connoisseur in the 1920s. The printing company, whose name is inscribed in red on the title page, shares the spotlight with the illustrator in this elaborate production. Based in Haarlem, The Netherlands, this company, which is still in operation nowadays, has gained since its inception an outstanding reputation as a printer of stamps, banknotes, and security documents. In the first decades of the twentieth century, the Dutch firm advertised widely its impressive collection of typefaces in an attempt to attract commissions from American publishers.[17] As a statement printed on the page facing the beginning of Chapter 1 informs the reader, 'This book has been set entirely by hand from type cast by Joh. Enschedé en Zonen from original Didot matrices'.[18] The Didot is, of course, the typeface originally fashioned and widely employed by the famous dynasty that dominated French printing around the time of the Revolution, the Didots. In a survey conducted by Sarah Hyndman, a specialist in the psychology of type, the modern Didot emerged as 'the diamond of all fonts', connoting luxury, craftsmanship, and elegance in the consumer's eye, and Bennett was certainly aware of its prestigious history and unique features.[19] With an attractive typeface marked by clarity and refinement the book designer paired a page layout unencumbered by ornamental features, a combination recalling Pierre Didot the Elder's Louvre editions. The illustrations are separated from the text by tissue guards with the captions printed in italics and red ink. In the deluxe print run, the images appear in colour, although there are significant variations from one copy to another that extend beyond what one might expect to encounter in a hand-coloured print run. To the options offered to the consumer in paper and illustration, the Bennett Libraries added a selection of bindings: copies of the deluxe print run in crimson, azure, and navy blue morocco have resurfaced on the rare book market; copies of the ordinary print run in marbled boards with gilt decorated cloth spine exist in a predominantly brown or blue pattern. Although special copies were also on sale in Voltaire's time (for example, with the plates *avant la lettre* or printed on large vellum paper), the availability of editions in a wider range of configurations based on format, paper, illustration, and binding emerged in the nineteenth century and continued in the following fifty years, as a result of the publishers' need to adapt the book as a consumer product to the market's demand for more choices and the buyers' desire to possess special objects.

Clara Tice's visual adaptation of *Candide* is characterized by her feminist convictions and predilection for erotic art. A New York Dadaist, Tice blatantly defies convention and adopts a critical viewpoint in regard to the source text: her series of etchings is striking in that it places female characters, whose roles in the overall economy of the narrative are secondary, at the forefront, thus endowing them with unprecedented visual agency. In fact, the eponymous protagonist only appears in two of the illustrations: a plate representing his first kiss with Cunégonde behind the screen (Chap. 1); and an image showing the wealthy Persian seducing him (*Part II*, Chap. 2). Instead of observing Candide in action, the reader-viewer encounters Cunégonde receiving a cut in her left flank from the Bulgarian soldier's sword before being sexually attacked (Chap. 8), a woman whose buttock is cut by a janissary while his companion devours a fresh morsel from another piece of human flesh (from the old woman's story, Chap. 12), two stark naked women chased by monkeys who bite their backsides (Chap. 16), Paquette as a prostitute in Venice (Chap. 24), three Circassian beauties from Candide's seraglio with their veils just lifted (*Part II*, Chap. 6), Cunégonde, who has recovered her former outward appearance, in the Sultan's harem (*Part II*, Chap. 10), and finally, Zénoïde and her mother preyed upon by masculine desire (*Part II*, Chap. 13). Using her unique pictorial language and repertoire, the American artist draws compositions brimming with femininity and sensuality that fearlessly exploit the visual topoi and iconographic system of eroticism. The first kiss, boudoir encounters, homosexuality, violent sexual confrontations, cannibalism, prostitution, harem pleasures — no subject belonging to the traditional erotic repertoire is taboo. The frontispiece (Figure 7.2) is even more incendiary: it represents a tame tiger embracing a naked female figure in a seductive pose, which refers to a fleeting textual scene that only the brief caption allows the reader-viewer to associate with Zirza's story (*Part II*, Chap. 7). It is highly unusual in the extensive iconographic corpus associated with *Candide* to discover an image chosen as a frontispiece that relates to the continuation of Voltaire's philosophical tale and not to the original text, especially when the two are published in a single volume, as is most often the case. By making this choice not to focus on Candide, the artist once again diverges from tradition and furthermore does not abide by the general principle governing book illustration, which dictates that the visual narrative be constructed around the principal character's actions. If Candide's banishment from Baron of Thunder-ten-tronckh's castle leads this disciple of Leibnizian optimism to engage in a series of adventures that test his beliefs and endurance, in Voltaire's text female characters are only obstacles or adjuvants in the protagonist's global itinerary and personal development. Refusing to overlook their involvement or transpose them as passive silhouettes, the American artist, who is unafraid to depict sex and sexuality in all its facets and milieus, instead chooses to endow female characters with visual agency in the etchings that she creates for this edition of *Candide*. This is particularly clear if one compares Tice's female figures to their counterparts in mainstream erotica: in the edition produced by the Bennett Libraries, they appear distinctly less passive and less victimized despite the scenarios in which they are depicted. In sum, Tice's compositions are elegant but scandalous, even provocative in light of their feeble textual anchorage and overt eroticism. They reflect the artistic context in which they were created — Greenwich Village of the 1920s — as much as the illustrator's preoccupations and imagery. Inserted in this typographic replica of an eighteenth-century edition, they create a marked dissonance between text and image, material support and graphic adaptation, tradition and originality.

Random House's *Candide* (1928), Designed and Illustrated by Rockwell Kent: Adaptation as Collector's Item

In a letter dated 24 January 1927, Bennett A. Cerf informed the Moby Dick Book Shop of the establishment of Random House, 'an organization that will be devoted to the creation and distribution of books of typographic excellence in America'.[20] Upon its inception, Random House was a business partnership of the highly respected proprietor of Pynson Printers, Elmer Adler, and the new owners of the Modern Library, Bennett A. Cerf and Donald Klopfer, who had purchased the lucrative collection in 1925. The first book published by Random House was this edition of *Candide*, which would indeed be recognized as a masterpiece of book design and illustration by collectors, bibliophiles, critics, and general readers. Although it is highly probable that the idea of publishing an edition of *Candide*

FIG. 7.2. Colour frontispiece by Clara Tice for Voltaire, *Candide* (Haarlem: Joh. Enschedé en Zonen, 1927), from the deluxe print run, unnumbered copy. Private collection.

initially came from Cerf because the text was a bestseller in the Modern Library collection, and we know that the then-overwhelmingly popular artist Rockwell Kent (1882–1971) jumped on board because he had always wanted to illustrate this classic, the mastermind behind the practical side of this publishing venture was in fact Adler, a gifted printer with an exquisite sense of style, an eye for detail, and a dedication to perfection.[21] It is certain that Adler fully understood how to adapt successfully a classic for American bibliophiles. A passionate advocate for 'typographic excellence', he had built a solid business on his knowledge of the elaborate formula that transformed a combination of words and images into a collector's item through book design, fine printing, and original illustration.

Every material detail of this adaptation of *Candide* was carefully crafted and endowed with significance. This limited quarto edition consists of 1470 numbered copies printed on all rag French paper, bound in gold-embossed maize buckram, and 95 special copies, hand-coloured 'in the studio of the artist' (primarily by artist Ione Robinson), bound in decorated cloth with leather backstrip, and sold in custom-made slipcases.[22] All the copies contained Rockwell Kent's signature on the colophon page. The text was hand-set in a type created by the German graphic designer Lucian Bernhard (1883–1972), who had emigrated from Berlin to New York in the early 1920s. The colophon informs the reader that the paragraph designs were executed by Kent and cast by the Bauersche Giesserei (a German firm established in Frankfurt in 1837, with an office newly opened in New York). By naming the type designer and the foundry on the colophon page, Adler no doubt seeks to confer an aura of prestige on his edition, to link it to the illustrious tradition of European book design and fine printing. The iconographic component of this edition, executed entirely by an American artist, is not only copious but also polymorphous. It comprises four categories of images: ornate capitals (inserted at the beginning of each chapter), dingbats (a unique typographical feature of this edition), in-text vignettes (reproduced at the bottom of pages), and paratextual illustrations (half page, title page, copyright, bibliographical note, and colophon). As they narrate the story of Candide while dramatizing the theory of optimism, the images form a complementary and strategic alliance with the verbal component of the edition. For example, the infratextual vignette depicting the lashing administered to Candide by a Bulgarian soldier fuses on the page with the brief textual fragment upon which it is loosely based, to create a perfectly balanced block in which the visual does not overpower the verbal (Figure 7.3). This is not a scene described with any precision by Voltaire but entirely orchestrated by Kent's imagination. In an expressive fashion, the artist creates an opposition between the dynamic, vigorous persecutor and his suffering victim, situating this interaction at the forefront of the image, upon relatively flat but rough terrain devoid of any visual detail that would distract the reader's attention. The destruction caused by war is inscribed in the background, where extensive smoke billows into the sky and a distant village unnaturally perched on a mountain occupies a precarious position. If Clara Tice's etchings are purposefully disconnected from *Candide*, offering what in her time could be construed as a feminist rewriting of the canonical work, Rockwell Kent's

12

figure and merit never pay anything; are you not five feet five tall?" "Yes, gentlemen," said he, bowing, "that is my height." "Ah, sir, come to table; we will not only pay your expenses, we will never allow a man like you to be short of money; men were only made to help each other." "You are in the right," said Candide, "that is what Doctor Pangloss was always telling me, and I see that everything is for the best." They begged him to accept a few crowns, he took them and wished to give them an IOU; they refused to take it and all sat down to table. "Do you not love tenderly..." "Oh, yes," said he. "I love Mademoiselle Cunegonde tenderly." "No," said one of the gentlemen. "We were asking if you do not tenderly love the King of the Bulgarians." "Not a bit," said he, "for I have never seen him." "What! He is the most charming of Kings, and you must drink his health." "Oh, gladly, gentlemen." And he drank. "That is sufficient," he was told. "You are now the support, the aid, the defender, the hero of the Bulgarians; your fortune is made and your glory assured." They immediately put irons on his legs and took him to a regiment. He was made to turn to the right and left, to raise the ramrod and return the ramrod, to take aim, to fire, to double up, and he was given thirty strokes with a stick; the next day he drilled not quite so badly, and received only twenty strokes; the day after, he only had ten and was looked on as a prodigy by his comrades. Candide was completely mystified and could not make out how he was a hero. One fine spring day he thought he would take a walk, going straight ahead, in

FIG. 7.3. Page number 12 with an untitled vignette by Rockwell Kent, from Voltaire, *Candide* (New York: Random House, 1928), copy no. 84. Private collection.

line drawings are discreet additions and echo Voltaire's satire, creating a peaceful symbiosis between text and image.[23]

Any reader who has held in her hands a copy of this edition will not be surprised to learn that it garnered critical accolades immediately after its publication. The Literary Guild, established in 1927 by Samuel W. Craig and Harold K. Guinzberg as a competitor to the Book of the Month Club, selected it as its special Christmas book in 1929. Four short articles published in the Literary Guild's *Wings*, which discuss this prestigious selection, provide us with information on the features that distinguished a successful book adaptation in 1920s America. In many respects, these articles resemble the additional features normally included on a DVD of a film adaptation and serve similar purposes. In an article explaining the selection of this edition as the Literary Guild's special Christmas book, Carl Van Doren, the organization's chairman, praises the literary merit of 'an established masterpiece, the quintessence of all the books in which wisdom, wit, and malice are brought to bear upon the spectacle of human life', thus underlining the originality and merit of the source text as a classic.[24] After declaring this edition 'what is generally agreed to be the finest piece of book-making ever achieved in the United States', the American critic highlights the relevance of Voltaire's philosophical tale to a contemporary society politically confronted with 'a kind of official optimism in power'.[25] The determining factor in this selection, however, was 'the incomparable dress in which [this *Candide*] has been presented by its printer and illustrator', and the new edition published by the Literary Guild replicated it as closely as possible.[26] The issue of the magazine *Wings* in which Van Doren's article appears also includes a brief introduction to Voltaire and a note on Rockwell Kent, whom the anonymous author of this brief commentary proclaims 'justly the most popular living American artist today'.[27] Another complimentary piece, 'The Story of Your "Candide"', offers a behind-the-scenes look at its production, praises its unique material qualities, and accentuates the affordability of the product.[28] In sum, book design and illustration play a crucial role in the adaptation of a classic for the 1920s American public, who can appreciate fine workmanship, high-quality materials, distinctive typography, and creative illustration.

Ives Washburn's *Candide* (1929), Illustrated by Howard Simon: Adaptation as Remake

In film studies, a 'remake' refers to an adaptation that is based on a previous cinematic production not a literary source.[29] *Remaking* as a practice, however, can also extend to illustrating a book, and the edition that I discuss in this section can be considered a remake of the edition of *Candide* published by the Bennett Libraries. From a typographical perspective, the 1929 *Candide* bears a close resemblance to its 1927 precursor and it reveals the same preoccupations with material presentation (the edition published by the Bennett Libraries was already on sale when Ives Washburn's was being designed); and in regard to its series of illustrations, it exemplifies a similar desire to offer a distinguished, albeit deliberately less provocative, visual supplement while banking on the artist's reputation. The status of this edition as a remake is apparent when you place the editions side by side and examine their features. Ives Washburn, who had just launched his own publishing enterprise in 1926, produced an edition of Voltaire's tale that appeared just three days after the Wall Street Crash.[30] In the decades following, Washburn would make his mark as the publisher of detective fiction and children's literature, but in those formative years he was experimenting with various genres and specialized markets. As a newly minted publisher, Washburn had to exercise extreme caution in his editorial choices, and it thus comes as no surprise that he made his publishing debut with two safe bets: Théophile Gautier's *Mademoiselle de Maupin*, a hedonistic romance of love and passion that had become a commercial success after 1850 and a *fin-de-siècle* cult text; and Voltaire's *Candide*, a philosophical tale that had achieved the status of international bestseller immediately after its initial publication in 1759 and afterwards inspired a wealth of illustrated editions throughout Europe. The dust jacket designed for this edition of *Candide*, a rare surviving copy of which I was fortunate to locate, contains significant information about this book, its context of production, and the publisher's motivations (Figure 7.4).

It is unusual to find such a long editorial justification on a dust wrapper, but its presence could be explained by the fact that this protective element of the book was often discarded by readers and seldom preserved once the item entered a public collection, so the publisher did not think it inappropriate to use it primarily for marketing purposes. On a sinuous tree-of-life green motif decorating the front side of the dust wrapper, a series of three simple frames consecrates the creative triumvirate responsible for this book, the decreasing size of the rectangles connoting the order of importance attributed to each creator of meaning: at the top, the author responsible for the source text ('Voltaire | *Candide*'), to whom the most visible place of honour is typographically assigned; in the middle, the adaptor who produced the visual complement ('wood engravings by | Howard Simon'); and at the bottom, the publishing figure who engineered the publication of the edition ('Ives Washburn | New York'). Curiously, the front flap, which seeks to give an idea of what the book is about to the purchaser, unabashedly plagiarizes verbatim excerpts from Philip Littell's preface to the 1918 Boni & Liveright edition forming part of the celebrated Modern Library collection, including its memorable beginning:

> Ever since 1759, when Voltaire wrote 'Candide' in ridicule of the notion that this is the best of all possible worlds, this world has been a gayer place for readers. Voltaire wrote it in three days, and five or six generations have found that its laughter does not grow cold.[31]

Washburn's edition thus bears the trace of multiple previous editions as well as being a remake of a specific one.

On the back cover of the dust wrapper, Washburn carefully carves out his niche in the specialized book market and presents the context in which his venture was launched: 'During the past few years there has been an increasing demand for books strictly modern in spirit although classic in the best sense of the word, printed in beautiful format and bound for the most fastidious collector'.[32] The American editor

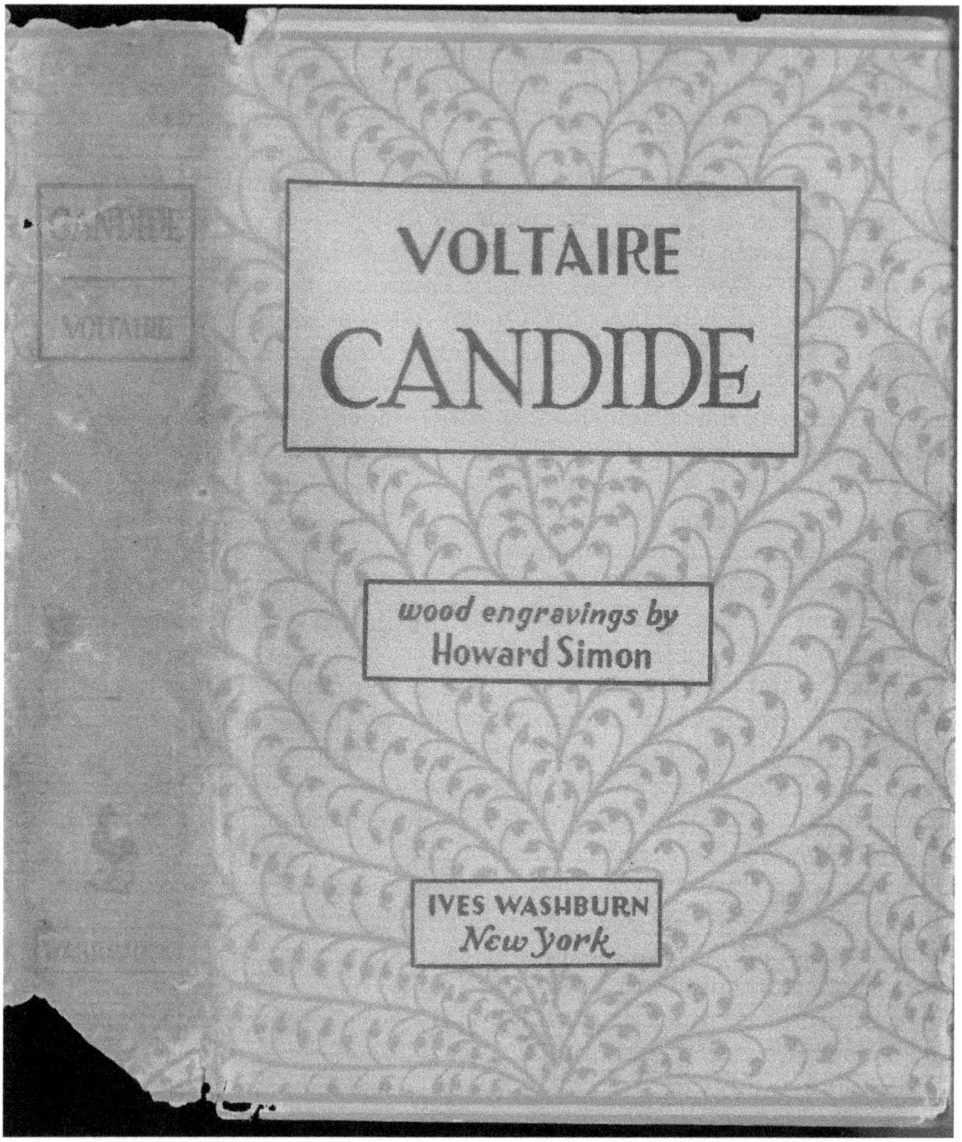

FIG. 7.4. Partial dust jacket (front and spine covers) for Voltaire, *Candide* (New York: Ives Washburn, 1929). Private collection.

then remarks that fine press books published in limited quantities 'at prices usually far beyond the reach of the average man's pocket-book'[33] were conceived to meet the demand for this type of materially appealing consumer product. Washburn states his mission as a publisher in clear terms:

> It will be the policy of Ives Washburn from now on to issue trade editions, unlimited and easily available, of the classics which are most in demand. It will be the publisher's endeavor to make these books as fine in typography, layout and binding as any of the press books the prices for which range from fifteen to over one hundred dollars, and to offer them to the public at a price that all book-lovers can afford. All books issued in The Chantecler Library will be printed on fine paper, from type particularly chosen to fit the character of each individual work. They will be uniformly bound in black vellum cloth, will be die-stamped in silver and will have stained tops.[34]

This quotation is taken from the first of two relatively long paragraphs that market this edition as a compromise between the fine press book, issued in a limited edition for book collectors who can afford its hefty price tag, and its affordable counterpart, the trade edition that aims to appeal to the reader as an aesthetically pleasing and materially appealing consumer product but is less expensive and more widely distributed. In this statement, Washburn additionally references a specific triad — 'typography, layout, and binding' — when addressing the presentation of the book, and those are distinguishable aspects of the edition published by the Bennett Libraries as well. The observation concerning expensive press books could be seen as a veiled reference not only to the Bennett Libraries' *Candide* but also to Random House's original edition of the same title, from which Washburn seeks to distinguish his product on the basis of price and distribution. Furthermore, Washburn's edition of *Candide* was part of the Chantecler Library of Illustrated Classics, which is not without significance in an era when book collectors constituted a large segment of the market. By forming a collection, publishers hoped to incite buyers to purchase it in its entirety, even though some of its components might interest them less than others, or not at all. What is moreover interesting about this paratextual editorial statement is that it reveals the transitional phase in which editions of the classics would find themselves in the immediate aftermath of the Wall Street Crash. Washburn expects that some of his editions will contain a limited print run 'for those especially interested in the work of the artist chosen, printed in larger format [which is not the case for *Candide*] with illustrations personally made by the artist' — an appeal to both the book collector and the iconophile, whose purchasing power was still of consequence at the time.[35]

To the triad of book arts mentioned above Washburn then adds illustration. As we have seen before, the choice of illustrator is instrumental in the process of adaptation and an important selling point for any edition. Washburn endeavours to commission 'the best artist available for the specific book in mind' and, by also entrusting him with the design of the book, desires a uniformity of creative vision.[36] Below a brief advertisement for *Mademoiselle de Maupin* on the rear flap of the dust jacket, Washburn astutely comments, as a marketing strategy, on Howard Simon's reputation, praising his appeal to American and international collectors as well as signalling the acquisition of his work by important museums:

> Mr. Simon's work has been collected both on this side of the Atlantic and abroad by museums as well as by individuals. One of his wood engravings was included in the fifty best prints of the year for 1928. An illustration he has made for *Mademoiselle de Maupin* is in the collection of wood-engravings at the Baltimore Museum, and his work is in The British Museum collection.[37]

Trained in prestigious American and French institutions, Howard Simon (1902–1979), who would later author an important contribution to the study of book illustration (*Five Hundred Years of Art and Illustration: From Albrecht Dürer to Rockwell Kent*, 1942), learnt his woodblock technique from Japanese instructors and excelled in its application to book illustration.

The dust wrapper highlights similarities between Ives Washburn's creative vision and that of his predecessor, Whitman Bennett, which one can infer from the material and aesthetic qualities of his 1927 edition of *Candide* in the absence of surviving archival documentation. This material adaptation of *Candide*, a work that Washburn places among 'the classics which are most in demand' in his paratextual intervention, imitates the edition published by the Bennett Libraries in other respects as well. *Candide* ('Part One', pp. 3–133) is again followed by a continuation ('Part Two', pp. 137–208; the same translation is used); surprisingly, however, since this is not announced on the dust jacket or the title page, the edition also features *Zadig* (pp. 211–326), another philosophical tale by Voltaire frequently edited in America, but which does not surpass in popularity the star title of this product. The choice of also offering *Zadig* might have been motivated by the editor's desire to distinguish his remake from the edition that had otherwise inspired it in form and content. The colophon page contains further specifications concerning this octavo edition. The deluxe print run consists of 160 copies (of which 150 were on sale), containing sixteen tipped-in wood-engraved plates on india paper; these special copies were numbered by hand and printed on all rag deckle-edge paper.[38] The ordinary print run remained relatively modest but was more than double the size compared to its precursor: 2000 copies on watermarked rag paper with the illustrations printed from the original wood engravings. The price inscribed on the dust wrapper of this print run was $5.00. Similarly to the two editions examined in the previous sections of this chapter, the text is set in a special font: 12-point Granjon, a revived typeface with its origins in the sixteenth century, which matches in style and aesthetics the wood engravings inserted in the book. Linking it to the Garamond typeface in a seminal study published in *The Fleuron*, Beatrice Warde declares it 'worthy to rank with Caslon for usefulness, with Centaur for beauty; sharp enough for publicity, clear enough for a dictionary'.[39] At the time, the printer chosen by Washburn, Vail-Ballou Press (located in Binghamton, NY), was mailing out booklets with specimens of new typefaces (including the Granjon) and decorative material to interested publishers who could use these advertisements to update their *Specimen Book*, previously circulated by the press.[40] The novelty appeal of this typeface, in conjunction with its illustrious origins in the French Renaissance and its typographic qualities, increased its market value. On the colophon page,

Washburn also mentions the paper supplier, Herman Scott Chalfant, and repeats the illustrator and book designer's name before affixing his emblem, a rooster on an open book (a synonym for rooster or cockerel being 'chantecler' or 'chanticleer'). Not coincidentally, the watermark also echoes the same image.

Another feature reprised from the Bennett Libraries edition is the bicolour title page. In green and black, this title page reiterates the informational content of the front dust wrapper in the exact same descending order, but a humorous vignette representing Pangloss holding a book and discoursing between two naked young children, probably intended to be Candide and Cunégonde, is inserted after the title. Infratextual decoration consists of ornate initials, a distinctive feature also of the Random House *Candide*, with stylized motifs of vegetal origin superimposed on landscape fragments of marine, mountainous, or desert origins; emblematic elements evoking the themes of voyage and the exotic are scattered throughout (e.g. village, bridge, ship, oriental palace, and tropical tree). As expected, given the relatively small number of full-page illustrations (sixteen in total for both *Candide* and its continuation, as mentioned above), sizable gaps mark the visual continuum and the images are inserted at uneven intervals throughout the book. Interestingly, Simon's wood engravings earned the praise of a contemporary critic, Winfred Porter Truesdell, who finds them to be 'strong in literary content as befits their use as illustrations', without leaving the reader-viewer 'wanting in understanding', and 'cover[ing] a wide range of subject'.[41] The table of illustrations (p. ix), an element lacking in the edition produced by the Bennett Libraries, establishes a direct link between the uncaptioned images and the text from which they are adapted, although the wood engravings do not always face the exact page from which the caption is extracted. For the frontispiece (Figure 7.5), Simon places the content of his adaptation under the moral gravitas of the famous Voltairean dictum urging readers to cultivate their gardens; the artist interprets literally a phrase that the 1920s educated reader undoubtedly recognized, and visually exploits this familiarity to advocate for a (re)reading of the classic while implicitly highlighting through his work the uniqueness of this new incarnation of *Candide*. The medium chosen by the artist allows him to create a particularly distinctive adaptation of this closing scene: shading, line, and composition are carefully used to delineate four main planes, clearly separated from one another, and each embodying its own meaning. On an agrarian background, an earnest Candide is portrayed preparing his land, while a nearly naked Pangloss by his side (seemingly transported from a medieval painting), his shovel reposing in the earth, is still engaged in futile discourse, as he previously was in the vignette on the title page. The two intermediary planes — the land already toiled and the farmhouse on the banks of the Propontis — connote stability, simplicity, and order. However, the sun symbolically setting in the background and thick layers of clouds cleverly foreshadow the continuation of the main character's troubles in Part Two.

Whereas Tice was irreverent to tradition in her artistic choices, Simon consistently illustrates the *sine qua non* scenes in the iconographic corpus formed by the illustrated editions of *Candide*. His images are closely linked to their verbal

FIG. 7.5. Frontispiece by Howard Simon for Voltaire's *Candide* (New York: Ives Washburn, 1929), from the deluxe print run, copy no. 14. Private collection.

support, a connection that circumscribes the semantic polyvalence of the image and allows the reader-viewer familiar with the text to identify the scenes represented even when examining the edition at a glance; in contrast, Tice's etchings conserve a high degree of autonomy in relation to the text. Within his infratextual sequence, Simon first represents three scenes of violence: the carnage of war (Chap. 3), the Lisbon earthquake (Chap. 5), and the auto-da-fé (Chap. 6). He then expands this visual narrative of destruction to include the stories of female characters: Cunégonde's adventures are referenced in the image showing the bargain concluded by the Jewish Don Issachar with the Great Inquisitor (Chap. 8); and the tangential account of the old woman is visually transposed in the overtaking at sea by the corsairs of the ship carrying the daughter of Pope Urban X (Chap. 11). To continue the visual sequence, Simon focuses his attention on the Eldorado episode, showing the travellers leaving in the machine built by the king's engineers to allow them to traverse the impenetrable mountains (Chap. 18). For the remaining three illustrations, Simon visibly draws his inspiration from Clara Tice, remaking three of her images that focus on erotic encounters: Paquette and Brother Giroflée frolicking in a Venetian pleasure house (Chap. 24); the homoerotic seduction of Candide by the wealthy Persian (*Part Two*, Chap. 2); and finally, Candide in his lascivious seraglio, after having found complete happiness in carnal pleasure in the midst of a terrestrial paradise resembling Eldorado (*Part Two*, Chap. 6). To conclude his iconographic series, the illustrator adapts an image with the Leibnizian caption 'All things are good: everything is best' (Pangloss's last words pronounced when Candide discovers him at death's doorstep in a hospital), an image that thematically recalls the *ars moriendi* iconography appreciated during the Middle Ages. In his images, Simon effectively transposes the accumulation of striking descriptive details that mark Voltaire's style with carefully chosen visual elements characterized by great evocative and symbolic power. What is lost in this visual adaptation, where forms of dark behaviour are accentuated by the artist through the use of thick lines and large black surfaces, is the 'gaiety' lavished on the page by a 'pen [that] runs and laughs', referenced on the inner front flap of the dust wrapper. In the artist's vision, *Candide* as a classic imparts vital lessons to a twentieth-century audience that could benefit from it as much as Voltaire's contemporaries and other generations had done in France and throughout the world since the Age of Enlightenment. Visually disconnected from the eighteenth century but still linked to the *Ancien Régime*, Washburn's edition of *Candide* is a remake that does not convey a preoccupation with historical authenticity through font choice or page design, as did the edition produced by the Bennett Libraries. Nevertheless, like its precursor, it distances itself from period-inspired visual representation for the sake of novelty.

Williams, Belasco, and Meyers's *Candide* (1930), Illustrated by Mahlon Blaine and Arthur Zaidenberg: Adaptation for the Mass Market

Published in 1930, this illustrated edition of *Candide* marks a turning-point in the American section of the iconographic corpus to which it belongs. From fine press book-objects and limited editions, illustrated classics transition into the realm of consumer products designed for the mass market, and the illustrious colophon page is no longer deemed of interest. Devoid of a note containing bibliographical details about its publication and material presentation, this edition of *Candide* also discards its customary textual pendant — Part II. The edition commissioned by Williams, Belasco, and Meyers contains, however, a frontispiece and five full-page plates designed by Mahlon Blaine, as well as twenty-one vignettes executed by Arthur Zaidenberg, the first of which is placed at the beginning of the tale and the rest at the end of chapters, like tailpieces in *Ancien Régime* books, except that their function is not merely ornamental. Robert Arrington recalls that 'around 1930 [Blaine] was asked by Williams, Belasco and Meyers to do drawings for their re-issues of classic works, such as *Candide*'.[42] There were at least eight other New York editions modelled on the Williams, Belasco, and Meyers prototype and published in the same year, which indicates that it was an extremely popular product.[43] On the front side of the modern dust jacket designed specifically for the edition issued by the Illustrated Editions Company (Figure 7.6), above the illustrator's name the publishers have strategically placed a laudatory quotation about Voltaire's *Candide* attributed to W. Somerset Maugham; using a similarly exalted tone, the front flap elaborates on the text as a world classic, with the following conclusion:

> *More* than a satire, more than a daring buffoonery, CANDIDE ranks among the foremost narratives of pure adventure and masterly exercise of imagination in any language — in any age. In addition to all the unblushing realism and the Rabelaisian humor, there is also the fascination and consummate interest of one of the world's finest *stories*.[44]

The lavishing of praise continues in the brief introduction which, in addition to listing other defining qualities that enhance the readability of the text, highlights its relevance to contemporary readers. When comparing the commercial editions modelled on the Williams, Belasco, and Meyers prototype, it becomes apparent that they differ primarily in their exterior appearance, composition of the title page, the type of paper used, and the overall quality of the printing. Surprisingly, in American university libraries, these small-size books illustrated by Blaine and Zaidenberg seem to be amongst the most favoured by students, if one judges by the abundance of marginalia filling their empty spaces, which demonstrates engagement with the product and thus suggests its success as an adaptation. My observation is, of course, based on empirical evidence and it needs to be verified more widely.[45]

A powerful means of adapting the text, illustration is also an aspect of the product that effectively incites consumers to purchase it in interwar America. In all the editions in this section, the illustrator's name is featured prominently in the visual-paratextual framing, but Arden Book Company goes even further by marketing its product as 'profusely illustrated'.[46] A prolific and eclectic artist, Mahlon Blaine

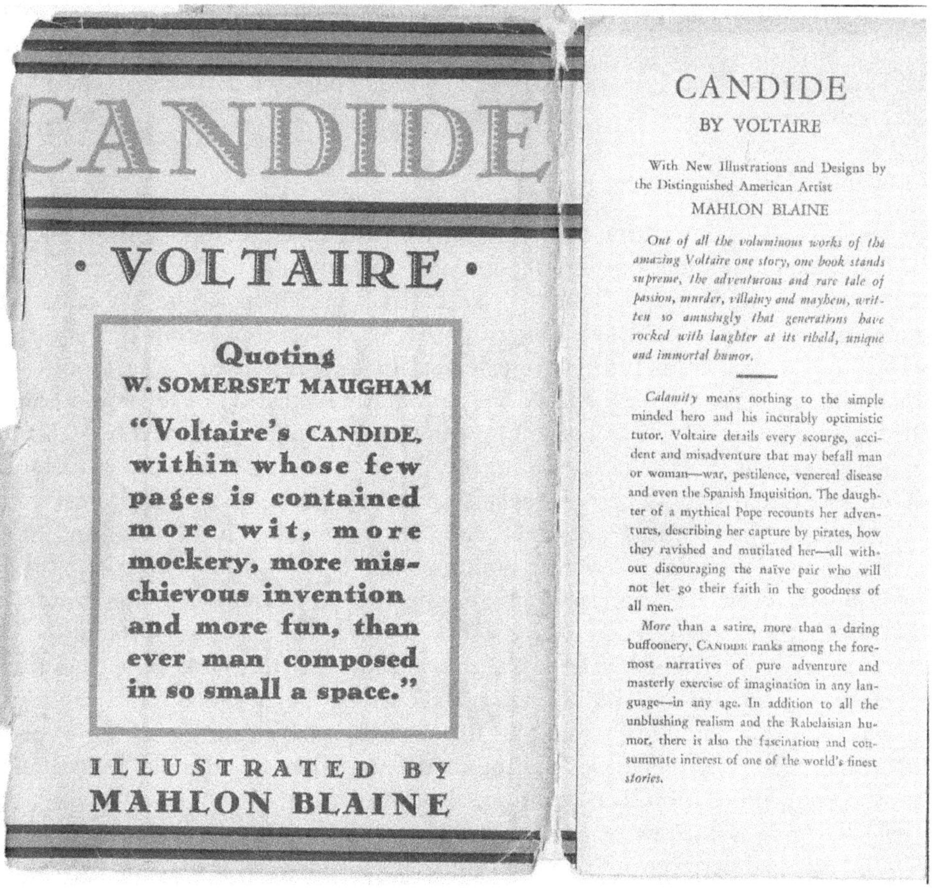
CANDIDE
• VOLTAIRE •
Quoting
W. SOMERSET MAUGHAM
"Voltaire's CANDIDE, within whose few pages is contained more wit, more mockery, more mischievous invention and more fun, than ever man composed in so small a space."
ILLUSTRATED BY
MAHLON BLAINE
CANDIDE
BY VOLTAIRE
With New Illustrations and Designs by the Distinguished American Artist
MAHLON BLAINE
Out of all the voluminous works of the amazing Voltaire one story, one book stands supreme, the adventurous and rare tale of passion, murder, villainy and mayhem, written so amusingly that generations have rocked with laughter at its ribald, unique and immortal humor.
Calamity means nothing to the simple minded hero and his incurably optimistic tutor. Voltaire details every scourge, accident and misadventure that may befall man or woman—war, pestilence, venereal disease and even the Spanish Inquisition. The daughter of a mythical Pope recounts her adventures, describing her capture by pirates, how they ravished and mutilated her—all without discouraging the naïve pair who will not let go their faith in the goodness of all men.
More than a satire, more than a daring buffoonery, CANDIDE ranks among the foremost narratives of pure adventure and masterly exercise of imagination in any language—in any age. In addition to all the unblushing realism and the Rabelaisian humor, there is also the fascination and consummate interest of one of the world's finest stories.

FIG. 7.6. Partial dust jacket (front cover and front flap) for Voltaire, *Candide* (New York: Illustrated Editions Company, 1930). Private collection.

(1894–1969) favours scenes copiously treated by his predecessors, but he filters them through his own lens to produce decadent compositions with an erotic emphasis and wrought with visual details. Blaine's focus is on the following subjects: the Oreillon girls posing with half-human monkeys at their feet (frontispiece, Chap. 16); the baron witnessing the amorous encounter between Candide and Cunégonde (Chap. 1); an attractive Cunégonde wearing only a necklace and shoes shared by the Jew and the Grand Inquisitor (Chap. 8); the pillaging of the galley carrying Pope Urban X's daughter by the pirates (Chap. 11); the marquise asking Candide to take off her garter in Paris (Chap. 22); and Paquette and Friar Giroflée strolling in Venice (Chap. 24). Although his name was not advertised like that of his collaborator, Arthur Zaidenberg (1903–1990) added elaborate tailpieces executed in clear lines that parody characters, themes, and actions, while accentuating the dramatic tension, humorous quality, and excessive cruelty of the satire. In the heterogeneous series that they designed for this edition, the artists embrace a predilection for fantastic art and the macabre, adopt a caricatural style that works well with a text characterized in the introduction as 'literary caricature', and portray feminine characters through the prism of fantasy and eroticism.[47] In terms of representation and subject matter, these images have much in common with comic books, popularized in the United States during the 1930s.

Conclusion

As we have seen, illustration is merely one of the adapted components of an illustrated book and it needs be considered in relation not only to the text surrounding it but also to the material context in which it is presented to the reader-viewer-consumer. For researchers who have approached book illustration by relying on word and image, book history, intermediality, and reader-response theories, an examination of the transfer, transformation, and remediation of form and content through the prism of graphic adaptation not only offers them a new lens through which to extend their analyses to hitherto largely ignored material considerations of the illustrated book as an object *and* consumer product, but also an incentive to include in the accepted paradigm this vital participant in the local and global marketplace — the reader-viewer-consumer. The book as a physical object has traditionally been the primary focus of the discipline known as the history of the book, in particular descriptive bibliography, while artistic production has conventionally been the terrain of art history, but the illustrated book has always fallen into a no man's land. It has not generally been studied integrally as a bimodal entity made up of words and images in a material configuration of paper, ink, binding, text, and artwork through the processes of editorial intervention, book design, illustration, and printing, for the purpose of being sold to and, to a variable degree, valued by readers-viewers-consumers. It is thus important to move beyond material descriptions that are informative, and word and image studies that generally ignore the material envelope of the text, as interesting as they may be in and of themselves, to consider as meaningful the choices made independently or in collaboration by various adapters in their attempt to adapt a text to a target readership. In simple terms, a page typeset in elegant Didot roman characters, bereft of typographic ornamentation, and facing a full-page provocative etching will not have the same aesthetic and cognitive effect on the reader as a page laid out in a new typeface such as the Bernhard classic on a page with exquisite typography, eye-catching dingbats, and an ornamented initial or integrated vignette that blends in and discreetly accompanies the text. One edition is not better than the other; they are simply different but just as important as products of adaptation. It is equally essential to consider illustration as part of this process of adaptation because images provide a powerful means by which to adapt a classic for a specific readership.

As this study has demonstrated, publishing an illustrated edition of *Candide* in interwar America means capitalizing on the value of the text as a literary classic and emphasizing its relevance to contemporary society in paratextual materials such as dust jackets and introductions, determining a material configuration that the intended buyers will find tempting and worth investing in, and commissioning plates that are germane to Voltaire's philosophical tale and add a new layer of meaning to or critical commentary on it. In adapting this canonical work for book collectors and the cultural elite, American publishers such as the Bennett Libraries, Random House, and Ives Washburn opted to use high-quality materials (paper, ink, and binding) and alluring typefaces with classic or modern undertones, limited the print run to a relatively small number of special and ordinary copies, and invested in the services of a book designer and illustrator with star power or recognized talent. During this period, it was normal to find numbered copies and artwork that were signed by publishers, printers, or artists, which enhanced their value as unique products and valuable collectibles. By proceeding in this fashion, publishers tapped into the considerable market for fine press, illustrated, and signed books. At the other end of the illustrated book production spectrum, however, are commercial products like the edition commissioned by Williams, Belasco, and Meyers, which aimed to appeal to a large segment of the public and did not rely considerably on their material presentation as a selling point (although the artist's name, and by extension the illustrative component, warrants special mention on the title page). Even if the details of the adaptation process are in this case obscure — their traces to be potentially uncovered in archives — those inexpensive consumer products are just as much the product of fashioning a text to suit the tastes and interests of a specific segment of the public as their attractive and expensive counterparts. Presented with a wealth of editions, readers-viewers-consumers of *Candide* as adapted by the Bennett Libraries, Random House, Ives Washburn, and Williams, Belasco, and Meyers will certainly not share the same reading experience because the act of reading is not only a cognitive process but also a tactile and visual experience.

Notes to Chapter 7

1. The field of adaptation studies primarily deals with adaptations that exist independently of their source of inspiration or verbal foundation (plays, films, operas, etc.). The illustrated book, which is the subject of this chapter, is different from those types of adaptation in that it is a 'source-bound' product, by virtue of containing illustrations inserted alongside the text of origin to which they are connected to a variable degree.
2. I would like to thank Ann Lewis and Silke Arnold-de Simine for their insightful and generous feedback on this chapter.
3. Elleström, 'Adaptation Within the Field of Media Transformations', p. 114.
4. Murray, *The Adaptation Industry*, p. 13.
5. Hutcheon, with O'Flynn, *A Theory of Adaptation*. The example mentioned in this context is Aubrey Beardsley's illustrations for Oscar Wilde's *Salomé* (p. 15). The epilogue contains a more detailed discussion of the medium of the book as interactive adaptation (as in the form of an eBook for example) (pp. 201–06).
6. Brigitte Friant-Kessler proposes the following useful definition of 'graphic afterlife': '*a fluctuating spectral reshaping of a recognisable visual motif or rendering which is either reproduced, re-interpreted, adapted and/or put to another use.* A print after a painting can thus be seen as a first-degree graphic afterlife. A character from an identified literary illustration that resurfaces in the context of political satire is also a graphic afterlife; as such, it may be given a new rhetorical sense but is acknowledged as the ghost of a previously circulated representation'. For details, see her article 'Visual Sterneana: Graphic Afterlives and a Sense of Infinite Mobility', *Journal for Eighteenth-Century Studies*, 39.4 (December 2016), 643–62 (p. 644).

7. Elleström, 'Adaptation Within the Field of Media Transformations', p. 114. For an interesting article that examines book illustration side by side with cinematic adaptation through the lens of intermediality, see Ann Lewis, 'Intermedial Approaches to Marivaux's *La Vie de Marianne*: Text, Illustration, Film', *Journal for Eighteenth-Century Studies*, 39.4 (December 2016), 621–42.
8. Mary-Céline Newbould, *Adaptations of Laurence Sterne's Fiction: Sterneana, 1760–1840* (Farnham: Ashgate, 2013). See, in particular, Chapter 5, '"An Illustration to the Mind's Eye": Sterneana and the Visual', pp. 153–213.
9. This chapter is a revised version of a paper originally presented at the Legenda conference *Adapting the Canon* (October 2014, Institute for Modern Languages Research, London), which advanced in significant ways our collective thinking about the expansion of adaptation studies. Recent scholarly efforts to consider the intersection of illustration studies and adaptation studies include Kate Newell's groundbreaking *Expanding Adaptation Networks: From Illustration to Novelization* (2017) and Illustr4tio's fifth conference (*Illustration and Adaptation*, October 2019, Université de Bourgogne, Dijon, France). While illustration as a form of adaptation has received more attention from scholars such as Newell after this chapter was submitted, it should be noted that *the illustrated book* — the material support of the text and its illustration — remains largely unstudied as a product of adaptation, as I argue below.
10. Murray, *The Adaptation Industry*, p. 12.
11. By using in this context the composite term 'reader-viewer', inherited from word and image studies, I am referring specifically to a book with a visual component. From my own argument that the book itself is an adapted product, one can infer that a non-illustrated book is also the direct result of adaptation.
12. See, for example, the following exhibit catalogues and bibliographical inventories: Angela Graas and others, *Candide: Illustrierte Ausgaben eines Klassikers. Katalog einer Ausstellung der Universitätsbibliothek Trier* (Trier: Universitätsbibliothek Trier, 2000), with a complementary website <http://candide.uni-trier.de> [accessed 30 December 2019]); Marie-Laure Chastang, 'Rencontre des œuvres de Voltaire et de leurs illustrateurs (1796–2002): essai bibliographique à l'intention des futurs chercheurs', *Revue Voltaire*, 3 (2003), 131–214; J. Patrick Lee, 'Bibliographie des éditions illustrées américaines des œuvres de Voltaire', *Revue Voltaire*, 5 (2005), 285–307; and Gernot Uwe Gabel, *Voltaires 'Candide': die illustrierten Ausgaben des 20. Jahrhunderts aus den deutschsprachigen Ländern* (Hürth: Gemini, 2012). For an informed and perceptive survey of this iconographic corpus, see Peter Tucker, *The Interpretation of a Classic: The Illustrated Editions of 'Candide'* (Oxford: The Previous Parrot Press, 1993). Some in-depth studies on a more limited (from a temporal or geographical perspective) scale have also engaged with these illustrations. For example: Robert Vilain, 'Images of Optimism? German Illustrated Editions of Voltaire's *Candide* in the Context of the First World War', *Oxford German Studies*, 37.2 (2008), 223–52; Ghislain Chaufour, *Candide antérot: Voltaire commenté à partir des vingt-six 'Images à Candide' de Paul Klee* (Paris: Cerf, 2009); David Adams, 'L'Illustration de *Candide* dans les *Romans et Contes de M. de Voltaire* (1778)', in *Les 250 ans de 'Candide': lectures et relectures*, ed. by Nicholas Cronk and Nathalie Ferrand (Leuven: Peeters, 2014), pp. 561–75; Eric Gatefin, '*Candide* vu par Joann Sfar: illustration, commentaire et caricature d'un "texte sacré"', in *Les 250 ans de 'Candide'*, ed. by Cronk and Ferrand, pp. 605–16; Christina Ionescu, '*Candide* à New York: éditions illustrées américaines de l'entre-deux-guerres', in *Les 250 ans de 'Candide'*, ed. by Cronk and Ferrand, pp. 577–603; and Kathrin Baumeister, *Die beste aller Welten: Künstler illustrieren Voltaires Candide. Chodowiecki — Monnet — Moreau — Unold — Klee — Kubin* (Berlin: Reimer, 2015).
13. See Marie T. Keller, 'Clara Tice, "Queen of Greenwich Village"', in *Women in Dada: Essays on Sex, Gender, and Identity*, ed. by Naomi Sawelson-Gorse (Cambridge, MA: MIT Press, 1998), pp. 414–41. The sobriquet is attributed to Frank Crowninshield, at the time editor of *Vanity Fair*, who influenced the artist's career.
14. Voltaire, *Candide, or All for the Best. Translated from the French of M. de Voltaire* (Haarlem: Joh. Enschedé en Zonen, 1927), colophon page.
15. I am most grateful to David Stern who sent me scans from copy no. 4, then in the stock of the Boston bookseller Peter L. Stern & Company, now sold; the excerpt quoted is from the colophon page of this copy. In addition to these eleven unique copies, there are apparently five copies (as stated on the spine of a different binding, executed in a more traditional fashion than

the modern one that reproduces the nudes), which contain ten hand-coloured original etchings on vellum as well as hand-coloured plates of the etchings inserted throughout. One such copy resurfaced at the Rare Books Signature Auction, Heritage Auctions, 4–5 October 2012, Beverly Hills (CA), lot 36202.

16. It was translated into English in 1761. For an erudite introduction to this continuation, see Édouard Langille, 'Introduction', *Candide, ou l'optimisme. Seconde partie*, ed. by Édouard Langille (Exeter: University of Exeter Press, 2003), pp. ix–xxvii.
17. The printing house also owned a foundry, which became internationally known in the twentieth century for Jan van Krimpen's work as a designer of typefaces (distributed in the United States by the Continental Typefounders Association). This edition of *Candide* is included in a list of books entirely designed by van Krimpen, but his name is not mentioned on the colophon page perhaps because he was not well-known to American collectors. See John Friedrichs, 'Preliminary Checklist of the Early Work of Jan Van Krimpen' <http://home.planet.nl/~johnf/home.html#1927> [accessed 15 November 2019].
18. See *Spécimen des caractères de la fonderie normale à Bruxelles, provenant de la fonderie de Jules Didot et de son père Pierre Didot* (Haarlem: Joh. Enschedé en Zonen, 1914).
19. Madeleine Morley, 'The World's Most Expensive-looking Font Might Surprise You', 27 October 2015 <https://eyeondesign.aiga.org/the-worlds-most-expensive-looking-font-might-surprise-you/> [accessed 15 November 2019].
20. Bennett A. Cerf, letter to Moby Dick Book Shop, 24 January 1927, Random House Records, Columbia University (New York City), box 118, folder 'Booksellers'. Similar letters were mailed to other booksellers as well.
21. Bennett Cerf, *At Random: The Reminiscences of Bennett Cerf* (New York: Random House, 2012), p. 70.
22. Voltaire, *Candide* (New York: Random House, 1928), colophon page.
23. I have analysed this edition from a word and image perspective in two publications: 'Narrative Form and Iconographic Sequence: Rockwell Kent's *Candide* (1928) in Text and Image', *Image & Narrative*, 17.1 (2016), 15–28; and 'Exploring the World with Rockwell Kent's *Candide*: Intermedial Translation, Paratextual Framing, and Iconographic Landscape', in *Art and Science in Word and Image: Exploration and Discovery*, ed. by Keith Williams and others (Leiden: Brill, 2019), pp. 309–22.
24. Carl Van Doren, 'Why the Editorial Board Selected "Rockwell Kent's *Candide*"', *Wings*, 3.12 (December 1929), 4–5.
25. Ibid., p. 5.
26. Ibid.
27. [Anon.], 'Rockwell Kent — The Artist', *Wings*, 3.12 (December 1929), 3.
28. [Anon.], 'The Story of Your "*Candide*"', *Wings*, 3.12 (December 1929), 6–7.
29. On the phenomenon of cinematic remaking, see especially Constantine Verevis, *Film Remakes* (Edinburgh: Edinburgh University Press, 2006).
30. Library of Congress, *Catalogue of Copyright Entries: New Series, Volume 27, Group 1* (Washington, DC: United States Government Printing Office, 1931), notice 14255, p. 2171.
31. Philip Littell, 'Introduction', in Voltaire, *Candide*, Modern Library of the World's Best Books (New York: Boni & Liveright, 1918), pp. vii–xi (p. vii). In the original introduction, it is 'old' not 'cold'.
32. Voltaire, *Candide* (New York: Ives Washburn, 1929), dust wrapper (rear), my collection.
33. Ibid.
34. Ibid.
35. Ibid.
36. Ibid.
37. Ibid., back flap of the dust wrapper.
38. In my copy of this edition (numbered 14 in green ink), the frontispiece contains the artist's signature in pencil on the left-hand side, but the other images do not, which does not correspond to the description supplied by the colophon: 'The illustrations for these copies have been proved and signed by the artist'.

39. Paul Beaujon [Beatrice Walde's pseudonym], 'The "Garamond" Types: Sixteenth and Seventeenth Century Sources Considered', *The Fleuron: A Journal of Typography*, 5 (1926), 131–79 (p. 176).
40. The untitled and undated pamphlet that I have in my collection devotes considerable space to the Granjon.
41. Winfred Porter Truesdell, 'The Modern Woodcut and Howard Simon', *The Print Connoisseur: A Quarterly Magazine for the Print Collector*, 10 (April 1930), 136–65 (p. 158).
42. Not much is known about Mahlon Blaine because he took pleasure in creating an unusual existence for himself in the interviews that he gave during his lifetime. The absence of archival documentation about his life and the context of his creative output is detrimental to scholarship on his book illustrations. One of his friends, Gershon Legman, published a useful monograph about him, *The Art of Mahlon Blaine* (East Lansing, MI: Peregrine Books, 1982). The excerpt quoted is on p. 5.
43. These publishers are: Three Sirens Press, Grosset & Dunlap, Illustrated Editions Company, Hartsdale House, Book Collectors Association, Arden Book Company, World Pub. Co., and Parnassus. In the same year, Three Sirens Press also published an edition of *Candide* paired with *A Sentimental Journey*. My account contradicts J. Patrick Lee's identification of the Three Sirens Press edition as the original one in 'Bibliographie des éditions illustrées américaines des œuvres de Voltaire' (p. 296).
44. Voltaire, *Candide* (New York: Illustrated Editions Company, 1930), front flap of the dust jacket.
45. It is worth noting that there is usually a proliferation of editions of *Candide* on open shelves in North American libraries, including the cheaper Random House reissues or new editions with Kent's line drawings, but my informal survey suggests that they do not all bear these traces of student engagement in the same way as those illustrated by Blaine and Zaidenberg.
46. Voltaire, *Candide* (New York: Arden Book Company, 1930), title page.
47. B. B., 'Introduction', in Voltaire, *Candide* (New York: Illustrated Editions Company, 1930), p. 11.

CHAPTER 8

❖

Pride and Prejudice: Permutations as Adaptation

Jeremy Strong

Introduction

With the exception of Shakespeare, few English writers have a greater claim to canonical status than Jane Austen. Always in print, frequently adapted, taught, studied, and referenced, she is widely understood as a 'national treasure' of Britain's literary heritage, and one of the most prominent features of our cultural landscape. Roger Gard suggests that Austen transcends the literary as, simply, a 'great national figure'.[1] Of her six published novels, *Pride and Prejudice* (1813) is undoubtedly the best known. Even for those who have not read the original, the essentials of its characters and story are often familiar through film, television and web adaptations, as well as through other texts that use the novel as a foundation for their own narratives — for example *Bridget Jones's Diary* (1996, adapted 2001), *Lost in Austen* (2008), and the YouTube series *The Lizzie Bennet Diaries* (2012–2013).

This chapter considers three recent novels that rework *Pride and Prejudice* in very different ways. Jo Baker's *Longbourn* (2013) imagines events as seen from the perspective of the servants, constructing a parallel narrative for figures only briefly glimpsed in Austen's account. *Death Comes to Pemberley* (2011) by P. D. James (itself adapted for television in 2013) takes the form of a murder mystery 'sequel' that uses more recent genre conventions to cast suspicion on a number of characters. Finally, Seth Grahame-Smith's *Pride and Prejudice and Zombies* (2009, adapted for cinema in 2016) is a comic mash-up of text from the original with new material in which a plague of zombies afflicts Britain. Underpinning all three engagements with *Pride and Prejudice* is the extent to which a reader's working knowledge of the original is central to the construction of meaning in, and a pleasurable engagement with, the new works.

Perhaps unsurprisingly, the notion of a novel adapting another novel is far less familiar than the conventional trajectory of novel-to-film or the diverse trans/inter/cross-media traffic that has come to be encompassed by adaptation studies. Yet my claim for these texts, and the reading experiences they provoke, to be understood in terms of adaptation does not rest on the presence of illustrations in

Pride and Prejudice and Zombies, nor the fact that *Death Comes to Pemberley* and *Pride and Prejudice and Zombies* have been (and *Longbourn* may be) adapted for the screen. Rather, it rests on the relationship between the antecedent text and those which follow. Linda Hutcheon argues for adaptations as 'announced' and 'specific'; texts which clearly state their foundational relationship with other, particular texts, and it is here contended that the three novels examined amply meet these defining characteristics.[2] They announce their relationship to *Pride and Prejudice* firstly through their titles and sustain that claim to a filial connection through narratives that assume their particular shapes in direct response to the original work; parallel narratives that operate within or just beyond the same timeframe as the action of the original text, interacting with and shaping our perspective on that original. Likewise, the specificity of the adaptive source is never in any doubt. Although all three may be said to engage with a broader canvas that includes, inter alia, Austen's entire *œuvre* and its adaptations as 'heritage film', the core connection to a single anterior work is indisputable.[3] Whilst the shift across media that is conventionally associated with adaptation is absent, this chapter will examine how the three new texts open up equivalent transformative operations through their different uses of genre. Finally, questions of adaptation and canonicity combine in the choice of source text. In using *Pride and Prejudice*, the three novels invite interpretation in terms of adaptation by engaging with a serially re-versioned behemoth of both the cultural landscape and the adaptation industry, the significance and canonical standing of which is to a great degree determined by its torrent of adaptations and their associated critical commentary.

Prior Knowledge and Pleasure

When, towards the end of *Longbourn* an 'express' arrives at the house at midnight bearing an important message, the housekeeper, Mrs Hill, hopes that it may bring news of her vanished son, James.[4] Readers too have expectations of a development in respect of this character, most particularly that the central relationship between James and the maid, Sarah, one of two housemaids listed but not named in *Pride and Prejudice*, will be satisfactorily secured. However, the reader familiar with Austen's original will also be aware that the express in question actually bears the news of Lydia Bennet's elopement (or worse) with the charming but untrustworthy Wickham.[5] The anxiety of Mrs Hill and the pleasurable anticipation of the reader for the advancement of the James/Sarah story — a pairing of initially clashing but ultimately complementary personalities which deliberately echoes the Elizabeth/Darcy romance — must continue. In keeping with the pattern established throughout Baker's novel, we see that, a) the events of *Pride and Prejudice* form an immutable template into which the new work's innovations are woven, and b) as *Longbourn*'s revisionist political sensibilities insistently demonstrate, the cares and tribulations of the servants are subordinate to the lives of those they serve. Baker plays with the comedy staple of having two pairs of lovers (one of higher rank, one of lower) to show how the lower, servant-class pairing will have to wait, like us, for their story.

P. D. James's *Death Comes to Pemberley* employs an equivalent reliance on the primacy of *Pride and Prejudice* in its development of a murder mystery narrative, though its events only begin in the post-marriage period that consistently marks the conclusion of Austen's stories. Indeed, James's work acquires a significant degree of its effect precisely from the deliberate eruption of problems (murder, suspicion, shame, acrimony) into a space conventionally rendered and understood as a secure settlement. The Austen ending in general, and Pemberley in particular, represent a version of 'happily ever after' that resolves perfectly in married love, financial security, and a benign social order. Historically, many responses to Austen, both popular and scholarly, have emphasized the mutually-sustaining interrelationship between the writer's style and the trajectory of her marriage plots. Cheryl Nixon, for example, observes that 'Austen criticism rests on the foundation of Austen's "balance", "unity", and "harmony"'.[6] Hence, death coming to Pemberley in the form of a murdered minor character from the original, with Wickham seemingly the prime suspect, upsets this balance, re-introducing and magnifying the themes that provided obstacles to the Elizabeth/Darcy union in *Pride and Prejudice*. Readers are presented not merely with a continuation of *Pride and Prejudice* but with the potential for the undoing of its famous resolution, an effect on which the ubiquity and popularity of the earlier novel is wholly reliant.[7]

Wickham's unsuitability as a brother-in-law to Darcy is compounded by his connection to this new and dreadful crime, a transgression far greater than the defaulting and un-chastity that have defined him to date. Likewise, the qualities that make Lydia undesirable as a relation (but exquisitely enjoyable to readers as a trial for Elizabeth) — imprudence, vulgarity, silliness — are afforded full expression by a scandal that commences with her appearance at Pemberley as a 'wild shrieking apparition' shortly after the violent event.[8] It is our knowledge of *Pride and Prejudice*, far more than the initial pages of the new novel, that primes us for the full heft of what this means, and what it threatens, for Elizabeth and Darcy. The next morning, when a somewhat recovered Lydia is presented with breakfast and 'discovered that grief had made her hungry and ate avidly' (p. 130) we recognize a deliberately Austenian voice — barbed, funny — reminding us of Lydia's capacity for selfishness, and we anticipate that a continuation of the behaviours that defined her in the original and its previous widely-viewed screen adaptations will also inform the new work. We might also observe that the presumed 'knowing' quality of the author/reader relationship in *Death Comes to Pemberley* is shared with the flurry of Austen adaptations that began in the 1990s.[9] Of course, by the time of the three novels central to the present study, that mid-1990s cycle had itself become part of the web of texts and prior knowledge that afford structure and nuance to how readers understand and enjoy the most recent offerings. Equally, the tagline of James's novel ('Dancing, Merriment... and Murder') seems to gesture (at least in its first two words) to the earlier, frothier style of Austen adaptations (for example, the 1940 MGM *Pride and Prejudice*), before colliding that account with 'murder'.

Pride and Prejudice and Zombies is simultaneously the closest and the most removed from Austen's original of the three works; being, as its tongue-in-cheek cover blurb describes, 'an expanded edition of the beloved Jane Austen novel featuring all-new scenes of bone-crunching zombie mayhem'. Although, as a mash-up, it borrows a significant proportion of the text directly from the original, the intention is to make the additional material as wildly divergent from the themes and possibilities of *Pride and Prejudice* as conceivable while still retaining other central elements, principally the Elizabeth/Darcy relationship. Comedy is generated through the unlikely combination of gore and horror on the one hand, and Austen's subtle social commentary on the other, producing a new narrative that continually invites the reader to compare the mash-up with its polite predecessor and its various screen renderings. Hence, Grahame-Smith's resolution of the Wickham/Lydia elopement still involves the intervention of Darcy who settles Wickham's debts and provides a sum of money for his marrying Lydia, thereby restoring the Bennet family reputation. However, we additionally learn that Darcy, now highly-proficient in the martial arts, beats Wickham lame, broken, impotent, and incontinent, able neither to 'lay another hand in anger, nor leave another bastard behind'.[10] While many modern readers might feel that the original outcome for Wickham is insufficiently punitive, as indeed other dangerous Austen chancers like Willoughby and Frank Churchill escape comparatively unscathed, the mash-up affords a (literally) thumping resolution more in tune with mainstream movie finales in which virtue is rewarded and villainy is comprehensively punished. In this respect, *Pride and Prejudice and Zombies* shares an impulse with the otherwise very different 1995 film adaptation of *Sense and Sensibility*. Rather than settle for Austen's comparatively mild summary of the future that awaits the faithless Willoughby after he abandons Marianne, the ending of the Lee/Thompson adaptation cuts from the joyous double wedding of the Dashwood sisters to a miserable Willoughby on horseback, surveying the happy scene from far away. This revised version, like Grahame-Smith's worked-over Wickham, is not merely content to deny the deceiver a share in the principal marriage, but elects to rub his nose in it too.

Themes, Theory, and Criticism

Longbourn is notable for the extent to which its preoccupations are shared with those of scholarly responses to Austen over recent decades as well as with the more politically-engaged screen adaptations. Issues of gender and sexuality, property and power, race and blood, as well as their various intersections, are at the heart of its narrative polemics. Dwelling precisely on what Austen elides — from the material facts of work, to the condition of the bodies that do (or do not) perform it — the novel is a *Pride and Prejudice* re-examined through influences and critical prisms as diverse as E. P. Thompson's *The Making of The English Working Class* and postcolonial theory. From its opening pages in which the housemaid, Sarah, begins dealing with the Bennets' washing at half-past four on a cold morning, reflecting that 'no one should have to deal with another person's dirty linen' (p. 14), the intention to problematize the foundations (economic, physical, moral) of the lives of Austen's principal characters is made clear. In taking this approach, Baker's work is as much a challenge or corrective to comfortable nostalgic adaptations-as-readings of Austen, especially their sumptuous imagery, as it is to the original novel. As H. Elizabeth Ellington observes of the screen versions:

> The beauty of these films, the visual pleasure of lavish costumes and interiors, lush gardens and landscapes, beautiful and beautifully-lit actors and actresses, is what is so seductive about them. We are seduced by the prettiness of the film and overlook its questionable subtexts for the scopophilic pleasures we find in the cinematic experience of England's landscapes.[11]

For example, Baker's Bennet sisters are not, their servants know, 'as rarefied as angels' (p. 15) despite their public appearance, which in this context is also synonymous with the entirety of *Pride and Prejudice* and of many adaptations. Rather, they are 'frail, leaking, forked, bodily creatures' (p. 14) whose gentle existence is predicated upon the labour and privations of others. In an emphatically non-Austen moment, Baker has her heroine, Sarah, slip in 'hogshit' (p. 15) while taking out the laundry, ruining all her previous work, and signposting for readers how the new text will relate to the values of its predecessor. More specifically, this calculated besmirching of the languorous pleasures of landscape and costume drama with excrement underfoot, fouled clothing, and never-ending work could not more deliberately repudiate the pillars of heritage film, especially where Austen is concerned.

Matters of sex, class, and property coalesce in *Longbourn*'s invention of a backstory that includes a sexual relationship between Mr Bennet and housekeeper Mrs Hill prior to his marriage to Mrs Bennet. James, their resulting son, who is not publicly acknowledged by Mr Bennet, is therefore (or was potentially) the missing male heir to Longbourn, a property which, owing to the legal entail endlessly complained of by Mrs Bennet, cannot pass to a female relative. William Blackstone's *Commentaries on the Laws of England (1765–1769)* lays out the stark facts of the condition and difficulty of being a bastard: 'A bastard, by our English laws, is one that is not only begotten, but born, out of lawful matrimony'.[12] Mr Bennet, by not marrying his housekeeper in the interval between his son's conception and birth has determined the latter's status for a lifetime. Outlining 'the rights and incapacities which appertain to a bastard', Blackstone explains: 'The rights are very few, being only such as he can acquire; for he can inherit nothing, being looked upon as the son of nobody'; '(K)in to nobody, (he) has no ancestor from whom any inheritable blood can be derived'.[13] The fundamental narrative premise of *Pride and Prejudice* enabled by the device of the entail — five unmarried daughters, their problematic parents, and the potential for a slip into comparative destitution — is transformed by Baker's invention. By having James literally beneath the Bennets' noses, working as a footman and unaware of his paternity, the novel both points up the absurd (gendered) unfairness of the inheritance and compounds it by contrast with James's even worse predicament as an unacknowledged natural son.

The gulf between Elizabeth Bennet's condition and that of James is most fully, and ironically, expressed in the exchange between Elizabeth and Sarah in which the latter asks if there has been any news of 'Mr Smith' (Smith being the surname James uses).[14] Elizabeth cannot recall him, until she finally grasps that Sarah is talking of a servant: 'Oh! *Smith!* You mean the *footman!* [...] You called him *Mr* Smith, that's why

I misunderstood you: I thought you meant someone of my acquaintance. I thought you meant a gentleman' (pp. 353–54). Though Smith may not be a gentleman, and though neither of them know it, he is nevertheless Elizabeth's half-brother. Readers of *Longbourn* are inevitably prompted to reflect ironically upon the exchange in *Pride and Prejudice* between Elizabeth Bennet and Lady Catherine de Bourgh in which the former makes specific reference to her paternity as the key factor that affords a species of social parity between herself and Darcy and, hence, makes their union not-inconceivable: 'He is a gentleman; I am a gentleman's daughter; so far we are equal'.[15]

Race is introduced into Baker's novel through the device of having the Bingley family money come from being 'in sugar' (p. 71). This manoeuvre allows a chime with another of Austen's monied families, the Bertrams of *Mansfield Park*, who have holdings in Antigua. Patricia Rozema's 1999 adaptation of that novel developed this into a substantial theme, stressing how the family's luxury and indolence are made possible by slavery and offering harrowing glimpses of lives there defined by cruelty and sexual violence.[16] Linda Troost and Sayre Greenfield note how Rozema's *Mansfield Park* turned:

> A novel concerned with the effects of particular upbringings on individual happiness and morality into a film concerned with the effects of broader social forces on the content and discontent of entire classes of people, as well as their individual representatives.[17]

Longbourn performs an equivalent operation in its rewriting of *Pride and Prejudice*, broadening its scope to encompass a wider social orbit and encouraging readers to interpret characters as representative of others. The Bingleys' close associations with the Caribbean, its plantations, and the slave trade are emphasized by having one of their footmen, Ptolemy Bingley, be of mixed race and, it is clearly implied, the natural son of Bingley's father and one of his slaves: 'Mr Bingley, Senior, God rest him, brought me back here [...] He was always very fond of me. And of my mother, too, though he left her there. I was just a boy' (p. 147).

Just as the Bennet household and its supposedly absolute distinctions between family and servants are collapsed (in theory, though not in practice) by the existence of James, so the Bingleys — and despite Caroline Bingley's contempt for the Bennets — are shown to be commingled with those they would regard as lesser. Though Ptolemy formally bears the Bingley name via his enslaved mother according to the conventions of slave ownership, his blood connection to the family could have afforded him the name as of right. The potential joining of families and their mutual suitability, so exhaustively considered in *Pride and Prejudice,* not least by the domineering Lady Catherine de Bourgh, is shown to be comprehensively complicated, in fact rendered a nonsense, by prior relationships altogether different from any union of the 'respectable, honourable, and ancient'.[18] Of course, the non-sanctioned relationships that *Longbourn* describes, including a gay Mr Hill, are not a matter of public knowledge and their biological truth does not alter the condition of the haves or have-nots. Their secrecy, and the means by which their human consequences are dealt with, bear critical testament to the web of power relations in Regency England; of the power of men over women, white over black, rich over poor. Austen, as Baker implies, may often have been concerned with a particular facet of this — the precarious situation of the relatively impoverished gentlewoman — but the broader landscape of interlocking unfairnesses she essentially figured as natural.[19] The 'natural' is a category exhaustively problematized in the field of cultural studies and, relatedly, in critical approaches to texts, their consumers, media, and institutions since the latter third of the twentieth century. Graeme Turner describes how:

> Cultural Studies defines itself in part through its disruption of the boundaries between disciplines, and through its ability to explode the category of 'the natural' — revealing the history behind those social relations we see as the products of a neutral evolutionary process.[20]

Longbourn, itself a category-blurring compound of reading, writing, and criticism, seeks to effect such a disruption to the social fabric of *Pride and Prejudice*, albeit in the context of an evident affection for the work and its author. A raft of assumptions that underpin the world of the original — who chooses? who owns? who instructs? who obeys? who even appears? — are unsettled in a welter of innovations that pointedly reverse traditional popular readings of the Austen milieu as desirable, decorous, and proper. If *Longbourn* may be said to have a target (as opposed to a target readership), it seems to have in its sights the parallel traditions of reading and adapting Austen that perpetuate cosy interpretations of the author, her works, and her time, what Troost and Greenfield describe as 'a reactionary escapism to a simpler time as it was lived by a comfortingly wealthy and leisurely class'.[21]

War and the Wider World

Perhaps the most enjoyable aspect of Grahame-Smith's mash-up is his success in stitching together an account of England in the grip of a decades-long Zombie apocalypse with a (generally) genteel romance plot in which the participants endeavour to ignore, endure, and carry on despite the over-arching situation. In this respect, Austen is the ideal zombie co-author, plucked from the grave to serve ends to which, in life, she would not likely have given her assent. Beyond a general sense in which 'Austen' summons for the popular imagination a particular agglomeration of attitudes and manners — of profound feelings judiciously expressed, of taking tea, carriages, drawing rooms and lawns — it is the looming but unspoken backdrop that makes *Pride and Prejudice* so apt for zombification. Countless critics and commentators have observed the relative absence of an explicitly acknowledged geo-political context from the world of Austen's novels. (Though, of course, the works are simultaneously amenable to readings that locate characters in terms of social forces and competing ideologies.)[22] The French Revolution, its resulting wars, and the bogeyman figure of Napoleon Bonaparte — events and entities which dominated public life and collective fears for most of Austen's adult existence — are scarcely shadows on her pages. The appearance of a militia regiment, a newly-returned colonel, or the long absence of a naval post-captain, are matters of consequence essentially in terms of their relevance to small communities, of the altered prospects for households with unmarried young ladies, but never, for example, in terms of an explicit discussion of one of the invasion scares which Austen lived through. That Grahame-Smith frequently has his zombies termed 'unmentionables' plays with this condition of absence/presence. Recurring narrative elements in the original, such as the sending of servants with notes between houses, acquire comic value because of the state of affairs (new to readers, but a long-standing fact of life for characters) in which solitary travellers are especially vulnerable to the depredations of the 'manky dreadfuls':

> She (Elizabeth) requested to have a note sent to Longbourn, desiring her mother to visit Jane, and form her own judgment of her situation. The note was immediately dispatched, but the rider was met with a group of freshly unearthed zombies on the road and dragged off to his presumable demise. The note was dispatched a second time. (p. 36)

The expendability of servants in *Pride and Prejudice and Zombies* hinges on the original's sense of their non-existence as characters and unimportance as subjects. Grahame-Smith plays for humorous effect the casual thoughtlessness with which anonymous servants are shuttled between properties on the whim of their employers (and, indeed, the author of the text), unobtrusively facilitating the social gatherings that, in turn, advance the story.

The comic approach of *Pride and Prejudice and Zombies* stands in sharp contrast to *Longbourn*'s aim to recuperate the servants' and other peripheral characters' previously hidden experience. Although they function in different ways, both texts' foregrounding of hitherto occulted or absent dimensions of the original constitutes a strand of the claim made by the present study to understand these works as adaptations. Here, the *Longbourn/Pride and Prejudice* adaptive relationship may usefully be compared with the equivalent relationship between Jack Gold's *Man Friday* (1975) and Defoe's *Robinson Crusoe*. Gold's film — separated, like *Longbourn*, from the cultural mores of its source by a significant span of history — critiques the ideological framework of the original novel by a pointed relocation of the 'supporting' character to the centre.[23] In *Longbourn* we see how the same unpleasant weather that leads to Jane Bennet catching a chill and a fever in the original is also responsible for the maid, Sarah, becoming seriously unwell. But, compared to the solicitude and worry that Jane's condition occasions, for Sarah 'it was not often that someone could get away, and there was certainly little time to stay and comfort her' (p. 121).

The danger of Wickham to Lydia is likewise figured as less substantial than the danger he poses to much younger and poorer girls. The advances of Wickham, a frequent visitor to the Longbourn kitchen where he plies the twelve-year-old maid Polly with sweets and small talk, grooming her for sex, are only prevented by the timely intervention of James. For Lydia, who connives in her own fall, the consequences of which are in any case patched-up within the above-stairs social orbit, Wickham is a charming rogue. For Polly he is nothing less than a predatory paedophile. Similarly, the briefly-mentioned flogging of a private in *Pride and*

Prejudice becomes a two-page *Longbourn* sequence with close attention to physical and textural details that Austen eschews: 'His skin was lurid in the dull light, his cheek hazed with greying stubble and flattened against the dark weathered wood. His eyes were wide and rolling, his jaw clenched' (p. 112).[24] However, the most substantial intervention in terms of 'restoring' a broader historical and political context in *Longbourn* is the sustained flashback sequence set in the Iberian peninsula in 1808–1810 in which James serves in the army, becomes (technically, though not morally) a deserter, and eventually returns to England by joining a merchant ship which carries him back via the New World. This fifty-page section and numerous other references indicate the permeability of Austen's ostensibly self-contained story-world to global narratives of empire, war, and trade.

Death Comes to Pemberley also effects an opening-up of Austen's world through a conclusion that involves Wickham and Lydia deciding to start over in America, where Wickham will work for a Jeremiah Cornbinder of Virginia. In part this resolves the obvious worry that *Pride and Prejudice*'s original distancing of the problematic couple at the novel's close had not been sufficient to prevent their disruptive re-entry into Elizabeth and Darcy's life. Readers are invited to believe that several thousand miles of intervening ocean should finally allow for that settled separation that the end of *Pride and Prejudice* had promised but which P. D. James wilfully unpicked. Equally, contemporary readers and audiences accustomed to sequels and sequels-to-sequels may also recognize in this resolution the opposite narrative device in which even the most seemingly absolute and final conclusion may prove merely a caesura to be hastily glossed and overturned (i.e. the villain's return, replacement, even resurrection!) at the commencement of the next instalment.[25] Wickham and Lydia's relocation to America also alludes to another recognizable motif that merges literary, fictive, and historical dimensions: the notion of emigration, exile, or a sustained overseas sojourn as an opportunity, variously punitive and redemptive, to reboot a life marked by failure or disgrace. Narratives as diverse as *Moll Flanders*, *Great Expectations*, and the *Flashman* novels employ this narrative device and, significantly, frequently see their protagonists return.[26] Attractive, plausible, and prepared to take risks, Wickham and Lydia are ideal candidates for a New World makeover and James's suggested future for the couple brings out the allusive qualities of this form of narrative closure in allowing readers to draw upon other narratives to imagine the picaresque adventures that await them. The epilogue allows us a brief return of Lydia's voice, and of her capacity to blithely forget past troubles to focus on present pleasures: 'Williamsburg,' Lydia writes, 'was in in every way an improvement on boring Meryton' (p. 314).

Style and Quotability

All three of the novels considered embark upon a strongly self-conscious engagement with what might be termed the 'Austen voice' in their opening sentences. *Pride and Prejudice and Zombies* adapts her original opening in a fashion that signals the tone of the new work and provides an explanation for the narratively convenient availability of nearby Netherfield Park:

> It is a truth universally acknowledged that a zombie in possession of brains must be in want of more brains. Never was this truth more plain than during the recent attack at Netherfield Park, in which a household of eighteen was slaughtered and consumed by a horde of the living dead. (p. 7)

Death Comes to Pemberley echoes the familiar 'universally acknowledged' in a largely redundant prologue that recaps the events of *Pride and Prejudice* before summarizing the key developments in Elizabeth and Darcy's life prior to the new action proper: 'It was generally agreed by the female residents of Meryton that Mr and Mrs Bennet of Longbourn had been fortunate in the disposal in marriage of four of their five daughters' (p. 1).

While *Longbourn* commences with a direct statement of its revisionist focus on the material reality of work, it does so in a fashion that, syntactically, in its consciously archaic sound, in its deployment of a practical maxim, and in immediately locating events in an English county, is highly suggestive of Austen: 'There could be no wearing of clothes without their laundering, just as surely as there could be no going without clothes, not in Hertfordshire anyway, and not in September' (p. 13).

Death Comes to Pemberley offers the reader familiar with Austen's *œuvre* other nudges and winks to suggest an author 'at play' — albeit very respectful play — with her predecessor's work as part of the adaptive process, principally through the over-arching premise of translating Elizabeth's qualities of intelligence and spunkiness to a different genre, making her the detective. James also gently directs the cognoscenti to Austen in-jokes. These include a backstory for Wickham for the years after *Pride and Prejudice* but before the events of *Death Comes to Pemberley* that has him working for a short and unsuccessful spell as secretary to Sir Walter Elliott of *Persuasion* (pp. 196–97), while Wickham's illegitimate baby son is eventually found a suitable and loving home with Harriet and Robert Martin of Highbury, characters from *Emma*.[27] These half-hidden references serve to glue *Death Comes to Pemberley* into a broader textual mosaic than the single source adaptation, enabling readers to participate in a game of 'spotting' in which both prior reading of Austen's novels and viewing of the adaptations will have served as relevant priming. James is also alive to the potential for reflexive humour and genre-bending in offering readers the entertainment of seeing familiar aspects of her contemporary procedural crime thrillers adapted to suit the technologies and protocols of Austen's period setting. Bloodstains, a narrative staple of the post-DNA forensic procedural, are invoked ironically in an exchange between the investigating magistrate and the physician summoned to examine the corpse: 'I take it [...] that your clever scientific colleagues have not yet found a way of distinguishing one man's blood from another's?' (p. 108)

The perpetual awareness of *Pride and Prejudice* as a structuring presence in the new texts is rarely more apparent than in those sequences of the original that have been rendered iconic both by frequent quotation and by their inclusion as must-be-there scenes in multiple screen adaptations. The initial, failed proposal by Darcy to Elizabeth becomes in *Pride and Prejudice and Zombies* an even angrier episode in which the verbal exchanges of the original are supplemented with kicks and blows that result in Darcy crashing into the mantelpiece. In the same spirit, Elizabeth's memorable confrontation with Lady Catherine de Bourgh, in which the latter hopes to scupper the Darcy/Elizabeth union, takes place not in that 'prettyish little wilderness on one side of (the) lawn' but in the Bennet family's 'prettyish little dojo' (p. 284) and results in the interfering aunt being bested both in word and in a protracted contest of martial arts. *Longbourn* relies wholly on readers' prior knowledge of Darcy's visit to the Collins's house to make his first proposal. Sarah answers the door for him ('his big glossy self', p. 267) and returns immediately to thinking about her lover James. None of the key proposal scene is presented directly. Later, when Darcy strides from the house and Sarah can hear 'the quiet sounds of Elizabeth crying' (p. 268), readers understand that one of the principal events of the parallel narrative has taken place. It may have been 'off-page' but is nonetheless a presence in the act of our reading, precisely because of its status as a central moment in one of our most canonical and frequently-adapted stories.

Conclusion: Genre and Respectability

Despite taking a single canonical novel as their springboard, it is apparent that the three novels considered occupy very different places in a genre spectrum (detective story, parody, novel) or literary hierarchy, and perform their particular narrative operations in a fashion heavily determined by the norms of those genres. *Pride and Prejudice and Zombies* unabashedly revels in the collision between 'high' (English, period, literary) and 'low' (horror, gore, comedy). With illustrations throughout and a 'Reader's Discussion Guide' at the conclusion including tongue-in-cheek questions, Grahame-Smith delights in a bringing-low that continually draws attention to the unlikeliness of the mash-up (a 'towering work of classical zombie literature', p. 318).[28] *Death Comes to Pemberley*, as a whodunit detective novel, occupies a somewhat more elevated place in a conventional hierarchy of the genres or putative pecking order of the contemporary publishing trade. Equally, it is by far the least successful of the three novels considered, hamstrung by the author's fannish devotion to Austen. James's reluctance to jeopardize too much of *Pride and Prejudice* results in a somewhat wooden story in which the victim was a minor character (Denny) in whom readers would have little invested, too few original characters are potential suspects, and the eventual culprit is a servant plucked from the narrative margin. In contrast to Grahame-Smith's boundless irreverence, James seems simply to have wanted *Pride and Prejudice* to go on and on and to have effected this the only way she knew how, although it is the failure to adhere to the conventions of her 'home' genre, detective fiction, that renders the new work unsatisfactory. Although *Death Comes to Pemberley* is, like *Pride and Prejudice and Zombies*, a collision between the original and a newer genre, the terms of engagement are so skewed towards a sense of the original work's canonical status that the impact of this collision between genres is but slightly felt. Like a page-to-screen adaptation constrained by notions of fidelity, the new work fails to push at the boundaries it opens up.

In its realist seriousness, *Longbourn* has positioned itself successfully within the contemporary canon of 'literary fiction', albeit at the expense of the deft wit so much in evidence in Austen. Whilst its particular adaptation of the tenets of *Pride and Prejudice* is thoughtful and provocative, the impulse to respond to, revisit, and revise the terms of a canonical literary work through a parallel narrative focusing on secondary characters has itself been a recognizable tendency, a genre of sorts, for some time. Tom Stoppard's play *Rosencrantz and Guildenstern Are Dead* (1966) employed the device of relocating minor characters (from *Hamlet*) to the centre of events. In the same year, Jean Rhys's novel *Wide Sargasso Sea* (1966) created a prequel to Charlotte Brontë's *Jane Eyre* (1847) emphasizing many of the postcolonial themes that Baker explores, including racial and gender inequality, the ownership of names, dislocation, and assimilation. More recently, Peter Carey's *Jack Maggs* (1997) took Charles Dickens's *Great Expectations* as the inspiration for a novel in which the title character (a reworking of Dickens's Magwitch) actually encounters a version of Dickens himself. Relatedly, Jasper Fforde's series of novels featuring literary detective Thursday Next (2001–12), commencing with *The Eyre Affair* (2001) imagines a parallel universe in which characters from literary works threaten to spill from the pages of their originals, to cross between and rewrite texts, and generally upset the canon. This is a tradition of adapting within which *Longbourn* self-consciously inserts itself, at the same time as engaging with the multiple previous adaptations of Austen's texts.

In a postmodern era of interlocking multi-platform franchises, reboots and origin-stories, spin-offs and sequels, Henry Jenkins describes how the themes and content of each property 'extends outward from its originating medium to influence many other sites of cultural production'.[29] Although he refers here to corporate practices of extending and exploiting synergies across multiple media platforms, in which the intellectual property of franchise owners is rigorously defended against unauthorized use, these forms of dissemination may also be observed in respect of out-of-copyright materials such as Austen's original novels. Certainly, Austen is available for making-over and adaptation in a way that the world of *Batman* or *Harry Potter* is not, though our shared — and of course varying — sense of Austen's work is as much shaped by subsequent adaptations as it is by her originals.[30] Indeed it is now all but impossible to approach her in any other way.

Notes to Chapter 8

1. Roger Gard, *Jane Austen's Novels: The Art of Clarity* (New Haven, CT: Yale University Press, 1994), p. 12.
2. Hutcheon, with O'Flynn, *A Theory of Adaptation*, p. 16.
3. The term 'heritage film' was first used by Andrew Higson and others in the 1990s to define a cycle of nostalgic and visually sumptuous costume dramas, including, but not limited to, many adaptations and films by Merchant Ivory; see Andrew Higson, *English Heritage, English Cinema: Costume Drama Since 1980* (Oxford: Oxford University Press, 2003).
4. Jo Baker, *Longbourn* (London: Penguin, 2013), p. 361; further references to this work are given in the text.
5. Information which Elizabeth Bennet receives in a letter from her sister Jane whilst in Derbyshire.
6. Cheryl Nixon, 'Balancing the Courtship Hero: Masculine Emotional Display in Film Adaptations of Austen's Novels', in *Jane Austen in Hollywood*, ed. by Linda Troost and Sayre Greenfield (Lexington: University of Kentucky Press, 2001), pp. 22–43 (p. 28).

7. Notably, the television adaptation stressed the potential rupture of the Elizabeth/Darcy relationship far more powerfully than P. D. James's original.
8. P. D. James, *Death Comes to Pemberley* (London: Faber & Faber, 2013), p. 59; further references to this work are given in the text.
9. As Rachel Brownstein observes, 'you are invited and assumed to be in the know by the mid-1990s Austen films' ('Out of the Drawing Room, Onto the Lawn', in *Jane Austen in Hollywood*, ed. by Troost and Greenfield, pp. 13–21 (p. 18)). Whilst there had been a steady stream of Austen adaptations up until this point, the mid-1990s saw a florescence of Austen-mania, with adaptations including the films *Sense and Sensibility* (Lee, 1995), *Clueless* (Heckerling, 1995), and *Emma* (McGrath, 1996) and the television productions of *Persuasion* (Michell, 1995), *Pride and Prejudice* (Langton, 1995) and *Emma* (Lawrence, 1996), the last two both scripted by Andrew Davies.
10. Jane Austen and Seth Grahame-Smith, *Pride and Prejudice and Zombies* (Philadelphia: Quirk Books, 2009), p. 260; further references to this work are given in the text.
11. Elizabeth H. Ellington, 'A Correct Taste in Landscape: Pemberley as Fetish and Commodity', in *Jane Austen in Hollywood*, ed. by Troost and Greenfield, pp. 90–110 (p. 109).
12. William Blackstone, *Commentaries on the Laws of England (1765–1769)* <http://www.lonang.com/exlibris/blackstone/> [accessed 4 January 2020].
13. Ibid.
14. Significantly it is also the surname of the illegitimate Harriet Smith in *Emma*, whom the title character mistakenly assumes to be the unacknowledged child of a gentleman.
15. Jane Austen, *Pride and Prejudice*, ed. and with an introduction by Vivien Jones (London: Penguin, 1996), p. 287.
16. *Mansfield Park* (Patricia Rozema, 1999).
17. Linda Troost and Sayre Greenfield, 'The Mouse that Roared: Patricia Rozema's *Mansfield Park*', in *Jane Austen in Hollywood*, ed. by Troost and Greenfield, pp. 188–204 (p. 188).
18. Austen, *Pride and Prejudice*, p. 287.
19. The precarious situation of impoverished gentlewomen was a theme in particular substantially developed in the 1995 adaptation of *Sense and Sensibility* with much new dialogue.
20. Graeme Turner, *British Cultural Studies: An Introduction* (London & New York: Routledge, 1992), p. 6.
21. Linda Troost and Sayre Greenfield, 'Introduction: Watching Ourselves Watching', in *Jane Austen in Hollywood*, ed. by Troost and Greenfield, pp. 1–12 (p. 5).
22. See, for example, Mary Poovey, *The Proper Lady and the Woman Writer: Ideology as Style in the Works of Mary Wollstonecraft, Mary Shelley and Jane Austen* (Chicago: Chicago University Press, 1984).
23. In this context 'supporting' signifies not merely a narrative subsidiarity, but the assumption that Friday's (black) labour should naturally be at the service and direction of the white Crusoe.
24. In Austen and Grahame-Smith, *Pride and Prejudice and Zombies*, the flogging of a private is subverted into 'a private had been flogged for engaging in base acts with a headless corpse' (p. 49)!
25. Though P. D. James's own death in 2014 does make it less likely that Pemberley will be troubled again.
26. Generally, though not invariably, it is the more deserving figures from fiction who stay put in their new country, for example Mary and Jem of Elizabeth Gaskell's *Mary Barton*.
27. Interestingly, the 2013 BBC adaptation of *Death Comes to Pemberley* omits both these references, perhaps regarding them as liable to be missed by a majority of viewers.
28. For example: 'Due to her fierce independence, devotion to exercise, and penchant for boots, some critics have called Elizabeth Bennet "the first literary lesbian". Do you think the authors intended her to be gay? And if so, how would this Sapphic twist serve to explain her relationships with Darcy, Jane, Charlotte, Lady Catherine, and Wickham?' (p. 319).
29. Jenkins, *Convergence Culture*, p. 19.
30. Unauthorized and especially fan-based adaptations of contemporary franchise texts (so-called 'fanfiction') do, of course, exist, and are often shared via the web.

CHAPTER 9

❖

Re-routing *Hamlet*: From the Canon to Consumer Culture[1]

Jozefina Komporaly

Following bold stagings of British 'in-yer-face' theatre — including *Blasted* by Sarah Kane and *Shopping and Fucking* by Mark Ravenhill — that consolidated Thomas Ostermeier's reputation as an *enfant terrible* of German theatre, the director turned his attention to European classics: Ibsen, Büchner, and, indeed, Shakespeare. Ostermeier contends that the 'anger, the desperation, the longing for beauty, the longing for another world' so prevalent in Shakespeare is also to be discovered in Georg Büchner, Edward Bond, and Sarah Kane;[2] and he approaches canonical texts 'through the lens of Sarah Kane', aiming to shake up the conventions of theatre-making and spectatorship.[3] Ostermeier's primary goal is not to offer modern takes on classics, but an interpretation of the society in which he lives. As he declared, he aims to 'understand more about the complexities of things going on in the world', alongside 'the complexity of human relationships'.[4] In this sense, he is a social and political commentator first and foremost, and a theatre director second.[5]

I argue that Ostermeier's stagings of canonical texts are active interventions on what could be termed, in Genette's taxonomy, as hypo-texts, and that they belong to a category defined by various forms of recontextualization, reformulation and re-use.[6] Ostermeier's *œuvre* as a whole offers a contemporary re-evaluation of the canon, and his adaptative strategies are based on creative engagements with translation, *mise en scène*, and dramaturgy. As such, these strategies define his working methods and collaborations to a high degree, and at the same time broaden the boundaries of how we may understand adaptation in artistic terms.

For the purposes of this chapter, I adopt Linda Hutcheon's definition of adaptation as 'a creative and interpretive transposition of a recognizable other work', 'a kind of extended palimpsest', and 'a transcoding into a different set of conventions' (though not necessarily a different medium).[7] In the case of Ostermeier's *Hamlet,* bold interlinguistic transfer is braided with (significant) textual editing and updating, and filtered through a relational dramaturgy that encourages audience involvement. These elements are underpinned by a *mise en scène*, affiliated to an intermedial practice celebrating the continuity between old and new media, that operates as a form of adaptation, as Ostermeier's distinctive directorial approach privileges above all the reimagining and recontextualizing of the source text. Ostermeier's theatre 'never stops adapting its features to the world and the world to its features',[8] and indeed, aiming to engage in an uncompromising social and political analysis, the director is concerned with exploring the possibility of truth and truthfulness in a bourgeois society,[9] and the potential for radical thought and for genuine democracy in a capitalist system dominated by neo-liberalism.[10] He favours plays that are centred on confrontation and interrogation, rather than the clear-cut advocation of a particular position, so the audience is invited to take up the challenge of considering opposing points of view.[11] For Ostermeier, when staging historical or indeed contemporary authors, pre-existing texts constitute mere points of departure for the development of an autonomous work of art, inspired but independent from the source text, and created in collaboration with the company. Reflecting his strong political convictions, Ostermeier aims to run the theatre as a collective of equals where the company is nurtured and work is developed gradually, over a period of time, which adds a further dimension to the adaptive process. He notes:

> The prime function of the director is to describe and communicate with the actor. You discuss a dialogue, you agree on a situation in a play — and then it's up to the actor. [...] When something happens in rehearsals which I don't control, when something is liberated in the actors, then I leave the rehearsal room in bliss. I don't get that from feeling 'fine, my concept works'.[12]

Ostermeier's *Hamlet* provides a complex and multi-faceted case study for exploring this approach to adaptation. It was conceived as a high-profile, internationally relevant production, commissioned for the Avignon Festival, and is still touring the world after twelve years in repertory. This reflects the reputation of the Schaubühne theatre company and its artistic director as one of the major export successes of German subsidized theatre. Ostermeier chose to direct the play to counteract the frequent representation of Hamlet as an honest romantic hero in a corrupt world. His approach — though not altogether new, as Tom Stoppard (*Rosencrantz and Guildenstern Are Dead*, 1966) and Charles Marowitz (*The Marowitz Hamlet*, 1968), for instance, had used it previously — transforms the protagonist into an obnoxious and impulsive character who interrogates the very category of the heroic and is unable to break out from his dysfunctional immediate family.

Ostermeier stated in his manifesto when he took over the direction of the Schaubühne in 2000 that theatre 'can be a place for society to gain consciousness', 'to be repoliticised', and for that aim 'we need a contemporary theatre' which is 'not the simple depiction of the world as it looks [...], it is a view on the world with an attitude that demands change'.[13] Ostermeier's productions aim to politicize spectators by engaging an often young audience with ongoing issues of their time. This does not mean that Ostermeier considers theatre to be a political event or that it is capable of sparking a revolution, rather that he treats it as a forum for observing human behaviour.

Ostermeier, Translation, and Adaptation

Over the years, Ostermeier has worked with several in-house dramaturgs to make a significant contribution to the Schaubühne's agenda; these partnerships bear the hallmarks of a shared artistic platform, and a mutual interest in contemporary playwriting (represented by the likes of Sarah Kane, Mark Ravenhill, Franz Xaver Kroetz) and a desire to revisit canonical texts in a fresh light. In other words, reinterpreting the canon for the twenty-first century, by including relatively contemporary work, is a hallmark of Ostermeier's artistic approach, and so is his concern with the reception of historically distant material in languages other than their original. Endorsing the generally accepted view that translations lose their relevance and immediate connection with contemporary culture much faster than original works, Ostermeier basically re-evaluates the canon in the light of translation and adaptation. Laera points out, referencing Venuti, that 'transferring pre-existing material into another language, culture or medium involves an exercise in self-definition through an act of appropriation of the foreign, which raises issues around a given society's self-representation and the reiteration of ideological exclusions'.[14] As a rule of thumb, despite the existence of several alternative German versions, Ostermeier tends to commission fresh translations of canonical works to be used as a basis for his productions, so that these can resonate with the flavour of the German language as spoken at present and reference, as much as possible, contemporary concerns. Indeed, as Hutcheon stresses, drawing on Bassnett, 'translation involves a transaction between texts and between languages and is thus "an act of both inter-cultural and inter-temporal communication"'.[15] Marius von Mayenburg's new version of *Hamlet* is intended as a blueprint for contemporary self-representation, and confirms and consolidates the ideologically motivated role of translation and adaptation as creative strategies for addressing the present through the lens of the past.

As Michael Billington observes in his essay 'Shakespeare in Europe', 'something strange happens when you lose the English language and context: you release the play's metaphorical power'.[16] Indeed, if we look at examples of Mayenburg's translation strategies, taken from Act 1, scene 3, what becomes instantly apparent is the opening up of an interpretive space in the wake of the ruthless excision of well-known lines. To put it differently, Mayenburg's direct manner of translating allows for additional creative freedom in the *mise en scène*, and avoids the static productions often seen in English-language stagings. In Shakespeare, this is how Laertes addresses Ophelia in the opening of the scene:

LAERTES: For Hamlet and the trifling of his favour,
Hold it a fashion and a toy in blood,
A violet in the youth of primy nature,
Forward, not permanent, sweet, not lasting,
The perfume and suppliance of a minute; No more. (*Hamlet*, 1.3)

For the Schaubühne production, translator and (at the time) in-house dramaturg Marius von Mayenburg does away altogether with the blank verse and opts for transparent contemporary prose, rendering the entire speech via a single compact sentence: 'Was Hamlet betrifft und sein Flirten, Ofelia, das hältst du am besten für eine Laune und triebhafte Spielerei, einen Duft, eine Zerstreuung für den Augenblick, mehr nicht'.[17] The backtranslation into English of his version would be something like, 'As far as Hamlet is concerned and his flirting, Ophelia, you'd better take this to be a whim and [a form of] toying with (sexual) desire, a scent, a distraction for the moment, nothing more'. It is instantly evident that the translation eliminates the allegorical overtones and focuses directly on the ephemeral nature of instinctual (sexual) urges and desires. Of course, being familiar with the cultural code of the time, Shakespeare's original audience would have had no difficulty in accessing such explicit allusions inherent in the text (be it here or in other plays); however, instead of inviting a decoding of historically and culturally distant conventions, Mayenburg chooses a directness characteristic of our age. This directness and overtness is metaphorically matched in the *mise en scène* by a simple, rectangular earth-filled set, a site of rot and corruption in which the characters slip and stumble. Soil is smeared by Hamlet onto the players, envelops the entire cast and gradually threatens to smatter the audience. Mud is also the visible revelation of Hamlet's madness, and, more obviously, acts as a non-verbal double to the negotiation of lust and desire that underpins the play.

Ostermeier's staging of the translation addresses the feeling of being out of control in a world governed by excess, where there are no clear allegiances anymore and where conspicuous consumption and the cult of celebrity is the new ideology. This is exemplified by the following dialogue between Ophelia and Polonius:

> OPHELIA: He hath, my lord, of late made many tenders
> Of his affection to me.
> POLONIUS: Affection! pooh! you speak like a green girl,
> Unsifted in such perilous circumstance.
> Do you believe his tenders, as you call them?
> OPHELIA: I do not know, my lord, what I should think.
> POLONIUS: Marry, I'll teach you: think yourself a baby;
> That you have ta'en these tenders for true pay,
> Which are not sterling. Tender yourself more dearly;
> Or — not to crack the wind of the poor phrase,
> Running it thus — you'll tender me a fool. (*Hamlet*, 1.3)

Mayenburg opts to do away with the multiple puns and language games that characterize the original, and condenses the passage into sober and colloquial language, which is marked by a matter-of-fact tone even when psychologically informed. In this way, the sparse simplicity of the set is reflected and further amplified by the simplicity of language, and draws attention to the actors and the moral questions at the core of the play:

> OFELIA: Er hat mir in letzter Zeit oft seine Zuneigung signalisiert.
> POLONIUS: Zuneigung, puh! Du redest wie ein Mauernblümchen, das mit so gefährlichen Situationen keine Erfahrung hat. Glaubst du seinen Signalen, wie du es nennst?
> OFELIA: Ich weiss nicht was ich denken soll.
> POLONIUS: Dann werd ich es dir sagen: Denk, das du selbst ein Baby bist,

> wenn du diese Signale, die Falschgeld sind, für bare Münze nimmst; mach dich rar, sonst machst du mich zum Idioten.[18]

The back-translation into English would read as follows:

> OPHELIA: Recently he has often signalled his affection.
> POLONIUS: Affection. Pooh! You talk like a shy young thing, inexperienced in such situations. Do you believe his signals, as you call them?
> OPHELIA: I don't know what I should think
> POLONIUS: Then I will tell you. Imagine you are a baby when you take these fake signals at face-value; make yourself scarce, otherwise you make me look like an idiot.

Patrice Pavis calls attention to a paradox whereby 'Shakespeare is easier to understand in French and German translation than in the original, because the work of adapting the text to the current situation of enunciation will necessarily be accomplished by the translation'.[19] Susan Bassnett concurs, stating that 'Chinese, Czech, Italian and Japanese translations [...] are not bound to the text by a sense of reverence, but motivated to ensure that Shakespeare reaches a new audience'; and indeed the Schaubühne's new version has successfully tried and tested this premise of accessibility.[20] The main changes engineered by Mayenburg in his German version thoroughly de-poeticize Shakespeare's dramatic language, institute vulgarity as a legitimate mode of expression, behaviour, and perception (even in places where Shakespeare is not himself vulgar), and destroy any hint of theatrical illusion. Polonius describes Hamlet to Claudius as a 'depressive' figure, who displays such modern-day symptoms as 'lack of appetite, sleeplessness, exhaustion and dizziness', thus offering an up-to-date diagnosis of contemporary ailments typical of an affluent society.[21] As Ostermeier contends, translations can:

Rewrite how people talk. English people always have to deal with the fact that it is probably the most beautiful literature that was ever written but at the same time it sounds a bit awkward and dated, and even some English audiences don't understand when they hear the lines on stage for the first time. We don't have this problem. That's my overall and highest aim when I'm doing Shakespeare: to have a translation where you understand every line.[22]

This ambition to make the play comprehensible on a textual level is paralleled by the production's carefully chosen performance aesthetic.

Editing the Plot, Updating the Scenario: The Postdramatic and the Metatheatrical

Ostermeier follows an 'inductive approach' in his work, through which the '*Stoff* [material] of the playtext and the present (of director, actors, audiences) communicate'.[23] In his view the very purpose of direction (*Regie*) is 'to stage a play in the present', and the production's aim to is to 'fill the dramatic situation (*Spielsituation*) [...] with our life and actions'; which is why presenting Hamlet 'as a spoilt brat [...] is only possible on the back of our own time' and staging a play becomes 'translating literature into a dramatic process (*Vorgang*) that happens in the here and the now'.[24]

Ostermeier recalls that for Ibsen's *Nora*, for instance, they wanted to 'change the text, do a modern adaptation of the language, change the surroundings, and the end — having Nora shoot Torvald'.[25] Eventually, though, he chose not to edit but to retain Ibsen's text and, together with dramaturg and translator Maja Zade, focused on adapting aspects of plot and staging by adding contemporary elements to it while removing outdated contexts. In the case of *Hamlet*, at Ostermeier's request, Mayenburg produced a highly trimmed stage script, with several plotlines and characters removed, that in performance runs under three hours with no interval — as opposed to five-hour long versions created by numerous companies when using the full Shakespearean text. This reflects Ostermeier's view that, from a playwriting perspective Shakespeare's plays pose problems for contemporary audiences: they are 'much too long, [there are] too many plots [...]. Hamlet is [...] the worst-made play. But genius'.[26] As we have seen, his radical version is achieved through various modalities of adaptation, including textual editing paired with *mise en scène* as an additional layer of adapting the source material to a new context through contemporary references. For example, by blurring the boundaries between funeral banquet and wedding celebration, staged as an orgy featuring takeaway food and drinks served straight out of cartons and cans, and alluding for instance to (then) celebrity gossip involving French president Nicolas Sarkozy and Carla Bruni, whom he later married, Mayenburg's contemporary German text is further contextualized and brought into the realm of the here and now. This new irreverent and funny version not only chimed with its modern audience, but also invited a fresh engagement with Shakespeare and theatre as an art form, making the audience delight in the live qualities of theatre-making, as in Shakespeare's day, and experience a wide spectrum of sensations from the uncomfortable to the perplexed and mystified, but above all engaging and drawing them into the flow of the performance.

This *Hamlet*'s aesthetic is to some extent indebted to postdramatic theatre, in its essentially fragmented structure (there is no climactic point in the production, even Hamlet's iconic monologue has been uprooted), its ongoing celebration of the artifice of theatre, its experimentation with form and genre, its integration of intermediality, its body-centredness, and its constant blurring between performer and audience fault-lines.[27] Audience participation or involvement is a constant, either via direct engagement (by responding to cues from the protagonist) or, more often, through the indeterminacy of meaning. As David Barnett argues, explicating Lehmann, the postdramatic:

> Proposes a theatre beyond representation, in which the limitations of representation are held in check by dramaturgies and performance practices that seek to *present* material rather than to posit a direct, representational relationship between the stage and the outside world.[28]

Indeed, Ostermeier contends:

> In a world where there are no more coherent narratives, because there are no more acting subjects that could be properly identified, I can't build up any dramatic action. My experience of the world is disoriented, I don't know who

is responsible for what's happening; yet this is the world I try to reflect and I can only do it through postdramatic theatre.[29]

Scaling the cast down to only six performers — five male and one female — meant that the same actress was cast as both Ophelia and Gertrude. The Schaubühne marketed the production by focusing on the actors' constant changing of roles, making the defining point that 'Hamlet's progressive loss of touch with reality, his disorientation, the manipulation of reality and identity are mirrored in the acting style, which takes pretence and disguise as its basic principles'.[30] Ostermeier's theatre celebrates the theatricality of theatre, it places the exploration of meta-theatricality — as a revelation of the inner processes of theatre-making and a self-conscious examination of the relationships between theatre and reality — at the core of this production of *Hamlet*.

Staging Media, Mixing Genres, and Audience Interaction

We have seen how Ostermeier utilizes creative interventions rooted in translation and dramaturgy, which he underpins by *mise en scène* as a form of further adaptation and cultural appropriation; to this, we should also add the key ingredient of intermediality. In his production of *Hamlet*, he draws on consumer culture as a potent point of reference and offers his audience a diet they are all too familiar with from their own daily lives, many examples of which dramatize the interactive dimension of multi-media experiences: a mash-up of reality and television game shows, video recording and projection, references to the world of showbusiness, accompanied by the ongoing consumption of fast-food and drinks, whose packaging is still in evidence, all to the tunes of contemporary pop music orchestrated by real-life DJ Lars Eidinger (Hamlet). Songs such as 'Theater', a German Eurovision song from the 1980s, or the hip hop number 'Krawall and Remmidemmi' [Ruckus and Riot], which topped the German charts at the time of rehearsals, were found intuitively and ended up seamlessly fused into the production. Likewise, a moment of fooling around led to the creation of an iconic moment: Eidinger's scratching, using paper plates, a casual replication of a DJ's gestures, became adopted as part of Hamlet's on-stage vocabulary. Moreover, on a monthly basis, *Hamlet* performances were followed by a complimentary event of sorts, called *Autistic Disco* and bearing the motto 'Pop is pop, and art is art', which was essentially a late-night party, held at the theatre venue, with DJ Lars Eidinger. Thus, Eidinger further transcends the boundaries of his role as Hamlet and fuses his public and private persona with that of the Shakespearean protagonist. Through DJ'ing this event, he also assumes further ownership of the material, musical and otherwise, presented in the production, encouraging a mixing-up and a hybridity that is quintessentially contemporary.

As Ostermeier notes, Shakespeare also collated heterogeneous material from many pre-existing sources, presented in a broad variety of styles, and in the Schaubühne's *Hamlet*, intermedial references and borrowings abound: Claudius confesses his crime in the style of live television chat shows, and Hamlet/Eidinger urges the audience to chant with him or to volunteer their contribution, such as naming the play-within-the-play or commenting on how evil Claudius looks. Through the 'bodily co-presence of actors and spectators',[31] this *Hamlet* production celebrates a feature that is unique to live performance: the active or 'emancipated' spectator (as Jacques Rancière terms it), who possesses the capacity to interpret the spectacle on offer, and generate their own associations and contextual updates.[32] Rancière's notion of emancipation blurs the boundaries between looking and doing, and grants agency to the aesthetic experience inherent in the pleasure of spectating. It shows an affinity with the concept of 'porous dramaturgy', articulated by Cathy Turner and Duska Radosavljevic, who draw attention to 'attempts to engage the audience in co-creation through [...] interactivity, immersion and site-specificity'.[33]

Ostermeier's production titillates the audience with memorable and spectacular scenes that have an immersive and interactive quality, tapping into our fascination with the visual. 'The Mousetrap' scene, which could be classed as an autonomous piece of live art, is a case in point. Hamlet, shedding the physical attributes associated with his character, transforms into a potentially neutral performer, who then engages with the performer previously playing the part of Horatio, covers him in clingfilm and pours tomato juice-cum-blood and milk down his constrained body. Another example of immersive and interactive dynamic can be seen in the opening of the production, where we see the full cast smoking and drinking at a table behind a gold screen-cum-curtain. This tableau is held for the entire duration of the spectators' taking their seats in the auditorium, and then morphs into the funeral and wedding banquet scenes. Remnants of cheap consumer products (cartons of tomato juice and milk, beer cans, plastic cups and plates) are abundant throughout, chiming in with the tone of the improvised dialogue with the audience (some of the chanting Eidinger initiated in December 2013 included 'we want to party/we want some pussy').

Ostermeier has argued that the problems and conflicts he is scrutinizing are primarily sociological rather than psychological, and his inclination is to look at society in its broader context. As Peter M. Boenish claims, in Ostermeier's theatre 'playtexts provide a (dramatic) narration whose constituent situations are put into theatral play(ing) so that they offer models of the existential conflicts within our societies'.[34] Ostermeier reveals that his ultimate directorial approach is 'to be honest with the writer, with the text, and get to the core of the play'.[35] Crucially, though, Ostermeier parallels his serious intentions — to read Shakespeare's plays as inherently political — with a laid-back manner, and thus makes *Hamlet* profound and entertaining at the same time. This is a version of *Hamlet* where the audience is encouraged to interact with the performers and to reward their jokes with laughter as and when they see fit, thus inviting a well-tried pattern of spectatorship common in Shakespeare's day, though often neglected in so-called canonical productions. Arguably, Ostermeier's *Hamlet* constitutes a trans-generic form as it refuses to conform to traditional genre markers, and what was written as tragedy by Shakespeare is played, at least in places, as comedy. This is rooted in postdramatic attempts to trouble contemporary expectations of how to interpret a text, and its rejoicing in the disruption of the hierarchical order: generic and political alike. In this way, when Lars Eidinger as Hamlet places the crown upside down on his head, he challenges the symbolic importance of royal lineage, status, and privilege, and invests a moment rooted in tragic solemnity with irreverent comedic accents.

Ostermeier's touring production takes advantage of the monumental scale offered by venues such as Avignon's Palais des Papes or London's Barbican, and designer Jan Pappelbaum utilized an enormous moving frame holding a beaded-curtain composed of long gold chains, allowing for dramatic entrances and the projection of film captured by Hamlet's invasive hand-held camera. The incorporation of digital technology into theatre practice is a significant feature of late twentieth- and twenty-first-century performance, and we live at a time when social and political action is firmly framed by documentation and media capture. Practically nothing can take place in contemporary life in the Western world, be it public or private, that is not recorded or documented in some way or other; and in this production of *Hamlet* video-cam technique establishes the protagonist as a documenter of other characters' actions. In addition, as Hamlet carefully records everyone (including himself), he not only creates an archive arguing against the ephemeral nature of live performance, but also unravels the mechanisms through which everything and everybody can be amplified to larger than life scale. Images are projected onto the mesmerizing gold bead curtain, while simultaneously the action unfolds on the stage behind the curtain — both of which are visible to the spectator.

Live theatre has become, in Elleström's terms, a 'strongly multimodal media', having acquired, according to Chiel Kattenbelt, the additional capacity to be a hypermedium which 'stages' other media.[36] Consolidating over the last decade and a half, and known as digital, multimedia, mixed-media, and, most frequently, intermedial theatre, this form reflects on the increasing impact of new technologies in a globalized world and acts as a platform for raising pertinent social and aesthetic concerns. *Hamlet's* intermedial dimension — whereby live and documented performance is situated side by side — offers some of the most striking moments in the production. The audience watches Hamlet film his co-performers, whilst they also watch the live footage generated by the latter, thus witnessing the way in which documentation is superimposed upon live events. The use of this type of technology and methods is far from unique to Ostermeier; Katie Mitchell and Franz Castorf, to name but two other directors, tend to make much more consistent use of intermediality in performance; however, they all have in common a preoccupation with experimenting with the boundaries of staging classical works. In addition to textual and cultural adaptation, these directors adapt the canon to a new medium and constantly-changing audience expectations, arguing for correspondences between the importance of creating a fresh version sited in the target culture that resonates with the here and now, and speaking a new visual language tuned in to current technological developments.

At the same time, as Aneta Mancewicz points out, new media often 'refashions stage practice by evoking strategies of old media'.[37] This claim to continuity can be usefully illuminated by Jay David Bolter and Richard Grusin's theory of remediation, which contends that a medium 'is that which remediates [...] and appropriates the techniques, forms, and social significance of other media and attempts to rival or refashion them in the name of the real'.[38] Although Bolter and Grusin do not specifically address theatre, their claim that a medium in our culture can no longer operate in isolation is paramount; endorsing this view Mancewicz argues that 'the ongoing relationship between pre-digital and digital technologies contributes to refashioning thematic resonances in Shakespeare's plays and their performance in contemporary Europe, while calling for a redefinition of live performance in relation to other forms of communication and production'.[39]

As Peter M. Boenisch contends, though, the relations between various types of media in a multi-tracked text — a self-consciously postmodern text which operates on several layers and mediatic levels — are ultimately a matter of perception and interpretation, in that intermediality in the context of the theatre is an 'effect of performance [...] created in the perception of observers because the relational aspect between thing and sign is a matter of experiencing'.[40] On the one hand, mediatization is essentially taken for granted and, hence, almost invisible in day-to-day life, but in Ostermeier's *Hamlet,* the multiple levels of performance, live and mediated/mediatized, have the potential to make us aware of these different layers: if one concentrates only on the live performer on stage, Judith Rosmair/ Lucy Wirth (as Gertrude) wearing dark glasses appears as a woman of undefined age, but the (simultaneously) projected video image of her hugely magnified face (reminiscent of cinematic as well as painterly techniques) references current tabloid images of celebrities beleaguered by pestering paparazzi.[41] In live performance, Urs Jucker is first and foremost Claudius; however, when filmed images of him playing the ghost of old Hamlet are projected onto the screen, he excels at rendering the haunting quality of the ghost, which is then juxtaposed with the seediness and moral corruption of Claudius. The production's opening image is Hamlet reciting his iconic monologue with his face blown up so large that only his eyes and nose can be squeezed onto the screen. This separation-cum-emphasis of the performer's key facial features, again rooted in old media forms such as painting or cinema, resonates with the renown of the lines, which have taken on an independent life of their own, being used to such an extent outside the context of the play that they have become devoid of meaning.

'To be, or not to be' are the first words spoken in the performance; however, instead of being glorified they are made insignificant by a softly-spoken Hamlet, squatting behind the bead curtain, ignoring both audience and onstage cast, and filming himself. His focus is the creation of a document through which he can witness the events taking place, and by opting to film himself and, later on, the other guests at the table, he draws attention to the importance of perspective. Since the production deliberately uses a transmitter with a bad and noisy signal, the streamed images come across as dark and rough, thus helping to interrogate the question of Hamlet's madness as well as reiterate the idea of chaos in a world out of joint. As for Hamlet's most famous lines, they are repeated twice more in the production, in instances different from Shakespeare's original text. Hamlet warns the audience in an aside that he has a monologue to deliver; and the speech, rather than uttered with romantic solemnity, is delivered with contempt: Eidinger gets through it while standing on a table, drunk, no skull in hand, and with a plastic crown placed upside down on his head.

Improvised Roles

The production not only restructures Shakespeare's text by relocating elements of this most iconic of plays, by changing the flow of the original Shakespearean text, and by exploring various facets of intermediality, as explored above; it also blurs the boundaries between performers embodying characters and performers as individuals. Lars Eidinger, cast as Hamlet, has ongoing interactions with the audience as an actor playing the role of Hamlet, thus transcending his position as an actor playing a role and becoming an emblem of sorts for the production in a personal capacity as well (Eidinger preceded Ostermeier at the Schaubühne, starting there in 1999, and has been a staple of his productions over the years). Ostermeier references Polish director Krystian Lupa's metaphor of the actor dancing with their character, and indicates a similar dramatization of the relationship between Eidinger and Hamlet: the actor's and the character's identities each being foregrounded at different moments of the production.[42] Eidinger chats to the audience, requests instant feedback, and acknowledges foreign languages and locations when touring. In fact, Eidinger even integrated genuine accidents into the fabric of the performance. When he smacked his head into a pillar, a dialogue with the audience ensued in which he asked whether he should continue and when urged to do so, he did despite the obvious pain and bleeding. It is unclear whether it was he who did not want to stop or if the audience pressurized him to continue to perform, but, on the whole, performances have become slightly longer over time as Eidinger has settled into his role and developed a taste for this interactive platform with his audience. This interactive potential inherent in canonical works has its origins in the asides frequently used by Shakespeare himself; and from Eidinger's, and Ostermeier's, point of view, adapting the canon can legitimately include the amplification of interactive elements to an improvisational level in response to actual circumstantial concerns. These, seemingly trivial, references simultaneously connect the world of live performance with that of the immediate present and of the original dramatic text, not to mention that they help us consider what might be defined as 'truthful' versus 'theatrical' in performance. According to Lehmann:

> In the postdramatic theatre of the real the key point is not the assertion of the real as such [...] but the disconcert that occurs through being unable to establish whether one is dealing with reality or fiction. Both the theatrical effect and the effect on consciousness derive from ambiguity.[43]

As spontaneous ideas and observations make their way straight into the texture of the performance, we are witnessing a situation whereby rehearsals are, to a degree, bypassed. Ostermeier, in his preface to *Eidinger (Backstage)*, affectionately calls Eidinger a 'Berliner Schnauze mit Herz' [an outspoken Berliner with a heart and charm], and amongst his key qualities notes being 'outspoken, dry, often coarse, charming, rude, with an absurd humour, edgy, non-conformist, boundary pushing'.[44] Indeed, Eidinger alters the tone of the improvised dialogue with the audience between apparent small talk and explicit incitement or even provocation. This, in principle, is part of the production's dramaturgy that integrates prompts for creative input for performers and indeed the audience; however, the degree to which Eidinger carries out these improvisational interactions varies significantly from place to place, and occasion to occasion, and involves an element of chance and unpredictability. These factors affiliate this production of *Hamlet* to relational art as theorized by Nicolas Bourriaud, and locate it in 'the space of interaction, the space of openness that ushers in all dialogue', producing 'relational space-time elements, inter-human experiences trying to rid themselves of the straightjacket of the ideology of mass communications, in a way, of the places where alternative forms of sociability, critical models and moments of constructed conviviality are worked out'.[45]

In this sense, Eidinger's spontaneous integration of a genuine accident into the fabric of the performance is the epitome of avoiding clichés and formulaic approaches, and ushers in an unprecedented degree of agency for an actor engaging with text-based theatre. In this way, in addition to ambiguity regarding the boundaries between Hamlet the character and the actor playing Hamlet, Eidinger's increasing authorial investment in the production has started to rewrite the rules of director-actor relationship and moves towards collaborative practice.

Conclusion

As we have seen, Ostermeier addresses his society's social, moral, and political concerns through *Hamlet*, and invests Shakespeare's text with up-to-date contemporary references. Jan Kott's thesis that Shakespeare is our contemporary is surely borne out in this production, which shows how *Hamlet* remains emblematic in many different areas.[46] Aiming to stage a balance between indigenous and canonical drama, the question of translation and adaptation is central for Ostermeier, and his version is a thoroughly contemporary project both in its language and *mise en scène*. It has attracted an unprecedented interest from young audiences due to its hybrid qualities, and features an adolescent tantrum-throwing talk-show host who blatantly embodies the fallibility of his generation. This Hamlet is in the mould of Sarah Kane's Hippolytus in *Phaedra's Love*, who is by definition incapable of genuine emotion or action. Instead, he is an observer and documenter of contemporary mores driven to madness, not least through the constant intrusion of his camcorder with which he records everyone's actions, his own included. Capturing images references contemporary society's excessive preoccupation with celebrity as well as our obsession with the self, but also points to surveillance through omnipresent CCTV cameras and a resulting sense of persecution. As these images are then instantly blown up and streamed live onto a large screen, behind which the actual live action continues, live and documented performance continues to exist side-by-side, and invites a discussion on the modes and potential of performance. This intermedial dimension of Ostermeier's adaptation, emblematic for the prevalence of technology in contemporary performance, demonstrates an increasingly popular approach to contemporary ways of adapting the canon. Ostermeier opens up points of contact between long-established canonical staples and fresh demands of the contemporary context. Ultimately, as he situates intermediality and interactivity at the core of his production, he asserts the need for dialogue in multiple ways: between the canon and translation, adaptation, and new dramaturgies; between source and target texts; between languages; between performers and audiences; between the past and the present; as well as between various theatre, media, and performance cultures. As a handful of performers slip in and out of almost two dozen parts, with the full awareness and participation of the audience, this *Hamlet* invites us to attempt all of the above, and, in addition, makes us want simply to rejoice in its playful reflection on identity, simulation, and theatricality.

Notes to Chapter 9

1. This essay reworks material discussed in the Ostermeier section of the chapter 'Adaptive Recontextualisations: *Hamlet* for the Here and Now, or Reappropriating the Canon', in Jozefina Komporaly, *Radical Revival as Adaptation: Theatre, Politics, Society* (London: Palgrave, 2017), pp. 36–49. Many thanks to Palgrave Macmillan and Springer Nature for their kind permission to reuse content from the above.
2. Andrew Dickson, 'Thomas Ostermeier: "Hamlet? The Play's a Mess"', *Guardian*, 13 November 2011 <https://www.theguardian.com/stage/2011/nov/13/thomas-ostermeier-hamlet-schaubuhne> [accessed 5 January 2020].
3. Thomas Ostermeier, in Emma Hogan, 'Deutsche Bard: Are you Ready for "Hamlet" in German? Thomas Ostermeier Talks About his Controversial Staging of Shakespeare', *Financial Times*, 25 November 2011 <https://www.ft.com/content/6f0ea1b4-edc5–11e0-a9a9–00144feab49a> [accessed 20 November 2019].
4. Thomas Ostermeier, in James Woodall, 'Thomas Ostermeier: On Europe, Theatre, Communication', in *Contemporary European Theatre Directors*, ed. by Maria M. Delgado and Dan Rebellato (Abingdon & New York: Routledge, 2010), p. 374.
5. For the latter, the director has been regularly critiqued in his native Germany, where the predominant aesthetic of fragmentation and discontinuation pushes him to the periphery of fashionable norms, despite overwhelming international acclaim. As an exiled artist of sorts, to use Georges Banu's term, Ostermeier does not shy away from the ever-deepening rift between his own form of theatre-making and the current institutional opinion in German theatre.
6. Gérard Genette, *Palimpsests: Literature in the Second Degree*, trans. by Channa Newman and Claude Doubinsky (Lincoln: University of Nebraska Press). p. 5.
7. Hutcheon, *A Theory of Adaptation*, p. 35.
8. Margherita Laera makes this claim about theatre more generally, see 'Introduction: Return, Rewrite, Repeat: The Theatricality of Adaptation', in *Theatre and Adaptation: Return, Rewrite, Repeat*, ed. by Margherita Laera (London: Bloomsbury, 2014), pp. 1–18 (p. 1).
9. He has approached this central topic in several productions based on canonical sources, including Ibsen's *An Enemy of the People* and Shakespeare's *Measure for Measure* and *Hamlet*, as he considers it to be *the* fundamental question to come to terms with, in our market-driven society.
10. Thomas Ostermeier, in Jean-François Perrier, 'Entretien avec Thomas Ostermeier', Avignon Festival, 2008, p. 1 <fa2008_entretien_avec_thomas_ostermeier.pdf> [accessed 21 November, 2019].
11. Ibid., p. 2.
12. Thomas Ostermeier, in Michael Merschmeier and Franz Wille, '"Ich muss es einfach versuchen": ein Theater Heute-Gesprach mit Thomas Ostermeier', *Theater Heute*, 5 (1998), 26–30, also quoted in Peter M. Boenisch, 'Thomas Ostermeier: Mission (Neo)Realism', in *Contemporary European Theatre Directors*, ed. by Delgado and Rebellato, p. 355.

13. Schaubühne am Lehniner Platz, 'Der Auftrag' [The Mission], originally published in the inaugural programme brochure for the theatre's Spring season 2000, reprinted as 'Wir müssen von vorn anfangen' [We have to start afresh], *Die Tageszeitung*, 20 January 2000, p. 15.
14. Laera, 'Introduction', p. 9. Cf. Venuti, *The Translator's Invisibility*, and *The Scandals of Translation: Towards an Ethics of Difference* (London & New York: Routledge, 1998).
15. Hutcheon, *A Theory of Adaptation*, p. 16; Susan Bassnett, *Translation Studies*, 3rd edn (Abingdon & New York: Routledge, 2002), p. 9.
16. Michael Billington, 'Shakespeare in Europe', in *One Night Stands* (London: Nick Hern Books, 1993), p. 357.
17. Marius von Mayenburg, *Hamlet*, German version for the Schaubühne, Henschel Schauspiel <http://www.henschel-schauspiel.de/de/media/media/theater/TI-3314_LP.pdf > [accessed 6 September 2016].
18. Ibid.
19. Patrice Pavis, 'Problems of Translation for the Stage: Interculturalism and Post-modern Theatre', trans. by Loren Kruger, in *The Play Out of Context: Transferring Plays from Culture to Culture*, ed. by Hanna Scolnicov and Peter Holland (Cambridge: Cambridge University Press, 1989), p. 28.
20. Susan Bassnett, 'Neither Rhyme nor Reason', *ITI Bulletin* (September-October 2015), pp. 26–27.
21. Mayenburg, *Hamlet*; my back-translation into English.
22. Hogan, 'Deutsche Bard'.
23. Thomas Ostermeier, in Thomas Ostermeier and Peter M. Boenisch, *The Theatre of Thomas Ostermeier* (Abingdon & New York: Routledge, 2016), p. 133.
24. Ibid.
25. Woodall, 'Thomas Ostermeier', p. 371.
26. Thomas Ostermeier, in Andrew Dickson, 'Thomas Ostermeier: "Hamlet? The Play's a Mess"'.
27. It is worth saying, though, that despite the influence of the aesthetic of the postdramatic, this *Hamlet* engages too much with the world outside the theatre to qualify as a case of pure postdramatic theatre.
28. David Barnett, 'When is a Play Not a Drama? Two Examples of Postdramatic Theatre Texts', *New Theatre Quarterly*, 24.1 (February 2008), 15. Cf. Hans-Thies Lehmann, *Postdramatic Theatre*, trans. by Karen Jürs-Munby (Abingdon & New York: Routledge, 2006). Ostermeier's work, especially his recent output, has also been viewed (by Boenisch, 'Thomas Ostermeier', for instance) as an instance of neo-realism in the theatre — an interpretation the director also welcomes.
29. Thomas Ostermeier, 'Der Kapitalismus liebt die Stille nicht: Gespräch mit Byung Chul-Han', *Schaubühne Spielzeit für 2013–14*, p. 4.
30. Schaubühne website <http://www.schaubuehne.de/en/productions/hamlet.html> [accessed 14 November 2013].
31. Erika Fischer-Lichte, *The Transformative Power of Performance: A New Aesthetics*, trans. by Saskya Iris Jain (Abingdon & New York: Routledge, 2008), p. 138.
32. Jacques Rancière, *The Emancipated Spectator* (London: Verso, 2009).
33. Cathy Turner and Duska Radosavljevic, 'Porous Dramaturgy: "Togetherness" and Community in the Structure of the Artwork', 2012 <http://expandeddramaturgies.com/?p=687> [accessed 20 November 2019].
34. Ostermeier and Boenisch, *The Theatre of Thomas Ostermeier*, pp. 6–7.
35. Thomas Ostermeier, in conversation with Peter Cramer, *Talking Germany* programme, Deutsche Welle, broadcast on 15 April 2012 <http://www.youtube.com/watch?v=vaUHxKXjkwI> [accessed 20 November 2019].
36. Elleström, 'The Modalities of Media', p. 38; Chiel Kattenbelt, 'Theatre as the Art of the Performer and the Stage of Intermediality', in *Intermediality in Theatre and Performance*, ed. by Freda Chapple and Chiel Kattenbelt (Amsterdam & New York: Rodopi, 2006), pp. 29–39 (p. 37).
37. Aneta Mancewicz, *Intermedial Shakespeares on European Stages* (Basingstoke: Palgrave, 2014), p. 108.

38. Jay David Bolter and Richard Grusin, *Remediation: Understanding the New Media* (Cambridge, MA: MIT Press, 2000), p. 65.
39. Mancewicz, *Intermedial Shakespeares on European Stages.*
40. Peter M. Boenisch, 'Aesthetic Art to Aisthetic Act: Theatre, Media, Intermedial Performance', in *Intermediality in Theatre and Performance*, ed. by Chapple and Kattenbelt, pp. 103–16 (p. 113).
41. The link with celebrity culture is further amplified by the insertion of a Carla Bruni song: after the funeral, Gertrude dedicates a song by the (at the time) new wife of then French president Nicolas Sarkozy to her own new husband, Claudius.
42. Thomas Ostermeier, *Teatrul şi frica / Theatre and Fear*, ed. by Georges Banu and Jitka Goriaux Pelechová, trans. by Vlad Russo (Bucharest: Nemira, 2016), p. 32.
43. Lehmann, *Postdramatic Theatre*, p. 101.
44. Thomas Ostermeier, 'Foreword', in Michael Eberth, *Eidinger: Backstage* (Berlin: Verlag Theater der Zeit, 2011), pp. 1–3. 'Berliner Schnauze' refers to a person who speaks in the local Berlin and Brandenburg dialect, and who embodies a certain roughness by being outspoken and making use of coarse humour.
45. Nicolas Bourriaud, *Relational Aesthetics*, trans. by Simon Pleasance and Fronza Woods with the participation of Mathieu Copeland (Dijon: Presses du réel, 2002), pp. 44–45.
46. See Jan Kott, *Shakespeare our Contemporary*, trans. by Bolesław Taborksi (London: Routledge, 1988); first published in Polish in 1961.

CHAPTER 10

❖

François Villon on the Radio: Ezra Pound's Adaptation of *The Testament* for the BBC

Claire Pascolini-Campbell

The fifteenth-century Parisian versifier and fabled *poète maudit*, François Villon, is remarkable for the number of creative adaptations across genres, time periods, languages, and media that his poetry and poetic persona alike have inspired. His verse has served as creative fodder to the sculptor Auguste Rodin, who immortalized Villon's 'Belle Heaulmière' in a bronze figure cast in 1887, known first as 'The Old Woman' and latterly as the 'Belle qui fut Heaulmière'. His *ballades* and *rondeaux* have been set to music by such diverse artists as Claude Debussy (1910), Georges Brassens (1953), the rock band Eiffel (2009), and the Russian bard singer Bulat Okudzhava, whose 'Molitva Fransua Viyona' was covered by Regina Spektor in 2012. The legend of his life has moved from page to stage in adaptations by Justin Huntly McCarthy (1901), Rudolf Friml (1925), and Samuel Aaron DeWitt (1956), while Bertolt Brecht's famous character, Mack the Knife, quotes liberally from Villon in *The Threepenny Opera* (1928). In the nineteenth and twentieth centuries, novels or short stories taking Villon as their protagonist have appeared both in English and in French, issuing from the pens of writers such as Robert Louis Stevenson (1877), John Erskine (1937), Babette Deutsch (1942), and Jean Teulé (2006). The medieval French poet has also graced the silver screen, first in the silent film *The Oubliette* (1914), and most recently in Kichitaro Negishi's *Villon's Wife* (2009), which transplants a Villon persona into 1940s post-war Tokyo.

What accounts for Villon's enduring popularity as a source for adaptation? On the one hand, much of his appeal is due to his captivating narrative persona, a pseudo-autobiographical character present throughout *Le Testament* and *Le Lais* who seems to offer a rare glimpse into the lives of medieval Paris's common folk. Moreover, together with the apparent 'authenticity' of his narrative voice, audiences have been drawn to the colourful personal history memorialized (and no doubt embellished) in his poetry — from his alleged association with loose women and petty thieves, to his multiple incarcerations and brushes with the hangman's noose. Often unwilling to separate the 'real' Villon from that of the eponymous testator who figures in his verse, a fascination with the myth of the man is the driving force behind many Villonian adaptations.

Nonetheless, despite the frequency with which his work has been adapted, Villon has not always been viewed as a canonical poet. Indeed, Harold Bloom omits him from his survey of canonical writers, a surprising decision given Bloom's own rationale that canonicity is quantifiable and can be verified by the number of 'progeny' a writer inspires. For instance, he writes of Dante:

> Dante's progeny among the writers are his true canonisers, and they are not always an overtly devout medley: Petrarch, Boccaccio, Chaucer, Shelley, Rossetti, Yeats, Joyce, Pound, Eliot, Borges, Stevens, Beckett. About all that dozen possess in common is Dante, though he becomes twelve different Dantes in his poetic afterlife. This is wholly appropriate for a writer of his strength; there are nearly as many Dantes as there are Shakespeares.[1]

Much of the above quotation might be applied to Villon: like Dante, he multiplies and fractures. Villon's presence in the Western canon ought then to be conspicuous, illustrated as it is by the many adaptations of his work. For Bloom, however, the canonical strength of a writer is also dependent on the status of those who engage with them. While both Dante and Villon may count Rossetti and Pound amongst their progeny, a significant portion of Villon's heirs have existed below the surface of canonical tradition. Although recent criticism has done much to restore the failing fortunes of some of his Victorian acolytes (Algernon Swinburne, for example), others, such as John Payne, the first to transpose the entirety of Villon's text into English, remain only minor figures.

Marginality is itself a theme in Villon, whose own *œuvre* emphasizes his exclusion from normative society — both because of his failure to harness patronage and his criminality. Indeed, the perception of Villon as 'marginal' or 'other' has itself been a motivation for many of those engaging with his work; adapting his poetry and adopting his voice have often been ways for Villon's heirs to express their own experiences of 'otherness'.

In adapting his text for the radio, then, Ezra Pound may justifiably have felt that Villon's was a reputation in need of puffing. As we shall see, his choice of medium can be understood as a deliberate attempt to bring Villon to the mainstream, complementing his efforts to canonize him in his 1934 anthology, *The ABC of Reading.*[2] Furthermore, in his choice of radio as medium, Pound is also formally experimental, exploiting a new technology to tell a very old story. Was this experiment a success? How did the encounter with radio open up creative possibilities for the process of adapting and transposing Villon's *œuvre* for a modern audience? This article will argue that Pound's choice of medium was based, in part, on his interest in 'melopoeia' and the idea that the sound of poetry is itself productive of meaning.

Pound and Villon, Multiple Encounters: Pastiche, Criticism, Translation, Opera

Pound holds a special place among Villon's many heirs. As well as being the first to attempt to bring Villon to the general public via the mass medium of radio, he was greatly influential in introducing his work to other poets and creative writers of the Modernist period and beyond.[3] Pound, himself, continually returned to the medieval French poet throughout his long and varied career as poet, critic, playwright and composer. Indeed, as far as adaptation studies is concerned, his creative encounters with Villon are particularly worth noting for the many generic forms that they take; in Pound's work Villon's text is renewed again and again as pastiche, translation, opera, and radio melodrama.

For instance, Villon first appears in Pound's *œuvre* through two 'Villonauds', imitative pastiches which reproduce the style, themes, and to some extent the form of the original poetry, published originally in *A lume spento* (1908) and later in *Personae: Collected Shorter Poems of Ezra Pound* (1926).[4] In 1910 Pound devoted an entire chapter to the medieval poet in his critical text, *The Spirit of Romance*.[5] The book was written during his brief tenure as a lecturer at Regent Street Polytechnic and focuses on medieval and early modern writers, including studies of the work of Arnaut Daniel, Guido Guincelli, Dante, Petrarch, Boccaccio, Chaucer, John Gower, Michael Agnolo, Camoens, Lope de Vega, and Shakespeare. It is significant that Pound's essay on Villon also includes his own translations from Villon's *œuvre*, exemplifying another form of creative engagement with his work. The *Cantos*, too, are laden with allusions to Villon, and his presence in this modern epic, a text that was to occupy Pound from 1924 until his death in 1972, is emblematic of the central role that Villon came to play in Pound's mission of re-evaluating and revising the Western canon.[6] In addition, Pound set Villon to music in his 1924 opera, *The Testament*, and it was this work that was later adapted for BBC radio as a melodrama, in 1931. In this context, the radio adaptation which is the focus of this article must be seen as a complex intermedial encounter — an engagement not only with the poetic 'source text', but also with a range of other genres and media, most strikingly the 1924 opera adaptation of the same text, which is itself at the nexus of a range of theatrical, musical, and poetic influences.

Performed in 1924 and 1926 at the Salle Pleyel in Paris, the opera version of *The Testament* was composed in collaboration with the avant-garde American composer, George Antheil. Pound and Antheil set Villon's work to music, stringing the sung poems together as a series of vignettes performed by Villon and characters from his world. The plot of the opera describes Villon's return to Paris as a wanted man and culminates in a 'final tableau' in which six hanged men perform the famous 'Ballade des pendus' [Ballad of the hanged men], as Pound explains: 'A final tableau depicts six lads hung by the neck. Each director mounting the production must decide if Villon is among the six, as history has left no trace'.[7] The source texts were primarily drawn from Villon's work known by the same name, *Le Testament*, although the 'Ballade des pendus' is from the miscellaneous poems editors have grouped together as the *Poésies*.

Pound's choice of opera as medium speaks to a long tradition of reading Villon as a 'musical' poet. This perception is partly bound up in ideas about the musical roots of the *ballade* (Villon's form of choice) and broader debates about poetry as an intrinsically aural/oral medium. For instance, more than fifty years earlier Swinburne had already commented on the synergies between music and poetry with regard to Villon in particular, describing his work as a source of 'spontaneous indefinable music' and 'inexplicable melody', 'faultless always as to form and harmony of natural utterance, from the tenderest note of piteous or even sacred song'.[8] Moreover, as we saw in the introduction, there have been multiple musical adaptations of Villon's *œuvre*. In fact, during the same period that Pound was producing his opera, Villon was also being renewed for contemporary audiences as the protagonist of Rudolf Friml's operetta, *The Vagabond King* (although Friml's libretto is based on McCarthy's 1901 novel about Villon, as opposed to being a direct musical transposition of the source text).

Where Pound's adaptation was especially innovative, however, was in his technique for setting Villon's words to music. Pound and Antheil's score attempts to replicate the precise cadences and speech patterns of Old French, their starting point being that rhythm and melody should emerge from the words themselves. This creative decision resulted in a mixed metre that challenged audiences and performers alike (a score so difficult that it had to be simplified for the radio version of the opera).[9] His technique differs significantly from how literature is usually rendered into opera, where the medium is used to heighten the expressiveness of the text, moving the text away from normal speech patterns in favour of rising emotional intensity. For instance, in *Literature as Opera*, Gary Schmidgall explains that:

> Opera has to do with heights. Exaggeration is part of its essence. [...] The composer [...] and his librettist must search for moments in literature — call them lyric or explosive or hyperbolic — which permit them to rise to an operatic occasion [...]. The realism of natural motion is one of the qualities we bargain away by taking opera seriously on its own heightened level of expression.[10]

Pound's artistic decisions, however, were not motivated by a desire to 'exaggerate' or 'heighten' the text, but by his interest in the relationship between music and literature, an interest that, as we have seen, he shared with Swinburne (who was himself influenced by French Aestheticism in the development of his theories). The music of poetry in particular is a crucial preoccupation of Pound's, a hybridity he attempts to define through his theory of 'melopoeia'. In his essay, 'How to Read', he describes melopoeia as a kind of poetry 'wherein the words are charged, over and above their plain meaning, with some musical property, which directs the bearing or trend of that meaning'.[11] The sound or 'musical property' of poetry can therefore serve to communicate meaning as:

> The melopoeia can be appreciated by a foreigner with a sensitive ear, even though he be ignorant of the language in which the poem is written. It is practically impossible to transfer or translate it from one language to another, save perhaps by divine accident, and for half a line at a time.[12]

Thus, by transposing Villon's *ballades* into sung poetry, Pound resolves what he perceives as the impossibility of translation between languages, arguing that the listener receives a more genuine experience of the poetry through musical transposition. Rather than using Villon's themes to inspire a score, a decision that would mute the melopoeia of the source texts, Pound's opera engages with the text at the lexical level. By retaining the same cadences and speech patterns he enables the sound of the poetry to resonate, amplified by music.

The staging was also calculated to focus attention on the sound of the poetry, and Pound used the stillness of Japanese Noh drama to encourage his audience to focus on the auditory experience of the opera. For instance, in a letter to W. B. Yeats, over the course of which he enquires about the possibility of staging the opera at the Abbey Theatre in Dublin, Pound emphasizes the opera's debt to the stylings of Noh: '*The Testament*'s source of emotional power lies within the poetry and music, inclining it toward the Noh drama'.[13] As in Noh, the actors wore masks and their movements (or lack thereof) were highly stylized. For instance, the Villon character was to remain immobile throughout the performance in order to focus the audience's attention on his words. That the words were in Old French did not matter — according to Pound's theory of melopoeia the sound of the poetry was enough to generate meaning. When Pound came to adapt his opera to radio melodrama, this conviction, that sound is productive of meaning, was to remain a guiding principal, as we shall see below.

From Opera to Radio Melodrama

As far as Pound's use of the technology of radio is concerned, he is generally known for his infamous wartime broadcasts.[14] His adaptation of *The Testament* opera into radio melodrama has garnered much less attention, despite it being, as Margaret Fisher points out, 'one of the first electronically enhanced operas to be broadcast in Europe'.[15] Pound had several motivations for adapting his opera for the radio and, in his statement for the BBC, where the adaptation would air, he describes his rationale as follows:

> As with 'Villon' [the radio melodrama] the poet here continues to follow his intention: that is, to take the world's greatest poetry out of books, to put it on the air, to bring it to the ear of the people, even when they cannot understand it or cannot understand it all at once. The meaning can be explained but the emotion and beauty cannot be explained.[16]

The first of his aims, then, is to apply the technology of radio to his agenda of disseminating the canon more broadly. Radio broadcasting offered the opportunity to reach more people than ever before, effectively bringing Villon into the commercial mainstream. The canonizing potential afforded by new technologies has been noted by multiple adaptation theorists, with Deborah Cartmell and Imelda Whelehan affirming that, 'commercially it is obvious that a popular film adaptation of a novel can transform the text's value, from esoteric object to object of mass consumption'.[17] This statement might equally be applied to the technology of radio.

Indeed, by 1932 the BBC had five million licence holders, more and more people having decided that it was necessary to buy a wireless set. According to Asa Briggs, author of *The BBC: The First Fifty Years*, the increased popularity of the wireless in the 1930s has a direct correlation to changing leisure patterns and attitudes towards the 'home':

> It is interesting also to relate radio to changing leisure patterns. The average working week was sixty hours when broadcasting began in 1922, but it had fallen by as much as ten to fourteen hours a week by 1939. This added to the time available for listening. So, too, did the increased emphasis on the 'weekend' at home [...] home-centred wireless provided everywhere a new shape not only for the day but for the week.[18]

The wireless, moreover, was presented as 'companionable' and a justifiable substitute for the experience of attending operas, plays, or the cinema. For example, in his verse about a lonely woman listener, a *Radio Times* poet hailed the wireless as a mechanism for connecting communities, bridging distances and social differences through a communal auditory experience:

> Into her lonely cottage every night
> Comes music, played a hundred miles away...
> And as she hearkens, unto her it seems
> That she is one with the vast listening throng
> Held rapt together by the strains of song,
> Made one in music, dreaming the same dreams.[19]

On the other hand, Pound's canonizing agenda was also bound up in his theory of melopoeia, to which his statement to the BBC implicitly refers in its insistence that the sound of the verse — its 'emotion and beauty' — transcends language. In this, the ambitions of the radio melodrama coincide with those of the stage opera: both adaptations seek to provoke their audience to engage in a type of active listening.

While both opera and radio melodrama relied on the sound of the poetry to convey meaning, opera-goers had the benefit of visual clues to aid their interpretation, helping them to contextualize the sung poetry and follow the progression of the story. Indeed, a series of Villonian backdrops (the tavern, the brothel, the church, the gibbet) hinted at the themes of the *ballades*, with costumes and characterization adding further to the picture. In the purely aural medium of radio, however, Pound was faced with a 'blind' audience who would have to distinguish between characters and settings by hearing alone. Moreover, there was some consternation on the part of the BBC producer that, to listeners unfamiliar with Villon, the Old French lyrics could be misinterpreted as 'pretty pretty' without additional context.[20] For instance, while some of the sung poems deal with themes of love and loss, many more focus on drunkenness, prostitution, and physical decay, a distinction that the listener might fail to appreciate. Pound therefore made the pragmatic decision to bolster the libretto with additional dialogue, a script written in English that would guide the listening audience through the events of the story and dispel any preconceptions about Old French as a language reserved for the treatment of delicate topics alone.

Creative Reinventions: Language

Pound's script sets about creating a soundscape of Villon's world for his 'blind' radio audience first at the level of language. It departs from Standard English in favour of a slang polylect, a linguistic variety that the *Radio Times* described as 'hobo': 'the libretto is taken from Villon's own poetry, interspersed with brief snatches of dialogue in 'hobo' language. These elements form a harmonious and interesting whole, depicting the life and character of the picturesque poet-drunkard-thief in the most vivid way'.[21] While the passage characterizes the choice of language as 'harmonious', not all contemporary commentators agreed, some appearing to have viewed the juxtaposition of slang and Old French as a 'difficulty to be got over':

> 'François Villon' was one of the best plays the BBC has given us. The play did not disappoint. There was only one small difficulty to be got over, and that was the modern idiom used by Mr. Pound for the conversations [...]. Taken in itself it was not wrong, but there was an incongruity with the poems of Villon, which were sung, and beautifully sung, in French.[22]

Pound's aim, however, was not to disrupt but to complement. His choice of language is intended to situate Villon and his companions as part of a timeless urban working class, updating their social, linguistic, and economic identities for the modern listener while avoiding direct association with a specific region or social group. In this, his method differs from that of other adaptors and translators who fully transplant Villon into modern linguistic settings. In 'Villon's Good-Night', for instance, the nineteenth-century poet W. E. Henley translates Villon's 'Ballade de merci' into Victorian Cockney slang, arguing that the language provides a 'sportsmanlike equivalent' to Villon's own:

> You bible-sharps that thump on tubs,
> You lurkers on the abram sham,
> You spunges miking round the pubs,
> You flymy titters fond of flam,
> You judes that clobber for the stramm,
> You ponces good at talking tall,
> With fawneys on your dexter famm —
> A mot's good-night to one and all![23]

Conversely, Pound brings a medley of different linguistic influences together to create a simulacrum of 'Villonian' English for his script, a technique similar to that he employed in his 'Villonauds'. For example, Old French, Old Norse, Middle English, and Modern English clash evocatively in 'A Villonaud: Ballad of the Gibbet':

> Drink ye a skoal for the gallows tree!
> François and Margot and thee and me,
> Drink we the comrades merrily
> That said us, 'Till then' for the gallows tree!
>
> Fat Pierre with the hook gauche-main,
> Thomas Larron 'Ear-the-less,'
> Tybalde and that armouress

Who gave this poignard its premier stain
Pinning the Guise that had been fain
To make him a mate of the 'Haulte Noblesse'
And bade her be out with ill address
As a fool that mocketh his drue's disdeign.[24]

The term 'skoal' is from the Old Norse *skál*, whereas the pronouns 'ye' and 'thee', the inflection on 'mocketh', and the phrase 'drue's disdeign' are Middle English. The poem is also peppered with words from Old French, including 'Haulte Noblesse' [high nobility], 'Larron' [thief] and 'gauche-main' [pairing dagger]. Moreover, the language of Victorian medievalism likewise seeps into the poem: the word 'armouress' is distinctly Swinburnian and an intertextual reference to his translation of Villon's 'Regrets de la belle Heaulmière', 'The Lament of the Fair Armouress'.

However, while the hybrid language of the 'Villonauds' is intentionally 'medievalizing', pairing words from medieval languages with the lexis of Victorian medievalism, the language of Pound's radio melodrama is 'modernizing' in that it is predominantly comprised of modern slang. For instance, the script opens with the following dialogue:

SERGEANT OF POLICE: For violence against particular, for violence
(*pompously*) against the King's officers, for deception of
the King's officers that he did in the city of
Paris...
CAPTAIN OF WATCH: Stt! not so loud, now.
SERGEANT OF POLICE: ...that he did speak with foul language...
(*softer*)
PRIVATE OF THE WATCH: A clerk, sir? Do you think he will plead
scortum ante?
CAPTAIN OF WATCH: I don't care if he pleads pickled halibut,
Your job is to run 'om in. Twenty of you for
The six of 'em, easy takin'.[25]

Although the archaic language of the Sergeant of the Police and the Sergeant's reference to the practice of 'scortum ante' (the medieval practice of being permitted to visit a prostitute before execution) appears to locate the action in the medieval past, this impression is soon complicated by the captain's speech. His 'cocknified' dialect signals his socio-economic identity but also escapes ready classification. His language approaches cockney in, for example, the dropping of the initial 'h' from 'hom' (him) and the final 'g' from 'taking' and in its apparent use of cockney rhyming slang ('pickled halibut'). However, there are subtle deviations from cockney too: 'him' should be ''im' and not ''om' and there is no obvious corresponding rhyme for 'pickled halibut', marking it as a Poundian invention. Elsewhere, the characters pair American slang ('git along!') with English ('the little torf') further dislocating the text from association with any one specific dialect (pp. 207, 214).

In creating what Fisher has termed a 'universal hybrid language' to render Villonian dialogue in English, Pound gives his Villon a contemporary social identity but refrains from domesticating him to the extent that other translators and adaptors have done.[26] Instead, in framing the Old French texts with a modern dialect, he stages an interaction between the medieval and the modern, presenting the source text as a body of work capable of straddling temporal and linguistic boundaries, as relevant here and now as it was there and then.

Experiments in Tone: Melodrama and Comedy

As the above discussion has shown, if the creation of a script was, to a certain extent, a concession to a new medium, it also provided a further site for creative engagement with the source text. This engagement extends to structure, the script enabling Pound to respond to the format of the original *Le Testament*, in which the *ballades* occur within an organizing narrative frame. While, in Villon's case, that frame is part mock-will, part pseudo-autobiography, a structure in which the *ballades* feature as (frequently ironic) bequests, in Pound's version, they are inserted into the plot of a modern melodrama. A popular type of theatrical entertainment in nineteenth-century Britain, the genre pairs sensational stories with musical accompaniment and simply-drawn 'stock' characters. Frequently associated with realism, working-class audiences, and salacious themes such as murder and criminality, melodrama is distinctly appropriate to Villon. Furthermore, the genre is also much invested in comedy and farce, aspects that Pound brings to the fore in his radio adaptation.[27] Indeed, his choice of melodrama as mode enables him to engage with the comedy of Villon's text — something that, in its sombre *mise en scène*, the stage opera ignores.

For instance, in addition to the Villon persona, his mother, the belle Heaulmière, and Ythier Marchant — all of whom are given voices in the source text — the script introduces a number of new characters whose central function is to act as comic relief. While these characters are distinctly 'Villonian' in that they are suggested by and respond to the themes of the source text, as in conventional melodrama, they appear as stock 'types' primarily distinguished by their function in society or in the world of the play. They include, for example, the Sergeant of Police and his posse, the Priest, the Barman, the Gallant, the Friend, Beauty, and Ganthière. It is not surprising to find this cast of characters peopling Villon's world: his persona's frequent entanglements with the law, penchant for wine and taverns, and censure of hypocritical clerics explain the presence of the Police Sergeant, the Barman, and the (lascivious) Priest. Meanwhile, the Gallant refers to the 'gracïeux gallans' with whom Villon spent his youth and Beauty is extrapolated from the testator's appeal to 'Faulse Beaulté' and speaks to the tradition of allegorical figures popularized by the *Roman de la Rose*.[28] The Friend could represent any of the acquaintances of whom the testator speaks well (such as, for example, the gangster Colin Cayeux), while Ganthière [The Glove Maker] is taken from the 'Ballade de la belle Heaulmière aux filles de joie'.[29]

Much of the comedy of the script is achieved through the manner in which the new characters interact with the Old French that constitutes the primary libretto. For instance, the dialogue that frames Villon's most famous *ballade*, the 'Ballade des dames du temps jadis', is openly comedic. The 'Ballade' in question is prefaced by a lyric on the inevitability of death, sung by the Villon character in Pound's adaptation. In response to his performance, the Barman character rejoins: 'you've got the 'ump' (p. 209). There is humour both in the understatement and in the manner in which it is expressed — having the ''ump' is a poor descriptor of Villon's painful awareness of human mortality. The text then segues into the 'Ballade des dames du temps jadis' whose refrain, 'Mais où sont les neiges d'antan?', was famously translated by D. G. Rossetti as 'Where are the snows of yesteryear?'. Performed by the Villon character, the poem is an evocative expression of nostalgia. However, Pound blunts the pathos of the piece, his Barman interrupting yet again with a witty, colloquial aside: 'I dunno, I dunno where yer snows are gone, I dunno' (p. 209). Pound's audacity in translating so canonical a phrase in this irreverent manner is, in itself, a source of comedy, as is the Barman's apparent misunderstanding of the hypothetical nature of *ubi sunt*.

Elsewhere, humorous commentary and witty asides function as exegesis. The audience is made aware, for instance, that Villon is engrossed in the activity of writing his will through the colourful exclamation, 'Ajh! Gees! I'm makin' my will' (p. 214). Further, when the Villon character sings 'Bien plein s'escuz', the Friend knowingly returns, 'And she's a-gettin' 'em' (p. 214). The comic interjection serves to elucidate the meaning of the text: the ''em' refers to the 'escuz' or money of the preceding line, the implication being that woman to whom the *ballade* refers is being paid for sex. This motif — that of the economics of female sexuality — is immediately picked up by the succeeding *ballade*, whose refrain compares old women to out-of-circulation coins.[30] The Friend also performs a simultaneous if somewhat interpretative translation to the Gallant's song, echoing his line 'je regnie Amours' [I renounce Love] with the statement 'he denies 'em', and picks up on the themes of blood and violence in 'Et deffie a feu et a sang' [and dare him by fire and blood] with the comment 'looks like he's a-bleeding' (pp. 217–18).

Finally, if the ending of Pound's adaptation is far removed from the happy resolution that audiences might expect of a melodrama, it is not without humour. The pathos of the final scene with its performance of the 'Ballade des pendus' is downplayed, the script drawing attention to the absurdity of a poem being performed by dead men as opposed to its sombre themes of punishment and remorse:

> WOMAN'S VOICE: Six lads of the village,
> hung by the neck until dead.
> Did you ever head a man sing on the gallows?
> VOICE: Hahj?
> WOMAN'S VOICE: I'm a-tellin' you. They're hung. They're
> hung by the necks.
> Can you HEAR 'em? (p. 220)

Moreover, the final words of the script are themselves light-hearted, consisting of the following pithy couplet: 'Here ends the will and testament, | It's all up with poor Villon' (p. 221).

As we have seen, scripting the melodrama allows Pound to respond to the comedy of the source text. On the other hand, Villon and Pound do not frequently overlap in their choice of comic moments. A notable exception, however, is the treatment of Ythier Marchant, a character who serves as the butt of the joke in the source text and the adaptation alike. For instance, in the melodrama, the Friend introduces Marchant with the line 'Ugh, 'ere comes your boy friend' (p. 209). If the humour here appears mean-spirited, it is because Pound is taking his cue from Villon who employs witty puns and comic innuendo to mercilessly poke fun at Marchant in both his *Lais* and his *Testament*. In *Le Lais*, for example, Villon's testator persona ironically bequests his 'branc d'acier trenchant' [blade of cutting steel] to Marchant.[31] On the face of it, the gifting of a powerful sword from one man to another is reminiscent of the chivalric tradition. In the context of the source text, however, the gift takes on phallic connotations. For instance, Marchant has often been suspected of having been Villon's love rival and, by bequeathing him his sword, Villon suggests that Marchant's own sword is not up to the task; that is, he is impotent.

The choice of melodrama as frame, then, speaks to the themes of the source text, enabling the comedy of the Old French *Le Testament* to surface, in particular. Pound's experiment with new technology is also an experiment with tone, as he tempers the sombreness of the opera libretto with moments of comic absurdity.

Aural Effects: Space and Time

While the script offers a platform through which to engage with the source text, it is noticeably sparse on visual description. Instead, Pound took advantage of new technologies to move his characters across the aural landscape. The advertisement in the *Radio Times*, for example, describes the radio melodrama as follows: 'The play is an interesting experiment in a kind of impressionism that is only possible over the microphone or, perhaps, in a sound film'.[32] Thus, in adapting his opera for the radio, Pound was able to explore the use of sound effects to represent space and time, colliding past and present, uncoiling temporal layers, and creating space through sound.

The radio melodrama's producer, Edward Archibald Harding, a noted radio pioneer, had coached Pound. The end result was a play that featured artificial echo and sound effects, and the operation of an electronic audio mixing board to combine pre-recorded passages with live performance. Harding's dictum was that 'the great point is to make the listener *experience* what he is hearing', a message fully absorbed by Pound in his creation of an auditory landscape for *The Testament*.[33]

The passage of time — an important theme in the poetry itself — is represented through radio technology primarily through the use of 'foley' or recorded sound effects. For instance, from the outset of the radio play, the sound of drums that signals a change in scene is linked to the movement of time, segueing into the sound of church bells marking the passage of time ('*Fade in church bell tolling, hold and stop; add drum theme, add full echo*') and then into a clock striking nine ('*Off echo, hold little drum theme and slow out. Let clock strike 9*') (pp. 206–07). The drum theme, which fades in and out of the narrative and the music, comes to signify the rhythm of time passing with changes in the pace and rhythm of the drums serving to heighten the sense of urgency, of time slipping away, and bringing Villon closer and closer to the hangman's noose. Indeed, given that the script opens with a warrant for Villon's arrest, the listeners are made aware from the outset that his time is limited.

Pound uses foley to represent space as well as time, substituting for the lack of visual details in the script. While the sound of church bells sets the first scene, the listener is soon transported from the town square to the house where Villon's love interest, Rosie, lives: '(*end with sound of door shutting* VILLON *out significantly; sharp out as door slams; off echo*) FRIEND: Did you see how she pulls the shutter?' (p. 213). On the other hand, the *ballade* performed by Villon's mother, 'Ballade pour prier Nostre Dame', moves the action of the narrative into a church, as suggested by the '(*Gregorian chants*)' which precede it, and the '(*Church Service music by Dufay*)' which closes the scene (p. 215). This is followed by a sharp knock on the door which marks an abrupt shift from church to brothel:

(*In knocking on door*)
(*Up echo high*)
BOZO: To hell with you... No, you will not go in
... For a tanner?
PRIEST: What are you to be stoppin' me?
BOZO: I'm the Boss.
PRIEST: Of the establishment. (pp. 215–16)

In the final scene of the radio play, Pound substitutes the haunting visual tableau of six hanged men for an aural experience of the same. The foley — the sound of wind and the creaking of the gibbet, in this instance — makes the audience aware that the drama has moved outdoors, before the dialogue reveals the exact nature of the sounds they are hearing:

(*Slow in drum theme, hold and slow out; pause; In a sighing of wind, hold, down a little, add creak, and no echo for* VOICE *of:*)
VOICE: What do you see there?
WOMAN'S VOICE: Six lads of the village,
hung by the neck until dead. (p. 220)

Furthermore, echo and fade effects as well as foley are used throughout the performance to distinguish scene location and the movements of the characters. For instance, the speakers' voices recede with the end of a scene: 'SGT: A skirt, sir? (*Fade in, to background, drum theme*)' (p. 207). Similarly, echo is used to mark distance, enabling Pound to collapse and expand his auditory landscape:

(*In Heaulmière's preliminary screech, 'Ha!' with full echo on.*)
(*off echo*)
YTHIER: Wot's 'at?
(*out drum theme*)
V'S FRIEND: It's the old 'un. They say she used ter work
for the blacksmith. (p. 211)

In the scene above, the use of echo suggests that the Heaulmière is being heard from 'off stage' by Ythier and the Friend. A comparable technique is used to mark the location of Villon's mother, her song seeming to echo within the cavernous space of the medieval cathedral:

(*Fade out on 'Amen', in echo*)
V'S MOTHER: Dame du ciel, régente terrienne.
(begins singing)
(*echo down for this*)
FRIEND: An' she's a-prayin'.
(sotto voce)
(*echo*)
V'S MOTHER: Emperière des infernaux palus,
(Contd. fast) ...En ceste foy je vueil vivre et mourir. (p. 215)

The impression created is of the Friend in the foreground, providing a commentary on the Mother's song. However, as the song continues the echo subsides, the presence of the Friend diminishing and Pound 'zooming in' on the Mother instead.

In this way, Pound's use of sound effects allows him to create an aural landscape in which the narrative unfolds. Foley is used to suggest distinct Villonian spaces (the church, the brothel, the gibbet) whereas echo and fade allow Pound to zoom in and out on characters, as in a film. Time as well as space is represented, moreover, with the drum theme and frequent chiming of bell towers propelling the story on towards its inevitable, macabre end.

Conclusion

Pound's use of the medium of radio as a means of adapting Villon's *Le Testament* for a modern, English-speaking audience provides a fascinating case-study for examining forms of transposition and translation of a medieval poetic text across genre, time, and place, and, at the same time, for considering the complex interplay between different media, languages, and genres in what is a multi-layered adaptation process. In particular, we have seen how, in adapting the source text as opera and then the opera as radio melodrama, Pound exploits the differences between the two media to draw out different aspects of the original poetry. While both adaptations focus on melopoeia — on the sound of the Old French poetry as productive of meaning — in the radio melodrama Pound's script adds layers of interpretation, repositioning the source texts within a timeless urban setting and framing them with comic dialogue. Furthermore, the technological possibilities of radio allow Pound to create a particular kind of aural experience, bringing Villon's Paris to life in an intensely evocative way. Indeed, in putting Villon on the radio Pound invites his audience to exercise their auditory imaginations, making them active participants in the recovery of the Old French poet and his world.

Notes to Chapter 10

1. Bloom, *The Western Canon*, p. 80.
2. Ezra Pound, *The ABC of Reading* (London: Faber & Faber, 1961).
3. Pound's influence on 'H. D.' [Hilda Doolittle], Williams Carlos Williams, Basil Bunting, and Robert Lowell are indicative of this trend.
4. Ezra Pound, *A lume spento* (Venice: A. Antonini, 1908); *Personae: Collected Shorter Poems of Ezra Pound*, second printing (New York: Boni & Liveright, 1926 [*recte* 1927]).
5. Ezra Pound, *The Spirit of Romance: An Attempt to Define Somewhat the Charm of the Pre-Renaissance Literature of Latin Europe* (London: J. M. Dent, 1910).
6. Ezra Pound, *The Cantos of Ezra Pound* (London: Faber & Faber, 1975).
7. Margaret Fisher, *Ezra Pound's Radio Operas: The BBC Experiments, 1931–1933* (Cambridge, MA: MIT Press, 2002), p. 34.
8. Algernon Charles Swinburne, letter to John Nichol, 2 April 1876, in *The Swinburne Letters*, ed. by Cecil Lang, 6 vols (New Haven, CT: Yale University Press, 1959–1962), III (1960), 165.
9. Fisher, *Ezra Pound's Radio Operas*, p. 23.
10. Gary Schmidgall, *Literature as Opera* (New York: Oxford University Press, 1977), pp. 10 & 11.
11. Ezra Pound, 'How to Read', in *Literary Essays of Ezra Pound*, ed. by T. S. Eliot (Norfolk, CT: New Directions, 1954), pp. 15–40 (p. 25).
12. Ibid., p. 25.
13. Fisher, *Ezra Pound's Radio Operas*, p. 37.
14. During World War Two, Pound broadcast frequent speeches over Rome Radio in which he criticized the American government and promoted Fascism. The speeches led to him being charged with treason.
15. Fisher, *Ezra Pound's Radio Operas*, p. 2.
16. Ibid., p. 20.
17. Deborah Cartmell and Imelda Whelehan, 'Introduction', in *Adaptations: From Text to Screen, Screen to Text*, ed. by Deborah Cartmell and Imelda Whelehan (Abingdon & New York: Routledge, 1999), pp. 1–19 (p. 4).
18. Asa Briggs, *The BBC: The First Fifty Years* (Oxford: Oxford University Press, 1985), p. 114.
19. Ibid., p. 111.
20. Fisher, *Ezra Pound's Radio Operas*, p. 94.
21. Ibid., pl. 4.
22. M. C., 'The Testament of François Villon', *Manchester Guardian*, 28 October 1931, in *BBC Written Archives Centre*.
23. W. E. Henley, 'Villon's Good-Night', in *Recreations of the Rabelais Club* (London: printed for the members, private circulation only, 1885–1888), pp. 6–7.
24. Ezra Pound, 'A Villonaud: Ballad of the Gibbet', in *Personae*, p. 11.
25. Ezra Pound, *The Testament of François Villon, A Melodrama by Ezra Pound, Words by François Villon, Music by Ezra Pound*, full text in Fisher, *Ezra Pound's Radio Operas*, pp. 206–21 (p. 206). Further references to this work are given in the text.
26. Fisher, *Ezra Pound's Radio Operas*, p. 93.
27. François Villon, 'Le Testament', in *Poésies complètes*, ed. by Claude Thiry (Paris: Librairie Générale Française, 1991), pp. 89–253 (p. 109, l. 225; p. 167, l. 942).
28. For a definition of 'melodrama' see Frank Rahill, *The World of Melodrama* (University Park: Pennsylvania University Press, 1967), p. xiv.
29. Villon, 'Le Testament', p. 133, l. 533.
30. See ibid., pp. 133–34, refr.
31. Villon, 'Le Lais', in *Poésies complètes*, ed. by Thiry, pp. 59–87 (p. 64, l. 83).
32. Fisher, *Ezra Pound's Radio Operas*, pl. 4.
33. Ibid., p. 93.

CHAPTER 11

Thérèse Raquin and the Anxieties of Adaptation

Kate Griffiths

Adaptations have the potential to be anxious artefacts. In his now seminal *The Anxiety of Influence* (1973), Harold Bloom famously outlines the way in which poets anxiously negotiate with their canonical precursors to wrest an authority, creative identity, and originality for themselves. Bloom's model is particularly powerful for the field of adaptation studies, where adaptive artists, anxiously or otherwise, seek a creative presence for themselves alongside or in place of the earlier authors whom they rework. Charles Spencer, writing on the National Theatre's 2006 reworking of Émile Zola's *Thérèse Raquin* (1867), underlines both this creative negotiation and the power of Zola and his text as canonical forebears. Spencer writes: 'Marianne Elliot's production, though often impressive [...] seemed like a dim shadow of the thrilling, lurid images already floating around inside my head. [...] Zola's original novel will haunt my memory far more potently than this [...] stage version'.[1] Zola's novel *Thérèse Raquin* both speaks to and allows us to evaluate aspects of Bloom's ideas on influence at various levels. Within the plot, characters enact the anxiety of influence as they seek to replace their precursors, only to find themselves haunted and destroyed by them. At the level of the novel as creative artefact, however, Zola embraces a far more positive, playful, and generative model of influence which contrasts starkly with the destructive emphasis of much of Bloom's writing on the subject. In *Thérèse Raquin*, Zola crafts for himself a creativity which revels in and reflects on the intricate influence of its reworked sources. Key adaptations of the novel in different media do likewise. Focusing on some of the novel's afterlives in film (Marcel Carné's *Thérèse Raquin,* 1953, and Charlie Stratton's *In Secret,* 2013); in television (the BBC's 1980 *Thérèse Raquin*, Caroline Huppert's *La Liberté de Marie,* 2002), and a BBC Radio 4 adaptation (*Thérèse Raquin*, 1998, dramatized by Melissa Murray), this chapter will evaluate their self-reflexive consideration of the play of influences from which they are formed. As creative artefacts, they knowingly evaluate the influence of earlier artists and authors on their own existence. But they also analyse the creative influence of their own adaptive medium, be it film, television, or radio, on their work. When read in association, these adaptations of a canonical forebear join with that forebear to embrace a vision of influence as a multi-faceted thing. They depict it not as a source of anxiety, but rather as a source of complex creativity.

Anxious Adaptations

Bloom's model of anxious influence in which writers wrestle with their canonical ancestors has itself become canonical. The poet, Bloom suggests, longs to establish him/herself as a solitary, innovative genius without predecessors or precedents, as an identity of pure, hermetically-sealed originality. But the reality of the past three hundred years, Bloom argues, is that every poem must be read 'as its poet's deliberate misinterpretation [...] of a precursor poem or of poetry in general'.[2] Poetry, in the modern era, is, for Bloom, an innately revisionary endeavour as writers work inescapably from the literature which comes before them. Their revisionary relationship with that literature may take different forms (Bloom envisions six possibilities — Clinamen, Tessera, Kenosis, Daemonization, Askesis, and Apophrades, pp. 14–16). It may be creative, but it is nearly always, Bloom underlines, ultimately anxious and combative. Bloom asks: 'Do strong poets gain or lose more, *as poets*, in their wrestling with their ghostly fathers?' (p. 88). Poetry, for Bloom, is generated from the struggle between great writers and the descendants who would take their place.

Bloom's vision of the anxiety of influence and the familial terms in which he couches it resonate with key elements of adaptation studies. The work of film scholar Millicent Marcus on post-war Italian film-makers is a case in point. Adaptations, Marcus suggests, inevitably contemplate their revisionary relationship with their source, a relationship which varies from adaptation to adaptation. Marcus makes the case that specific adapters both reflect on this revisionary relationship and integrate their reflections into the images, decor, and dialogue of the films they produce. They meta-textually encode and enact their relation to their precursor, to their source text, in the fabric of their fictions. In vocabulary which is as familial as Bloom's, Marcus focuses on what she calls 'umbilical scenes', scenes which self-reflexively refer to the elements of the source text which the adaptive offspring have altered or omitted.[3] Marcus makes clear the intellectual creativity of such scenes. However, in keeping with Bloom's reading, they concurrently mark adaptation as an artefact predicated on a lack, on the absence of elements of a pre-cursor/parent and his/her text.

If Bloom's *The Anxiety of Influence* makes for intriguing reading in the sphere of adaptation studies, Zola's *Thérèse Raquin* and its multimedia afterlives offer a fertile and ever-expanding case-study to which to apply it. First published in 1867, Zola's novel about a murderous love triangle in nineteenth-century Paris is amongst the most adapted of all Zola's novels. Zola adapted the novel himself for the stage in 1873, to little critical acclaim. Yet the play has proved resilient in theatrical terms. At least five stage adaptations have appeared since 2006.[4] The novel proved popular in the silent era of film — three known silent adaptations exist.[5] And the text continues to fascinate contemporary filmmakers, making two appearances on the larger screen in the last four years. It was reconfigured as a Korean vampire movie, *Thirst*, in 2009, and Charlie Stratton's *In Secret*, starring Elizabeth Olsen and Jessica Lange, appeared in 2013. Television too has capitalized on the influence of *Thérèse Raquin*, creating from it both made-for-televisions films and serials in Germany, Sweden, France, Britain, Mexico, Italy, and Belgium. While radio reconfigurations are harder to trace due to stark differences in national archiving strategies specific to this medium, the BBC radio archives list four separate radio adaptations of Zola's novel.[6] *Thérèse Raquin* clearly makes adaptive sense.

The cultural reception of the novel's adaptations in their varied forms, though, often testifies to anxieties amongst the audience in relation to influence. Charles Spencer's concerns about Zola's power and place as a precursor in a subsequent adaptation, cited at the beginning of this chapter, are far from isolated. Numerous critics of the recent Broadway performance of *Thérèse Raquin*, starring Keira Knightley in the lead role, testify to Bloom's assertion that 'the strong dead return, in poems as in our lives, and they do not come back without darkening the living' (p. 139). They felt the lack of Zola in an adaptation marked by his presence. Writing in the *New York Times,* Peter Marks suggests of a competing adaptation, the Neal Bell version directed by David Esbjornson, when it premiered on Broadway that 'still there is the nagging sense all through *Thérèse Raquin*, that even with some eloquent touches, something vital is missing'.[7] Even reviews which praise the adaptation often do so for its fidelity to Zola, lauding its ability to take us back to the source author and his novel. Whether lauded or decried, the adaptation still belongs to Zola. Esbjornson and Bell have not displaced him — the mechanisms of canonical adaptation and the cultural institutions via which it is evaluated will not allow them to do so. Zola's influence is so strong in death that critics find him lacking in works which no longer fully belong to him, in works which concurrently bear the creative signature of another.

This battle of identities which often characterizes the critical reception *of Thérèse Raquin* in adaptive form, in some respects echoes the battle of influence at the heart of the novel. In the twists and turns of its plot and characters' internecine relationships, *Thérèse Raquin* is particularly resonant when read via Bloom's combative framework. Laurent, a bad artist, offers to paint Camille in order to replace him and wrest a better material presence for himself. He uses art as a ploy to begin an affair with Camille's wife, Thérèse, and to avail himself of the affections, food, and comfort provided by her mother-in-law, Madame Raquin. He is driven, Zola makes clear, by 'l'espérance de se mettre à la place de Camille' ('the hope of putting himself in Camille's place').[8] Frustrated by Camille's continued presence in the space Laurent hopes to occupy, Laurent wrestles with and drowns the precursor whose space he covets. But even as he takes his predecessor's space, he cannot dispossess it of Camille's ghost, a presence strengthened by Camille's very death. Bloom, contemplating the question of literary influence, writes: 'The largest truth of literary influence is that it is an irresistible anxiety: Shakespeare will not allow you to bury him, or escape him, or replace him' (p. xviii). Camille rises from the grave and will not allow Laurent to escape or replace him either. Camille's influence triggers a powerful anxiety in the house from which he has been displaced: 'ce corps horriblement défiguré qui se tenait toujours là, les accablait d'une continuelle anxiété' ('This horribly disfigured corpse, ever present, overwhelmed them with continual feelings of anxiety') (p. 615; 126). This very anxiety transforms Laurent as an artist. His previously mediocre art acquires, thanks to the murder, a range and depth of talent previously unimaginable. Yet, in keeping with Bloom's model, so haunted is Laurent by his precursor that his art never fully belongs to him. When Laurent draws, his works, despite their quality, endlessly reproduce the identity of Camille: 'sa main, sans qu'il en eût conscience, traçait toujours les lignes de ce visage atroce' ('his hand, without his realizing it, was constantly drawing the lines of this frightful mask') (p. 630; 145). Such is the spectral influence of his predecessor that Laurent's creative hands are physically and grammatically alienated from him: 'Il lui semblait que cette main ne lui appartenait plus' ('It seemed to him that the hand no longer belonged to him') (p. 631; 146). In relation to poetic authorship, Bloom warns of the displacement which ensues if one allows the strong dead too much power. Laurent experiences precisely this displacement. He speaks Camille's name:

> Le cadavre, qui hantait déjà la maison, y fut introduit ouvertement. Il s'assit sur les sièges, se mit devant la table, s'étendit dans le lit, se servit des meubles [...]. Laurent ne pouvait toucher une fourchette, une brosse, n'importe quoi, sans que Thérèse lui fît sentir que Camille avait touché cela avant lui. Sans cesse heurté contre l'homme qu'il avait tué [...] il s'imagina [...] qu'il était Camille. (p. 650)

> The body, which was already haunting the house, was now brought into it openly. It sat on the chairs or at the table, lay down on the bed, and used the furniture [...]. Laurent could not pick up a fork, a brush or anything without Thérèse letting him know that Camille had touched it before him. Constantly running up against the man he had killed [...] he came to think that he was Camille. (p. 173)

Ultimately Laurent destroys both his own canvases and himself, so strong is Camille's influence. Laurent engages in, and loses, a Bloomian battle for his own identity, for the borders and boundaries of his own being under the anxious onslaught of a ghostly precursor.

The borders and boundaries of identity shift throughout the novel, triggering anxieties. Laurent is possessed/dispossessed by Thérèse: 'sa maîtresse [...] s'était glissée peu à peu dans chacune des fibres de son corps' ('his mistress [...] had gradually insinuated herself into every fibre of his body') (p. 556; 46). He kills Camille to assert a financial, sexual, and familial presence for himself. Yet, far from displacing Camille, he becomes him, the despised husband for whom Thérèse feels a complex repugnance. Early in the novel, and as a means to try to insinuate himself into Camille's home, Laurent paints Camille: 'Le portrait était ignoble [...]. Laurent [..] avait [...] exagéré les teintes blafardes de son modèle, et le visage de Camille ressemblait à la face verdâtre d'un noyé' ('The portrait was vile. [Laurent] had [...] exaggerated his model's pale features, and Camille's face looked like the greenish mask of a drowned man') (p. 546; 33). As a result of this portrait and the affair it facilitates, Camille will die and become the grimacing, green mass of matter Laurent depicts. But, so too will the portrait come to depict its creator. When Laurent gazes into the mirror having committed murder, his body assumes the hue and expression of Camille in painted form: 'le miroir verdâtre donnait à sa face une grimace atroce' ('the greenish mirror gave his face a frightful grimace') (p. 575; 70). In a fascinatingly alienated moment, Laurent becomes the portrait which is not of him.[9] The originary identity of which Bloom's poets dream proves impossible in *Thérèse Raquin* as identities shift and slip anxiously.

Zola and the Joy of Influence: Adaptation, Generation, and Intermedial Borrowing (Art, Theatre, and Myth)

For Laurent, the artist in Zola's novel, the return of the dead precursor triggers anxiety, prevents the production of art, and ultimately leads to death. Zola, the artist, in stark contrast, far from seeking to repress and replace his precursors, actively cultivates them. The nineteenth-century author casts his own authorship and originality precisely as the confluence of overlapping influences which, far from triggering anxiety, serve as a source of intertextual energy in their range and number. Zola borrows intermedially from the world of art. Robert Lethbridge writes persuasively on Zola's repeated attempts to link his name and work with Manet.[10] Such attempts were, Lethbridge underlines, clearly self-interested, generating publicity and renown. Yet Zola's claim to translate the Impressionists into fiction rings true in his fiction. The landscape of *Thérèse Raquin*, particularly in Saint Ouen, is clearly painterly as Zola highlights the visual *touches* and *taches* of his fiction: 'tout le paysage se simplifiait dans le crépuscule; la Seine, le ciel, les îles, les côteaux n'étaient plus que des taches brunes et grises' ('the whole landscape was simplified by the dusk: the Seine, the sky, the islands and the hills were now only brown and grey smudges') (p. 569; 62). Ekphrastic moments in which Zola recreates well-known canvases in print are, Henri Mitterand suggests, frequent in the textual art museum that is Zola's corpus.[11] Zola exhibits in *Thérèse Raquin* an adaptation in prose of Manet's highly visible and infamous *Olympia* (1863), which was controversial for the clear financial transaction it depicts between client and bored contemporary prostitute. Zola magnifies the controversy of his painterly source by having Laurent desire a dead naked woman whose means of death has metaphorically marked her neck in a manner reminiscent of Olympia's necklace. Laurent stares at the beautiful female corpse in the morgue and the corpse appears to offer itself to him seductively. Zola describes a 'corps frais et gras blanchissait avec des douceurs de teinte [...] la tête un peu penchée, [qui] tendait la poitrine d'une façon provocante' ('fresh, plump body [...] paling with very delicate variations of tint [...], her head slightly to one side, offering her bosom in a provocative manner'), with 'une raie noire qui lui mettait comme un collier d'ombre' ('a black stripe on her neck, like a necklace of shadow') (p. 577; 72). Lethbridge convincingly unpicks the ways in which the core tones of Manet's painting are adapted and reworked in the light and shade of Zola's morgue scene, as well as exploring Henri

Mitterand's suggestion that the bedroom scenes in which Thérèse offers herself to Laurent might also be read as adaptations of Manet's famous work.[12] The cat at Olympia's feet is transposed to the bedroom of Thérèse, the other female body which will later prostitute itself to all and sundry. The cat adapts a comparably hostile stance to Laurent as male interloper: 'François gardait une attitude de guerre: les griffes allongées, le dos soulevé par une irritation sourde' ('François was still in an aggressive posture: with his claws out and his back arched') (p. 612; 121). Zola chooses to adapt Manet's *Olympia*, a painting which italicizes its own very visible revisionary relationship with its highly canonical antecedents, with Titian's 1538 *Venus of Urbino* in particular, and with the contemporary conventions of female nude painting, conventions which it cites only to revise. Zola's *Thérèse Raquin* underlines the influence on its pages of Manet's *Olympia*, a painting which is itself centrally concerned with the creative reconfiguration of earlier sources.

The novel's intermedial borrowings extend beyond the visual arts to the world of theatre. Zola, as previously mentioned, adapted *Thérèse Raquin* for the stage. The theatre, though, already lies at the heart of the novel. Russell Cousins has written compellingly on the theatrical techniques which illuminate the novel's progress as Zola casts a luminous spotlight initially on Madame Raquin's hand as she attempts to denounce the lovers and then again on their dead bodies as she contemplates their destruction.[13] What has not been explored, though, is the novel's extensive borrowings from Shakespeare's *Romeo and Juliet*. As a standard bearer for the Romantics, Shakespeare loomed comparatively large in Zola's century and its cultural imagination. David Garrick's stage adaptation of *Romeo and Juliet* played at the Odéon in Paris in 1827 starring Harriet Smithson, Berlioz's future wife, and inspired Berlioz to compose his 'symphonie dramatique Roméo et Juliette'. In 1867 Charles Gounod and librettists Michel Carré and Jules Barbier staged their opera *Romeo et Juliette*. The influence of Shakespeare's play on Zola's novel is pronounced. Both are based on a premise whereby a family seeks to trap a young girl into marriage. In both, the object of her affections kills her cousin. In both, the male lover purchases poison to ensure death, while the female protagonist has recourse to a knife. In both, the denouement is predicted and decided from the outset, triggering a pervasive sense of entrapment. Thérèse enters the shop: 'elle s'imaginait qu'elle venait d'être enterrée vive [...] au fond d'une fosse commune où grouillaient des morts' ('she imagined that she had been buried alive [...] at the bottom of a communal grave') (p. 622; 135). What Juliet fears above all is being buried alive in her family's crypt and Shakespeare's play repeatedly has recourse to the vocabulary of immolation. Whereas Romeo and Juliet are pushed to their demise by the stars, by external forces acting upon them, the cause of the downfall of Zola's lovers is internal as their guilt consumes them. Yet Shakespeare's stars find a mocking reference in Zola's opening to the novel as the narrative contemplates the false gems sold opposite the Raquin shop: 'une bougie, plantée au milieu d'un verre à quinquet, met des étoiles de lumière dans la boîte de bijoux faux' ('a candle stuck in the glass mantle of an oil lamp puts glimmering stars in the box of costume jewellery') (p. 526; 10). If Romeo and Juliet are pure, lofty lovers, Thérèse and

Laurent are their debased, cheap copies. Both works caused consternation for their frank depiction of lust. In both *Romeo and Juliet* and *Thérèse Raquin* the lovers spend but one night together. Romeo and Juliet have but one night because Romeo has murdered Juliet's cousin. Thérèse and Laurent by contrast use their night precisely to plot the murder of the cousin. Both murder scenes take place in stifling heat as the sun drives murderous intents. Both works reflect on the shifting nature of identity. Laurent, Thérèse, Camille, and Madame Raquin all become other, as has already been suggested, in the course of the novel. Juliet, too, reflects on the futility of focusing on the fixity of names as a guide to the truth of identity. She appeals to Romeo:

> Deny thy father and refuse thy name,
> [...]
> 'Tis but thy name that is my enemy.
> Thou art thyself though, not a Montague.
> What's Montague? It is nor hand nor foot,
> Nor arm nor face nor any other part
> Belonging to a man. (*Romeo and Juliet*, II.2.34–41)

While Zola's literary name is writ large both in and via *Thérèse Raquin*, that name both interacts with and engages with the influence of Shakespeare as a canonical forebear.

Zola's engagement with Shakespeare's influence might be read as an anxious endeavour. Influence, for Bloom, may be creative, may take many forms, but it is always, ultimately, anxious: '"Influence" is a metaphor, one that implicates a matrix of relationships — imagistic, temporal, spiritual, psychological — all of them ultimately defensive in their nature' (p. xxiii). Zola though offers a more teasing, enabling vision of influence. He borrows from Shakespeare, the most canonical author of the past four centuries according to Bloom. But he does not struggle anxiously with Shakespeare's influence, he emulates its construction. Zola's chosen intertext is one of the most influential of all time. But it is also one of the most intertextual, fashioned from a range of overlapping influences. René Weis notes that 'Shakespeare would take from anyone and everywhere with both fists', asserting of *Romeo and Juliet* that it is 'a narrative that Shakespeare did not invent but one which he shaped, structured and mediated'.[14] He worked from Arthur Brooke's poem *The Tragical History of Romeus and Juliet* (1562), but critics also debate whether he was familiar with the range of Italian and French sources of the story — da Porto, Bandello, or Boaistuau's French translation of Bandello — claiming that he had almost certainly read the story 'Rhomeo and Julietta' from William Painter's *Palace of Pleasure* (1567).

Zola's *Thérèse Raquin* is as tellingly and teasingly intertextual in the range and breadth of its sources and influences. Myth should, David Baguley argues, be antithetical to Zola's naturalist/realist project, as it is a 'conventionalised narrative of superhuman accomplishments unrelated to a plausible realistic context'.[15] Myth, though, as Baguley and a variety of critics underline, is core to Zola's novels.[16] *Thérèse Raquin* is, as I have argued elsewhere, no exception to this trend. The novel situates Thérèse as Pasiphae, daughter of Helios the sun and the eldest of the Oceanids, who sleeps with a bull producing a monster who will be trapped in the labyrinth.[17] Attracted to Laurent's 'cou de taureau' [bull's neck], Thérèse falls pregnant by him with a monster child whom she incites Laurent to destroy *in utero* (p. 541; 27). What matters, though, is not what Zola borrows from myth but rather how and why his texts use myth as a textual source. Baguley suggests that Zola borrows from myth in a manner which 'both recontextualises, transmotivates, parodies idealistic literary constructs and creates its own mythical configurations'.[18] Zola borrows from myth visibly, adaptively, creatively. His use of such narratives resonates with adaptation theorist Julie Sanders's reading of myth as a metaphor for the adaptive process. According to Sanders '[myth] depends upon, incites even, perpetual acts of reinterpretation in new contexts, [it] embodies the very act of appropriation'.[19] It is the narrative which, in its ceaseless reconfigurations, has no end for it is, as Claude Lévi-Strauss points out, 'in-terminable'.[20] Far from being anxious victim to the play of influences from which he constitutes his own authorial identity, Zola's fiction emphasizes and reflects on them.

Self-reflexive Adaptations: Cinema, *Thérèse Raquin*, and the Multiplicity of Influence

Of the adaptations of *Thérèse Raquin* for cinema, Marcel Carné's 1953 *Thérèse Raquin* is perhaps the most canonical. It is also key to any study of the notion of influence in relation to Zola and the cinema. Influence, it makes clear, is not restricted to a single, linear interaction with a forebear. Rather, it is multiple, may be creative or anxious, and takes many forms. Carné's adaptation sits at the creative confluence of a variety of influences: its source, the director's artistic identity and body of work, the film's stars, as well as its contemporary era. While the film clearly positions Zola as its precursor in its opening credits, it also works to construct and ratify the directorial identity of Carné in its set-piece shots and the iconography which marks it as Carné's film in aesthetic terms.[21] The film is marked as Carné's too by the role of Roland Lesaffre, the actor playing the part of the blackmailing ex-serviceman Riton who threatens to expose the lovers' crime in murdering Camille. The actor became a recognizable, almost constant feature in Carné's films.[22] Yet the intersection of influences at the film's core is yet more complex as analysis of the role of Roland Lesaffre reveals. Lesaffre's presence marks the film as Carné's. Yet, in *Thérèse Raquin* Lesaffre is not an empty cypher, pointing solely to Carné, for the film, in its dialogue, adapts the life and memories of the actor as a war veteran.[23] Lesaffre too, Carmen Mayer-Robin argues, points to the influence of the film's contemporary era. Mayer-Robin reads the insertion of this 'jaded and profiteering' sailor, a character who has no counterpart in Zola's novel, as 'evidence of moral decay in post-war France'. Both Riton and the transference of Zola's nineteenth-century narrative to post-war Lyon mean that 'the adaptation, like so many *films noirs* of the era, becomes a statement about psychic damage in the aftermath of the world wars'.[24] Susan Hayward concurs that the influence of Carné's contemporary era is strong, reading the film as shaped by 1950s gender politics, a context which explains Thérèse's refusal to leave her husband. But for Hayward, the film is a key example of the influence and formative impact of the star personae of actors on the works in which they feature. Hayward writes: 'Signoret's luminous intelligence was never going to allow her to embody the raw bestiality of Zola's Thérèse. [Raf] Vallone's exotic otherness and Italian Communist Party credentials place him a long way away from the crude avaricious Laurent of the novel'.[25] The influences at play in the film are creatively and compellingly multiple. They do not function in binary relationship between source author and film director but rather encompass both the contemporary era of the film and the cumulative star personae of the prominent actors performing in them.

Carné's adaptation, however, does self-consciously contemplate the revisionary nature of its relationship with Zola as a source text. It draws attention, perhaps anxiously, perhaps playfully, to its alterations. The film contains a variety of scenes which might meet Marcus's aforementioned definition of 'umbilical' moments. Carné's *Thérèse Raquin* gestures to the aspects of Zola's novel which are no longer there, giving presence to their absence. In Zola's novel, Thérèse and Laurent's love affair is witnessed only by the cat François. Thérèse, laughing at the silent feline witness to her passion, exclaims: 'On dirait qu'il comprend et qu'il va ce soir tout conter à Camille... Dis, ce serait drôle, s'il se mettait à parler dans la boutique' ('You'd think he understood and that he was going to tell Camille everything this evening. Why, wouldn't it be odd if he were to start speaking in the shop one of these days? He could tell some fine stories about us') (p. 551; 40). Taking Thérèse's joke literally, Carné transforms Zola's silent animal witness into Riton, the sailor returning from war who blackmails the lovers, speaking his knowledge of their guilt in the shop itself, as Zola's heroine predicted. Underlining this act of substitution, Carné renames Zola's cat 'Pompom', the item the filmmaker uses to introduce the sailor when we first meet him asleep on the train, his eyes shaded by the pompom on his hat. Furthermore, Carné's Laurent speculates about different ways to be with Thérèse. He claims that, were he a different man, he would befriend Camille, take advantage of his hospitality, and then do away with him on a Sunday trip out. His hypothesis sets out precisely the behaviour of Zola's character Laurent, the behaviour which Carné has changed. Carné's film gestures in this umbilical scene to the elements of Zola's novel which it has omitted, audibly referencing its revisionary relationship with Zola as source influence.[26]

Carné's *Thérèse Raquin* is not only influenced by other works, be they previous Zola texts or adaptations, it has also influenced subsequent adaptations of Zola's novel. A 2006 theatrical adaptation of *Thérèse Raquin* produced by Marianne Elliot at the National Theatre adapted both Zola and Carné. In Carné's adaptation, when the lovers have killed Camille, the film predicts their subsequent destruction via a violent series of flashing lights as they realize what they have done. In Elliot's theatre production, shortly before dying, Camille shakes a box of dominoes. The theatrical adaptation advances in abrupt freeze frames accompanied by flashing lights. Characters hold fixed positions before disappearing into darkness and reappearing seconds later, their movements a few degrees advanced. The violence of these theatrical freeze frames replaces the murder that the play does not show. It also jars the audience's theatrical experience, abruptly pointing to the influence of another medium into the theatrical production: Carné's film.[27] Comparably, in the 2002 French television adaptation of *Thérèse Raquin, La Liberté de Marie* [Marie's Freedom], directed by Caroline Huppert, Huppert's Laurent character alludes and returns to Carné's film as his creative predecessor. In scenes which have no equivalent in Zola, Huppert's Laurent pretends to be a film hero and an Italian one at that. Both the character and the actor are clearly French. Such scenes only become meaningful when understood through the prism of Carné's film in which Laurent was played, with heavily-accented French (the actor refused to be dubbed), by the Italian Raf Vallone in what was a Franco-Italian co-production.[28] Carné's adaptation, like Zola's novel, not only works and reworks earlier sources, it is itself configured and reconfigured across time, nations and media.

The most recent reconfiguration of the novel takes the form of Charlie Stratton's film *In Secret* (2013). The value of Stratton's film to this chapter lies in the way in which, like that of Carné, it breaks away from any binary reading of influence as a closed, anxious relationship between precursor and creative descendant. In interviews, Stratton does explicitly claim to take the viewer back to Zola. Yet Zola's novel, as Laurent's recurrent dream about returning to the Raquin shop suggests, is precisely about the impossibility of returning fully to an earlier moment or situation. Stratton may seek to take the viewer back to nineteenth-century Paris, but he cannot for it is no longer there. What he actually offers the viewer is a reconstructed version created using historical parts of Belgrade. Stratton's film underlines the plurality of previous influences and sources from which it creates itself. His screenplay works not from Zola's novel directly but instead from a modern theatrical adaptation written by playwright Neal Bell.[29] It is simultaneously an adaptation and an adaptation of an adaptation. Zola's source novel is a receding play of origins and influences. So too is Bell's play. He originally wrote it as a libretto for a musical of the novel. While the musical was never produced, the play was picked up by regional and ultimately national theatres. Stratton himself staged the play in Los Angeles. Productions of Bell's stage play are now legion. These productions, although key to the adaptive evolution of *Thérèse Raquin* and Stratton's decision to film the text, are now inaccessible sources of influence. Having been staged, the physical performances exist only in the refracted form of printed stage reviews and the Bell play text on which they are based. Stratton's film is at once Stratton's, Bell's, and Zola's. It also points to other formative influences, embedding matter from a range of its televisual and cinematic forebears. Through the emphatic use of recognizable film noir techniques, Tay Garnett's *The Postman Always Rings Twice* (1946), a classic film noir piece indebted to Zola's *Thérèse Raquin,* clearly marks Stratton's film.[30] For example, elevated shots, so key to the film noir aesthetic, in their depiction of frail humans hopelessly trapped in their destiny, dominate Stratton's *Thérèse Raquin.* They visualize the literal entrapment of the paralysed Madame Raquin, a puppet in the lovers' hands, as she lies nearly drowning in the bath. They underscore the inexorable constraints on the lovers from the moment the murder sequence begins. The camera, elevated in a high-angle shot above the boat, traps the lovers in its towering gaze. The plethora of barred, blocked shots which characterize film noir and its entrapped protagonists are rife in Stratton's film. Thérèse is frequently filmed both in and beyond the shop through the bars of its window. She turns to drinking and whoring, seeking freedom in licentiousness. Stratton's camera makes a mockery of her endeavour, filming her against the bars of the tavern window. The whispering influences of earlier adaptations and sources are creatively embedded in Stratton's *Thérèse Raquin.* Far from expressing anxieties about his ability to adapt Zola as a single source, Stratton teasingly embeds traces of the broad range of shifting influences from which his creative artefact stems.

The Influence of Medium (i): Adapting *Thérèse Raquin* for Television

In the play of influences from which adaptations are formed, the effect of the formal qualities of different media cannot be overstated. The 1980 BBC television serial, *Thérèse Raquin,* dramatized by Philip Mackie, is a case in point. Television, with its traditionally spatially restrained aesthetic, does not appear to offer an obvious home for Zola's texts. Largely for budgetary reasons, in the 1980s and earlier, television adaptations traditionally relied on 4:3 boxy interior shots in studio-produced pieces, heavy in dialogue and close ups. Zola, by contrast, is famous for his panoramas, for the sheer breadth and depth of his realist fiction. *Thérèse Raquin*, though, is not only arguably the most claustrophobic of Zola's novels, and therefore perhaps the most suited to the television aesthetic, it also unveils the central claustrophobia of Zola's theorization of existence, his belief that humans are trapped in their destinies by their heredity, their era, and their environment. The Passage du Pont-Neuf, on which the Raquin shop stands, is 'une sorte de corridor étroit et sombre [...]. Ce passage a trente pas de long et deux de large, au plus' ('a sort of dark, narrow corridor [...]. This passageway is, at most, thirty paces long and two wide') (p. 525; 9). Laurent's lodgings, barely six metres across, prove comparably claustrophobic. Thérèse and Laurent, moreover, are doubly trapped both by the genetics which drive them and by the close focus of Zola's narrative as the novelist dissects his characters. In Mackie's 1980 BBC adaptation of *Thérèse Raquin,* the contemporary aesthetic of period television works to make the space of the novel even smaller. While Zola's novel details the characters' youth in Vernon, the adaptation, resolutely Paris-centric and interior in its focus, offers only a fleeting vision of Vernon in the stifled consciousness of Thérèse. The landscape, shot in close focus, is symbolically barred by the fence in the shot's foreground and by Camille's concurrent monologue as he overwrites and silences his wife's memory. In the visual grammar of film, low-angle shots from characters' feet monumentalize the characters in question, testifying to their potency and power. The BBC television adaptation, however, uses such monumentalizing shots in highly mocking form. Laurent waits desperately for Thérèse, the woman he can never have, in his tiny flat. The camera films him from below in a low-angle shot which allows this giant of a man to dominate, in aesthetic terms, a scene about his impotence, his inability to grasp the woman he so desires. Comparably, Thérèse, as she contemplates the claustrophobic misery of yet another Thursday night soirée at the Raquin house, is filmed from the floor beneath her, her visual dominance of the shot parodying the utter dispossession that is her life. Both low-angle shots are followed by extreme high-angle shots through the windows or roof above. Such high-angle shots, common in film noir in particular, visually convey the characters' entrapment. For Janey Place and Lowell Peterson, it is 'an oppressive and fatalistic angle that looks down upon its helpless victim to make him/her look like a rat in a maze'.[31] Moreover, occurring soon after an extreme low-angle shot, these high-angle shots encase the characters in a vertical reflective symmetry. As if to underline this, Laurent then appears in shadow bars, created by the light from the windows above, a visual indication of the ever more claustrophobic nature of his existence. The aesthetic of contemporary BBC period television influences Mackie's 1980 *Thérèse Raquin* in conjunction with Zola as precursor.

The influence of the BBC and its production values is also highly visible in Mackie's piece. Such is the potency of this influence that it allows the adaptation to make absent core elements of its source text. The shaping force of the corporation is visible in the BBC English spoken by the characters who retain their French names and a smattering of French vocabulary, vocabulary foreign enough to mark the adaptation as other but domesticated enough to be readily comprehensible. The French words and songs which perforate the adaptation's dialogue serve as signifiers for a French culture and influence that is acknowledged but ultimately occluded within this clearly BBC offering. The adaptation's sex scenes also underscore the creative signature of the BBC in this era. The novel's steamy, animalistic sex between Thérèse and Laurent is influenced and shaped by the contemporary production values of the BBC. The sights and sounds of the sexual commerce between Laurent and Thérèse are obfuscated by the adaptation's music and the dark skylight through which the scene is at times shot. The camera focuses on but then cuts insistently away from the sex act. Thérèse's sexual satisfaction is barred, comically displaced onto Madame Raquin as the adaptation rhythmically cuts from the fevered sexual commerce of the lovers to Madame Raquin's ecstatic and then somnolent face as she frenetically conducts literal commerce in the shop below. In scenes which might be argued to be umbilical in their acts of obfuscation — they point to what they cannot show — this BBC television adaptation teasingly underlines its necessary alteration of the influence of its source. The adaptation finds creative presence in pointing to the key absences it has created in its stated source of influence: Zola's novel.

The Influence of Medium (ii): Adapting *Thérèse Raquin* for Radio

If the visual aesthetic of television influences adaptive versions of *Thérèse Raquin* in that medium, Melissa Murray's 1998 adaptation for BBC Radio 4 offers a playful and extensive exploration of the shaping influence of radio on her work. She focuses on sound and silence, the core possibilities of radio as a medium. Thérèse is urged to be silent by each and every main character. The scene transitions which relate to Thérèse in Murray's adaptation are initially made up of 'dead ambience', a technical term in radio for ambient silence. Thus the scene transition between Thérèse's compelled marriage to Camille and her chaste wedding night, a scene transition of absolute silence, speaks both her inability to utter her opposition to events and the personal absence to which they condemn her. Despite this, Thérèse's voice comes to be the most dominant of this adaptation. It directs her affair with Laurent, it suggests and triggers the murder which will ensue. It revels in its ability to surpass the blindness of those around her as they ignore the truth of her murderous love. In a fascinatingly palimpsestuous scene, in which Camille silences Thérèse to show off his newly-acquired knowledge of the Egyptians to the assembled company, his monologue is overlaid by the following inner monologue from Thérèse. Her speech is at once silenced since it does not leave the confines of her skull, and powerful, for its contents will subsequently direct and dominate Camille's reality: 'what an exquisite delight it is to deceive you. Biting the pillows, biting my poor lover's arms in a frenzy of delight. If I concentrate hard I can recall the exact moment he pushed himself inside me, the exact words he spoke'. Radio allows Thérèse to speak even when she remains intradiegetically silent.

The influence of radio as a medium shapes the adaptation. Radio cannot show the breadth of the panoramas for which Zola is so famed, but it does offer a different type of vision, one highly suited to Zola's *Thérèse Raquin*: inner vision. Radio's vision (and indeed that of literature, Zola's medium) is interior in two key respects. First, radio infiltrates the heads of its listeners, inhabiting the recesses of their minds, recesses in which the action is staged. As Frances Gray puts it, 'the stage of radio is the darkness and silence of the listener's skull'.[32] However, radio's inner vision is not restricted to the mind of its listener. Radio blocks out the outside world and is consequently, in its ensuing darkness, particularly adept at the dramatization of thoughts. Dramatizing the novel in which Zola claimed to dissect the living cadavers of Thérèse and Laurent, Murray exploits the innate intimacy of radio to take us into the most private spaces of Thérèse's existence. We become part of her sex scenes, scenes which can be far more bestial, far racier, than their counterparts in cinema and television, precisely because they are beyond our sight. Still more intimately, we become part of Thérèse's consciousness itself as Murray, eschewing the widespread use of a narrator in such adaptations, allows us frequent and seemingly unmediated access to the confines of Thérèse's skull. Thérèse may claim, in response to Laurent's probing questions, 'my thoughts are my own', but the adaptation, in this most confessional of media, immediately violates Thérèse's fantasies as Laurent is violating the sanctity of her marriage, delivering her innermost thoughts to the listener. The intimate inner vision of radio enhances the searing intimacy of Zola's *Thérèse Raquin*.

Murray's medium, radio, is not only suited to *Thérèse Raquin*, but her reworking self-consciously explores her ability to adapt the influence of Zola. It reflects, meta-adaptively, on its own creative act. Meta-stories permeate this radio adaptation, imbuing it from the outset with a highly self-reflexive dimension. Madame Raquin tells the young Camille a bedtime story depicting his own life: 'Once upon a time, there was a little boy who lived with his Mama in a little house, all snug and cosy'. Laurent tells the truth of his affair with Camille's wife to Camille himself, fictionalizing the names:

> It's a rather amusing story if you like. I know the husband, but not well. We have little enough in common but we are acquainted. The wife is a strange creature. Still waters run deep. Calm and composed on the outside but underneath a torrent.

'Aren't you afraid of being found out?' Camille asks. 'He's hardly the type,' replies Laurent to and of Camille. Comparably, Laurent, shortly before committing murder, again confesses his desires and actions by displacing his own story on to the waiter who serves them:

> I think our waiter is rather taken with Thérèse. Madame Thérèse I mean. Look at him staring at her. Does that make you jealous? Yes, jealous, you, husband. Looking at her, perhaps thinking not very nice thoughts about your lovely wife, thinking of what he would do with her if he were alone with her in his attic, perhaps he hates you, look at his eyes.

In a work of adaptation, a work whose identity is always already displaced as the recreation of an ever- yet never-present earlier forebear, Murray places displacement in the narrative foreground. Murray's adaptation is a work of endless returns. The young Camille opens the adaptation contemplating the turns of the river which will subsequently return to drown him. Thérèse is repeatedly placed on her chair and urged to be a good girl first by her father and then by Madame Raquin who makes her stay there all night as punishment. At the adaptation's close, a paralysed Madame Raquin now occupies the same chair, unable, like Thérèse was, to move. Thérèse kills herself, urging her aunt to 'sit and watch how nice and quiet I am, what a good girl I can be under the right conditions'. Part of the seemingly endless returns of *Thérèse Raquin* in new forms and new media, Murray's adaptation self-reflexively places the turns and returns of a variety of influences in the forefront of her adaptive creation.

Conclusion

Zola offers us in *Thérèse Raquin* an exploration of the formative, multiple nature of influence. Influence, in the novel, is not a binary, linear, closed relationship between a single source and its subsequent creative descendant. Rather, in *Thérèse Raquin*, Zola borrows in highly visible, plural ways from a wide range of well-known sources. He borrows from myth, from Manet, and from Shakespeare — sources which loomed large in the nineteenth-century French cultural consciousness. He does not borrow anxiously, he borrows playfully, creating art from the web of earlier influences which he explores in his fiction.

The cinema, television, theatre, and radio adaptations explored in this chapter, as they rework Zola for a new medium, enter into a variety of dialogues with Zola's source novel precisely about the nature of influence itself. Carné's film adaptation underlines the complex, yet creative negotiation between the influence of the source author, the creative aesthetic of the adaptive director, and the influential role of a key actor and his star persona. Stratton's *In Secret* makes clear the influence of earlier adaptations both in film and in theatre on his creative reworking of the novel *Thérèse Raquin*, an influence also explored in Huppert's television adaptation *La Liberté de Marie*. The BBC television adaptation of the novel, dramatized by Mackie, demonstrates the influence of medium on the adaptation produced as part of the spatially-restrained period drama aesthetic of television of the 1980s. Medium too is key to understanding Murray's radio reworking of the novel, a reworking which places sound and silence, the key ingredients of radio, at its core. Murray's piece, like Zola's novel, is clearly self-reflexive in its adaptation. Zola contemplates the source texts whose influence he adapts to shape his own novel. Murray fills her dramatization with meta-narratives and doubles which gesture to the radio adaptation's own status as an altered double of Zola's source. Cumulatively, these reworkings of Zola's novel push, with their source author, for a reading of influence not only as a source of anxiety, but rather also as a positive, plural creative tool.

Notes to Chapter 11

1. Charles Spencer, 'Dim Shadows of Zola's Hellish Vision', *Daily Telegraph*, 15 November 2006 <www.telegraph.co.uk/culture/theatre/drama/3656552/Dim-shadows-of-Zolas-hellish-vision.html> [accessed 11 April 2016].
2. Harold Bloom, *The Anxiety of Influence: A Theory of Poetry*, 2nd edn (Oxford: Oxford University Press, 1997), p. 43. All further references will be to this edition of the text are given in the text.
3. Millicent Marcus, *Filmmaking by the Book: Italian Cinema and Literary Adaptation* (Baltimore, MD: Johns Hopkins University Press, 1992), p. 140.
4. The play appeared at the National Theatre, London, in 2006, at the Quantum Theatre, Pittsburgh, in 2007, at the Riverside Studios, London, in 2008, at the Edinburgh Fringe in 2009, and at the Roundabout Theatre, New York, in 2015.
5. Two silent versions of Zola's novel appeared within the space of four years in the early twentieth century. In 1911, Einar Zangenberg's *Thérèse Raquin* was made in Denmark. Nino Martoglio's *Thérèse Raquin* was released in 1915, made under the auspices of Milano Film and Morgana Films. In 1928, director Jacques Feyder added to the silent versions of Zola's novel by releasing *Thérèse Raquin/Du sollst nicht ehebrechen!*. The film was released in both France and Germany and was a product of the Deutsche Film Union.
6. In 1948, Mai Zetterling and Herbert Lom starred in a BBC radio adaptation created from Kathleen Boutall's translation. The adaptation was entitled *Guilty* and aired on the BBC Home Service. An adaptation produced by John Powell, *Thérèse Raquin*, was broadcast in 1969 on BBC Radio 4. In 1998, another version, again entitled *Thérèse Raquin*, dramatized by Melissa Murray and directed by Cherry Cookson, went out on BBC Radio 4. One of the corporation's most prolific adapters of Zola, Diana Griffiths, turned her hand to *Thérèse Raquin* in 2009, writing a radio play of the same name which was produced and directed by her frequent collaborator, Pauline Harris.
7. Peter Marks, 'It's Lust, but not Strictly Sexual', *New York Times*, 4 November 1997 <http://www.nytimes.com/1997/11/04/theater/reviews-theater-review-it-s-lust-but-not-strictly-sexual.html> [accessed 11 April 2016].
8. Émile Zola, *Thérèse Raquin*, in *Œuvres complètes*, ed. by Henri Mitterand, 15 vols (Paris: Cercle du Livre Précieux, 1966–1969), I (1966), 511–682 (p. 595); *Thérèse Raquin*, trans. by Robin Buss (London: Penguin 2004), p. 98 (all further quotations from *Thérèse Raquin* and its translation will be taken from these editions, unless otherwise indicated, and are given in the text).
9. Zola's study of the instability of identity extends beyond Laurent. Madame Raquin is a case in point. Poised in her paralysis between the states of life and death, she, like her ghostly son

Camille, stands between the murderers. The physical descriptions of mother and son coalesce. Madame Raquin's body takes on the watery, disintegrating tropes of her drowned son: 'on eût dit le masque dissous d'une morte' ('it was like the decayed mask of a dead woman') (p. 632; 127). As Madame Raquin compelled Thérèse to submit to the caresses of her feeble son, so Madame Raquin is forced to accept the caresses of the murderous Thérèse as she pleads disingenuously for forgiveness. From her prostrate position, Thérèse resembles Grivet, the man she so despises. Like Grivet, she pretends to decipher her aunt's thoughts from her gaze, imposing a meaning on them which they patently do not have. For further reading on Zola's novel, see D. F. Bell, '*Thérèse Raquin*: Scientific Realism in Zola's Laboratory', *Nineteenth-Century French Studies*, 24 (1995), 122–32; Susan Harrow, '*Thérèse Raquin*: Animal Passion and the Brutality of Reading', in *The Cambridge Companion to Émile Zola*, ed. by Brian Nelson (New York: Cambridge University Press, 2007), pp. 105–20; Jean Bourgeois, 'De *Thérèse Raquin* à *Germinal*: une structure obsédante', *Cahiers naturalistes*, 74 (2001), 43–59.

10. Robert Lethbridge, 'Zola, Manet and *Thérèse Raquin*', *French Studies*, 34.3 (1980), 278–99.
11. Henri Mitterand, 'Le Musée dans le texte', *Cahiers naturalistes*, 66 (1992), 13–22.
12. Henri Mitterand, *Zola journaliste: de l'affaire Manet à l'affaire Dreyfus* (Paris: Armand Colin, 1962), p. 71.
13. Russell Cousins, *Zola: Thérèse Raquin* (London: Grant & Cutler, 1992). See also Kate Griffiths, 'Mythical Returns: Televising *Therese Raquin*', *Nineteenth-Century French Studies*, 39.3–4 (2011), 285–95.
14. René Weis, 'Introduction', in William Shakespeare, *Romeo and Juliet*, ed. by René Weis (London: Arden Bloomsbury, 2012), pp. 1–115 (p. xxxiii).
15. David Baguley, *Naturalist Fiction: The Entropic Vision* (Cambridge: Cambridge University Press, 1990), p. 90.
16. Ibid.. See, inter alia, Philip Walker, 'Prophetic Myths in Zola', *PMLA*, 1.24 (1959), 444–52; Mario Maurin, 'Zola's Labyrinths', *Yale French Studies*, 42 (1969), 89–104; and Jean Borie, *Zola et les mythes* (Paris: Seuil, 1971).
17. See Griffiths, 'Mythical Returns', pp. 285–95.
18. Baguley, *Naturalist Fiction*, p. 90.
19. Sanders, *Adaptation and Appropriation* (2006), p. 63.
20. Claude Lévi-Strauss, *Mythologiques: le cru et le cuit* (Paris: Plon, 1964), p. 14.
21. For a fuller exploration of this point, see Kate Griffiths, 'Memories in/of Thérèse Raquin: Émile Zola and Marcel Carné', *French Studies*, 65.2 (2011), 188–99. The film's establishing shot, as Edward Baron Turk makes clear, cinematically references those of Carné's 1936 film *Jenny*, his *Hôtel du nord* (1938), *Les Enfants du paradis* (1945) and the director's later television film *La Bible* (1977). A child and a handcart appear shortly before the accident that kills the man blackmailing the lovers, the accident that seals the fate of the lovers. Children with handcarts serve as symbols of the forces of fate throughout Carné's work. See Edward Baron Turk, *Child of Paradise: Marcel Carné and the Golden Age of French Cinema* (Cambridge, MA: Harvard University Press, 1989).
22. Lesaffre's role, Susan Hayward makes clear, references Carné's creative vision and not that of Zola. The director uses Lesaffre to do away with Zola's vision of the lovers as driven by inherited characteristics. Hayward writes: 'Instead, Carné introduces a third person, the blackmailing sailor, as the instrument of fate. He externalises the inner fatal drive that Zola speaks of and gives human form to it' ('Literary Adaptations of the 1950s: *Thérèse Raquin* and *Les Diaboliques* (1955)', *Studies in French Cinema*, 3.1 (2003), 5–14 (p. 8)).
23. For a fuller exploration of this point, see Griffiths, 'Memories in/of Thérèse Raquin'.
24. Carmen Mayer-Robin, 'Framed! Fact, Fiction and Frame Tale in Adaptations of Zola's *Thérèse Raquin*', *Romance Studies*, 28 (2010), 158–68 (p. 162).
25. Hayward, 'Literary Adaptations of the 1950s', p. 8.
26. Part of this paragraph appeared in a different form in Griffiths, 'Memories in/of *Thérèse Raquin*', pp. 188–99, and I thank the editors of *French Studies* for their advice in the writing of that paper.
27. For more on this reading of Marianne Elliot's theatre version, see Griffiths, *Zola and the Artistry of Adaptation*.
28. For further details, see Griffiths, 'Mythical Returns', pp. 285–95.

29. Émile Zola, *Thérèse Raquin*, adapted by Neal Bell (New York: Broadway Play Publishing Inc, 2016).
30. Nick Smith (played by Cecil Kellaway), a middle-aged roadside diner owner, hires a drifter, Frank Chambers (John Garfield), to work in his restaurant. Frank begins an affair with Nick's beautiful wife Cora (Lana Turner) and the two conspire to kill Nick and seize his assets.
31. Janey Place and Lowell Peterson, 'Some Visual Motifs of *Film Noir*', in *Film Noir Reader*, ed. by Alain Silver and James Ursini (New York: Limelight Editions, 1996), pp. 65–76 (p. 68).
32. Frances Gray, cited in John Drakakis, *British Radio Drama* (Cambridge: Cambridge University Press, 1981), p. 142.

BIBLIOGRAPHY

ABEL, RICHARD, *The Ciné Goes to Town: French Cinema 1896–1914* (Berkeley: University of California Press, 1998)

ADAMS, DAVID, 'L'Illustration de *Candide* dans les *Romans et contes de M. de Voltaire* (1778)', in *Les 250 ans de 'Candide': lectures et relectures*, ed. by Nicholas Cronk and Nathalie Ferrand (Leuven: Peeters, 2014), pp. 561–75

ADORNO, THEODOR W., 'Notes to Kafka', in *Prisms*, trans. by Samuel and Shierry Weber (Cambridge, MA: MIT Press, 1967)

AGAR, JON, *Constant Touch: A Global History of the Mobile Phone* (Cambridge: Icon Books, 2003)

ALT, PETER-ANDRÉ, *Kafka und der Film: Über kinematographisches Erzählen* (Munich: C. H. Beck, 2009)

ANDREW, DUDLEY, *Concepts in Film Theory* (New York: Oxford University Press, 1984)

[ANON.], 'The Talent Histogram', *Movie*, 1 (1962), 10–11

——'Rockwell Kent — The Artist', *Wings*, 3.12 (December 1929), 3

——*Spécimen des caractères de la fonderie normale à Bruxelles, provenant de la fonderie de Jules Didot et de son père Pierre Didot* (Haarlem: Joh. Enschedé en Zonen, 1914)

——'The Story of Your "*Candide*"', *Wings*, 3.12 (December 1929), 6–7

ALBRECHT-CRANE, CHRISTA, and DENNIS RAY CUTCHINS, eds, *Adaptation Studies: New Approaches* (Madison, NJ: Fairleigh Dickinson University Press, 2010)

AOYAMA, YUKO, and HIRO IZUSHI, 'Hardware Gimmick or Cultural Innovation? Technological, Cultural, and Social Foundations of the Japanese Video Game Industry', *Research Policy*, 32.3 (2003), 423–44

ARAGAY, MIREIA, 'Reflection to Refraction: Adaptation Studies Then and Now', in *Books in Motion: Adaptation, Intertextuality, Authorship*, ed. by Mireia Aragay (Amsterdam: Rodopi, 2005), pp. 11–34

ARCHER, NEIL, and ANDREEA WEISL-SHAW, eds, *Adaptation: Studies in French and Francophone Culture* (Bern: Peter Lang, 2012)

ASSMANN, ALEIDA, 'Canon and Archive', in *Cultural Memory Studies: An International and Interdisciplinary Handbook*, ed. by Astrid Erll and Ansgar Nünning (Berlin & New York: de Gruyter, 2008), pp. 97–107

AUDEN, W. H., *Prose and Travel Books in Prose and Verse*, in *The Complete Works of W. H. Auden*, ed. by Edward Mendelson, 6 vols (Princeton, NJ: Princeton University Press, 2002), II

AUSTEN, JANE, *Emma* (London: John Murray, 1816)

——*Mansfield Park* (London: Thomas Egerton, 1814)

——*Persuasion* (London: John Murray, 1818)

——*Pride and Prejudice*, ed. and with an introduction by Vivien Jones (London: Penguin, 1996)

AUSTEN, JANE, and SETH GRAHAME-SMITH, *Pride and Prejudice and Zombies* (Philadelphia, PA: Quirk Books, 2009)

BAGULEY, DAVID, *Naturalist Fiction: The Entropic Vision* (Cambridge: Cambridge University Press, 1990)

Baker, Jo, *Longbourn* (London: Penguin, 2013)
Barnett, David, 'When is a Play Not a Drama? Two Examples of Postdramatic Theatre Texts', *New Theatre Quarterly*, 24.1 (2008), 14–23
Baron Turk, Edward, *Child of Paradise: Marcel Carné and the Golden Age of French Cinema* (Cambridge, MA: Harvard University Press, 1989)
Barthes, Roland, 'The Death of the Author', in *Image, Music, Text*, trans. by Stephen Heath (New York: Hill & Wang, 1977), pp. 142–48
—— 'Introduction à l'analyse structurale des récits', in *L'Aventure sémiologique* (Paris: Seuil, 1985), pp. 167–206
—— *S/Z* (Paris: Seuil, 1970)
—— *S/Z*, trans. by Richard Miller (New York: Hill & Wang, 1974)
Bassnett, Susan, 'Neither Rhyme nor Reason', *ITI Bulletin* (September-October 2015), 26–27
—— *Translation Studies*, 3rd edn (Abingdon & New York: Routledge, 2002)
Baudrillard, Jean, *Simulacra and Simulation*, trans. by Sheila Faria Glaser (Ann Arbor: University of Michigan Press, 1994)
Baumeister, Kathrin, *Die beste aller Welten: Künstler illustrieren Voltaires Candide. Chodowiecki — Monnet — Moreau — Unold — Klee — Kubin* (Berlin: Reimer, 2015)
Bay-Cheng, Sarah, and others, eds, *Mapping Intermediality in Performance* (Amsterdam: Amsterdam University Press, 2010)
Bazin, André, *Qu'est-ce que le cinéma?* (Paris: Éditions du Cerf, 2002)
Beaujon, Paul [Beatrice Walde's pseudonym], 'The "Garamond" Types: Sixteenth & Seventeenth Century Sources Considered', *The Fleuron: A Journal of Typography*, 5 (1926), 131–79
Beissner, Friedrich, *Der Erzähler Franz Kafka* [1952] (Stuttgart: Kohlhammer, 1958)
Bell, D. F., '*Thérèse Raquin*: Scientific Realism in Zola's Laboratory', *Nineteenth-Century French Studies*, 24 (1995), 122–32
Bellos, David, *Georges Perec: A Life in Words* (London: Harvill/Harper Collins, 1993)
—— 'Sounding Out *Les Misérables*', *Dix-Neuf*, 20.3–4 (2016), 241–51
Benjamin, Elizabeth, and Jessica Goodman, eds, *Fame and Glory: The Classic, the Canon and the Literary Pantheon*, special issue of *MHRA Working Papers in the Humanities*, 8 (2013) <http://www.mhra.org.uk/publications/Fame-Glory> [accessed 10 August 2019]
Benjamin, Walter, 'Franz Kafka: zur zehnten Wiederkehr seines Todestages', in *Gesammelte Schriften*, ed. by Rolf Tiedemann and Hermann Schweppenhäuser, 7 vols in 15 (Frankfurt a.M.: Suhrkamp, 1972–1989), II.2 (1977), 409-38
—— 'Das Kunstwerk im Zeitalter seiner technischen Reproduzierbarkeit', in *Gesammelte Schriften*, ed. by Rolf Tiedemann and Hermann Schweppenhäuser, 7 vols in 15 (Frankfurt a.M.: Suhrkamp, 1972–1989), I.2 (1974), 435–508
Bergson, Henri, *Œuvres*, ed. by André Robinet and Henri Gouhier, 4th edn (Paris: PUF, 1984)
Billington, Michael, 'Shakespeare in Europe', in *One Night Stands* (London: Nick Hern Books, 1993), pp. 355–60
Binder, Hartmut, 'Anschauung ersehnten Lebens: Kafkas Verständnis bildender Künstler und ihrer Werke', in *Was bleibt von Franz Kafka? Positionsbestimmung. Kafka-Symposion, Vienna 1983*, ed. by Georg Kranner and Wendelin Schmidt-Dengler (Vienna: Braumüller, 1985), pp. 17-41
Blank, Juliane, 'Erzählperspektive im Medienwechsel: visuelle Fokalisierung in Comic-Adaptionen von Texten Franz Kafkas', *kunsttexte.de*, 1 (2011) <https://edoc.hu-berlin.de/handle/18452/8106> [accessed 24 March 2020]
—— *Vom Sinn und Unsinn des Begriffs Graphic Novel* (Berlin: Ch. A. Bachmann, 2014)

Blin-Rolland, Armelle, *Adapted Voices: Transpositions of Céline's 'Voyage au bout de la nuit' and Queneau's 'Zazie dans le métro'* (Oxford: Legenda, 2015)
—— 'Re-inventing the Origins of the Boy Who Wouldn't Grow Up: Régis Loisel's *Peter Pan*', *Studies in Comics*, 5.2 (2014), 273–90
Blin-Rolland, Armelle, Guillaume Lecomte and Marc Ripley, eds, *Comics and Adaptation*, special issue of *European Comic Art*, 10.1 (2017)
Bloom, Gina, 'Videogame Shakespeare: Enskilling Audiences through Theatre-making Games', *Shakespeare Studies*, 43 (2015), 114–27
Bloom, Harold, *The Anxiety of Influence: A Theory of Poetry* [1973], 2nd edn (Oxford: Oxford University Press, 1997)
—— *The Western Canon: The Books and School of the Ages* (New York: Harcourt Brace & Co., 1994; Papermac, 1995)
Bluestone, George, *Novels into Films* [1957] (Baltimore, MD: Johns Hopkins University Press, 2003)
Boenisch, Peter M., 'Aesthetic Art to Aisthetic Act: Theatre, Media, Intermedial Performance', in *Intermediality in Theatre and Performance*, ed. by Freda Chapple and Chiel Kattenbelt (Amsterdam & New York: Rodopi, 2006), pp. 103–16
—— 'Thomas Ostermeier: Mission (Neo)Realism', in *Contemporary European Theatre Directors,* ed. by Maria M. Delgado and Dan Rebellato (Abingdon & New York: Routledge, 2010), pp. 339–62
Bokhove, Niels, and Marijke van Dorst, eds, *Einmal ein grosser Zeichner: Franz Kafka als beeldend kunstenaar* (Utrecht: Salon Saffier Saffier, 2002)
Bolas, Terry, *Screen Education: From Film Appreciation to Media Studies* (Bristol: Intellect Books, 2009)
Bolter, Jay David, and Richard Grusin, *Remediation: Understanding New Media* (Cambridge, MA: MIT Press, 2000)
Borie, Jean, *Zola et les mythes* (Paris: Seuil, 1971)
Bourgeois, Jean, 'De *Thérèse Raquin* à *Germinal*: une structure obsédante', *Cahiers naturalistes*, 74 (2001), 43–59
Bourriaud, Nicolas, *Relational Aesthetics*, trans. by Simon Pleasance and Fronza Woods with the participation of Mathieu Copeland (Dijon: Presses du réel, 2002)
Branigan, Edward, *Point of View in the Cinema: A Theory of Narration and Subjectivity in Classical Film* (Berlin, New York & Amsterdam: de Gruyter, 1984)
Briggs, Asa, *The BBC: The First Fifty Years* (Oxford: Oxford University Press, 1985)
Brine, Kevin R., 'The Judith Project', in *The Sword of Judith: Judith Across the Disciplines*, ed. by Kevin R. Brine, Elena Ciletti and Henrike Lähnemann (Cambridge: Open Book, 2010), pp. 3-21
Brombert, Victor, *Victor Hugo and the Visionary Novel* (Cambridge, MA: Harvard University Press, 1984), pp. 86–139
Brontë, Charlotte, *Jane Eyre* (London: Smith, Elder & Co., 1847)
Brownstein, Rachel, 'Out of the Drawing Room, Onto the Lawn', in *Jane Austen in Hollywood,* ed. by Linda Troost and Sayre Greenfield (Lexington: University of Kentucky Press, 2001), pp. 13–21
Bruce, Iris, 'Kafka and Popular Culture', in *The Cambridge Companion to Kafka*, ed. by Julian Preece (Cambridge: Cambridge University Press, 2002), pp. 242-46
Bruhn, Jørgen, Anne Gjelsvik and Eirik Frisvold Hanssen, eds, *Adaptation Studies: New Challenges, New Directions* (London & New York: Bloomsbury Academic, 2013)
Bruhn, Jørgen, Anne Gjelsvik and Eirik Frisvold Hanssen, 'There and Back Again': New Challenges and New Directions in Adaptation Studies', in *Adaptation Studies: New Challenges, New Directions*, ed. by Bruhn, Gjelsvik and Hanssen, pp. 1–16

BURDETT, ARNOLD, and DAN BROWN, *BCS Glossary of Computing and ICT*, 13th edn (London: British Computer Society Learning and Development Ltd., 2013)

CALÈ, LUISA, and ANTONELLA BRAIDA, eds, *Dante on View: The Reception of Dante in the Visual and Performing Arts* (Aldershot & Burlington, VT: Ashgate, 2007)

CAMERON, IAN, 'Films, Directors and Critics', *Movie*, 2 (1962), 4–7

CARABALLO, LAURA CECILIA, '*Docteur Jekyll & Mister Hyde* de Mattotti et Kramsky: briser la figuration', in *Bande dessinée et adaptation: littérature, cinéma, tv*, ed. by Benoît Mitaine, David Roche and Isabelle Schmitt-Pitiot (Clermont Ferrand: Presses Université Blaise Pascal, 2015), pp. 137–54

CARDWELL, SARAH, *Adaptation Revisited: Television and the Classic Novel* (Manchester: Manchester University Press, 2002)

——'Pause, Rewind, Replay: Adaptation, Intertextuality and (Re)defining Adaptation Studies', in *The Routledge Companion to Adaptation*, ed. by Dennis Cutchins, Katja Krebs and Eckard Voigts (Abingdon & New York: Routledge, 2018), pp. 7–17

CAREY, PETER, *Jack Maggs* (London: Faber & Faber, 1997)

CARROLL, LEWIS, *Alice's Adventures in Wonderland* and *Through the Looking Glass* (London: Penguin 1998)

CARTMELL, DEBORAH, '100+ Years of Adaptations, or, Adaptation as the Art Form of Democracy', in *A Companion to Literature, Film and Adaptation*, ed. by Deborah Cartmell, Blackwell Companions to Literature and Culture (Chichester: Wiley, 2012), pp. 1–13

CARTMELL, DEBORAH, ed., *A Companion to Literature, Film and Adaptation*, Blackwell Companions to Literature and Culture (Chichester: Wiley, 2012)

CARTMELL, DEBORAH, and IMELDA WHELEHAN, *Screen Adaptation: Impure Cinema* (Basingstoke: Palgrave Macmillan, 2010)

CARTMELL, DEBORAH, and IMELDA WHELEHAN, eds, *Teaching Adaptations* (Basingstoke: Palgrave Macmillan, 2014)

——*Adaptations: From Text to Screen, Screen to Text* (Abingdon & New York: Routledge, 1999)

CARTMELL, DEBORAH, and OTHERS, eds, *Pulping Fictions: Consuming Culture Across the Literature/Media Divide* (London: Pluto Press, 1996)

CATTRYSSE, PATRICK, 'Film (Adaptation) as Translation: Some Methodological Proposals', *Target*, 4.1 (1992), 53–70

CAVALLARO, DANI, *Anime and the Art of Adaptation* (Jefferson, NC: McFarland, 2010)

CERF, BENNETT, *At Random: The Reminiscences of Bennett Cerf* (New York: Random House, 2012)

CHASTANG, MARIE-LAURE, 'Rencontre des œuvres de Voltaire et de leurs illustrateurs (1796–2002): essai bibliographique à l'intention des futurs chercheurs', *Revue Voltaire*, 3 (2003), 131–214

CHAPPLE, FREDA, and CHIEL KATTENBELT, eds, *Intermediality in Theatre and Performance* (Amsterdam & New York: Rodopi, 2006)

CHATMAN, SEYMOUR, *Story and Discourse: Narrative Structure in Fiction and Film* (Ithaca, NY: Cornell University Press, 1978)

CHAUFOUR, GHISLAIN, *Candide antérot: Voltaire commenté à partir des vingt-six 'Images à Candide' de Paul Klee* (Paris: Cerf, 2009)

CHION, MICHEL, *Audio-Vision: Sound on Screen*, trans. by Claudia Gorbman (New York: Columbia University Press, 1994)

——*The Voice in Cinema*, trans. by Claudia Gorbman (New York: Columbia University Press, 1999)

COMOLLI, JEAN-LUC, and PAUL NARBONI, 'Cinema/Ideology/Criticism', trans. by Susan Bennett, *Screen*, 12.1 (1971), 27–36

CORBEYRAN, ERIC, and RICHARD HORNE, *La Métamorphose* (Paris: Guy Delcourt, 2009)
CORRIGAN, TIMOTHY, 'Defining Adaptation', in *The Oxford Handbook of Adaptation Studies*, ed. by Thomas Leitch (Oxford: Oxford University Press, 2017), pp. 23–35
COUSINS, RUSSELL, *Zola: Thérèse Raquin* (London: Grant & Cutler, 1992)
CREPAX, GUIDO, *Il processo* (Casale Monferrato: Piemme, 1999)
CRUMB, ROBERT, and DAVID Z. MAIROWITZ, *Kafka* (Berlin: Reprodukt, 2017)
——*Kafka for Beginners* (Cambridge: Icon Books, 1993)
CUTCHINS, DENNIS, LAWRENCE RAW and JAMES M. WELSH, eds, *The Pedagogy of Adaptation* (Lanham, MD: Scarecrow Press, 2010)
——*Redefining Adaptation Studies* (Lanham, MD: Scarecrow Press, 2010)
CUTCHINS, DENNIS, KATJA KREBS and ECKARD VOIGTS, eds, *The Routledge Companion to Adaptation Studies* (Abingdon & New York: Routledge, 2018)
DAVIS, COLIN, 'From Psychopathology to Diabolical Evil: Dr Jekyll, Mr Hyde and Jean Renoir', *Journal of Romance Studies*, 12.1 (2012), 10–23
——*Postwar Renoir: Film and the Memory of Violence* (New York & Abingdon: Routledge, 2012)
DEBONA, GUERRIC, *Film Adaptation in the Hollywood Era* (Urbana, Chicago & Springfield: University of Illinois Press, 2010)
DEHE, ASTRID, and ACHIM ENGSTLER, *Kafkas komische Seiten: ein Lesebuch* (Göttingen: Steidl Verlag, 2011)
DELEUZE, GILLES, *Cinema 2: The Time-Image*, trans. by H. Tomlinson and R. Galeta (London: Athlone Press, 1989)
DERRIDA, JACQUES, *Specters of Marx: The State of the Debt, the Work of Mourning and the New International*, trans. by Peggy Kamuf (New York & Abingdon: Routledge, 2006)
DIAMOND, ELIN, 'Stoppard's *Dogg's Hamlet, Cahoot's Macbeth*: The Uses of Shakespeare', *Modern Drama*, 29 (1986), 593–600
DICKENS, CHARLES, *Great Expectations* (London: Chapman & Hall, 1860)
DOBSON, MICHAEL, *The Making of the National Poet: Shakespeare, Adaptation and Authorship, 1660–1769* (Oxford: Clarendon Press, 1992)
DONALDSON-EVANS, MARY, 'The Colonization of *Madame Bovary*: Hindi Cinema's *Maya Memsaab*', *Adaptation*, 3.1 (2010), 21–35
——*Madame Bovary at the Movies: Adaptation, Ideology, Context* (Amsterdam: Rodopi, 2009)
DRAKAKIS, JOHN, *British Radio Drama* (Cambridge: Cambridge University Press, 1981)
DUPRÊTRE, EVELYNE, and GERMAN A. DUARTE, eds, *Transmédialité, bande dessinée & adaptation* (Clermont-Ferrand: Presses universitaires Blaise Pascal, 2019)
DUTTLINGER, CAROLIN, 'Film und Fotografie', in *Kafka Handbuch: Leben, Werk, Wirkung*, ed. by Manfred Engel and Bernd Auerochs (Stuttgart & Weimar: Metzler, 2010), pp. 72-79
——*Kafka and Photography* (Oxford: Oxford University Press, 2007)
EARHART, AMY E., 'Can Information Be Unfettered? Race and the Digital Humanities Canon', in *Debates in the Digital Humanities*, ed. by Matthew K. Gold (Minneapolis: University of Minnesota Press, 2012)
EASLEY, ALEXIS, *First Person Anonymous: Women Writers and the Victorian Print Media, 1830–70* (Aldershot: Ashgate, 2004)
EILITTÄ, LEENA, 'Kafka and Visuality', *KulturPoetik*, 6.2 (2006), 222-33
ELLESTRÖM, LARS, 'Adaptation Within the Field of Media Transformations', in *Adaptation Studies: New Challenges, New Directions*, ed. by Jørgen Bruhn, Anne Gjelsvik and Eirik Frisvold Hanssen (London & New York: Bloomsbury Academic, 2013), pp. 113–32
——'The Modalities of Media: A Model for Understanding Intermedial Relations', in *Media Borders, Multimodality and Intermediality*, ed. by Lars Elleström (Basingstoke: Palgrave Macmillan, 2010), pp. 11–48

ELLINGTON, H. ELIZABETH, 'A Correct Taste in Landscape: Pemberley as Fetish and Commodity', in *Jane Austen in Hollywood*, ed. by Linda Troost and Sayre Greenfield (Lexington: University of Kentucky Press, 2001), pp. 90–110

ELLIOTT, KAMILLA, *Portraiture and British Gothic Fiction: The Rise of Picture Identification, 1764–1835* (Baltimore, MD: Johns Hopkins University Press, 2012)

—— *Rethinking the Novel/Film Debate* (Cambridge: Cambridge University Press, 2003)

—— 'Screened Writers', in *The Blackwell Companion to Literature, Film, and Adaptation*, ed. by Deborah Cartmell (London: Blackwell, 2012), pp. 179–97

—— *Theorizing Adaptation* (New York & Oxford: Oxford University Press, 2020)

—— 'Theorizing Adaptations/Adapting Theories', in *Adaptation Studies: New Challenges, New Directions*, ed. by Jørgen Bruhn and others (London & New York: Bloomsbury Academic, 2013), pp. 19–45

—— 'The Theory of *Bad*aptation', in *The Routledge Companion to Adaptation Studies*, ed. by Dennis Cutchins, Katja Krebs and Eckard Voigts (Abingdon & New York: Routledge, 2018), pp. 18–27

ELLIS, JOHN, 'The Literary Adaptation', *Screen*, 23 (1982), 3–5

ENGEL, MANFRED, 'Kafka lesen — Verstehensprobleme und Forschungsparadigmen', in *Kafka Handbuch: Leben, Werk, Wirkung*, ed. by Manfred Engel and Bernd Auerochs (Stuttgart & Weimar: Metzler, 2010), pp. 411-27

—— 'Der Process', in *Kafka Handbuch: Leben, Werk, Wirkung*, ed. by Manfred Engel and Bernd Auerochs (Stuttgart & Weimar: Metzler, 2010), pp. 192-207

ERLL, ASTRID, 'Literature, Film, and the Mediality of Cultural Memory', in *Cultural Memory Studies: An International and Interdisciplinary Handbook*, ed. by Ansgar Nünning and Astrid Erll (Berlin: de Gruyter, 2008), pp. 389–98

FELLNER, FRIEDERIKE, *Kafkas Zeichnungen* (Munich: Wilhelm Fink, 2014)

FFORDE, JASPER, *The Eyre Affair* (London: Hodder & Stoughton, 2001)

FISCHER-LICHTE, ERIKA, *The Transformative Power of Performance: A New Aesthetics*, trans. by Saskya Iris Jain (Abingdon & New York: Routledge, 2008)

FISCHLIN, DANIEL, and MARK FORTIER, eds, *Adaptations of Shakespeare: A Critical Anthology of Plays from the Seventeenth Century to the Present* (Abingdon & New York: Routledge, 2000)

FISHER, MARGARET, *Ezra Pound's Radio Operas: The BBC Experiments, 1931–1933* (Cambridge, MA: MIT Press, 2002)

FLUSSER, VILÉM, *Does Writing have a Future?*, trans. by Nancy Ann Roth (Minneapolis: University of Minnesota Press, 2011)

—— *Writings*, ed. by Andreas Ströhl, trans. by Erik Eisel (Minneapolis: University of Minnesota Press, 2002)

FOUCAULT, MICHEL, 'What is an Author?', in *Modern Criticism and Theory: A Reader*, ed. by David Lodge and Nigel Wood (Edinburgh: Pearson Education, 1988), pp. 280–93

FRIANT-KESSLER, BRIGITTE, 'Visual Sterneana: Graphic Afterlives and a Sense of Infinite Mobility', *Journal for Eighteenth-Century Studies*, 39.4 (December 2016), 643–62

FRICK, CAROLINE, *Saving Cinema: The Politics of Preservation* (Oxford: Oxford University Press, 2011)

GABEL, GERNOT UWE, *Voltaires 'Candide': die illustrierten Ausgaben des 20. Jahrhunderts aus den deutschsprachigen Ländern* (Hürth: Gemini, 2012)

GARD, ROGER, *Jane Austen's Novels: The Art of Clarity* (New Haven, CT: Yale University Press, 1994)

GASKELL, ELIZABETH, *Mary Barton* (London: Chapman & Hall, 1848)

GATEFIN, ERIC, '*Candide* vu par Joann Sfar: illustration, commentaire et caricature d'un "texte sacré"', in *Les 250 ans de 'Candide': lectures et relectures*, ed. by Nicholas Cronk and Nathalie Ferrand (Leuven: Peeters, 2014), pp. 605–16

GENETTE, GÉRARD, 'Discours du récit', in *Figures III* (Paris: Seuil, 1972), pp. 65–273

——*Narrative Discourse: An Essay in Method*, trans. by Jane E. Lewin (Oxford: Blackwell, 1980)

——*Palimpsestes: la littérature au second degré* (Paris: Seuil, 1982)

——*Palimpsests: Literature in the Second Degree*, trans. by Channa Newman and Claude Doubinsky (Lincoln: University of Nebraska Press, 1997)

GERAGHTY, CHRISTINE, *Now a Major Motion Picture: Film Adaptations from Literature and Drama* (Lanham, MD: Rowman & Littlefield, 2008)

GIANNACHI, GABRIELLA, *Virtual Theatres: An Introduction* (London & New York: Routledge, 2004)

GIANNAKOPOULOU, VASSO, and DEBORAH CARTMELL, eds, *Intersemiotic Translation as Adaptation*, special issue of *Adaptation*, 23.3 (December 2019)

GIDDINGS, ROBERT, KEITH SELBY and CHRIS WENSLEY, *Screening the Novel: The Theory and Practice of Literary Dramatization* (London: Palgrave Macmillan, 1990)

GLEIZES, DELPHINE, ed., *L'Œuvre de Victor Hugo à l'écran: des rayons et des ombres* (Quebec: L'Harmattan/Presses de l'Université Laval, 2005)

GOETHE, JOHANN WOLFGANG VON, *Gedichte*, ed. by Erich Trunz, 2 vols (Frankfurt a.M.: Fischer, 1964)

GOGGIN, GERARD, 'Adapting the Mobile Phone: The iPhone and its Consumption', *Continuum: Journal of Media & Cultural Studies*, 23.2 (2009), 231–44

GRAAS, ANGELA, and OTHERS, *Candide: Illustrierte Ausgaben eines Klassikers. Katalog einer Ausstellung der Universitätsbibliothek Trier* (Trier: Universitätsbibliothek Trier, 2000)

GRAY, RICHARD T., 'Das Urteil: unheimliches Erzählen und die Unheimlichkeit des bürgerlichen Subjekts', in *Franz Kafka: Romane und Erzählungen*, ed. by Michael Müller (Stuttgart: Reclam, 2009), pp. 11–41

GRIFFITHS, KATE, '*Chez Maupassant*: The (In)Visible Space of Television Adaptation', in Kate Griffiths and Andrew Watts, *Adapting Nineteenth-century France: Literature in Film, Theatre, Television, Radio and Print* (Cardiff: University of Wales Press, 2013), pp. 143–71

——*Émile Zola and the Artistry of Adaptation* (Oxford: Legenda, 2009)

——'Memories in/of *Thérèse Raquin*: Émile Zola and Marcel Carné', *French Studies*, 65.2 (2011), 188–99

——'Mythical Returns: Televising *Thérèse Raquin*', *Nineteenth-Century French Studies*, 39.3–4 (2011), 285–95

——*Zola and the Art of Television: Adaptation, Recreation, Translation* (Oxford: Legenda, forthcoming)

GRIFFITHS, KATE, and ANDREW WATTS, *Adapting Nineteenth-century France: Literature in Film, Theatre, Television, Radio and Print* (Cardiff: University of Wales Press, 2013)

GRIFFITHS, KATE, BRADLEY STEPHENS and ANDREW WATTS, eds, 'Introduction: Multimedia Adaptation and the Pull of Nineteenth-century France', in *Adaptation*, special issue of *Dix-Neuf*, 18.2 (2014), 126–33

GRIGGS, YVONNE, *Adaptable TV: Rewiring the Text* (London: Palgrave Macmillan, 2018)

——*The Bloomsbury Introduction to Adaptation Studies: Adapting the Canon in Film, TV, Novels and Popular Culture* (London & New York: Bloomsbury Academic, 2016)

GROENSTEEN, THIERRY, *The System of Comics*, trans. by Bart Beaty and Nick Nguyen (Jackson: University Press of Mississippi, 2007)

GROSSMAN, Kathryn M., *Figuring Transcendence in 'Les Misérables': Hugo's Romantic Sublime* (Carbondale: Southern Illinois University Press, 1994)

GROSSMAN, KATHRYN M., and BRADLEY STEPHENS, eds, *'Les Misérables' and its Afterlives: Between Page, Stage and Screen* (Farnham: Ashgate, 2015)

GROSSMAN, KATHRYN M., and R. BARTON PALMER, eds, *Adaptation in Visual Culture: Texts, Images, and their Multiple Worlds* (London: Palgrave Macmillan, 2017)

Guillory, John, *Cultural Capital: The Problem of Literary Canon Formation* (Chicago: University of Chicago Press, 1993)
Hamery, Roxane, 'Rhétorique du double: les figures inquiétantes de Jean-Louis Barrault', in *Les Cinéastes français à l'épreuve du genre fantastique: socioanalyse d'une production artistique*, ed. by Frédéric Gimello-Mesplomb (Paris: L'Harmattan, 2012), pp. 109–28
Hand, Richard J., 'Paradigms of Metamorphosis and Transmutation: Thomas Edison's *Frankenstein* and John Barrymore's *Dr Jekyll and Mr Hyde*', in *Monstrous Adaptations: Generic and Thematic Mutations in Horror Film*, ed. by Richard J. Hand and Jay McRoy (Manchester: Manchester University Press, 2007), pp. 9–19
Harrow, Susan, '*Thérèse Raquin*: Animal Passion and the Brutality of Reading', in *The Cambridge Companion to Émile Zola*, ed. by Brian Nelson (New York: Cambridge University Press, 2007), pp. 105–20
Hartje, Hans, 'Georges Perec et le "Neues Hörspiel" allemand', in *Écritures radiophonoques*, ed. by Isabelle Chol and Christian Moncelet (Clermont-Ferrand: Cahiers de recherches du CRLMC/Université Blaise Pascal, 1997), pp. 73–86
Haskell, Eric T., 'Fusing Word and Image: The Case of the Cartoon Book, Wilde and Shenton', in *The Pictured Word: Word and Image Interactions 2*, ed. by Martin Heusser and others (Amsterdam & Atlanta, GA: Rodopi, 1998), pp. 245–54
Hayward, Susan, 'Literary Adaptations of the 1950s: *Thérèse Raquin* and *Les Diaboliques* (1955)', *Studies in French Cinema*, 3.1 (2003), 5–14
Heller, Reinhold, 'Rediscovering Henri de Toulouse-Lautrec's *At the Moulin Rouge*', *Art Institute of Chicago Museum Studies*, 12.2 (1986), 114–35
Henley, W. E., 'Villon's Good-Night', in *Recreations of the Rabelais Club* (London: printed for the members, private circulation only, 1885–88), pp. 6–7
Higson, Andrew, *English Heritage, English Cinema: Costume Drama Since 1980* (Oxford: Oxford University Press, 2003)
Hoffmann, Torsten, '"Das nicht, bitte das nicht!" Körperdarstellung in Comicversionen von Schnitzlers *Fräulein Else* und Kafkas *Verwandlung*', in *Graphisches Erzählen: Neue Perspektiven auf Literaturcomics*, ed. by Florian Trabert, Mara Stuhlfauth-Trabert and Johannes Waßmer (Bielefeld: Transcript, 2015), pp. 42-63
Hohlbaum, Christopher, *Kafka im Comic* (Würzburg: Königshausen & Neumann, 2015)
Horstkotte, Silke, 'Seeing or Speaking: Visual Narratology and Focalization, Literature to Film', in *Narratology in the Age of Cross-disciplinary Narrative Research*, ed. by Sandra Heinen and Roy Sommer (Berlin & New York: de Gruyter, 2009), pp. 170-91
Huber, Werner, Evelyne Keitel and Gunter Süss, eds, *Intermedialities* (Trier: Wissenschaftlicher Verlag Trier, 2007)
Hugo, Victor, 'Lettre à M. Daelli', 18 October 1862, in *Œuvres complètes: Roman II*, ed. by Annette and Guy Rosa (Paris: Laffont, 1985), p. 1154
——*Les Misérables*, trans. by Julie Rose (London: Vintage, 2008)
——*Re Mizeraburu*, Manga de Dokuha (Tokyo: East Press Co. Ltd, 2009)
——*Les Misérables: manga de Dokuha*, trans. by Anne Mallevay (Paris: Éditions Soleil, 2011)
Hutcheon, Linda, *A Theory of Adaptation* (New York: Routledge, 2006)
——, with Siobhan O'Flynn, *A Theory of Adaptation*, 2nd edn (Abingdon & New York: Routledge, 2013)
Inagaki, Naoki, 'Victor Hugo aujourd'hui au Japon', *Revue des Deux Mondes* (January 2002), 94–98
Ionescu, Christina, '*Candide* à New York: éditions illustrées américaines de l'entre-deux-guerres', in *Les 250 ans de 'Candide': lectures et relectures*, ed. by Nicholas Cronk and Nathalie Ferrand (Leuven: Peeters, 2014), pp. 577–603
——'Exploring the World with Rockwell Kent's *Candide*: Intermedial Translation,

Paratextual Framing, and Iconographic Landscape', in *Art and Science in Word and Image: Exploration and Discovery*, ed. by Keith Williams and others (Leiden: Brill, 2019), pp. 309–22

——'Narrative Form and Iconographic Sequence: Rockwell Kent's *Candide* (1928) in Text and Image', *Image & Narrative*, 17.1 (2016), 15–28

IONESCU, CHRISTINA, and ANN LEWIS, eds, *Picturing the Eighteenth-century Novel Through Time: Illustration, Intermediality and Adaptation*, special issue of *Journal for Eighteenth-Century Studies*, 39.4 (December 2016)

IWABUCHI, KOICHI, '"Soft" Nationalism and Narcissism: Japanese Popular Culture Goes Global', *Asian Studies Review*, 26.4 (2002), 447–69

JAGODA, PATRICK, 'Gaming the Humanities', *differences: A Journal of Feminist Cultural Studies*, 25.1 (2014), 189–215

JAMES, JEFFREY, 'Sharing Phones in Developing Countries: Implications for the Digital Divide', *Technological Forecasting and Social Change*, 78.4 (May 2011), 729–35

JAMES, P. D., *Death Comes to Pemberley* (London: Faber & Faber, 2013)

JANSEN, MARIUS B., *The Making of Modern Japan* (Cambridge, MA: Harvard University Press, 2002)

JENKINS, HENRY, *Convergence Culture: Where Old and New Media Collide*, rev. edn (New York: New York University Press, 2008)

KAES, ANTON, 'The Expressionist Vision in Theatre and Cinema', in *Expressionism Reconsidered: Relationships and Affinities*, ed. by Gertrud Bauer Pickar and Karl Eugene Webb (Munich: Wilhelm Fink, 1979), pp. 89–98

KAFKA, FRANZ, *Briefe April 1914–17*, ed. by Hans-Gerd Koch (Frankfurt a.M.: Fischer, 2005)

—— *The Metamorphosis and Other Stories*, trans. by Joyce Crick (Oxford: Oxford University Press, 2009)

——*Der Proceß*, ed. by Malcolm Pasley (Frankfurt a.M.: S. Fischer Verlag, 2002)

——'Das Urteil', in *Drucke zu Lebzeiten*, ed. by Wolf Kittler, Hans-Gerd Koch and Gerhard Neumann (Frankfurt a.M.: Fischer, 2002), pp. 43-61

——'Die Verwandlung', in *Drucke zu Lebzeiten*, ed. by Wolf Kittler, Hans-Gerd Koch and Gerhard Neumann (Frankfurt a.M.: Fischer, 2002), pp. 115-200

KAPP, KARL M., *The Gamification of Learning and Instruction: Game-based Methods and Strategies for Training and Education* (San Francisco: Pfeiffer, 2012)

KATTENBELT, CHIEL, 'Theatre as the Art of the Performer and the Stage of Intermediality', in *Intermediality in Theatre and Performance*, ed. by Freda Chapple and Chiel Kattenbelt (Amsterdam & New York: Rodopi, 2006), pp. 29–39

KELLER, MARIE T., 'Clara Tice, "Queen of Greenwich Village"', in *Women in Dada: Essays on Sex, Gender, and Identity*, ed. by Naomi Sawelson-Gorse (Cambridge, MA: MIT Press, 1998), pp. 414–41

KICK, RUSS, ed., *The Graphic Canon: The World's Great Literature as Comics and Visuals*, 3 vols (New York: Seven Stories Press, 2012-13)

KOLBAS, E. DEAN, *Critical Theory and the Literary Canon* (Boulder, CO: Westview Press, 2001)

KOMPORALY, JOZEFINA, *Radical Revival as Adaptation: Theatre, Politics, Society* (London: Palgrave, 2017)

KOTT, JAN, *Shakespeare our Contemporary*, trans. by Bolesław Taborksi (London: Routledge, 1988)

KOYAMA-RICHARD, BRIGITTE, *Mille ans de manga* (Paris: Flammarion, 2007)

KRAMSKY, JERRY, and LORENZO MATTOTTI, *Docteur Jekyll & Mr. Hyde*, trans. by Marc Violine (Tournai: Casterman, 2002)

——*Dr. Jekyll & Mr. Hyde*, trans. by Adeline Darlington (Nantier: NBM, 2002)

Kranz, David L., 'The Golden Continuum of Probability', in *In/Fidelity: Essays on Film Adaptation*, ed. by David L. Kranz and Nancy C. Mellerski (Newcastle upon Tyne: Cambridge Scholars Publishing, 2008), pp. 202–04

Kuper, Peter, *The Metamorphosis* (New York: Three Rivers Press, 2003)

Ladendorf, Heinz, 'Kafka und die Kunstgeschichte', *Wallfraf-Richartz-Jahrbuch*, 23 (1961), 293–326, & 25 (1963), 227–62

Laera, Margherita, ed., *Theatre and Adaptation: Return, Rewrite, Repeat* (London: Bloomsbury, 2014)

Lamarre, Thomas, *The Anime Machine: A Media Theory of Animation* (Minneapolis: University of Minnesota Press, 2009)

Lamping, Dieter, 'Franz Kafka als Autor der Weltliteratur', in *Franz Kafka und die Weltliteratur*, ed. by Manfred Engel and Dieter Lamping (Göttingen: Vandenhoeck & Ruprecht, 2006), pp. 9-23

Langille, Édouard, 'Introduction', *Candide, ou l'optimisme. Seconde partie*, ed. by Édouard Langille (Exeter: University of Exeter Press, 2003), pp. ix–xxvii

Larroche, Caroline, ed., *Toulouse-Lautrec*, exhibition catalogue (London: South Bank Centre; Paris: Réunion des Musées Nationaux, 1992)

Laurent, Franck, *Victor Hugo face à la conquête de l'Algérie* (Paris: Maisonnneuve & Larose, 2001)

Lee, J. Patrick, 'Bibliographie des éditions illustrées américaines des œuvres de Voltaire', *Revue Voltaire*, 5 (2005), 285–307

Legman, Gershon, *The Art of Mahlon Blaine* (East Lansing, MI: Peregrine Books, 1982)

Lehmann, Hans-Thies, *Postdramatic Theatre*, trans. by Karen Jürs-Munby (Abingdon & New York: Routledge, 2006)

Leitch, Thomas, 'Adaptation and Intertextuality, or, What isn't an Adaptation, and What Does it Matter?', in *A Companion to Literature, Film and Adaptation*, ed. by Deborah Cartmell (Oxford: Blackwell, 2012), pp. 87–104

—— 'Everything You Always Wanted to Know about Adaptation: Especially if You're Looking Forwards Rather than Back', *Literature/Film Quarterly*, 33.3 (2005), 233–45

—— *Film Adaptation and Its Discontents: From 'Gone with the Wind' to 'The Passion of the Christ'* (Baltimore, MD: Johns Hopkins University Press, 2007)

—— *The History of American Literature on Film* (New York: Bloomsbury Academic, 2019)

—— 'Is Adaptation Studies a Discipline?', *Germanistik in Ireland*, 7 (2002), 13–26

—— 'Jekyll, Hyde, Jekyll, Hyde, Jekyll Hyde, Jekyll, Hyde: Four Models of Intertextuality', in *Victorian Literature and Film Adaptation*, ed. by Abigail Burnham Bloom and Mary Sanders Pollock (Amherst, NY: Cambria Press, 2011), pp. 27–49

—— 'Panel Presentations and Discussion: "The Persistence of Fidelity"', in *In/Fidelity: Essays on Film Adaptation*, ed. by David L. Kranz and Nancy C. Mellerski (Newcastle: Cambridge Scholars Publishing, 2008), pp. 197–228

—— 'Review Article. Adaptation Studies at a Crossroads', *Adaptation*, 1.1 (2008), 65–68

—— 'Twelve Fallacies in Contemporary Adaptation Theory', *Criticism*, 45.2 (2003), 149–71

—— 'Where Are We Going, Where Have We Been?', in *The Literature/Film Reader: Issues of Adaptation*, ed. by James M. Welsh and Peter Lev (Lanham, MD: Scarecrow Press, 2007), pp. 327–33

Leitch, Thomas, ed., *The Oxford Handbook of Adaptation Studies* (Oxford: Oxford University Press, 2017)

Lethbridge, Robert, 'Zola, Manet and *Thérèse Raquin*', *French Studies*, 34.3 (1980), 278–99

Lévi-Strauss, Claude, *Mythologiques: le cru et le cuit* (Paris: Plon, 1964)

Lewis, Ann, 'Intermedial Approaches to Marivaux's *La Vie de Marianne*: Text, Illustration, Film', *Journal for Eighteenth-Century Studies*, 39.4 (December 2016), 621–42

LIBRARY OF CONGRESS, *Catalogue of Copyright Entries: New Series, Volume 27, Group 1* (Washington, DC: United States Government Printing Office, 1931), notice 14255, p. 2171

LINEHAN, KATHERINE, '"Closer Than a Wife": The Strange Case of Dr Jekyll's Significant Other', in *Robert Louis Stevenson Reconsidered: New Critical Perspectives*, ed. by William B. Jones, Jr. (London: McFarland & Co., 2003), pp. 85–100

LITTELL, PHILIP, 'Introduction', in Voltaire, *Candide*, The Modern Library of the World's Best Books (New York: Boni & Liveright, 1918), pp. vii–xi

LIU, SIYUAN, 'The Impact of *Shinpa* on Early Chinese *Huaju*', *Asian Theatre Journal*, 23.2 (2006), 342–55

LU, AMY SHIRONG, 'The Many Faces of Internationalization in Japanese Anime', *Animation*, 3.2 (2008), 169–87

MACDONALD FRASER, GEORGE, *Flashman* (London: Barrie & Jenkins, 1969)

MACCABE, COLIN, KATHLEEN MURRAY and RICK WARNER, eds, *True to the Spirit: Film Adaptation and the Question of Fidelity* (Oxford: Oxford University Press, 2011)

MCFARLANE, BRIAN, *Novel to Film: An Introduction to the Theory of Adaptation* (Oxford: Clarendon Press, 1996)

MCKNIGHT, ANNE, 'Frenchness and Transformation in Japanese Subculture, 1972–2004', in *Mechademia 5: Fanthropologies*, ed. by Frenchy Lunning (Minneapolis: University of Minnesota Press, 2010), pp. 118–37

MCLUHAN, MARSHALL, *Understanding Media: The Extensions of Man* (London: Routledge & Keegan Paul, 1964)

MACWILLIAMS, MARK W., ed., *Japanese Visual Culture: Explorations in the World of Manga and Anime* (Armonk: M. E. Sharpe, 2008)

MALRAUX, ANDRÉ, *Les Voix du silence* (Paris: Galerie de la Pléiade/NRF, 1951)

—— *The Voices of Silence*, trans. by Stuart Gilbert (Princeton, NJ: Princeton University Press, 1978)

MANCEWICZ, ANETA, *Intermedial Shakespeares on European Stages* (Basingstoke: Palgrave, 2014)

MANTEL, HILARY, *Wolf Hall and Bring Up the Bodies*, adapted for the stage by Mike Poulton (London: Nick Hern Books/Fourth Estate, 2014)

MARCUS, MILLICENT, *Filmmaking by the Book: Italian Cinema and Literary Adaptation* (Baltimore, MD: Johns Hopkins University Press, 1992)

MARKS, LAURA U., *Touch: Sensuous Theory and Multisensory Media* (Minneapolis: University of Minnesota Press, 2002)

MARX, KARL, *Das Kapital* (Washington, DC: Regnery, 2009)

MAURIN, MARIO, 'Zola's Labyrinths', *Yale French Studies*, 42 (1969), 89–104

MAYER-ROBIN, CARMEN, 'Framed! Fact, Fiction and Frame Tale in Adaptations of Zola's *Thérèse Raquin*', *Romance Studies*, 28 (2010), 158–68

MERSCHMEIER, MICHAEL, and FRANZ WILLE, '"Ich muss es einfach versuchen": ein Theater Heute-Gespräch mit Thomas Ostermeier', *Theater Heute*, 5 (1998), 26–30

MILLER, ANN, *Reading Bande dessinée: Critical Approaches to French-language Comic Strip* (Bristol: Intellect, 2007)

MITAINE, BENOÎT, DAVID ROCHE and ISABELLE SCHMITT-PITIOT, eds, *Bande dessinée et adaptation: littérature, cinéma, TV* (Clermont Ferrand: Presses universitaires Blaise Pascal, 2015)

—— *Comics and Adaptation,* trans. by Aarnoud Rommens and David Roche (Jackson: University Press of Mississippi, 2018)

MITTERAND, HENRI, 'Le Musée dans le texte', *Cahiers naturalistes*, 66 (1992), 13–22

—— *Zola journaliste: de l'affaire Manet à l'affaire Dreyfus* (Paris: Armand Colin, 1962)

MIZUNO, AKIRA, 'Stylistic Norms in the Early Meiji Period: From Chinese Influences to European Influences', in *Translation and Translation Studies in the Japanese Context*, ed. by Nana Sato-Rossberg and Judy Wakabayahsi (London: Continuum, 2012), pp. 92–114

MONTELLIER, CHANTAL, and DAVID ZANE MAIROWITZ, *The Trial: A Graphic Novel* (London: SelfMadeHero, 2008)

MURRAY, SIMONE, *The Adaptation Industry: The Cultural Economy of Contemporary Literary Adaptation* (New York & Abingdon: Routledge, 2012)

NAPIER, SUSAN J., *Anime: from Akira to Howl's Moving Castle*, 2nd edn (New York: Palgrave, Macmillan, 2005)

NAREMORE, JAMES, 'Introduction: Film and the Reign of Adaptation', in *Film Adaptation*, ed. by James Naremore (New Brunswick, NJ: Rutgers University Press, 2000), pp. 1–16

NEWBOULD, MARY-CÉLINE, *Adaptations of Laurence Sterne's Fiction: Sterneana, 1760–1840* (Farnham: Ashgate, 2013)

NEWELL, KATE, *Expanding Adaptation Networks: From Illustration to Novelization* (London: Palgrave Macmillan, 2017)

NIXON, CHERYL, 'Balancing the Courtship Hero: Masculine Emotional Display in Film Adaptations of Austen's Novels', in *Jane Austen in Hollywood*, ed. by Linda Troost and Sayre Greenfield (Lexington: University of Kentucky Press, 2001), pp. 22–43

NOGAMI, TERUYO, *Waiting on the Weather: Making Movies with Akira Kurosawa*, trans. by Juliet Winters Carpenter (Berkeley, CA: Stone Bridge Press, 2006)

O'FLYNN, SIOBHAN, 'Epilogue', in Linda Hutcheon, with Siohbhan O'Flynn, *A Theory of Adaptation*, 2nd edn (Abingdon: Routledge, 2012), pp. 179–206

O'SHAUGHNESSY, MARTIN, *Jean Renoir* (Manchester: Manchester University Press, 2000)

O'THOMAS, MARK, 'Turning Japanese: Translation, Adaptation, and the Ethics of Trans-National Exchange', in *Adaptation Studies: New Approaches*, ed. by Christa Albrecht-Crane and Dennis Cutchins (Madison, NJ: Fairleigh Dickinson University Press, 2010), pp. 46–60

OGI, FUSAMI, 'Female Subjectivity and Shōjo Manga', *Journal of Popular Culture*, 36.4 (2003), 780–803

ONEGA, SUSANA, and CHRISTIAN GUTLEBEN, eds, *Refracting the Canon in Contemporary British Literature and Film* (Amsterdam & New York: Rodopi, 2004)

OSTERMEIER, THOMAS, 'Foreword', in Michael Eberth, *Eidinger: Backstage* (Berlin: Verlag Theater der Zeit, 2011)

—— 'Der Kapitalismus liebt die Stille nicht: Gespräch mit Byung Chul-Han', *Schaubühne Spielzeit für 2013–14*, p. 4

—— *Teatrul şi frica/Theatre and Fear*, ed. by Georges Banu and Jitka Goriaux Pelechová, trans. by Vlad Russo (Bucharest: Nemira, 2016)

OSTERMEIER, THOMAS, and PETER M. BOENISCH, *The Theatre of Thomas Ostermeier* (Abingdon & New York: Routledge, 2016)

PAECH, JOACHIM, 'Intermedialität: Mediales Differenzial und transformative Figurationen', in *Intermedialität: Theorie und Praxis eines interdisziplinären Forschungsgebiets*, ed. by Jörg Helbig (Berlin, Schmidt, 1998), p. 16

PAREY, ARMELLE, and SHANNON WELLS-LASSAGNE, eds, *Adapting Endings from Book to Screen: Last Pages, Last Shots* (Abingdon: Routledge, 2019)

PAVIS, PATRICE, 'Problems of Translation for the Stage: Interculturalism and Post-modern Theatre', trans. by Loren Kruger, in *The Play Out of Context: Transferring Plays from Culture to Culture*, ed. by Hanna Scolnicov and Peter Holland (Cambridge: Cambridge University Press, 1989)

PEETERS, BENOÎT, *Case, planche, récit* (Tournai: Casterman, 1991)

PEREC, GEORGES, *Die Maschine: Hörspiel*, trans. and ed. by Eugen Helmlé, afterword by Werner Klippert (Stuttgart: Philipp Reclam jun., 1972)

PETTEY, HOMER B., and R. BARTON PALMER, eds, *French Literature on Screen* (Manchester: Manchester University Press, 2019)

PLACE, JANEY, and LOWELL PETERSON, 'Some Visual Motifs of *Film Noir*', in *Film Noir Reader*, ed. by Alain Silver and James Ursini (New York: Limelight Editions, 1996), pp. 65–76

POOVEY, MARY, *The Proper Lady and the Woman Writer: Ideology as Style in the Works of Mary Wollstonecraft, Mary Shelley and Jane Austen* (Chicago: Chicago University Press, 1984)

POPPE, SANDRA, 'Die Verwandlung', in *Kafka Handbuch: Leben, Werk, Wirkung*, ed. by Manfred Engel and Bernd Auerochs (Stuttgart & Weimar: Metzler, 2010), pp. 164–74

PORTER, LAURENCE M., *Victor Hugo* (New York: Twayne, 1999)

POULTON, M. CODY, *Spirits of Another Sort: The Plays of Izumi Kyōka* (Ann Arbor: Michigan Centre for Japanese Studies, 2001)

POUND, EZRA, *The ABC of Reading* (London: Faber & Faber, 1961)

——*A lume spento* (Venice: A. Antonini, 1908)

——*The Cantos of Ezra Pound* (London: Faber & Faber, 1975)

——*Literary Essays of Ezra Pound*, ed. by T. S. Eliot (Norfolk, CT: New Directions, 1954)

——*Personae: Collected Shorter Poems of Ezra Pound*, second printing (New York: Boni & Liveright, 1926 [*recte* 1927])

——*The Spirit of Romance: An Attempt to Define Somewhat the Charm of the Pre-Renaissance Literature of Latin Europe* (London: J. M. Dent, 1910)

——*The Testament of François Villon, a Melodrama by Ezra Pound, Words by François Villon, Music by Ezra Pound*, in Margaret Fisher, *Ezra Pound's Radio Operas: The BBC Experiments, 1931–1933* (Cambridge, MA: MIT Press, 2002), pp. 206–21

POWRIE, PHIL, and OTHERS, *Carmen on Film: A Cultural History* (Bloomington: Indiana University Press, 2007)

RAHILL, FRANK, *The World of Melodrama* (University Park: Pennsylvania State University Press, 1967)

RAJEWSKY, IRINA O., 'Border Talks: The Problematic Status of Media Borders in the Current Debate about Intermediality', in *Media Border, Multimodality and Intermediality*, ed. by Lars Elleström (Basingstoke: Palgrave Macmillan, 2010), pp. 51–68

——'Intermediality, Intertextuality, and Remediation: A Literary Perspective on Intermediality', *Intermédialités*, 6 (2005), 43–64

RANCIÈRE, JACQUES, *The Emancipated Spectator* (London: Verso, 2009)

RAW, LAURENCE, *Expanding Adaptation Studies* (Basingstoke: Palgrave Macmillan, forthcoming)

RAY, ROBERT B., 'The Field of "Literature and Film"', in *Film Adaptation*, ed. by James Naremore (New Brunswick, NJ: Rutgers University Press, 2000), pp. 38–53

——'Film and Literature', in *How a Film Theory Got Lost and Other Mysteries in Cultural Studies* (Bloomington: Indiana University Press, 2001), pp. 120–31

READER, KEITH A., 'Literature/Cinema/Television: Intertextuality in Jean Renoir's *Le Testament du Docteur Cordelier*', in *Intertextuality: Theories and Practices*, ed. by Michael Worton and Judith Still (Manchester: Manchester University Press, 1990), pp. 176–89

REICH-RANICKI, MARCEL, ed., *'Der Kanon': die deutsche Literatur. Romane*, 20 vols (Berlin: Insel Verlag, 2002)

RHYS, JEAN, *Wide Sargasso Sea* (London: André Deutsch, 1966)

RIPPL, GABRIELE, ed., *Handbook of Intermediality: Literature, Image, Sound, Music* (Berlin & Boston: de Gruyter, 2015)

ROSE, BRIAN A., *'Jekyll and Hyde' Adapted: Dramatizations of Cultural Anxiety* (Westport, CT: Greenwood Press, 1996)

ROTH, PHILIP, 'I Always Wanted You to Admire My Fasting, or, Looking at Kafka', in

The World of Franz Kafka, ed. by J. P. Stern (London: Weidenfeld & Nicolson, 1980), pp. 202-17

ROUSSO, HENRY, *The Vichy Syndrome: History and Memory in France since 1944* (Cambridge, MA: Harvard University Press, 1991)

ROWLANDS, ESTHER, *Cinematic Portraits of Evil: Christian de Chalonge's 'Docteur Petiot' and Jean-Pierre Jeunet's 'Delicatessen'* (Amherst, NY: Cambria Press, 2009)

SANDERS, JULIE, *Adaptation and Appropriation* (Abingdon & New York: Routledge, 2006)

SAVY, NICOLE, 'Cosette, un personnage qui n'existe pas', in *Lire 'Les Misérables'*, ed. by Guy Rosa and Anne Ubersfeld (Paris: Corti, 1985), pp. 173–90

SCHAUBÜHNE AM LEHNINER PLATZ, 'Der Auftrag' [The Mission], originally published in the inaugural programme brochure for the theatre's Spring season 2000, reprinted as 'Wir müssen von vorn anfangen' [We have to start afresh], *Die Tageszeitung*, 20 January 2000

SCHMIDGALL, GARY, *Literature as Opera* (New York: Oxford University Press, 1977)

SCHMITZ-EMANS, MONIKA, 'Kafka in European and US Comics: Intermedial and Intercultural Transfer Processes', *Revue de littérature comparée*, 78.4 (2004), 485–505

——*Literatur-Comics: Adaptationen und Transformationen der Weltliteratur* (Berlin: de Gruyter, 2012)

SCHNEIDER, GESA, *Das Andere schreiben: Kafkas fotografische Poetik* (Würzburg: Königshausen & Neumann, 2008)

SCHOBER, REGINA, 'Adaptation as Connection: Transmediality Reconsidered', in *Adaptation Studies: New Challenges, New Directions*, ed. by Jørgen Bruhn, Anne Gjelsvik and Eirik Frisvold Hanssen (London: Bloomsbury, 2013), pp. 89–112

SCHODT, FREDERIK L., *Dreamland Japan: Writings on Modern Manga* (Berkeley, CA: Stone Bridge, 1996)

——'The View from North America: Manga as Late-Twentieth-century Japonisme?', in *Manga's Cultural Crossroads*, ed. by Jacqueline Berndt and Bettina Kümmerling-Meibauer (New York & Abingdon: Routledge, 2013), pp. 19–26

SCHOLZ, ANNE-MARIE, *From Fidelity to History: Film Adaptations as Cultural Events in the Twentieth Century* (New York: Berghahn, 2013)

SCHÜWER, MARTIN, *Wie Comics erzählen: Grundriss einer intermedialen Erzähltheorie der grafischen Literatur* (Trier: Wissenschaftlicher Verlag Trier, 2008)

SEMENZA, GREG M. COLÓN, and BOB HASENFRATZ, *The History of British Literature on Film, 1895–2015* (London: Bloomsbury, 2015)

SHARP, JASPER, *Historical Dictionary of Japanese Cinema* (Lanham, MD: Scarecrow Press, 2011)

SHIVAS, MARK, 'Method: Vincente Minnelli', *Movie*, 1 (1962), 20–24

SILVER, MARK, *Purloined Letters: Cultural Borrowing and Japanese Crime Literature 1868–1937* (Honolulu: University of Hawaii Press, 2008)

SIMS, RICHARD, 'France', in *The Iwakura Mission in America and Europe: A New Assessment*, ed. by Ian Nish (Richmond: Curzon Press, 1998), pp. 45–55

SINYARD, NEIL, *Filming Literature: The Art of Screen Adaptation* (New York: St. Martin's Press, 1986)

SJOGREN, BRITTA H., *Into the Vortex: Female Voice and Paradox in Film* (Urbana: University of Illinois Press, 2006)

SONTAG, SUSAN, 'Against Interpretation', in *Essays of the 1960s & 70s*, ed. by David Rieff (New York: Library of America, 2013), pp. 10-20

STAM, ROBERT, 'Beyond Fidelity: The Dialogics of Adaptation', in *Film Adaptation*, ed. by James Naremore (New Brunswick, NJ: Rutgers University Press, 2000), pp. 54–76

——'Introduction: The Theory and Practice of Adaptation', in *Literature and Film: A Guide to the Theory and Practice of Film Adaptation*, ed. by Robert Stam and Alessandra Raengo (Malden, MA, & Oxford: Blackwell, 2005), pp. 1–52

——*Literature through Film: Realism, Magic and the Art of Adaptation* (Malden, MA, & Oxford: Blackwell, 2005)

STEPHENS, BRADLEY, '*Les Misérables* and the Twenty-first Century', in *'Les Misérables' and its Afterlives: Between Page, Stage, and Screen*, ed. by Kathryn M. Grossman and Bradley Stephens (Abingdon: Routledge, 2015), pp. 191–204

STERN, LESLEY, 'Fiction/Film/Femininity: Paper One', *Australian Journal of Screen Theory*, 8 (1981), 37–48

——'Fiction/Film/Femininity: Paper Two', *Australian Journal of Screen Theory*, 9–10 (1981), 51–68

STEVENSON, ROBERT LOUIS, 'The Strange Case of Dr Jekyll and Mr Hyde', in *The Strange Case of Dr Jekyll and Mr Hyde and Other Tales of Terror*, ed. by Robert Mighall (London: Penguin, 2002), pp. 1–70

STOPPARD, TOM, *Rosencrantz and Guildenstern are Dead* (New York: Grove Press, 1967)

SWINBURNE, ALGERNON CHARLES, *The Swinburne Letters*, ed. by Cecil Lang, 6 vols (New Haven, CT: Yale University Press, 1959–1962)

THOMPSON, E. P., *The Making of the English Working Class* (London: Victor Gollancz Ltd., 1963)

TRENCSÉNYI, KATALIN, and BERNADETTE COCHRANE, eds, *New Dramaturgy: International Perspectives on Theory and Practice* (London: Bloomsbury, 2014)

TROOST, LINDA, and SAYRE GREENFIELD, 'The Mouse That Roared: Patricia Rozema's *Mansfield Park*', in *Jane Austen in Hollywood,* ed. by Linda Troost and Sayre Greenfield (Lexington: University of Kentucky Press, 2001), pp. 188–204

TRUESDELL, WINFRED PORTER, 'The Modern Woodcut and Howard Simon', *The Print Connoisseur: A Quarterly Magazine for the Print Collector*, 10 (April 1930), 136–65

TUCKER, PETER, *The Interpretation of a Classic: The Illustrated Editions of 'Candide'* (Oxford: The Previous Parrot Press, 1993)

TURNER, GRAEME, *British Cultural Studies: An Introduction* (London & New York: Routledge, 1992)

UHLIG, BARBARA, 'Hidden Art: Artistic References in Mattotti's *Docteur Jekyll & Mr Hyde*', *Image & Narrative*, 17.4 (2016), 43–56

VALÉRY, PAUL, 'La Conquête de l'ubiquité', in *Œuvres II*, ed. by Jean Hytier (Paris: Gallimard, 1960), pp. 1284–87

VAN DOREN, CARL, 'Why the Editorial Board Selected "Rockwell Kent's *Candide*"', *Wings*, 3.12 (December 1929), 4–5

VARIETY ART WORKS, *Henshin* [= *Metamorphosis*] (Tokyo: East Press, 2008)

VENUTI, LAWRENCE, 'Adaptation, Translation, Critique', *Journal of Visual Culture*, 6.1 (2007), 25–43

——*The Scandals of Translation: Towards an Ethics of Difference* (London: Routledge, 1998)

——*The Translator's Invisibility: A History of Translation* (London: Routledge, 1995)

VEREVIS, CONSTANTINE, *Film Remakes* (Edinburgh: Edinburgh University Press, 2006)

VERGÈS, FRANÇOISE, 'Writing on Water: Peripheries, Flows, Capital, and Struggles in the Indian Ocean', *positions*, 11.1 (2003), 241–57

VERSACI, ROCCO, *This Book Contains Graphic Language: Comics as Literature* (New York: Continuum, 2007)

VERTOV, DZIGA, *Kino-eye: The Writings of Dziga Vertov*, ed. by Annette Michelson, trans. by Kevin O'Brien (London: Pluto Press, 1984)

VILAIN, ROBERT, 'Images of Optimism? German Illustrated Editions of Voltaire's *Candide* in the Context of the First World War', *Oxford German Studies*, 37.2 (2008), 223–52

VILLON, FRANÇOIS, *Poésies complètes*, ed. by Claude Thiry (Paris: Librairie Générale Française, 1991)

VOGL, JOSEPH, 'Kafkas Komik', in *Kontinent Kafka: Mosse-Lectures an der Humboldt-Universität zu Berlin*, ed. by Klaus R. Scherpe (Berlin: Vorwerk 8, 2006), pp. 72–87
VOIGTS-VIRCHOW, ECKART, *Introduction to Media Studies* (Stuttgart: Klett, 2005)
VOLTAIRE, *Candide, or All for the Best* (Haarlem: Joh. Enschedé en Zonen, 1927)
—— *Candide* (New York: Random House, 1928)
—— *Candide* (New York: Ives Washburn, 1929)
—— *Candide* (New York: Arden Book Company, 1930)
—— *Candide* (New York: Illustrated Editions Company, 1930)
—— *Candide* (New York: Williams, Belasco, and Meyers, 1930)
WAGENBACH, KLAUS, *Franz Kafka: Bilder aus seinem Leben* (Berlin: Verlag Klaus Wagenbach, 1983)
WAGNER, GEOFFREY, *The Novel and the Cinema* (Rutherford, NJ: Fairleigh Dickinson University Press, 1975)
WALKER, PHILIP, 'Prophetic Myths in Zola', *PMLA*, 1.24 (1959), 444–52
WEIS, RENÉ, 'Introduction', in William Shakespeare, *Romeo and Juliet*, ed. by René Weis (London: Arden Bloomsbury, 2012), pp. 1–115
WELLS, PAUL, 'Classic Literature and Animation: All Adaptations are Equal, but Some are More Equal than Others', in *The Cambridge Companion to Literature on Screen*, ed. by Deborah Cartmell and Imelda Whelehan (Cambridge: Cambridge University Press, 2007), pp. 199–211
WELLS-LASSAGNE, SHANNON, *Television and Serial Adaptation* (New York & Abingdon: Routledge, 2017)
WEST, MARK, and HAN EI CHEW, *Reading in the Mobile Era: A Study of Mobile Reading in Developing Countries* (Paris: UNESCO, 2014)
WILDE, OSCAR, *Salomé*, illustrated by David Shenton (London: Quartet Books, 1986)
WILLIAMS, RAYMOND, *Television: Technology and Cultural Form* (London: Routledge, 2003)
WISSE, RUTH R., *The Modern Jewish Canon: A Journey Through Language and Culture* (New York: Free Press, 2000)
WOLF, WERNER, 'Intermedialität', in *Metzler Lexikon Literatur- und Kulturtheorie: Ansätze, Personen, Grundbegriff*, ed. by Ansgar Nünning (Stuttgart: Metzler Verlag, 1998), pp. 327–28
—— *Selected Essays on Intermediality by Werner Wolf (1992–2014): Theory and Typology, Literature-Music Relations, Transmedial Narratology, Miscellaneous Transmedial Phenomena*, ed. by Walter Bernhart (Leiden & Boston, MA: Brill Rodopi, 2018)
WOOD, ROBIN, 'Minnelli's *Madame Bovary*', *CineAction!*, 7 (1986), 75–80
WOODALL, JAMES, 'Thomas Ostermeier: On Europe, Theatre, Communication', in *Contemporary European Theatre Directors*, ed. by Maria M. Delgado and Dan Rebellato (Abingdon & New York: Routledge, 2010), pp. 363–76
YANO, CHRISTINE R., 'Wink on Pink: Interpreting Japanese Cute as it Grabs the Global Headlines', *Journal of Asian Studies*, 68.3 (2009), 681–88
YARON, IDAN, and OMRI HERZOG, 'Kafka's Ruins in Popular Culture: A Story of Metamorphosis', *The Journal of Popular Culture*, 46.5 (2013), 1092-1105
ZIMMERMAN, ERIC, 'Gaming Literacy: Game Design as a Model for Literacy in the Twenty-first Century', in *The Video Game Theory Reader*, ed. by Bernard Perron and Mark J. P. Wolf (New York: Routledge, 2009), pp. 23–31
ZISCHLER, HANNS, *Kafka geht ins Kino* (Reinbek: Rowohlt, 1996)
ZOLA, ÉMILE, *Thérèse Raquin*, in *Œuvres complètes*, ed. by Henri Mitterand (Paris: Cercle du Livre Précieux, 1966–1969), 1 (1966), 511–682
—— *Thérèse Raquin*, adapted by Neal Bell (New York: Broadway Play Publishing Inc, 2016)
—— *Thérèse Raquin*, translated by Robin Buss (London: Penguin 2004)

Films, Television, and Radio Productions

Ah! Ah! Mujō, dir. by Kiyochiko Ushihara and Yoshinobu Ikeda (Japan, 1923)
La Bible, dir. by Marcel Carné (FR2, 1977)
Bridget Jones's Diary, dir. by Sharon Maguire (UK, 2001)
Das Cabinet des Dr. Caligari, dir. by Robert Wiene (Germany, 1920)
Le Chemineau, dir. by Albert Capellani (France, 1906)
Clueless, dir. by Amy Heckerling (USA, 1995)
David Copperfield, dir. by George Cukor (USA, 1935)
Death Comes to Pemberley, dir. by Daniel Percival (BBC, 2013)
Dr Jekyll and Mr. Hyde, dir. by John S. Robertson (USA, 1920)
Dr Jekyll and Mr. Hyde, dir. by Rouben Mamoulian (USA, 1931)
Emma, dir. by Douglas McGrath (UK, 1996)
Emma, dir. by Diarmuid Lawrence (ITV, 1996)
Les Enfants du paradis, dir. by Marcel Carné (France, 1945)
The Good Earth, dir. Sydney Franklin (USA, 1937)
Guilty (BBC Home Service, 1948)
Hôtel du nord, dir. by Marcel Carné (France, 1938)
In Secret, dir. by Charlie Stratton (USA, 2013)
Jenny, dir. by Marcel Carné (France, 1936)
Kyojin-den, dir. by Mansaku Itami (Japan, 1938)
La Liberté de Marie, dir. by Caroline Huppert (France 3, 2002)
Lost in Austen, dir. by Dan Zeff (ITV, 2008)
Madame Bovary, dir. by Jean Renoir (France, 1934)
Madame Bovary, dir. by Vincente Minnelli (USA, 1949)
Madame Bovary, dir. by Claude Chabrol (France, 1991)
Man Friday, dir. by Jack Gold (USA, 1975)
Mansfield Park, dir. by Patricia Rozema (UK, 1999)
Die Maschine, dir. by Georges Perec with Eugen Helmlé (Saarländischer Rundfunk, 1968)
Maya Memsaab, dir. by Ketan Mehta (India, 1993)
Les Misérables, dir. by Bille August (UK, 1998)
Les Misérables: Shōjo Cosette, dir. by Hiroaki Sakurai (Nippon Animation, 2007)
Nosferatu — eine Symphonie des Grauens, dir. by F. W. Murnau (Germany, 1922)
The Oubliette, dir. by Charles Giblyn (USA, 1914)
Persuasion, dir. by Robert Michell (BBC, 1995)
The Postman Always Rings Twice, dir. by Tay Garnett (USA, 1946)
Pride and Prejudice, dir. by Robert Z. Leonard (USA, 1940)
Pride and Prejudice, dir. by Simon Langton (BBC, 1995)
Le Procès, dir. by Orson Welles (France, 1962)
Sense and Sensibility, dir. by Ang Lee (USA, 1995)
Le Testament du Docteur Cordelier, dir. by Jean Renoir (France, 1959)
Thérèse Raquin, dir. by Einar Zangenberg (Denmark, 1911)
Thérèse Raquin, dir. by Nino Martoglio (Italy, 1915)
Thérèse Raquin/Du sollst nicht ehebrechen!, dir. by Jacques Feyder (Germany, 1928)
Thérèse Raquin, dir. by Marcel Carné (France, 1953)
Thérèse Raquin, dir. by John Powell (BBC Radio 4, 1969)
Thérèse Raquin, dir. by Simon Langton (BBC, 1980)
Thérèse Raquin, dir. by Cherry Cookson (BBC Radio 4, 1998)
Thérèse Raquin, dir. by Pauline Harris (BBC Radio 4, 2009)
Thirst, dir. by Park Chan-wook (South Korea, 2009)
The Trial, dir. by David Jones (BBC, 1993)

Victor Hugo et les principaux personnages des 'Misérables', dir. by the Lumière brothers (France, 1897)
Villon's Wife, dir. by Kichitaro Negishi (Japan, 2009)

Online Material

Anon. '250 Best iPad Apps: Books', *Daily Telegraph*, 3 June 2011 <http://www.telegraph.co.uk/technology/mobile-app-reviews/8552749/250-best-iPad-apps-books.html> [accessed 6 September 2014]
—— 'Novels Under Manga Cover: Convenience Stores Go Literary', *Daily Yomiuri Online*, 25 July 2008 <http://web.archive.org/web/20080802010605/http://www.yomiuri.co.jp/dy/national/20080725TDY13001.htm> [accessed 24 October 2019]
—— 'On the 150th Anniversary of the Sacking of the Old Summer Palace, China Reflects', *China Daily*, 18 October 2010 <http://www.chinadaily.com.cn/china/2010–10/18/content_11425824.htm> [accessed 24 October 2019]
—— '*The Alice App*' <http://thealiceapp.com/the-alice-app/> [accessed 14 July 2015]
A1000Castles, 'Alice in Wonderland, Arthur Rackham', YouTube, 24 January 2014 <https://www.youtube.com/watch?v=0vFweU5EA4M> [accessed 12 August 2015]
Asinine Games, 'Flapping Bard', YouTube, 23 March 2015 <https://www.youtube.com/watch?v=REbHoa_yM3Y> [accessed 12 August 2015]
Atomic Antelope, 'Alice for the iPad', YouTube, 12 April 2010 <https://www.youtube.com/watch?v=gew68Qj5kxw> [accessed 4 September 2014]
Baddeley, Anna, 'The Ebook is Dead: Long Live the Ebook', *Guardian*, 1 February 2015 <http://www.theguardian.com/books/2015/feb/01/the-ebook-is-dead-long-live-print-digital-sales> [accessed 7 August 2015]
Biersdorfer, J. D., 'New Apps Provide a World of Literature, One Chapter at a Time', *The New York Times*, 12 May 2017 <https://www.nytimes.com/2017/05/12/books/review/new-apps-provide-a-world-of-literature-one-chapter-at-a-time.html> [accessed 2 November 2018]
Blackstone, William, *Commentaries on the Laws of England (1765–1769)* <http://www.lonang.com/exlibris/blackstone/> [accessed 4 January 2020]
Boren, Zachary Davies, 'There are Officially More Mobile Devices than People in the World', *Independent*, 7 October 2014 <http://www.independent.co.uk/life-style/gadgets-and-tech/news/there-are-officially-more-mobile-devices-than-people-in-the-world-9780518.html> [accessed 10 August 2015]
Breccia, Alberto, 'Alberto Breccia, 20 ans après: entretien avec Lorenzo Mattotti' <http://www.alberto-breccia.net/breccia-20-ans-apres-entretien-lorenzo-mattotti/> [accessed 3 October 2015]
Cambridge University Press, 'Explore Shakespeare iPad Apps from Cambridge', YouTube, 28 November 2012 <https://www.youtube.com/watch?v=Uq9-OPDKtac> [accessed 6 September 2014]
Capelle, Sean, 'Party Like It's 1599 in Angry Bards', *AppAdvice*, 26 March 2013 <http://appadvice.com/review/quickadvice-angrybards> [accessed 12 August 2015]
Chion, Michel, '100 concepts pour penser et décrire le cinéma sonore', trans. by Claudia Gorbman <http://michelchion.com/download/new> [accessed 1 October 2015]
Corpuz, John, '15 Best E-book Reader Apps', *Tom's Guide*, 18 September 2018 <https://www.tomsguide.com/us/pictures-story/583-best-ereader-apps.html> [accessed 27 November 2018]
Cramer, Peter, *Talking Germany*, Deutsche Welle, broadcast on 15 April 2012 <http://www.youtube.com/watch?v=vaUHxKXjkwI> [accessed 20 November 2019]

Dailylit <https://www.dailylit.com> [accessed 3 November 2018]

Dickson, Andrew, 'Thomas Ostermeier: "Hamlet? The Play's a Mess"', *Guardian*, 13 November 2011 <https://www.theguardian.com/stage/2011/nov/13/thomas-ostermeier-hamlet-schaubuhne> [accessed 5 January 2020]

EverySteveJobsVideo, 'Steve Jobs Introduces Original iPad: Apple Special Event (2010)', YouTube, 30 December 2013 <https://www.youtube.com/watch?v=_KN-5zmvjAo> [accessed 9 August 2014]

Flacy, Mike, 'Amazon Doubles Kindle Paperwhite Storage', *Digital Trends*, 15 August 2014 <http://www.digitaltrends.com/mobile/amazon-doubles-internal-storage-within-kindle-paperwhite/> [accessed 10 August 2015]

Friederich, Ute, *Komik — Comic: komische Elemente in den Texten Franz Kafkas und ihre bildliche Umsetzung in verschiedenen Comic-Adaptionen* (unpublished Masters thesis, Universität Bonn, 2009) <https://docplayer.org/43758272-Komik-comic-magisterarbeit-zur-erlangung-des-grades-einer-magistra-artium-m-a.html> [accessed 24 March 2020].

Friedrichs, John, 'Preliminary Checklist of the Early Work of Jan Van Krimpen' <http://home.planet.nl/~johnf/home.html#1927> [accessed 15 November 2019]

Funnel27, '*Waiting for Godot*: The Video Game', YouTube, 16 June 2010 <https://www.youtube.com/watch?v=5N1kqtum5rI> [accessed 14 July 2014]

Gaddy, David, *Poe Mojis* <https://appadvice.com/app/poe-mojis/1182601024> [accessed 27 November 2018]

Google Play preview, *Shakespeare SwipeSpeare* <https://play.google.com/store/apps/details?id=com.swipespeare&hl=en> [accessed 27 November 2018]

Graas, Angela, and others, *Candide: Illustrierte Ausgaben eines Klassikers. Eine Ausstellung der Universitätsbibliothek Trier* <http://candide.uni-trier.de> [accessed 30 December 2019]

Gravett, Paul, 'Lorenzo Mattotti: The Magic & Music of Comics' <http://www.paulgravett.com/articles/article/lorenzo_mattotti> [accessed 14 December 2014]

Green, Hank, and Bernie Su, *The Lizzie Bennet Diaries* <https://www.youtube.com/channel/UCXfbQAimgtbk4RAUHtIAUww> [accessed 15 January 2020]

Grn Pod, 'iOS 11 AR Game Play', YouTube, 17 October 2017 <https://www.youtube.com/watch?v=lXY4pBxYcXY> [accessed 25 November 2018]

Hogan, Emma, 'Deutsche Bard: Are you Ready for "Hamlet" in German? Thomas Ostermeier Talks About his Controversial Staging of Shakespeare', *Financial Times*, 25 November 2011 <https://www.ft.com/content/6f0ea1b4-edc5–11e0-a9a9–00144feab49a> [accessed 20 November 2019]

hottrix, *iBeer 2.0. The REAL iBeer for iPod touch and iPhone*, YouTube, 10 July 2008 <https://www.youtube.com/watch?v=8b9PH55EtJI> [accessed 6 September 2014]

iClassics, *Charles Dickens* <http://iclassicscollection.com/en/project/charles-dickens/> [accessed 2 November 2018]

—— *Tactile Tales* <http://iclassicscollection.com/en/tactiletales/> [accessed 2 November 2018]

iOS App Stats, 'Miniville's Sounds of Alice in Wonderland', 12 August 2015 <http://www.iosmobileapp.com/john_jumper/minivilles_sounds_of_alice_in_wonderland/appId422778394> [accessed 12 August 2015]

Itbooks, 'Once Upon a Time' [n.d.] <http://eraseunavez.itbook.es/> [accessed 12 August 2015]

iTunes Preview, *Alice for the iPad* <https://itunes.apple.com/gb/app/alice-for-the-ipad/id354537426?mt=8> [accessed 6 August 2015]

—— *Fact Mountain: 19th Cent. British Literature* <https://itunes.apple.com/is/app/19th-cent-british-literature/id1422926555?mt=8> [accessed 2 November 2018]

—— *Shakespeare Pro* <https://itunes.apple.com/gb/app/shakespeare-pro/id341392367?mt=8> [accessed 27 November 2018]

JOHNSON, MEAD, and RB, 'Figures Show More People in the World Have Access to a Mobile Phone Than a Toilet', October 2018 <https://www.rb.com/media/news/2018/october/figures-show-more-people-in-the-world-have-access-to-a-mobile-phone-than-a-toilet/> [accessed 3 November 2018]

KEMP, SIMON, 'Digital in 2018: World's Internet Users Pass the 4 Billion Mark', *We Are Social*, 30 January 2018 <https://wearesocial.com/blog/2018/01/global-digital-report-2018> [accessed 2 November 2018]

MAYENBURG, MARIUS VON, *Hamlet*, German version for the Schaubühne, Henschel Schauspiel <https://henschel-schauspiel.de/de/werk/3314> [accessed 21 November 2019]

MARKS, PETER, 'It's Lust, but not Strictly Sexual', *New York Times*, 4 November 1997 <http://www.nytimes.com/1997/11/04/theater/reviews-theater-review-it-s-lust-but-not-strictly-sexual.html> [accessed 11 April 2016]

Merriam-Webster Dictionary, 'Kafkaesque' <http://www.merriam-webster.com/dictionary/kafkaesque> [accessed 24 March 2020]

MICROSOFT CORPORATION, *Adaptations*, *Microsoft Store*, [n.d.] <https://www.microsoft.com/en-us/store/apps/adaptations/9wzdncrddwg7> [accessed 16 July 2014]

MILNE-TYTE, ASHLEY, 'Shakespeare? There's an App for That', *VOA News*, 28 August 2013 <https://www.voanews.com/a/shakespeare-theres-an-app-for-that/1738809.html> [accessed 2 November 2018]

MORLEY, MADELEINE, 'The World's Most Expensive-looking Font Might Surprise You', 27 October 2015 <https://eyeondesign.aiga.org/the-worlds-most-expensive-looking-font-might-surprise-you/> [accessed 15 November 2016]

NIEKERK, PIET VAN, 'Is "Screen Fatigue" Really a Turn-up for the Books?', *Fipp: The Network for Global Media*, 13 November 2018 <https://www.fipp.com/news/features/screen-fatigue-books> [accessed 27 November 2018]

Open Education Database, 'The Very Best Book, Comics, and Manga Apps: Our Top 23 Choices', 18 December 2012 <http://oedb.org/ilibrarian/the-very-best-book-apps-our-top-15-picks/> [accessed 6 September 2014]

OTTMAN, JOHN, 'Two Wings of the Valkyrie', interview <www.tracksounds.com/specialfeatures/interviews/interview_john_ottman_2008.htm> [accessed 20 February 2020]

PALENTZ, EMMANUEL, '*The Alice App*: Renaissance Art meets the Alice World', *The Alice App*, 4 April 2014 <http://thealiceapp.com/the-alice-app/> [accessed 14 July 2015]

PERRIER, JEAN-FRANÇOIS, 'Entretien avec Thomas Ostermeier', Avignon Festival, 2008 <fa2008_entretien_avec_thomas_ostermeier.pdf> [accessed 21 November 2019]

PEW RESEARCH CENTER, 'Communications Technology in Emerging and Developing Nations', 19 March 2015 <http://www.pewglobal.org/2015/03/19/1-communications-technology-in-emerging-and-developing-nations/> [accessed 7 August 2015]

Prague Minos Guide <http://www.digital-guide.cz/de/realie/die-stadtviertel-der-hauptstadt/die-judenstadt---josefov-1/> [accessed 24 March 2020]

ROB, 'Bringing Shakespeare to Life through Technology', 30 June 2015 <http://www.samsung.com/uk/discover/news/bringing-shakespeare-to-life-through-technology/> [accessed 5 August 2015]

RUBIS, FLORIAN, 'Lorenzo Mattotti: "Je n'ai pas honte de le dire: le dessin est, quand même, une discipline spirituelle!" ', ActuaBD <http://www.actuabd.com/Lorenzo-Mattotti-Je-n-ai-pas-honte> [accessed 10 August 2017]

SAMSUNGTOMORROW, 'Samsung Reveals RE:Shakespeare App: An Encounter of Digital and Literature', 20 June 2015 <http://global.samsungtomorrow.com/samsung-unveils-reshakespeare-app-an-encounter-of-digital-and-literature/> [accessed 5 August 2015]

Shakespeare at Play, 8 October 2013 <http://www.shakespeareatplay.ca/> [accessed 6 September 2014]

Shakespeare Birthplace Trust, 'Eye Shakespeare App', *Shakespeare Birthplace Trust*, [n.d.] <http://shakespeare.org.uk/visit-the-houses/eye-shakespeare-app.html> [accessed 14 July 2014]

Sharwood, Simon, 'Developing World Hits 98.7 per cent Mobile Phone Adoption', *The Register*, 3 August 2017 <https://www.theregister.co.uk/2017/08/03/itu_facts_and_figures_2017/> [accessed 27 November 2018]

Spencer, Charles, 'Dim Shadows of Zola's Hellish Vision', *Daily Telegraph,* 15 November 2006 <www.telegraph.co.uk/culture/theatre/drama/3656552/Dim-shadows-of-Zolas-hellish-vision.html> [accessed 11 April 2016]

Statista <www.statista.com> [accessed 2 November 2018]

Stewart, Eric, 'Steve Jobs Introduces iBooks for the iPad', YouTube, 29 January 2010 <https://www.youtube.com/watch?v=3G31PSNhVUM> [accessed 6 September 2014]

Swaney, Mark, 'Ebooks on Course to Outsell Printed Editions in the UK by 2018', *Guardian*, 4 June 2014 <http://www.theguardian.com/books/2014/jun/04/ebooks-outsell-printed-editions-books-2018> [accessed 6 Sep 2014]

theavatarbook, 'Avatarbook Alice in Wonderland — iPad App', YouTube, 13 September 2011 <https://www.youtube.com/watch?v=FN67aEUb02M> [accessed 1 August 2015]

Touch Press, 'A Walk through *The Waste Land*', YouTube, 7 June 2011 <https://www.youtube.com/watch?v=rlhosnfP-Jw> [accessed 9 July 2014]

Turner, Cathy, and Duska Radosavljevic, 'Porous Dramaturgy: "Togetherness" and Community in the Structure of the Artwork', 2012 <http://expandeddramaturgies.com/?p=687> [accessed 20 November 2019]

Vanhée, Olivier, 'The Production of a "Manga Culture" in France', *Asia Culture Forum* (2006) <http://www.ceri-sciencespo.org/themes/manga/documents/texte_production_vanhee.pdf> [accessed 24 October 2019]

Volans, Henry, 'Building the Wasteland', *The Thought Fox*, Faber & Faber, 2011 <http://thethoughtfox.co.uk/building-the-waste-land/> [accessed 3 August 2015]

Wattpad <https://www.wattpad.com> [accessed 2 November 2018]

Wired, 'The Best e-Readers and Kindles', 9 July 2018 <https://www.wired.co.uk/article/best-e-readers-kindles> [accessed 27 November 2018]

INDEX

www.ingramcontent.com/pod-product-compliance
Lightning Source LLC
Chambersburg PA
CBHW081424090426
42740CB00017B/3169
* 9 7 8 1 7 8 1 8 8 3 9 6 9 *